D0055887

DATE DUE

HIGHSMITH #45231

STEPDADS

STEPDADS

Stories of Love, Hope, and Repair

William Marsiglio

ROWMAN & LITTLEFIELD PUBLISHERS, INC.
Lanham • Boulder • New York • Toronto • Oxford

ROWMAN & LITTLEFIELD PUBLISHERS, INC.

Published in the United States of America
by Rowman & Littlefield Publishers, Inc.
A wholly owned subsidiary of The Rowman & Littlefield Publishing Group, Inc.
4501 Forbes Boulevard, Suite 200, Lanham, MD 20706
www.rowmanlittlefield.com

P.O. Box 317, Oxford OX2 9RU, UK

British Library Cataloging in Publication Information Available

Library of Congress Cataloging-in-Publication Data

Marsiglio, William.
  Stepdads : stories of love, hope, and repair / William Marsiglio.
    p. cm.
  Includes bibliographical references and index.
  ISBN 0-7425-2673-9 (cloth : alk. paper)
  1. Stepfathers. 2. Father and child. I. Title.
  HQ759.92.M38 2004
  306.874'2—dc21

                                    2003013676

Printed in the United States of America

♾™ The paper used in this publication meets the minimum requirements of
American National Standard for Information Sciences—Permanence of Paper for
Printed Library Materials, ANSI/NISO Z39.48-1992.

CONTENTS

PREFACE

When I first thought about writing a book on stepfathers, I assumed I would be writing largely for an academic audience, as I am accustomed to doing. However, after completing several interviews, I began to realize that the story I wanted to write—felt compelled to share—begged to be told to a much wider audience. My motivation to reach out to the more general reader was reinforced each time I interviewed a participant. I was touched deeply when I heard men speak candidly, sometimes emotionally about their personal experiences. The men who shared their stories were at times euphoric, indifferent, or distressed. On balance, though, most left me with the impression that they were rather pleased with their lives as stepfathers. With a few exceptions, they were grateful for their romantic relationships and the stepchildren who had entered their lives. In fact, many were exceedingly proud of these kids; some professed to love them as if they were their own offspring.

Affected by the stepdads' detailed stories, as well as the passion with which they told them, I expanded the borders that define my audience. Although professors, researchers, therapists, and students remain important to the way I frame my project, I also want to speak to those intimately familiar with stepfamily life. My audience includes those who deal firsthand with the joys, struggles, and fears of negotiating this unfamiliar and personal terrain, as well as members of the academic community. My book is intended to appeal to a broad range of persons who may be imagining what their life would be like if they were to create a stepfamily, including formal and informal stepfathers, single moms, remarried or cohabiting moms, adults thinking about the prospects of forming a stepfamily, and even nonresident biological fathers whose children are involved with a stepdad. I especially want to speak to stepfathers, men similar to those who shared their personal stories with me.

To reach this broad audience, I downplay the explicit use of theoretical perspectives in the main body of the text and I use a somewhat selective referencing style. Still, I use endnotes to cite key source materials, direct the interested reader to relevant readings, and provide brief reviews of related substantive points. Source materials beyond my own data come primarily from two genres of scholarly literature, one dealing with fatherhood, the other, stepfamilies.

During the past two decades I have actively theorized about and studied fatherhood. However, aside from publishing an empirical article using national data on stepfathers (1992; revised in 1995), my familiarity with stepfamily research prior to my current study was rather limited. My 1992 article was based on national survey data that addressed issues involving stepfathers' perceptions about stepparenting as they relate to their own family. Based on secondary survey data, this research limited my ability to explore the social psychological processes associated with men's experiences as stepfathers. Fortunately, the in-depth interviews I use in my current study enable me to explore more deeply the social psychology of stepfatherhood. My study also helps bridge the gap between the fatherhood and stepfamily literatures.

Not wanting to shortchange my academic audience, I tailor the substantive appendices to scholars and students interested in a more systematic approach to the issues I address. Readers who so choose can consume the book's ten chapters without ever looking at the appendices—though I believe the information is valuable in its own right. Appendix A provides a self-reflexive, detailed analysis of how I recruited participants, conducted and analyzed the interviews, and decided on a writing style. The interview guides I used in my study are also displayed in appendix B. By providing these materials, I invite the reader backstage to observe the process that determined how I represent and interpret men's descriptions of their lives as stepfathers. I offer suggestions, too, for how future researchers might extend this work.

In addition to the participants, a number of persons earned my appreciation for having a hand in moving this book through the various stages of the research process, culminating in the actual writing and final editing of the manuscript. I would first like to thank the director of the National Center on Fathers and Families, Dr. Vivian Gadsden, as well as the Annie E. Casey Foundation, for their funding support (grant no. 16-21-481-12). I am also grateful for receiving a University of Florida sabbatical for fall 2001 that provided me the flexibility to conduct a large percentage of the interviews myself. Kanitra Perry's conscientious efforts in administering the grant supporting my research were quite helpful. I had the good fortune of working with Dean Birkenkamp, editor, and his assistant, Jessica Gribble. Each offered enthusiastic and timely support for my project. In particular, Dean helped me navigate the awkward path of producing a book that appeals to both academics and general readers. I also appreciate the sound guidance I received from Jehanne Schweitzer and Chrisona Schmidt on polishing my prose to reach this broad audience.

I relied on Robin Bludworth, Carla Edwards, and Jim Faubel to interview sixteen of my fifty-one participants, with Robin doing ten. I am fortunate that they were so dedicated and good-natured about this important task. Robin also proved to be an asset in interpreting the birth mother interviews. Her unwavering moral support throughout the entire project, as well as her editorial comments on the full manuscript, proved invaluable. In addition to interviewing four participants, Jim provided excellent assistance in several areas, including recruitment, library research, and compiling demographic summaries of the sample. Two other people played a pivotal role in helping me recruit participants. Nicole Cassisi Yucht recruited individuals using a newsletter from a local hospital. Her help was particularly valuable in the early stages of the recruitment process. Dana Bagwell played an important role in developing and initiating recruitment strategies that helped me identify a number of participants at various stages of the project. He also transcribed twelve interviews, took charge of entering and managing the data using a qualitative computer software package, and edited the entire manuscript. I appreciate Arupa Freeman, my main transcriptionist, for completing her work in a timely and meticulous fashion, and similar thanks go out to Constance Jylanki, who stepped in to complete a handful of transcripts.

Several students provided excellent assistance during the writing phase of this project: Jeanne Anne Collins, Leslie Condrey, MacGregor Meyer, Kacy Mixon, Malena Summers, and Erin Sweet. They helped with library and Internet research, editing, indexing, and various administrative tasks. In addition to her keen editorial comments, Leslie, a single mother entering a new stepfamily arrangement, was particularly helpful in providing feedback that enabled me to enhance this book's appeal to stepfathers and birth mothers. The final manuscript also benefited from substantive and editorial comments from two anonymous reviewers who read portions of the manuscript, and a colleague, Sally Hutchinson, who read a complete draft.

While doing this research, I had the good fortune of interviewing a

number of men who, in their everyday lives, challenge the negative stereotypes often assigned to stepfathers. This book owes much to these men who
took the time to share their engaging stories with me. I have made a concerted effort to represent and interpret their stories, as well as the stories offered by the birth mothers and children who participated, in a manner consistent with how they were shared. If the feedback I received from the five
men who reviewed sections of the book pertaining to their individual comments is an accurate barometer, I am confident that I have captured the
lives of the stepfathers in my study in a nuanced and meaningful way. Their
enthusiastic feedback was a welcome stamp of approval. Four of these men
have allowed me to use their real names to acknowledge my deep gratitude
to them: Tom Bedard, Ric Brandt, Jonas Oliver, and Kenny Stokes. I offer a special thanks to Tom (with stepson) and Kenny (with stepdaughter)
for enthusiastically spending several hours posing for pictures so that I could
have real-life participants illustrate my book's jacket cover.

I dedicate this book to the stepfathers in my study, as well as others
like them around the world, who are comfortable looking beyond the absence of shared DNA to embrace the challenges and opportunities of acting as a positive force in stepchildren's lives.

1

TALKING TO STEPDADS

D addy." This word, at first glance, appears so simple, so familiar. We've all heard it, most of us have used it, and some of us have had others say it to get our attention. Yet, when looked at with a discerning eye, much more can be seen. If the lens is focused to look beneath the surface, we find that the word "daddy," and its more mature rendition, "dad," are embedded in a dynamic, complex web of sentiments and relationship issues.

From one perspective, it makes no difference whether the word of choice is "daddy" or "dad." In each case a process, usually subtle, is at work. Often hidden from our conscious awareness of everyday life, this process helps shape the way we structure and manage our relationships. Those who whisper, beckon playfully, or shout "daddy" or "dad" do so because they aim to assign an image or a status to a man. The image is one of a male parent—father—as well as nurturer, playmate, disciplinarian, and protector. These roles carry messages that help people learn their rights and responsibilities. "What can I do?" "What should I do?" The messages, however, are not always clear and are sometimes challenged.

Social life and the labels (stepfather, dad, single, gay) that individuals use to assign meaning to people's lives, their own included, are often messy. Crude black-and-white descriptions fail to do justice to the nuances of people's lives and relationships; shades of gray seem more appropriate. Things are seldom as simple as they first appear. Those who contest and negotiate the common everyday terms they use to order their worlds feed this confusion. Concepts offered to embrace the essence of fatherhood speak volumes on this issue. There's far more to fathering and its labels than sperm and DNA.

To bring these abstract matters into focus, let's listen to one man's real-life story, shared with me during the course of my research for this book, which explores what I loosely label "stepfathering." With this story, we begin an intriguing journey into stepfathers' and their partners' inner worlds. More stories will follow in due course.

Eighteen months after his first date with Angela, Terry, in his mid-thirties at the time, formally committed himself heart, soul, and wallet to being a first-time "dad" to his new bride's six-year-old son, Zack. Although Terry's bond with Zack deepened quickly after they met, it was fostered initially by Terry's involvement with Zack's mom. As classmates in nursing school, Terry and Angela forged a friendship that led to a few casual dates. Terry describes how, on their third date, he boldly confessed to Angela how he felt about her:

> I just laid a bomb on her. I said this may scare you away, but I don't care if it does. It was meant to be. I'm not going to fool around. I've been there, and I know what I'm looking for and this is it. I told her the whole scene. I said you're going to think I'm crazy but I'm telling you, it's all over [he wanted to develop a committed relationship].

Terry's words proved to be prophetic; both his romantic love for Angela and his fatherly love for Zack flourished.

This story hints at how personal experiences with stepfathering can be linked to a dramatic transformation in lifestyle and perspective for some people. Terry's young adulthood was distinguished by a ten-year stint as a member of the elite Special Forces unit of the U.S. military machine. During those years, Terry lived a life laced with extensive international travel, intrigue, danger, and sexual exploits with countless foreign women in faraway lands. Upon leaving the military he married hastily and then divorced after seven difficult years.

Although he never seriously considered having children with his first wife, that all changed when he met Angela. Thinking back to when he met Angela, Terry remarks, "I really couldn't find anyone my age to start a family with, because of my situation, being in the military so long and then coming out and going to school seven years here. I was finally catching up with age, saying 'well this is going to happen now.'" Terry stumbled on a new way of life. It was both a practical and symbolic path; one marked by his commitment to being a devoted family man, in his case, to a woman who had given birth to another man's child.

Though he had virtually no experience with kids, Terry quickly evolved into a man who felt at home with his coparenting responsibilities and with the fatherly way he interacted with Zack. This transition had its conditions. Ironically, Terry, a seasoned veteran of nighttime parachuting into high-risk, hostile arenas, was not keen on jumping blindly into a stepfather arrangement. Several years prior, he had experienced a difficult breakup with a single mom who had an eight-year-old daughter. This breakup taught him a valuable lesson about guarding his emotions. It was precarious to love a child and invest deeply in a relationship when someone else controlled access to the child—both during the relationship and after it ended. Following their uncoupling, Terry recalled missing the child more than the mom. Terry was also leery about getting too involved in Zack's life because he knew that he did not want to be "half a father." He was intensely eager to marry Angela, but unleashing his unabashed enthusiasm hinged on receiving a green light to make a total commitment to Zack. His commitment to fathering would be all the way or no way. Angela made this possible by sitting back and giving Terry free rein to accept Zack into his life.

The thought of having other children with Angela comforted Terry. It also inspired him to treat Zack as though he were his own son. According to Terry's way of thinking, language that calls attention to the unique status of stepparents and half siblings is unappealing and counterproductive for family dynamics. All the kids in his household were going to be his children and see each other as "full" siblings. As Terry puts it,

> She's [Angela] got someone that loves her son and her son looks up to me and we get along real well. We're having more kids, so it's been very, very fortunate. I've seen [a] lot of other stepparents, and that term is not allowed in our house. Step, there's no such thing as step. He's [Zack] not a stepson, he's not a half brother. He doesn't have half brothers. We are a religious family and in God's eyes there's no such thing as half people. This is your brother, this is your mother, this is your father. Nothing wrong with him having two fathers.

Why tell this idyllic story? Because it reminds us that people sometimes build families in ways that transcend biology. For some, the meanings of family and fatherhood anchored by bonds of the heart are as powerful as ties created by images of shared bloodlines and DNA. One meaningful line of inquiry that speaks to this reality asks: How do men in family settings develop and negotiate fatherly relations with children who are not their biological offspring?

Terry's story, which we will return to later, raises the question of what makes a man a father. Does a genetic bond based on shared DNA, a legal tie, a state of mind, a set of actions, a specific type of relationship with a child's mother, or some combination of these markers supply the logic for defining fatherhood? Compared with those of an earlier era, professionals working with families, family scholars, and the average person on the street are more conscious of the borders that differentiate genetic, legal, and social fatherhood as well as the controversies surrounding these distinctions.[1]

Nancy Dowd, a legal scholar, offers a detailed definition of social fatherhood that focuses specifically on the expression of nurturance and does not distinguish between biological and stepfather status. To her, nurture represents "care—physical, emotional, intellectual, spiritual—gauged by one's conduct and the consequences for children's positive development. It is responsive to the different needs of children at different ages. Thus nurture is not a static conception. It means more than simply doing; it also means the manner in which things are done, and their results for children."[2] She goes on to define social fatherhood as the "practice of nurture, either alone or in combination with other caretakers, as the sole or primary parent, or contributing as closely as possible to an equal amount of caregiving in partnership with the other primary parent or parents."[3] I revisit the importance of nurture in the final chapter when I consider the prospects for supporting and improving men's lives as stepfathers.

Regardless of which path men take, expressing themselves in a fatherly way and experiencing a subjective sense of being a father is part of a multilayered process affected by, among other things, biology, social customs, and rituals, interpersonal dynamics, personality, love, and law. As more men get involved with children in unconventional ways, understanding this process will become increasingly important for the family members directly involved as well as the professionals who work with them.

Because we know so little about men who act as fathers or male mentors outside the borders of biology, this book highlights these men's experiences.[4] Trying to understand the challenges they face and how they use different types of resources to deal with their situations is a timely undertaking. The proportion of men who think and feel about children in this fashion has grown as patterns of family formation have changed. It appears too that the proportion of men who adopt children who are not related to their romantic partners has remained fairly constant over the past decade or so. These demographic patterns are strengthened by public and scholarly concern about how children's well-being is affected by their involvement with various types of nonbiological fathers. In the pages to follow, I explore many of the social, psychological, and interpersonal dimensions of the stepfathering process while focusing specifically on men's identities as stepfa-

thers. In some cases, the men may not perceive themselves specifically as father figures, but their activities and self-perceptions in some ways draw
them close to the borders of what is typically associated with fathering.[5]

These issues provide a backdrop for the timely questions that guide my
study of stepfathers. How do men get romantically involved with women
who have children from previous relationships? What enables these men to
come to see themselves, and have others perceive them, as acting in a fatherly way toward children who are not their own offspring? What takes
place that enables men to develop rights and obligations typically associated
with biological fathers? How does acting fatherly when genetic ties are absent influence men's sense of self? In what ways do men manage their relationships with their stepchildren in private and public contexts? And how
do men perceive the impact that stepfathering has for their children and
themselves?[6]

As with many things social, answers to these and similar questions about
fatherhood and stepfatherhood depend on who is asked, when they're asked,
where they're asked, and why they're asked. What is clear is that the ambiguity about what fatherhood means and how fathers should behave induces
people in both formal and informal settings to grapple with issues related to
paternal rights and responsibilities. Some of these struggles raise their head in
a court of law, for example, the married woman whose extramarital lover
pursues legal recourse to lay claim to the child he contends is his genetic offspring. Other struggles play out in the company of administrators at schools,
day care centers, sporting venues, hospitals, and other sites where children
spend time. Personnel working in these environments increasingly must deal
with disgruntled stepfathers and nonresident biological fathers who expect to
have access to "their" children's records as well as the option of making decisions on their children's behalf. Many difficulties arise and then repeat
themselves as men interact with family, romantic partners, and friends.
Much of this activity occurs in or around the home as people go about their
daily lives. Although efforts to negotiate the meaning of fatherhood often
take place at home, these experiences can have lasting implications for children that extend beyond these encounters and family settings.

In recent years, the public has grown more curious about the meaning and practice of fatherhood because divorce, single parenthood, out-of-
wedlock childbearing, cohabitation, remarriage, and modern reproductive
technologies have altered the social landscape of families and fathering.
Conventional definitions of fatherhood that rely on a blood tie or a legal
document to establish paternity or make an adoption official work just fine
in most settings. However, rigid definitions of fatherhood (or stepfather-

hood) oversimplify the everyday realities and personal relationships of an increasing number of people in the United States and other industrialized societies. A close look at one's own families, friends, and neighbors will reveal to many that becoming and being a father or stepfather means different things to different people. This kaleidoscope of fatherhood[7] is accentuated through popular culture and the news media. Television sitcoms, cinematic dramas and plays, documentaries, and daytime talk shows like *Oprah, Montel Williams,* and *Jerry Springer* provide a window into the complex, often bizarre world of family relations and fatherhood. So, too, the symbolic power of language can bring to light the competing meanings people associate with different fatherhood labels. The paths men take to become fathers in unconventional settings, the types of negotiations they have with partners about their partner's children, and men's feelings about various linguistic conventions that earmark them as family ("dad," father, and same surname) or limit them to the status of adult friend (first name, different surname, and Mr. so-and-so) each add a layer of complexity to whether and how men come to see themselves and treat others in a fatherly way.

Having a blood tie (or the presumption of a blood relationship in most cases) is without question a key element that many people use to bestow fatherhood status. Some may see the blood tie as a necessary but insufficient condition. Others downplay or dismiss the centrality of biology altogether. They focus instead on a man's functional involvement with a child above all else. Does he act like a "father" by assuming specific responsibilities? Does he pay for a child's diapers, food, clothes, toys, day care, and so on? Does the child or mother see the man as a father to the child? If a biological father has done little or nothing to establish his connection to a child, then others may be quick to say that another man has been the only father a child has ever known.

Everyday language reveals much about the subjective realities of men and others in situations where the practical borders of fatherhood are being negotiated repeatedly. Some men, for example, have an emotional and psychological need to be a "real father." Like Terry, they feel awkward being labeled a step, adoptive, or foster father. These labels may seem inappropriate because they conjure up a type of "fatherhood lite" image. Men who carry these labels are fathers, kind of, but they are not perceived as the real deal. In essence, they're a watered-down version of the physically present, biological father. However, not all men react in this way to the adjectives that are sometimes used to define certain types of nonbiological fathers. Some men freely accept labels that distinguish them from conventional biological fathers. From the broader perspective of social science and law, labels that distinguish categories of fatherhood from the physically present, biological father model clarify the social demography of men's relationships to children. They do so by muting the social psychology of how men experience their lives as "fathers." They say nothing about how men think, feel, and act.

When a cross-cultural and historical lens is used to study the meaning and practice of fatherhood, the complexity of the "father" category and fathering experience is magnified. We can learn much about the flexible ways fatherhood is defined by studying cultures far different from our own. For instance, the Indian peoples of the lowland region of South America offer a distinct contrast to a Western view of fatherhood. The Ache of Paraguay, the Barí of Venezuela, and the Canela of Brazil each provide unique, though similar, examples of the plasticity of the social conventions surrounding the meaning of fatherhood.[8] Anthropologists who have studied these horticultural and foraging societies tell us that each has a kinship system allowing a child to have multiple biological fathers. A review of all cultures acknowledging some form of partible paternity shows that the public recognition of secondary fatherhood is often discreet because it might cast unfavorable light on the mother and her husband/partner. Often, though, it is acceptable so long as another man's presence does not lead to situations that are perceived to be bad luck.

This concept of multiple fatherhood (partible paternity), reinforced by the larger community, may serve various purposes, including the improvement of children's well-being and, ironically, the reduction of sexual jealousy among men in some cases. Among the Ache, primary fathers are represented by the person named as the "real father." This man is thought to be the one who had sexual intercourse most often with the mother immediately prior to her first missed period; women often have multiple sex partners prior to and during pregnancy. Secondary fathers include all the other men who had sexual intercourse with the mother near the time of conception, but presumably are not the father because of the specific timing of those episodes. Some secondary fathers include men who have had sex with the woman after she was already clearly pregnant. The Canela call these late arrivals "contributing" fathers, and they actively encourage women to take on many sex partners during pregnancy. They believe the prospects for producing a viable fetus are enhanced by multiple semen contributions. In all three of these South American cultures, being a father of any type carries responsibilities (provision of food) and rights (sexual access to the mother of the child). Even though some fathers do not meet their responsibilities, many do. Ethnographic research with the Ache, for example, indicates that children with two fathers (one primary and one secondary) have the lowest age-specific rate of mortality compared to children who have only one father or more than two. A similar pattern is found among the Barí. Eighty percent of Barí children survive to age fifteen if they have a secondary father, whereas only 64 percent of children without a secondary father live to see their fifteenth birthday. The advantage for children with two fathers is even more dramatic when children are compared to their siblings. Those with a secondary father are 2.6 times more likely to survive to age fifteen than their brothers and sisters who do not have a secondary father. Researchers speculate that one of the main reasons for this difference is that children with multiple fathers are better nourished because they have more adult fathers providing them with animal protein. However, those who have studied the Ache find that having exactly two fathers is ideal in terms of child mortality rates; they speculate that having more than two fathers lessens the certainty of paternity for all possible father candidates and thus lowers individual men's investments in children.[9]

Although none of these cultures appears to have specific provisions for designating men as stepfathers per se, the idea that multiple males can play a simultaneous and significant fatherly role in a child's life is tangentially related to a number of the issues I discuss in this book. Those of us living in Western cultures have lives that differ profoundly from those of the South American Indians, but we touch common ground when we realize that our cultural definitions of fatherhood, just like theirs, are ultimately socially constructed.[10] These matters can be defined in various ways according to ever changing cultural and historical forces.

Models of fatherhood tied to a particular culture or historical era may also differ according to a child's age and developmental needs, but acting like a father most fully reflects a man's commitment or obligation to act as a male parent who protects, supports, teaches, and cares for a child. However, acting like a male parent and identifying oneself as a father figure do not always go hand in hand. When men's everyday lives are scrutinized, it is sometimes difficult to differentiate forms of paternal commitment or obligation from the investments men make on behalf of children whom they value but do not claim as their "own." Men may do things that others view as fatherly, but the men themselves may not see the children they are involved with as their children. They do not think of themselves as fathers to these kids.

Men, too, can wrestle with a partial identity as a father. They may feel like a father because they change diapers, pack lunches, or get involved in carpooling kids to and from soccer practice. But they may feel awkward about disciplining children or balk at taking on formal or informal financial obligations for children who are not their "own." Take for instance Tim, a thirty-one-year-old father of two preschool boys. The mother of his boys has physical custody of them while Tim lives with his fiancée and her two youngest daughters who are two and three years of age. Tim feels like and acts like a dad to these two girls; they call him "daddy." He diapers them, dresses them, feeds them, and disciplines them as though they were his own children. But he is reluctant to act on the biological father's suggestion that he legally adopt them, a suggestion that the children's mother has reservations about as well. Tim has concerns about assuming official financial responsibility for the girls at this point because it would terminate the biological father's child support obligations. He is also worried because he is not yet married to their mother. So Tim, in many respects, has come to see himself as a father, in part because the biological father is largely out of the picture. But he is still contemplating whether it makes sense to take on the financial role completely. His partner, Melanie, pretty much agrees with the decision to hold off on adoption, but she too hopes that Tim will assume a fatherly role toward her children. Despite Melanie's generally upbeat view of Tim's efforts to be there for her children, she feels that he should treat them more lovingly. She has doubts that he, or any man who is involved with kids who are not his offspring, could ever love them as his own. Ironically, she realizes that compared with her two former husbands who fathered her children, Tim treats her children rather well.

Meanwhile, in Terry's case, he felt that crafting his identity as a father to a nonbiological child meant that he needed the freedom to go all the way. There could be nothing incomplete about his identity as a father. Asked if he had negotiated with Angela the type of rights and responsibilities he would have with Zack, Terry forcefully replies:

> It was going to be all or nothing, and that was my negotiation. It was like, if I'm coming into this relationship, then I'm coming in a hundred percent. I'm either going to be an all husband and an all father or nothing at all. I can't have like half a relationship. I can't be half a father. Where do you draw the line? At what point do you stop and say, "Oh well, I'm being a little bit too harsh here." Or, "I can't tell you you can't go to baseball tonight. Only your mother can do that." If I'm going to love you, I'm going to be your father. I'm going to be there all the way. I'm going to be there when your teachers need to see me; I'm going to be there when it's time to take you to baseball; I'm going to be there when you need some breakfast made; I'm going to be there

when you need me. But in the same respect, you're going to have to be there when it's my turn. When it's like, you need to get your homework done now. You need to clean your room now; you need to go out and feed the dog now. These are things that—I treat him exactly like my father treated me.

Terry's comments illustrate that the nature of the "claiming" process for fathers is critical, but poorly understood. Some men get to the point of feeling as though a particular child (or children) is theirs. They see the child as their responsibility. They, in a sense, see the child as belonging to them. Other men, for various reasons, only scratch the surface of that feeling; they never fully claim the child as theirs. This multifaceted process of claiming a child is associated with the social construct of "father." It helps individuals differentiate forms of "fathering" from seemingly similar expressions of friendship and mentorship between a man and a child (or perhaps an adult who is younger than the man). In other words, when are men perceived to be acting in a fatherly way rather than as male adult authority figures? Unfortunately, we know little about why individuals perceive some men as establishing fatherlike relationships to children who are not their biological offspring.

Though important in many circles, biological paternity or its presumption plays only a minor role in the stories and analysis presented in this book. Because I examine men's experiences with children that are not grounded on shared biology, the processes that shape men's subjective experiences with partners and children in a family context take center stage. These processes are created and sustained through various types of interactions and reflective thinking. The meanings men and others associate with particular interpersonal and family rituals, domestic arrangements, parenting decisions, and interpersonal bonds are crucial to understanding men's behaviors and identities as stepfathers.

A key assumption to the way I frame my discussion of men's lives is that men's self-images are shaped in part by how others see and treat them. It becomes quite difficult, sometimes impossible, for men to sustain images of themselves as being fatherly toward children if significant others resist their efforts. Men often find themselves immersed in a matrix of interwoven influences, some big and others small. They come in the form of family laws, teachers' expectations, family members' perceptions, involvement with biological children, mothers who play the gatekeeping role, nonresident fathers' personalities as well as their commitment to be involved with their kids, various forms of social support, and stepchildren's personalities. These influences structure men's lives, though men and others may not fully understand their true impact, for themselves or for others. This matrix of influences can change over time, so learning more about how and why men's lives as stepfathers change is a decidedly important, though difficult task.

For me, embarking on a project that focuses on stepfathers is part of my larger mission to understand the rhythms and patterns of fathers' lives. For seventeen years, I have researched and written about different aspects of men's lives as fathers. My main goal has been to develop a clearer picture of the social psychology of men's experiences as persons capable of creating and fathering human life. In other words, how do men's self-perceptions influence how they act as fathers, and how do men's actions as fathers influence the way they see themselves? The broader question on which my work centers is, How do men's social environments affect the way men develop and express their identities as fathers?

Although I have used a scholarly perspective to guide my previous writing and my research for this book on stepfathering, my insights about fatherhood are leavened by my firsthand experiences with family life. The seeds for my interest in studying fathering can be traced to my early years as a sports-crazed, working-class kid. During my youth, I lacked the tools of science to grasp, as I do today, what my father and I meant to each other. But I cherished our time playing catch and watching sports. My dad was on my mind a lot then as I plotted to increase the chances of his playing with me. Some of my most vivid childhood memories are of me anxiously sitting at the sidewalk curb waiting for my sweaty, exhausted father to walk home after his 7–3 shift as a blue-collar worker at a local factory. In my mind's eye I see myself counting the minutes until my father's return, playing with his old-fashioned 1930s baseball glove that he purchased as a teenager. With my smallish fist pounding away, I try to round out the contours of the deep circular pocket in his worn and cracked leather glove. The glove's odd-looking shape makes it seem more like a catcher's mitt than a fielder's glove. My own contemporary glove, resting by my side, serves as a neat point of reference. As I compare our gloves, both in appearance and smell, nostalgia fills me with sensitivity to the thirty-six years that separate our lives and baseball histories. Babe Ruth was the hero of my father's day, Hank Aaron mine.

Because my father is a man of very few words, he expressed his fatherly ways with me through the quiet rituals of our daily lives. Aside from the thumping sound of the ball hitting leather, we played catch in silence. Without the trappings of words, we solidified our timeless bond as father and son. I am convinced that even though we share a bloodline, with similar facial expressions to remind us, it was my father's manly presence during my childhood, not our genetic relatedness, that fostered our bond.

In a previous book I wrote about how becoming a father at age eighteen provided me with a new generational focus, one that pointed my attention toward my future involvement with my own son.[11] The personal insights I shared spoke specifically to the struggles young men face when they become adolescent fathers in a Western society. Those thoughts were relevant to young men's experiences with their own sons and daughters.

As I turn my attention to stepfathers for this book, I am reminded of experiences that affected me after I became, at age twenty-two, a divorced father to a child who moved a thousand miles away. Within a few years, I found myself adjusting to my son forming a close relationship with the man who married my ex-wife. I was faced with knowing that a stepfather had entered my son's daily life and was bonding with him in ways that I could not. Each summer, our three-week visit reaffirmed for us the emotional and physical distance that separated us. These visits reminded us too that my son's stepfather was present and intimately involved in his everyday life throughout the rest of the year. I'm happy to say that, despite these geographical, psychological, and emotional hurdles, we managed to nurture a bond that has persisted throughout the years.

It was during this earlier period, about seventeen years ago, that I experienced the other side of the nonresident-stepfather equation, the side most germane to this book. My turbulent but committed relationship with a woman who had a ten-year-old daughter, Alli, and a nine-year-old son, Josh, opened my eyes and heart to a brand-new style of fatherly love. I grew attached to and began to love these children as though they were mine even though they were not my own flesh and blood. Alli even began to play around with calling me "daddy." As I interviewed participants for this project, I found myself time and time again revisiting my own memories of Alli and Josh that resonated so clearly with the powerful stories participants shared with me. Where appropriate, I will weave my own voice and experiences into the mosaic I craft to represent men's stories about stepfathering. My experiences with Alli and Josh many years ago not only served as motivation to write this book but helped me refine my understanding of the complex inner worlds of stepfathers and those associated with them. In subsequent years, other dating experiences have sensitized me to the delicate aspects of developing relationships with a single mom's young children whose biological father remains actively involved. By commenting on my experiences, particularly with Alli, I incorporate a kind of self-reflective interview into my discussion. My story, though meaningful to me, plays only a minor role in my larger effort to paint a portrait that captures men's diverse experiences as stepfathers.

The best way to get at what being a stepfather means to men, and to figure out how they have managed their lives as stepfathers, is to ask them. If we are to develop a better sense of the challenges stepfathers face, and the types of resources that come into play when they deal with those challenges, stepfathers' voices need to be heard. They are a diverse bunch indeed. In addition to the basic differences that catch the eye of demographers—such as age, race, marital status, number of children, and level of education—many other conditions differentiate stepfathers from one another. These differences are likely to influence the family dynamics stepfathers encounter. Some of the obvious factors include whether stepfathers have their own biological children; whether their biological children were born before or after they became stepfathers; whether the biological fathers remain involved in their children's lives; what kinds of decisions were made about where the new family lives; the ages of the children when stepfathers entered the picture; how long mothers and their children lived without a father figure present in the home; what efforts were made to blend children from both sides of a romantic union; and whether the couple anticipated or ended up having children of their own together.

Much of what I have to say is based on my in-depth interviews with a diverse sample of thirty-six men, thirteen of their partners, and two children.[12] As my assistants and I talked to participants, we sought to uncover the deep meanings men associate with their evolving identities and life circumstances as stepfathers. The men I spoke with represent a diverse sample of stepfathers living in north central Florida. To be included, the men had to describe themselves as being actively involved in the lives of their romantic partner's children who were nineteen years of age or younger and living with the mother. Beyond these criteria I did not employ any litmus test to identify the men as social fathers, nor did I systematically try to clarify for all men how their perceptions of the stepfather label resonated with them. Given my sample's diversity in terms of the kinds of relationships and living arrangements the men report, the label "romantic partner social father"[13] may be a more precise way of categorizing the men. However, I refer collectively and individually to my participants by using plural and singular versions of the terms "stepdad" and "stepfather" because these terms are less cumbersome and more meaningful to both my participants and the general population. Where appropriate, I explore the nuances of men's experiences with children in those relationships that muddle the typical borders associated with stepfathering or stepfamilies.[14]

Unlike survey studies based on large, nationally representative samples, I make no specific claims about how comparable the experiences of the men in my sample are to the larger population of stepfathers in the country or other Western societies. My intent is not to generalize in a rigorous way to a larger population of stepfathers. Rather, I want to highlight key aspects of the processes that enable men to experience their varied lives as stepfathers. In doing so, I am able to describe stepfathers' inner worlds as they wrestle with the circumstances of their unconventional, though increasingly common, daily lives.

One important way my sample is probably not representative of all stepfathers is that, to my knowledge, I did not interview physically and sexually abusive stepfathers. Abusive stepfathers were probably reluctant to step forward and volunteer to be interviewed about their relationships with their stepchildren. Even if they did, the ethics review board that monitors research projects at my university instructed me to inform my participants in writing prior to interviewing them that if they described any abusive behavior toward their child, I was required by state law to report this behavior to the appropriate authorities. Thus I have no way of knowing for sure whether men belonging to the well publicized subset of abusive stepfathers participated in my study. I do know that none of my participants confided in me that they were abusive, although a few of the female partners indicated that they had been abused as children by stepfathers.

The stereotypical image of the abusive stepfather is clearly etched into the public psyche. It has become commonplace to assert that stepfathers and boyfriends are more likely to physically and sexually abuse the children of their romantic partners than the children's biological fathers.[15] Some go so far as to say that "stepfathers are far more likely than fathers to do so [sexually molest children]."[16] Though a majority of studies appear to find that stepchildren are indeed at greater risk of abuse than biological children,[17] various researchers have challenged the scientific validity of these claims.[18] I, for one, tend to think that it is premature to draw definitive conclusions about how stepfathers compare to biological fathers. I can say with confidence, though, that the nature of my sample narrows the range of stories I am able to discuss. That said, the stories men shared with me are quite diverse and were not all presented through rose-colored glasses. A number of stepfathers talked about their struggles and in some cases outright despair with their family circumstances.

Notwithstanding my caveat about the underrepresentation of abusive stepfathers, I intentionally secured interviews with a diverse group of men. Many of them, though living in Florida at the time of the interview, had been raised in other states or spent significant periods of time as adults living outside of Florida. I made sure that I spoke with men from different social classes who worked at a range of occupations. I spoke with at least one lawyer, professor, director of computer services, registered nurse, minister, realtor, vending machine technician, computer programmer, office manager, supervisor of laundry services, and heavy equipment operator, as well as several men who were either permanently unemployed because of a disability or temporarily unemployed and homeless. Consistent with this occupational diversity, sixteen of the men had completed college, twelve had some college experience, and eight had either completed high school and not attended college or had not obtained a high school diploma. Twenty-seven self-identified as white, nine were African American, and a few indicated that they had some Hispanic ancestry. The youngest man I interviewed was twenty while the oldest was fifty-four, with an average age of thirty-six. Twenty-five were currently married and living with their partner, seven cohabited with their partner but were not married, and four lived in a residence separate from their partner. Twenty-two had fathered their own biological child, and eleven were actually living with at least one of their biological children at the time of the interview. Of those living with biological children, three men had children with their current partner. Finally, I spoke with stepfathers of sons and daughters who were infants, toddlers, young children, and adolescents of all ages. Two men had partners who were currently pregnant with their first child. Excluding these pregnancies, the average age of the oldest child living with the stepdad's partner was 10.3. These children were roughly five and a half years old on average when stepfathers began their relationships with the children's mothers. Of the thirteen mothers my research team interviewed, nine were white and four were African American. Three were college graduates while eight had some college experience. As for their financial situation, eight indicated they were average, four thought they were a little below average, and one said poor. Eight were married.[19]

Those who are interested in knowing more about my methodology may consult the appendices to this book, which include a detailed description of how I conducted my study as well as my reflections on the research process. If you are not interested in this study's methodology, feel free to skip it and move on to chapter 2.

2

A LENS FOR STEPFATHERING

As we journey into the stories that bring this book to life, our view of stepfathering will be sharpened as we view it though a demographic and theoretical lens. What is the larger social backdrop for how men's and children's lives are demographically organized today? How common is it for children to live with their mother's new husband or boyfriend? How common is it for men to live with kids who are not their biological offspring? How common are blended families in which men live with stepchildren and biological children—those conceived with their partner or a previous partner?[1]

When we listen to men's personal stories about their experiences in different stepfamily arrangements, we should remain aware that how men experience their lives as stepfathers can be affected by the types of resources they bring to the table when they date women. In addition to their educational and financial resources, how men treat children can be interpreted as part of their effort to develop romantic relationships with the children's mothers. That men who become stepfathers differ in several important ways from men who do not draws attention to the larger social context in which stepfathers live.

DEMOGRAPHICS

Research shows that in recent decades men have been spending less time living with children.[2] In the mid-1960s, 60 percent of adult men were living with children; this declined to 45 percent in the late 1990s. Although this decline summarizes all men's residential living arrangements, men's chances of living with or spending time with children who are not biologically related to them have actually increased during the same period. Men's living arrangements with stepchildren are further complicated when we consider that some women produce children with more than one man. One recent study found that 32 percent of mothers age 20–24, 45 percent of those 25–29, and 40 percent of mothers 30 or older have children with at least two different fathers.[3] A stepfather, for many of these mothers, becomes the additional biological father for one of her children. However, some stepfathers are involved with multiple stepchildren who have different biological fathers.

High rates of divorce and growing numbers of romantic partners who live together mean that a higher proportion of children have been living with or exposed to stepfathers during the past several decades.[4] Unfortunately, census data collected before 1990 does not permit demographers to identify whether children living with men were their own biological children or stepchildren.[5] Demographers have shown that children are present in the households of about 50 percent of the people who currently live together and have been married before (almost always to someone else). Kids are also present in 35 percent of the households where the partners have never been married. When these two types of households are combined, 70 percent include children who are related to only one of the partners. Though not formalized by marriage, these families are essentially stepfamilies.[6] Increasingly, stepfamilies that include married or cohabiting partners include fathers who are involved with both stepchildren and biological children.

One study of 7,107 men conducted in the early 1990s in Albuquerque, New Mexico, revealed that among this sample of men who were at least twenty-five years of age, almost 21 percent had helped raise a child who was not their own for at least one year.[7] Whereas 16 percent had raised their own offspring as well as other children, roughly 5 percent had raised only other men's children. When this 21 percent was broken down, 64 percent of the men had been involved with children from their partner's previous relationship. The other children were either their partner's dependent kin (5 percent), adopted from an agency (9 percent), or the children of friends or neighbors (6 percent).

Demographers estimate that before children living in the United States turn eighteen, about one-third will live with a stepparent.[8] The vast majority of these stepparents will be stepfathers.[9] In addition, about 2.2 million children live with an unmarried parent and the parent's partner (a large percentage of whom are not the child's biological parent).[10] This number is likely to grow as an increasing proportion of stepfathers will be cohabiting with the mothers of minor children for at least some of the time the children and stepfathers live together.

National data also help us develop a portrait of stepfathers who are married to women with children or cohabitate with mothers. These men, on average, have completed less education and have lower incomes than biological fathers who live with their children. Stepfathers are more likely to have been divorced and to already have children compared with men who are not stepfathers.[11] Some scholars interpret these patterns to mean that women who already have children are perceived to be less desirable or rank lower in the "marriage market." In everyday language, they're seen as less attractive because they have more baggage. Consequently, the men who pursue these women are more likely to have limited educational and financial resources. Men with greater resources are more likely to be involved in relationships with women with whom they have produced their own children or women who are childless. Thus men with fewer resources may use their willingness to become stepfathers as a way of securing women's investment in them as romantic partners and spouses. Some may do so in hopes of having their own children.

These resource differences between stepfathers and biological fathers come into play when researchers consider the different outcomes stepchildren experience when they are compared to their peers living in families with both of their biological parents. Some of the negative outcomes that stepchildren experience may be related to stepfathers' limited resources rather than life in a stepfamily per se. At the same time, others have suggested that men who go on to have their own children with women who have children from a previous relationship(s) may have better relationship and fathering skills than other men.[12] Recent evidence shows that stepchildren living in blended families where the stepfather is involved with both stepchildren and biological children receive better treatment than do stepchildren in families with a stepfather who does not have children of his own.[13]

As demographers begin to document the pervasiveness of stepfathering in the United States and provide a more complete profile of these men, it is also useful to explore their inner worlds—the purpose of this book. The stories of stepfathers I share will help provide a clearer sense of the symbolic worlds that give meaning to the notion of fathering for men who are involved with other men's offspring. Those worlds can be viewed more clearly by highlighting different aspects of the process of fathering.

BECOMING A FATHER, BEING FATHERLY

For many men, the process of becoming and being a father is relatively straightforward because it follows a well-established cultural script and proceeds in an orderly fashion. This process, typically, begins informally for a man when his partner announces, "I think I'm pregnant." Although these words may or may not be a pleasant surprise, they serve to alert a man to the presumption that he has played an active role in creating human life; life that is genetically related to him. Reproductive physiology being what it is, a man can only presume his paternity until the child is born. This situation can leave a man feeling unsure about his relationship to this future child. Despite varied responses to hearing about a partner's pregnancy, the moment itself can anchor a man's self-perceptions. With this news, a man can gain an up-close and personal appreciation for his procreative potential and become more intimately acquainted with the paternity status that awaits them—father.

Other paths to becoming a father are more circuitous. Men who take less direct routes venture down paths on which they become involved in the lives of children who are not biologically related to them. Many of these children are the biological offspring of their romantic partners, but some are not. Whether or not the children are connected to men's romantic partners, men can become a part of these children's lives at various points.

Step, adoptive, and foster fathers forge a fathering identity without relying on a genetic bond to a child or children. They are unable to solidify their sense of being fathers by depending on many of the conventional symbols and experiences associated with biological paternity. Instead, they must take an alternative route if they are to experience a paternal consciousness.

When these men get involved in a fatherly way in children's lives, any distinctive type of fatherhood "click" or "snap" that often enables biological fathers to think of themselves as fathers is less likely to occur. If it does, it will be embedded in a more muddled and gradual process than is the case for biological fathers. We usually think of men launching their new, tangible visions of being fathers when they are directly faced with the realization that they have played a role in conceiving a child. Although the meaning of this experience may be colored by whether men are involved in pregnancies that are planned or unplanned, wanted or unwanted, the powerful symbolism of their genetic connection is likely to leave an indelible impression on most men. Whether this initial impression is strong enough to affect men's paternal consciousness in a fundamental and long-standing way obviously varies among men. Some men may not experience any dramatic change until a doctor shows them a visual image of their child-to-be in a sonogram picture or they hear the heartbeat. Although a fetus appears as a relatively formless mass in the early months of a pregnancy, this obscure picture can inspire men, as well as women, to see themselves in a fresh way as they contemplate their intimate involvement in the miracle of life. This may be a turning point that helps men establish their paternal identity, or it may merely reinforce their perception of being capable of creating human life. Similarly, feeling a fetus kick for the first time during their partner's pregnancy can activate their paternal identity in a tangible fashion. A significant moment for men is participating in their partner's labor and delivery. Watching the birthing process unfold and then holding their children in their arms, men are likely to feel their paternal identity crystallize. Taken separately or collectively, these experiences usually help men solidify their experiential sense of being fathers.

Men tend to assume, sometimes incorrectly, that the pregnancy involves a baby that is "theirs," one that is biologically related to them. They can, if they wish, psychologically and emotionally take ownership of the child they helped conceive. They can tell themselves and others that the child belongs to them. As with most patterns, though, there are exceptions. Previous interviews I used for a book on young men, *Sex, Men, and Babies: Stories of Awareness and Responsibility*, confirmed the complex avenues men travel in the procreative realm. From these interviews and other sources, it appears that men confront the uncertainties of paternity and develop identities as fathers in unconventional ways far more often than the average person probably realizes.[14] Although some of the possibilities are more relevant than others to my discussion of stepfathering, a quick review of some of the possibilities reveals several ways men can orient themselves toward a pregnancy and birth. Looking at the various ways men develop fatherlike identities brings the stepfathering experience into sharper focus.

A man can walk into the life of an unattached woman after she has been impregnated by another man but before the child is born. He may do "identity work" to claim the child as his, though he will do so knowing that he is not genetically related to the child.[15] A man may dig deep into his emotional reservoir, step forward if others allow this to happen or are unable to impede his involvement, and unconditionally claim the child as his—even before the pregnancy is brought to term. This man assumes his new roles in a straightforward, unambiguous fashion. For other men, some of whom I met when I was interviewing stepfathers, the process may not be so clear-cut. Some of these men may not see themselves as fathers per se, but they may still play the role of fathers-in-waiting. I learned much from Neal, a mature and understanding twenty-two-year-old who provides an intriguing case study. Neal was the boyfriend of a young woman, Maria, who had an eight-year-old son with one man and was eight months preg-

nant with another man's child. As Neal talked about his experiences with
his girlfriend, whom he befriended when she was seven weeks pregnant, he
commented that, aside from phone conversations and some financial contributions, the biological father was not involved in Maria's life once she
announced the pregnancy. Without any apparent signs of jealousy, Neal
hoped and expected that the father would visit his child after the child was
born, sign the paternity papers, and be involved in the child's life. He describes his own confusion and outlook on the biological father's behavior
this way:

> Why wouldn't he want to be related to, why wouldn't he want to be in-
> volved with his child? I can't imagine. Even if it's, you are seeing some-
> body or whatever and you become pregnant with your partner. If you're
> not involved in a relationship for quite a long time or even if it's just a
> chance that you get pregnant, how could you not want to be involved
> with your child? That's what gets me, and I don't know if he realizes what
> it all entails as far as when he sees his child, the emotions. But from what
> I get from Maria, he's sort of immature about those types of things—that's
> what she tells me. That's why I have an opinion that I think it'll change
> as he sees his child and grows to know it; I think his opinion will change
> on not wanting to be part of his life and I hope it will. I don't think he's
> a bad person, but I think he should probably really think about how he's
> involved with his child. And I hope that he is in a positive way. She asked
> me, "Should I have him around or should I not?" I don't know what to
> tell her; I don't know. First of all, I'm new, being pregnant and on top of
> that, the situation with the dad, this is just, I don't know the answers to
> these questions. . . . I'm not strongly opinionated one way or another
> when it comes to whether he should be there for the child. But I'm more
> leaning on the side of yeah he should be there for the child. It's his child,
> and I think he will be after the baby is born.

Later in the interview, when asked about how his involvement in the pregnancy affected his relationship with Maria, Neal replies with conviction,
"We kind of have a mission, to have a baby, and now it's my mission as
well to help her, and be there for her and the baby. I think it has contributed to kind of a rapid involvement . . . of how we feel." Neal's demeanor and words throughout the interview made clear how invested he
is in his relationship with Maria and his role in helping her through the
pregnancy. He has verbally professed his love to her, and she has done the
same. From where I sit, it seems obvious that Neal is indeed on a mission.
He has discussed the choice of names for the baby with Maria on countless

occasions, faithfully gone with her to childbirth preparation classes, has been invited by Maria to take a ringside seat during the child's delivery, and has been comfortable discussing with Maria the prospects of the biological father getting involved in the child's life.

The unique set of circumstances Neal faces extend beyond his one-on-one interactions with Maria. There have been plenty of private and public opportunities for Neal to reflect on whether he sees himself having some type of fatherly presence in this child's life. Being with Maria in public, especially in the latter months of her pregnancy, has drawn attention to him as the man who presumably is responsible for her "condition." He notes how people sometimes congratulate him and Maria on the pregnancy when they're out at a restaurant, play, or elsewhere. With a flare for irony, Neal conveys how he responds, "Well thanks!" He continues with this rationalization:

> Because I'm putting up with her being pregnant, I feel like I should get a little credit, even just the slightest little bit would be fine with me. I don't wish the child was mine; I can't change what has happened, or what's going on. It would be, with her, I think she likes that I tell her that I really wouldn't mind if the child was mine. She is comforted by that. That kind of tells her that I'm accepting of the baby. Because I know, being a single mom, she's got to be concerned about that. Even though she says she doesn't, I can't imagine not being concerned whether the person [I'm] in a relationship with is going to be interested in hanging around when the baby [is born] or even with Stanley [Maria's other son].

As I listened to Neal's thoughts it became clear that he is traversing murky waters. At one point he comments that he "doesn't wish the child was mine," but then he quickly asserts that he wants Maria to know that he "wouldn't mind if the child was mine." This subtle distinction is apparently fueled by his intense feelings for Maria, and to a lesser extent his feelings for her eight-year-old son. His romantic love grounds him as he figures out how he feels about this pregnancy and the baby that connects her to another man. Although Maria has allowed Neal to be a part of her pregnancy in an intimate way, he does not believe that she sees him as the father of this child. However, he anticipates that her feelings may change after the child is born.

> She'll see in time, and I know she knows this, she'll see in time I'll accept that baby just like I do Stanley. As far as helping her with taking care of the baby, I'm going to do as much as I can. Hopefully in time she'll see that, she'll understand it's not something that I don't want to

do, like I won't mind helping and being there for her. She knows this
but I think actually doing it and participating makes a big difference.

With time, Neal will have his answer and I suspect a clearer sense of how
Maria wants him to fit into her life and that of the child. Though Neal's
circumstances are uncommon, there are others like him who face similar
questions about dating pregnant women who knowingly are carrying another man's child.

Other scenarios depicting how men get involved with children who
are not biologically related to them are worth mentioning, even though
some are less relevant for the stepfathers I interviewed. Listing these scenarios reminds us that men's involvement with children who are not biologically related to them can be achieved in various ways.

For starters, men may be involved in their partner's fertility treatments
and pregnancy that use donor sperm. In these situations, men have agreed up
front to establish an identity as a prospective father as well as a supportive co-
parent without the benefit of a personal genetic tie. Other men may begin to
think of themselves as prospective fathers because they have arranged to adopt
a baby that is being carried by a birth mother, not their partner. Adopting infants or older children as part of a couple can also provide men opportunities
to develop a paternal identity. These cases differ from the "normative" path-
way described earlier because they involve postnatal events that extend beyond the hours surrounding the labor and delivery process. A final scenario
finds some men suspicious about whether they are in fact responsible for their
partner's pregnancy. These men are concerned that their partner may have
had sex with someone else and conceived a child with this person. Such
doubt can inhibit the extent to which these men embrace a paternal identity.
In general, though, men who are involved with pregnant partners assume that
they personally have played a role in creating human life. They construct
their identity with this presumption in mind. Although the early-twentieth-
century anthropologist Margaret Mead informed us long ago that motherhood is a biological reality while fatherhood is a social convention, the presumption of paternity carries much weight in defining men's procreative
identity unless there are overriding suspicions to the contrary.

A MODEL OF FATHERING

As I began my research with stepfathers I had some ideas about how to con-
ceptualize their lives and structure the interviews. Interested in how men

become stepfathers and act in a fatherly way, I wanted to explore the inner worlds and social processes that give meaning to stepfathers' lives. Recall that I emphasized how these processes are similar in some ways to biological fathers' experiences, but different in others. Drawing on a model I used previously, I had a broad template of questions that would get men to talk about their lives as stepfathers.[16] This model focuses on young men's identities as persons capable of creating human life and their actual experiences as fathers. It also highlights the complexity of men's experiences with family-related issues and their perceptions of themselves as fathers. The model suggests that three different, though often overlapping trajectories or paths, can capture men's experiences as fathers. I describe these trajectories and show how they are useful to my research with stepfathers. By presenting this material here, I provide a framework for issues addressed in subsequent chapters that delve into men's personal accounts of stepfathering.

Before discussing the three specific trajectories (self-as-father, father–child, and coparental), I shall clarify terminology. Some social scientists have used the trajectory concept to represent a course or path of experience for individuals.[17] Trajectories imply that the experiences and processes that define them take place over time; people's lives change in various ways. However, people do not always see a course laid out before them with a specific destination in sight. They may simply be going through the rhythms of their lives, one day, one week, one month at a time. For this study, I do not use the "trajectory" metaphor to mean that men change by moving through a prescribed set of stages. Instead, I think of men's lives as unfolding in countless ways along three distinct, yet often interconnected substantive paths related to fathering. These paths represent life domains or specific areas of personal experience. They have no predefined end point. As I'll show later, significant life events may, on occasion, reinforce or alter men's identities as fathers and their perspective on fathering.[18] In my interviews with stepfathers and their partners, they were asked to talk about fathering issues related to these three trajectories.

The broad trajectories that I explore in this book involve men's inner worlds related to their thoughts about creating babies and, most importantly, about their experiences with acting in a fatherly way toward children not biologically related to them. These thoughts and experiences help define the personal context in which men construct their identities as fathers and act like fathers. How men experience these different trajectories can be studied at various points in men's lives, including crucial transitional periods such as marriage, divorce, and childbirth. Though particular trajectories may be irrelevant to men at given times, some take on meaning intermittently as men's life circumstances change.

What are these three trajectories? One is what I call a *self-as-father* trajectory. This path includes a man's philosophy about fathering, his desire and intention to have children, and his visions about how he would father his children. What is distinctive about this trajectory? A man who is in this life space or frame of mind is not tied directly to any particular relationship he has with a romantic partner or specific child. This self-as-father trajectory reflects how he sometimes embraces fathering as an amorphous set of roles or an abstract image, not a concrete, interpersonal connection to a specific child. A man does not have to be a father to experience this life domain of fatherhood; he just needs to be able to daydream and see himself as a father. When a man thinks about prospective fatherhood images, those he anticipates or hopes to realize some day, he often does so in a general way. Sometimes he relies on how he thinks and feels about his own father's past and present involvement in his life. How did his father raise him? What valuable lessons did he learn? What lessons does he want to duplicate or avoid with his own children? And how does his father relate to him now that he is an adult? The nature and direction of the self-as-father trajectory can also be affected by a man's life experiences and personal development. These experiences can involve work, military service, religious encounters, drug addictions, legal problems, traumas, disabilities, and others. As a man grows emotionally, psychologically, and spiritually as an individual, he may come to see himself, others, and the world around him in fresh ways. This change in outlook can affect his attitude toward fathering.

When looked at through a social psychological lens, whatever thoughts and feelings a man develops about having children typically begin when he learns, usually during adolescence, that he is capable of impregnating a sex partner.[19] Many boys may have a vague sense, prior to learning about the mechanics of their ability to procreate, that they will be fathers someday. They may look at their own dad and assume that they will be like him someday, older, bigger, married, and with a son or daughter of their own—a family man. Those raised without an involved father may take their cues from an uncle, grandfather, their mother, or a man in the public eye.

Looking further down the adult life course, theorists point out that developmental and motivational forces sometimes propel men to seek opportunities to nurture children.[20] For most men this means that they want to have their own biological children. Other men may find themselves becoming aware of these needs as they spend time with children who are not their biological offspring. Although some men search for romantic partners with whom they would feel comfortable having children, most men do not intentionally look for women to date who already have kids. As men move into their late twenties and beyond, they may assume that many of the women they date will already be mothers. According to Emmit, a twenty-eight-year-old African American, "There's a large percentage out there now these days of women; usually it's hard to find a woman without a child these days." But this is not the same as actively looking for women to date who already have children. Certain types of men, especially those with high social status, may actually use motherhood as a red flag that serves to exclude women from their dating circles. That said, men sometimes find that getting romantically involved with women who are mothers offers them insights about their own developmental needs. Men may discover or confirm that they enjoy being connected to children in a fatherly way. Their involvement with the children may help strengthen their attraction to particular women. Further, some may take advantage of their opportunity to evaluate firsthand their partner's mothering skills with someone else's child. Emmit jumped at the chance to express how impressed he was with his wife's "very good motherly instincts" that she displayed when they were dating. "That's one of the reasons why I'm going to say I married [Robin] well, one of the reasons I fell in love with my wife, because there's nothing that she wouldn't do for either one of the kids."

Once men become fathers or stepfathers, their personal experiences deepen their concept of what fathering means to them. The abstract ideas they have cultivated about fathering will be infused with practical significance by their real-life, hands-on experiences with specific children. Thus whatever broad sentiments they have about fathering will no longer be based solely in their imagination. Not only will kids make a difference in how fathers view fathering, but men's involvement with their romantic partners will too.[21]

One key aspect of the self-as-father trajectory is that men will associate images of their future fathering roles with images of their "possible selves."[22] With their sights set on these future-oriented self-images, they may ask: What do I want? Who can I be? What can I achieve? What role might children play in my life? Thus men's perceptions of how they would like to think, feel, and behave as fathers will come into play. Men can link their ideas of "possible selves" with the images they build from their life experiences. For Emmit, it was watching his father, a deacon in his childhood church, recover from a nearly fatal work accident when Emmit was a teenager. Reflecting on his five-year-old stepson, Jake, Emmit says, "I realized my dad, he is a man of his word and he believes in God Almighty, and I was asking the Lord, 'Can you please bless me like my father and have a heart like my father.' That's what I hope I can do with Jake, is be—have that unconditional love which I think I am slowly growing towards that way."

This self-oriented type of trajectory does not necessarily end when a man's first child is born or he expresses a willingness to assume fatherly roles toward a stepchild. It can evolve far beyond these experiences. However, once a man becomes a father or stepfather, his self-reflections about what type of father he would like to be are more likely to be connected with his "own" child (biological or nonbiological), at least for the period of time in which he sustains an identity as a father and commitment to the child.[23]

Of course, some commitments end abruptly and others fade away. Familiar to most of us are sad stories about fathers who lose touch with their children over time when they do not live with them. Some of these men make the choice to walk away from their children; they simply don't care. Others find that their commitments to their children wane as they take on the time-consuming and financial responsibilities that go along with getting involved with new families. Yet other fathers feel marginalized because they are pushed away. They reluctantly distance themselves from their children because the children's mother, her relatives, or the children themselves make it exceedingly difficult to maintain the kind of contact they would like. Each of these patterns is usually talked about in reference to biological fathers, but each can apply to stepfathers as well. Whatever the reason or reasons may be for nonresident fathers' declining involvement in their children's lives, some men eventually find themselves thinking about fathering in abstract terms again. The idea of becoming a father once more, perhaps couched in the hopes of doing a better job the next time around, may influence their thinking. Others may long for another chance to father a child with a more compatible romantic partner. And then there are men who never again seriously entertain the idea of fathering children. Feelings of grief, remorse, anger, guilt, or discomfort about an earlier fathering experience may lead them to suppress their desire to imagine what it could be like to become a father again. Obviously, a wide range of experiences shape how men think about, act on, and articulate their willingness to father their own children or become stepfathers.

Some of the emotional, cognitive, and physical energy that a man expends is part of their effort to act responsibly on his child's behalf. Images of "possible selves" may motivate a man to undertake projects to improve himself so he might have a better chance of being a responsible family man. A man facing the prospects of becoming a stepfather can visualize fathering roles typically associated with biological paternity and use these images to establish a point of reference or a guide for their self-evaluation.

The second trajectory deals specifically with a man's real-life relationships with each of his children.[24] These *father–child* trajectories can include both biological and nonbiological children. In most cases, a man develops and sustains relationships with specific children that evolve over time, although he may produce offspring with whom he never develops a father identity. For a biological father, these relationships typically begin prenatally. For most stepfathers, these relationships begin months or usually years after children are born. They may deteriorate to the point that a man no longer plays an active role in his children's lives. With time, however, a father may rekindle his connection to and involvement with these children. He may also develop new relationships with other children. Simply put, a father is likely to develop individual relationships with his children that are complex and fluctuate over time.

A father can develop and be aware of personal bonds he shares with individual children, a reality that may be both cause and consequence of the different ways a man can involve himself in his child's life. The bond a father develops with a child can affect how he interacts with that child. Conversely, how a father interacts with a child can go a long way in shaping the type of bond that binds the two.

Having relationships with more than one child provides a father unique opportunities to perceive, compare, and evaluate his fatherly involvement and his sense of self. A father with more than one child is likely to forge unique relationships with each of the children. Much can be gained by studying how a father subjectively manages and verbally constructs his sense of fathering based on multiple father–child trajectories. For the man who is involved in his children's lives, being a father to more than one child differs fundamentally from being a father to only one child.

By doing in-depth interviews with stepfathers, I was able to explore the different types of relationships men had with children and how these relationships affected each other—even though I spent extra time talking to men about their relationships with one target child. Unless men are encouraged to describe their experiences with different children, researchers often will be left with only a broad account of their fathering experiences or an account based only on a target child. In everyday life, and some interview settings, men may downplay their awareness of their child-specific fathering identities and activities unless they are directed explicitly to do otherwise. Men's diverse experiences with sons and daughters often highlight different types of fathering experiences with particular children. Presumably men with children by different mothers *may* use the mothers as a reference point to compartmentalize the way they consider and represent their fathering experiences. Likewise, men may use the biological or nonbiologogical status of their children to organize their subjective understanding of themselves as fathers. Because many of the stepfathers in this study were also biological fathers—with different mothers being involved in a number of cases—I was conscious of situations in which two or more mothers were involved in the stepfather's life history as a father figure.

A man's interactions with the mother (or mothers) of his children based on shared parenting responsibilities represents the third trajectory that is useful for studying fathers' and stepfathers' lives. At its core, this *coparental* trajectory represents dyadic, coparental processes targeting biological or nonbiological children, or both.[25] The man who has children with different mothers may experience different coparental trajectories that either intersect or coexist independently of one another. When these trajectories intersect, how a father interacts with one mother can affect how he interacts with another mother. A father's interactions with the mother who serves as a gatekeeper to his children are essential to the coparental trajectory.[26] The dyadic parenting processes that often emerge in a father's life—discussions about discipline, values, monitoring, financial support, and so forth—are intertwined with a father's efforts to involve himself in his child's life.

To understand men's lives as stepfathers, and the nuances surrounding their involvement with their stepchildren, we must be sensitive to how the self-as-father, father–child, and coparental trajectories overlap and influence one another at different times, including transitional periods. From a methodological perspective this framework poses the intriguing challenge of how to study father involvement for fathers with multiple children, especially when some of these children have different mothers.

For this study, I consider a man to be involved in stepfathering only if he entertains the thought of becoming friends with and eventually dates a woman who is a mother. In the beginning, it is the mother who decides if a man is allowed to get involved with her children. The mother decides if a man will be permitted to feed, clothe, bathe, and discipline her young children. The mother makes the choice as to whether a man will spend the night and have her children wake up to the sights and sounds of an adult man in the home. The mother is the gatekeeper who either invites a man to enter her children's life or shuts him out. To understand a stepfather's experiences we must go back to the early days when he first sought the companionship of a woman who happened to be a mother. His desire to become romantically involved with a woman even though she had children is key. Without this initial interest, a man will take the path of least resistance that allows him to avoid the additional responsibility children will bring to his life.

3

GETTING STARTED

Dating is basically a crapshoot; there are no guarantees. Those who think otherwise are fooling themselves. The odds are even more daunting when children are factored into the equation because the phases of "getting started," "moving things along," and "being involved" are more complex.[1] From the perspective of a birth mother or stepfather, life together as a stepfamily seldom begins on a given day; it evolves from the bits and pieces of experience woven into the fabric of their dating relationship. Thus the threads of a stepfamily's success or failure can be sewn long before adopting a formal or informal stepfamily label.

Unfortunately, developing meaningful and lasting romantic relationships, whether kids are involved or not, is no easy task in the modern era. It was refreshing to discover, then, that some of my participants had established wonderful relationships with partners who had children from previous relationships. Even though many faced unique and often difficult challenges because of their family circumstances, they were happy with their relationships.

Since the latter twentieth century, moving into and out of relationships has become an unspoken emblem of the human experience in Western cultures, America in particular.[2] With each successive generation, adults have become increasingly likely to experience a growing number of romantic involvements during their lifetime. Because people are postponing marriage, most young persons experience several serious relationships before they tie the knot for the first time—which the vast majority still do. Over the course of a lifetime, people are likely to have a number of unions that are quite serious, whether they marry or not. In fact, it is not uncommon for persons to experience multiple engagement proposals and marriage ceremonies. More and more, they are moving in and out of serious and not so serious romantic involvements just as they change jobs, homes, and even hairstyles. Gone are the days when most young sweethearts jointly tackled family, work, and health challenges as they moved side by side through their early, middle, and later years of life. Children, increasingly, are being pulled into and out of these serial relationships.[3]

DATING WITH CHILDREN

Many who explore the dating market today must deal with the everyday realities of single parenthood for themselves, their partners, or both. Some dating stories of single parents as well as their partners are relatively simple, others exceedingly convoluted. In one way or another, dating partners who have minor children living at home will eventually have to take their children into account as they manage their romantic relationships, especially if the relationship progresses to the point of living together or marriage. James Feldman, the national director of public education at KidsPeace, a nonprofit corporation helping kids in crisis, says that single parents' dating "has a quiet but profound impact on millions of people, both adults and children. A child's resistance to parents' dating is one of the most difficult scenarios faced by divorced, dating parents."[4]

Various factors can affect how people try to manage their relationships in the face of having children. Whatever those factors may be, some people go about their dating in a mindful manner, thinking about their kids every step of the way. They try to protect children's feelings at all costs. One man was particularly conservative in his approach to dating a woman with children; he chose not to allow his partner's children to know that anything romantic was happening for about three years. Barry describes how he and his wife molded an impression that he was a good friend who came over to the house and spent time with her and her children. He never spent the night when the kids were home but would take his partner and two kids out to dinner and spend time with everyone doing other things. Although he could not recall having any explicit discussions with his wife about this process during their early years of dating, he noted that they both thought it was best that they not go public with their relationship because the kids were having a difficult time with their mother's divorce.

Those at the other end of the spectrum go through the motions of dating without giving any thought to how their dating practices may influence their children. At best, the kids are a passing afterthought. One extreme example comes by way of a story told to me by a forty-two-year-old man,

Ray. He recalls how his most serious relationship began ten years ago when he met a woman, Angie, in a bar. The next day Angie asked Ray to move in to her apartment with her and her five-year-old daughter. He did. They ended up getting married within the year in order to retain their eligibility to live in the family housing provided by the local university. They also had a child of their own. Now, ten years later, they have divorced and no longer maintain a sexual relationship, but they manage to be active coparents for two children: their own nine-year-old daughter and the woman's four-year-old daughter by another man who was conceived after she and Ray divorced. Ray and Angie also stay in contact with Ray's original step-daughter, now fifteen, who lives with her father in another state.

Located somewhere between these extreme dating examples are folks who give some thought, especially early in the dating process, to how their children will respond or are responding to their dating. These people do not obsess about or ignore how their children will respond. Of course, dating strategies may be modified as people gain experience dating different people where their children or their partner's children are involved.

Men can act on their own while being sensitive to how mothers feel about their potential involvement in their lives and their children's lives. They can be extra careful in getting involved with mothers because they do not want to send the wrong message about their willingness to be a family man. They know that their involvement could imply expectations as a romantic partner as well as a father figure. Jesse, a twenty-year-old boyfriend of a young woman with a year-old child, illustrates this dynamic when he talks about how he weighed his priorities and carefully developed his relationship with his partner.

> There's no way I'm going to lead her on to the point that she's think-ing, "Well maybe, you know, this could be a dad for Shaun. This could be great." . . . You don't want to lead anybody on anyway, but if I'm not serious enough to know that someday I would look at marriage [with] her . . . then there's no point in going through this. There's no point in putting her through all that.

Jesse shares these thoughts as he describes how he began to reorganize his life priorities. He came to see that by not going on expensive surf trips he could devote his time and money to his girlfriend and Shaun in meaning-ful ways. His roles as a boyfriend and an emerging father figure enabled him to adopt a less egocentric view of life. In doing so, he began to express a more mindful approach to human relations.

Other men talked about decisions they made not to spend the night at their partner's house if the children were at home. Robby recalls avoiding these overnights for a long time, but then eventually stayed the night and helped his partner get her children ready for school. Speaking about the kids, Robby says, "Their eyes were like this big when they seen me, and wondered what are you doing here? There, it was weird, real weird." Another man, Juan, spoke about how he and his partner improvised because they did not want to give his partner's child the impression that a man had spent the night. Juan would wake up early and walk outside and knock on the door to wake up the child and signal to him that he had just arrived early that morning. This little trick apparently worked.

Obviously, compared to single persons or those with grown children, the dating process is more complex for people with minor children. Studying the context that shapes how people get romantically involved in each other's lives when one or both of them have minor children produces useful insights. What types of discussions, if any, do people have about their circumstances? What are their major concerns and fears? What types of expectations do people have? What types of logistical concerns surface? Although I focus primarily on men's involvement with women who are mothers, I also consider how men's own parental status affects their involvement with children who are not biologically related to them.

Because the "getting started" process for romantic relationships has its own unique trials and tribulations when children are involved, I devote special attention to several events and processes that affect the context for building and navigating dating relationships. Some of these experiences may be viewed differently through the eyes of individual men, women, and children. Here I emphasize the male perspective when considering how men get involved with partners who are mothers. The various events and processes I discuss sometimes occur in different sequences or overlap in specific ways depending on how particular people orchestrate their friendship and dating experiences.

For a man to be considered a stepfather in the way I'm defining the study population for this book, several things need to happen. He eventually must be romantically involved with a woman who has one or more children living with her at least part of the time. Thus how a man meets and then develops a romantic relationship with a partner who has a child is one of the fundamental processes related to stepfathering. A part of this meeting process involves the man becoming aware that the woman is a mother. At some point, the man must also take the initiative to meet and get involved with the child if he is ever to assume a significant role in the child's life. The mother of the child often plays an active role, in many cases suggesting a meeting or agreeing to arrangements that would enable the man and child to meet. When a child meets a potential stepfather, he or she may or may not realize that the mother is romantically interested in or involved with this person. One of the more memorable and comical first meetings I heard about was when Harry went to Jennifer's (his future wife) apartment to have dinner and meet her four-year-old daughter, Kelly. Jennifer vividly remembers the first words Kelly spoke to Harry as he entered the door: "Are you going to be my new daddy?" From Jennifer's perspective Kelly's comment "was kinda scary for me cause I'm thinking this guy's gone. He'll eat dinner and I won't see him again. . . . She had never talked like that, so it was a real eye-opener for me that she was thinking about somebody being her daddy." Jennifer's fears proved to be unfounded; Harry came back and they eventually married.

When a man acts in a fatherly way toward the child and the child is old enough to realize the essential elements of what it means to be "dating," the child eventually will learn that the mother is dating a particular man. Being introduced to a mother's dating partners and learning that she is dating someone are processes that sometimes occur simultaneously, although in many instances they do not. A child could be under the impression for a period of time, correctly or incorrectly, that a man is the mother's friend. In Barry's case, he was able to hide his dating relationship from his future stepchildren for three years!

The final process involves a man's interactions with the child. How does he start to connect with a child in a fatherly way? One path shows the man making a transition from the status of friend to casual romantic partner, to boyfriend, to boyfriend who has adult authority to direct a child's behavior, to a stepfather figure who may, in some cases, even be seen as a full-fledged father minus the blood connection. In special cases, this last status may be achieved without the "step" label being used to identify the man. Individuals and entire family units are likely to negotiate these crude distinctions and assign meaning in each particular situation. The transition from one status to another is also highly variable. Some people move slowly from the start whereas others move quickly. Some begin slowly or quickly and then either speed up or put on the brakes. Then there are those who follow no clear path for any extended period of time. They experience vacillation in their relationships and move in different directions. Those who experience life this way often do so because they are reacting to unpredictable life events involving romantic relationships, separations and divorces, births, employment, moving, illnesses, personal growth issues, and other circumstances.

My interviews reveal that people vary greatly in how they start their relationships and factor their children into the dating equation. With increasing numbers of single mothers living in Western countries, a woman's motherhood status has become a more prominent aspect of the predating and dating experience for many adults in recent decades. This characteristic was important over a century ago because of spouses' shorter life spans but became less significant in the mid-1900s.

Women's disclosures and men's discoveries about women being mothers can occur in any number of ways. This knowledge is often blended with the other bits of information people casually take in during the course of getting to know someone. In many situations, learning that a woman is a mother may be unrelated to dating. This information may be discovered before men (or women) make or even consider making an overture that could be seen as part of the dating ritual. Men can learn about a woman's maternal status as part of the common knowledge or gossip that is channeled through informal networks in neighborhoods, workplaces, or school settings. Internet and newspaper dating ads usually disclose information about a woman's motherhood status. Men may also form assumptions about a woman being a mother after seeing her with kids in public places such as the local mall, grocery store, or children's recreational events. In some cases, men may use multiple sources over a period of time to develop assumptions and learn details about a woman's motherhood status. And then there is the more direct route. Women can simply tell potential suitors that they are mothers in order to put them on notice from the start that they are part of a package deal, children included. Whatever the source or sources may be, men eventually learn that they are getting involved or have already become involved with someone who has kids.

SO, YOU HAVE KIDS

Almost all of the stepfathers in my study knew early in the "dating game" that their future partners had children. Many actually knew before they went out on a date or considered approaching the women about a romantic outing. Some men I interviewed learned about the women having children in the course of their initial meeting at a bar, a store, a prayer group, on the Internet, or in self-help groups.

Men's reactions varied a bit, but most took it in stride. For men who had kids of their own, learning that women had children was of little consequence. Yes, some men, whether they were fathers or not, acknowledged that they saw red flags at times and were a bit cautious, but very few spent much time worrying about women having children. For instance, Doug, a man who had no children, was not fazed in the least that his future wife had a child. He demonstrated this when he first met her toddler. Both Doug and his wife recalled this event similarly. Doug remembers that

> I was sitting home on the couch and her son came home and tapped on my knee with a toy, as little kids do, and she said "Yeah, that's my son Sammy." I said, "Okay," and she said, "That doesn't bother you?" I said, "No, should it? Is there a particular reason behind this questioning?" She said "No, some people when they see a kid want to go back home and run the other way." I said "Well, you don't see me heading for the door so." But she told me "Okay; I'm just laying the cards on the table." "Okay, they're out. I see them."

Doug's openness to his dating partner having a child foreshadowed how he aggressively took an interest in being a full-fledged father when he proposed marriage.

Learning about a dating partner being a mother sometimes gave other men, like Neal, reason to pause, but they were not affected in any significant way. Neal felt that his partner's motherhood status "put a new spin on dating somebody for sure." Although he said that it didn't "bother" him, he did have "questions." Some of these questions had to do with how a couple would manage their social activities while taking the child into account. He was relieved to find out then that the process of growing accustomed to dating a woman with a child was "absorbed into the relationship."

Some men with kids of their own reasoned that if they have kids, even if they weren't living with them, then they shouldn't hold it against women if they had children of their own. Keep in mind, though, that most of the men who said they felt comfortable knowing that the women they were eventually going to date had children were the same men who wound up getting involved seriously with these women. A self-selection process is at work here. Many men who are not willing to date women with children, or have serious reservations about doing so, would be ineligible for my study because they never allowed themselves to become seriously involved with women who had children in the first place, or they quickly ended the relationship. Thus the men who volunteered for my study on stepfathering may differ in some ways from those men who shy away from involvements with women who are mothers. Much could be learned from interviews with men who choose not to get involved with single mothers.

Having children provided some men with the opportunity to relate more easily and quickly to single mothers. Rodney, a thirty-seven-year-old father of two, captures this sentiment when he comments on how his initial interactions with his wife were enhanced because they both had kids. "It really brought us together quicker than it would have if neither one of us had had kids, because it was a common presence between us. We both had a boy and a girl. So we had, we could discuss the similarities and how we were raising our kids and that kind of thing. It led to a lot of good talks." Rodney saw his children quite a bit so he could relate to the practical, day-to-day issues associated with parenting. Men who live apart from their children much or all of the time can also offer insights about how the biological father who does see his child may be thinking and feeling. This can be a valuable perspective for single mothers who may have a hard time looking objectively at their former partner and his relationship to their child or children. Thus the new romantic partner who has experience as a father is often in a unique situation to relate to his partner or offer advice early in their relationship as well as throughout the time they are together (a point I elaborate on later).

FIRST IMPRESSIONS

Because we often hear that first impressions are important in many types of social relations, I was interested in stepfathers' first sightings and impressions of the children they would end up acting fatherly toward. Overall, men tended to report that they felt at least reasonably comfortable with their partner's kids when they first met. Because these meetings varied in place, context, length, and type of activity, there are various ways to identify what constitutes a first meeting. Does it count, for example, if children are half asleep and being carted back to bed when they and the future stepdads meet? Emmit, for instance, told about the time when he was introduced to his stepson, Jake. His future wife was toting Jake to his bedroom after she and Emmit had been out on a date. He recalled that Jake "kind of reached for me and I picked him up, held him—it felt weird at first. I'm holding some other man's child. It was a weird but warm feeling at the same time." What about men who come into their partner's home prior to going out on a date, meet the kids and exchange a brief hello and pleasantries, and then leave. What if the kids are engrossed in playing video games or some other activity that limits their focus? Differences in context can involve such things as the kids' or stepdads' home, public or private spaces, and indoor versus outdoor environments. Some first encounters are much more superficial than opportunities where men, mothers, and children go to a park for a social outing and have an extended period of time to interact and get to know one another.

Notwithstanding the various ways in which men meet children for the first time, none of the men clearly had negative things to say about the kids with whom they later became involved. Among those who had anything bordering on negative to say, the most common observations were that the kids appeared to be spoiled or disrespectful to their mothers. When men saw the kids as spoiled, they tended to blame the mothers and grandparents, rather than the kids per se. Some assumed that these adults were overcompensating for the disruption and emotional turmoil the kids experienced because of a divorce or a failed romantic relationship. Another man, Mark, was simply not enthralled with children in general. He described how the first time he met his future stepchildren, who were between three and five years of age at the time, he played with them at a park with his own kids. He added in a matter-of-fact way, "I'm not a real kid person. . . . kids that young, I mean there's not a whole lot, you can play with them a little bit, you can't carry on conversations to any great extent."

Many men who formed a clear-cut first impression, because they had the opportunity to spend time interacting with the kids, had decidedly positive things to say. The youngest man I spoke with was Jesse, the twenty-year-old boyfriend of the woman who had a year-old child, Shaun. Although Jesse had first seen Shaun briefly when he was getting "dedicated" at a church service, it was several months later that he actually spent time with Shaun. Jesse, Shaun's mother, and Shaun went to a local park for a picnic lunch when Shaun was seven months old. Jesse recalled this first outing with delight:

> We played with him for a day at the park and it was like a blast! It was fun. . . . It was just a lot of fun going to the park with Shaun and everything. It was neat. . . . I was like—oh my goodness, this thing is—he's awesome, you know. I was still, I guess, kind of uneasy because I wasn't around kids a lot. I don't know what they do and what they don't do and everything. But it was just a really fun day for both of us. . . . Most of the time Shaun would—he's a really friendly baby. He'll let anybody hold him. He doesn't cry a lot and stuff like that so she [girlfriend] didn't have a problem with me holding him some.

As Jesse told his story, it was clear that he had been captivated by this unique opportunity to interact with an infant in this playful, intimate way.

His glowing opinion of Shaun and the time he spends with him has become even more positive over the past several months. Since the first meeting, Jesse has spent a lot of time with Shaun and has been the primary caretaker on numerous occasions when his girlfriend is working. In this instance, first impressions did ring true.

Although a few men in my sample met stepchildren who were infants, most came into contact with children who were at least several years old. On average the kids were five and a half. For the most part, men's first impressions emphasized various types of positive traits. Men said things such as, "He was a cute kid. Real smart, articulate." "The kids were clean and they were well-mannered and those were for me good things." "Very, very intelligent, right here, right now, type of kid where—I sat and talked with her for about two hours, when she was five, and she was with me just like you and I are right now."

MOVING THINGS ALONG

Learning that women have children is one thing, seeing the kids for the first time is another, and having the opportunity to interact with them on a regular basis is sometimes entirely different. When things go well, as they often did for my sample of stepfathers, fond memories about the child during the early dating experience with the birth mother are not uncommon. Emmit, flashing a broad grin, recalls the time shortly after his current wife started to bring her three-year-old son to his house to spend the night. "Woke up one morning, had no hairbrush, no toothbrush, and I'm missing my wave cap, a stocking cap that I used to sleep with. Come to find out, Jake had flushed it all down the toilet. So right there I knew I was dealing with a little character in a sense. He's kind of mischievous but lovable. You can't help but love him." Emmit's feelings during this early period were indicative of the deep connection he later developed and currently maintains with Jake.

The intriguing stories men and women shared about how they met and navigated the single-parent dating scene illustrate how complex people's lives have become. Some people I interviewed were much more successful than others in the way they incorporated children into their dating and relationship development. For some, the stories take on an added layer of complexity because they involve children in the same household who have different fathers as well as specific children who may have experienced more than one father/stepfather or mother/stepmother.

When men walk into the lives of mothers and their children, they typically find themselves walking alongside a troupe of family members already in motion. The size of this troupe varies widely, the mother and her lone child being the smallest unit I considered in my research.[5] Whatever their number, family members can be perceived as being involved in a *family dance*[6] where they are moving through time as part of an interconnected unit. Of course, the extent to which individual family members are integrated into this unit varies considerably. Although their movements may not always be coordinated or predictable, and their level of involvement may be limited, all the members play some role in the family dance.

As they share in this family dance, they adjust individually to the ebb and flow of life, weaving their way through their daily routine under a common label of being a "family." Most of the time, those involved will embrace a similarly defined label of "family." When this occurs the dance is more likely to appear choreographed, though specific family performances may not always be smooth. Situations may arise that lead the people involved to challenge the family label or aspects of it. Even when this label provides people with a sense of identity and belonging, they may feel as though they, and perhaps others, are out of sync with the rest of the family troupe. In their eyes, family members may appear equivalent to a potpourri of hip-hop dancers, country line enthusiasts, and ballet performers. Just as one dancer may have a difficult time finding a common rhythm that fits with the others, so too incompatible family members may struggle to find common ground as they try to manage their disparate personalities and needs within one household.

Usually people spend years together, sometimes many years, gaining experience in their family dance as they learn to love, cry, sleep, eat, play, laugh, talk, and argue as part of a family. Some of these families are vibrant and healthy, others dysfunctional; most fall somewhere in the middle. A subset of those in the middle will teeter from time to time on the edges of being content or troubled. People with years of experience in a healthy family tend to build up a reservoir of family capital in the form of shared positive memories about holidays, birthdays, vacations, and other special events. In times of fun or crisis, these family memories can be recalled on a moment's notice to strengthen family ties. Healthy families obviously have much deeper reservoirs built on trust than unhealthy families that have been poisoned by repeated friction and hostilities. However, struggling through bad times can bring families together in the long run. The camaraderie family members can build from surviving adversity may offer them a ray of hope when sickness, death, poverty, crime, abuse, or some other malady pays a visit. All things considered, extended amounts of time in unhealthy families will tend to strengthen the negative sentiments people have about themselves and their family relations. Their poor coping strategies and confrontational decision-making dynamics will be reinforced.

Those who share time and take part in this dance of family life have an opportunity to establish their own rhythms, routines, and rituals—for better or worse. During this time they are exposed to family rules and promises, some of which are honored, others broken. Most of us, including stepdads, establish routines in our daily lives. As creatures of habit, we enjoy finding peace and familiarity in what we do in relationships and families. We search for ways to simplify our lives. When we're familiar with our world and can anticipate what will happen next, we tend to be less anxious. We feel safe. People feel differently about how much order they want, but everyone thirsts for a taste of consistency and order in life—even if they are unaware of it. The routines people establish in families can provide them with guidelines for their behavior in a way that helps individuals as well as the larger family. Establishing routines means that the range of choices is narrowed so that fewer decisions have to be made. If family members are making fewer decisions they may argue less, though they may not necessarily be happy.[7]

Not all routines are created equal. Being entrenched in certain types of family routines, such as abuse, humiliating discipline, and excessive individualism, can be destructive. The objective then is to establish safe, supportive, and generally healthy routines that are inclusive of those who matter, including those who are not biologically related to some family members.

Whether they are good, bad, or indifferent, family routines in one form or another exist prior to a stepdad joining a family's evolving dance.[8] So how do stepdads manage their lives when they enter this new circle of people who have already been at work establishing routines and living their lives as a self-contained family unit, one that sometimes includes the birth father and his family as well? Much of what takes place involves stepfathers and other family members trying to clarify and negotiate family boundaries involving "who, when, and how members participate in family life."[9] Various issues must be considered to get a good sense of what men grapple with in these types of stepfamily situations. They may include the biological father's past and current relationships with the mother and children, stepdads' relationships with the mother and children, and logistical concerns involving housing arrangements, work schedules, and children's personal needs and schedules.[10]

LEARNING ABOUT THE BIOLOGICAL FATHER

Embedded within a single mother's family dance are her memories of the man (or men) with whom she had a child. A woman typically gives voice to these memories when she tells her relationship and fertility story to a new partner. If she dates often and over a period of time, she is likely to find herself repeatedly sharing accounts about the father of her child with each new partner.

From the perspective of the romantic partner who enters a single mother's world, especially those who stick around for a while, this exchange is virtually inevitable. The only one who can sidestep the discussion is the man who knew the biological father prior to getting involved with the mother. Although there may be no need for him to be informed about the biological father's involvement in the mother's earlier life, the new partner will probably still hear his partner speak about her child's father from time to time.

A man who learns for the first time about the biological father of his partner's child can respond in numerous ways. He may be disturbed, pleased, or indifferent to what he hears. Much is likely to depend on his personality and life experiences, feelings for the woman, and the nature of how and what he learns about the biological father. The new romantic partners can be exposed in countless ways to information about the father. A woman may, at the outset, provide a detailed, lengthy account of her involvement with her former partner and his relationship to their child or children. She may highlight the key transitional points and memorable events in their lives together as well as her thoughts about the biological father's character. Or, with the passing of time, she may make occasional comments about the biological father in reference to current conversations and events. These disclosures allow the new partner to piece together an image of how the man related and perhaps still relates to the single mother and the child. Finally, a woman can elect to say next to nothing about the biological father other than to acknowledge his existence or, in rare situations, death.

Just as the disclosure can unfold in different ways, so too the tone and nature of what is said can vary. Shifts over time may result from the woman's mood or the circumstances of her continued interactions with the biological father. In many cases, a single mother's story is peppered with angry and frustrated remarks about the biological father's poor character, inadequacies as a partner, or lack of commitment to his child. In candid moments she may also comment on her former partner's wonderful qualities as a father or person.[11]

Whatever the single mother has to say, her new romantic partner is likely to learn relatively quickly how she feels about the biological father. Initial disclosures set the tone for how a man processes subsequent information about the biological father. The woman is the gatekeeper of this critical information. Typically the mother begins by sharing memories about her former partner that were created apart from the new partner, before they started dating or at least before they became friends. Sometimes the set of memories the mother brings with her into a new romantic involvement will be reinterpreted and also expanded after the new relationship begins. As for the latter, the mother's new accounts about the father may incorporate his reactions to her new dating situation and partner. The mother may fold into her emerging family dance her experiences with the new romantic partner, including her perception of the father's reactions to them. If the father is still involved in her life and the life of her child in some way, whatever new family dance develops may never completely be free and clear of his influence. What the biological father thinks and feels about the new partner, and vice versa, can affect to varying degrees how the mother continues to construct her family dance. The father's impact will be nil, of course, if the mother does not stay in contact with him, or does so only superficially.

With time, the man who eventually becomes the stepfather may supplement what he hears about the father from his partner with his own first-hand experience. These encounters should, for better or worse, deepen his perceptions of the biological father. He will then be in a better position to judge the accuracy of his partner's comments. Contrary to the popular stereotype, the stepfather may on occasion develop an active and healthy relationship with the biological father, though a reserved and civil relationship is usually as good as it gets.[12]

The single mother's initial and subsequent disclosures can be significant if they shape the new partner's impression of how he might or does fit into the single mother's family dance. In addition to these disclosures, a man will be affected by his perception of what the child or children may have to say about the father. A man may size up the situation and adapt himself as he tries to establish his comfort zone for being involved with a single mother and her child or children. He may adjust his expectations and level of interest without even knowing it. The new partner may even decide against pursuing a specific relationship because of the anticipated hassles he would encounter dealing with a particular father. The man may conclude that the father would make it exceedingly difficult for him to feel comfortable in a stepfamily situation.

As I reflect on my early involvement with Alli, whom I first met when she was ten, I realize how important her mother's description of the father was to me. It affected the way I saw and approached the family dance I was entering because it led me to believe that the father was devoted and responsible in his traditional fatherly roles, but that his style of communicating with Alli was somewhat detached. The mother was disappointed that the father did not have more of an engaged, spontaneous, and emotional connection to Alli. In some ways, I saw this as an invitation to reach out to Alli and provide her with a more playful and emotionally expressive adult male friend. I could also see for myself that Alli was a sensitive, loving, mature, and communicative child who wanted to connect with people in meaningful ways. Even though our bond probably would have deepened had her mother never uttered a word about the father's reserved personality, her comments paved the way for me to feel more comfortable about my initial attempts to be attentive and affectionate to Alli as we formed our friendship.

Unlike my situation, a significant number of the stepfathers in my study entered a woman's family dance at a point when the biological father was out of the picture completely or was sufficiently removed from the everyday life of the family to be inconsequential. Sometimes mothers' and children's memories of how biological fathers and/or previous stepfathers mistreated them provided stepfathers with a window of opportunity. Given the previous men's poor track records as partners and fathers, stepfathers often elicited favorable responses because they were available and treating the mothers and stepchildren well. They could shine brightly in their stepchildren's and partner's eyes in contrast to men who had mistreated family members and in some cases were still doing so. Many stepfathers were the main attraction without paternal competition. Some stepfathers seized this opportunity, relishing their chance to exert a fatherly presence, to be a co-parent, and to be accepted into this new stepfamily arrangement.

Because my interviews with these mothers tended to focus on their current relationships, my information about their perceptions of what their lives were like when they were with the biological fathers of their children is limited. Several mothers harbored distinctly negative images of their previous partners and the fathers of their children. Although their stories sometimes revealed distinctions between how they evaluated their former partners as romantic partners and how they saw them as fathers, many of their comments integrated these perceptions.

> Looking back, I think he was jealous. He didn't want me to pick him [son] up a lot. He said I was going to spoil him. It was kind of difficult

showing my son the attention I thought he needed. . . . when I look back I see nothing positive about this man. [Lisa]

And I knew that when Monica saw that [father physically abusing the mother], I knew that it could do damage to her, but I thought it would do more damage if she didn't have a daddy. . . . I wasn't fully thinking about them [children] or comprehending what the relationship was doing to them—Monica spilled some juice on the floor and he like grabbed her little arm and yelled at her—I just freaked out and left that night. [Melanie]

When he was drunk, he would say all kinds of mean and hateful things, and when he was sober, he was okay. He never did treat Sammy the same as he treated his daughter. Mike had been married once before me, and he had a little girl. [Patricia]

A number of mothers also shared their thoughts about their children's perceptions. One notable comment was that some children had no vivid memories of their fathers because the fathers had never played an active role in their lives. Consequently, these children were unable to contrast their stepfathers to other men in a detailed way. They could, however, still experience the comfort and excitement of having gained the attention of a father figure. Kristen, a mother of a ten-year-old girl, commented on her daughter's lack of connection to her long-forgotten birth father. The father had not been actively involved in his daughter's life since she was one and had only talked to her once since then, by phone when she was two. "How could she miss what she never had? She was one when I got the divorce. She can't miss that because she never had it." Kristen went on to describe a situation where her daughter recently came upon a picture of her father and said, "Can I tear this up and throw it away now?" Kristen interpreted this request as her daughter's way of saying, "Why do I need it? I have a daddy now." In instances similar to this one, children tended to receive stepfathers fairly well.

Not all men who begin to nudge their way into stepfather roles benefit immediately from poor behavior by biological fathers and previous stepfathers. Mothers and stepchildren, when exposed to these negative experiences, may sometimes form rigid, preconceived notions about men's involvement in their families. They may then apply them somewhat indiscriminately to all men. Although this did not appear to be a pervasive practice among the mothers interviewed in my study, I suspect that overcoming these types of perceptions is a challenge that some men face as they become stepfathers.

Doug learned early on that the biological father of Sammy, the child Doug would eventually adopt, was out of the picture. As Doug recalls, the father would only come around in the early days for money, and when he didn't get it from his ex-wife [Patricia] he tried to "beat up on her." This unpleasant history set the stage for an eventful day, the only time Doug ever saw the father. At some point near the time when Doug and Patricia got married, Doug, Sammy, Patricia, and the father were at Sammy's cousin's birthday party. It was here that Doug reluctantly asserted himself in a protective role toward Sammy. Patricia leaned on Doug to help her make a decision about whether she should allow the biological father, who was drunk at the time, to take Sammy to see Sammy's grandmother that day. Taking Doug's warnings to heart, Patricia decided that the biological father was in no condition to be with Sammy. Then the biological father "started throwing a fit and called her [Patricia] a bad name." Though others at the party physically restrained Doug, his aggressive reaction forced the biological father to leave. In the course of describing this event, the nature and depth of Doug's feelings are revealed.

> Naturally my concern was, keeping him [Sammy] and her [Patricia] safe. And I knew that, the guy being the way he was and the way he drank, that him being around them two equals disaster. So, that's the, in my opinion, the reason I was glad he didn't come around. Because I knew if he had came around he would have caused trouble because him and I would have gotten into it.

Doug made it quite clear that he took his protector role seriously. Though this key role is often associated with biological fathers, Doug's story illustrates how some stepfathers take it upon themselves, usually with the support of the child's mother, to step up and assume this responsibility. Those stepfathers, who referred to the biological father as a "derelict," "deadbeat dad," or something similar, either confronted the biological father directly or tried to assume responsibilities they felt the biological father had neglected. Taking on the biological father in this way is obviously risky; it may either cause additional friction within the household or minimize it.

"I was trying to get his dad to grow up" is how Thomas explains the conversations he has had with his stepsons' biological father. He continues, "I want Don to take responsibility for his children. I want him and Stephanie, even though they're divorced, to get along like me and my first wife." Thomas recalled one particular encounter, precipitated by the biological father telling his ex-wife (Thomas's current wife) that she should not be thinking about having more children because she couldn't take care of the ones she had. Outraged, Thomas called the biological father back and remembers saying:

> You're never around. You've never been around. You've proved that. You dropped Danny off. I asked you to come over to the house, sit down. You didn't come over. You sent your momma. You ain't got no balls. Let's face it. You can't come to me man to man over your child's issues. . . . It's like, these are your kids. You made 'em, you know. Now whether you pay your child support or whatever, that's fine. But don't go getting on the phone and telling her that if I can't afford the ones I got, they're not mine, my brother. They're yours, and I am raising them. I am sending them to school. I am buying them clothes. I'm buying their shoes. I buy them . . . and I don't ask you for nothing. Never have and never will. And I'll take care of this one too.

Thomas's personal dealings with the biological father over time reinforced the negative feelings he initially developed from what he had heard from his wife. He interprets his own experiences with the biological father through a gender lens as he forcefully challenges the father's manhood for not sitting down and talking to him about the boys. Though not the boy's biological father, Thomas indirectly claims his own manhood because of his willingness to act in a responsible, fatherly way.

Interestingly, several men walked into a situation where the biological father was a prison inmate. Given the growing male prison population, more and more men are finding themselves getting involved with single mothers faced with this situation. Coming into the family dance under these circumstances generally offered a stepfather a unique opportunity to shine because he was being compared to a father behind bars. This was the situation Emmit walked into three years ago. Emmit places his experience in context by describing a conversation he had with his wife very early in their dating.

> [She] was letting me know that Jake has a father and he knows that— he's a very intelligent child so he knew at the age of three, knew who his biological father was. [The father] went to the federal pen for a while, and when I met Jake and my wife, I think his father had about— a little bit under a year to go on his sentence. She explained the whole situation to me. His father would call him about three, four times a week, trying to keep in touch with him, because he basically told her he didn't want Jake to grow up the same way he did, without a father. After we started dating and she kind of informed him that me and her,

we were going to get married, his contact or his communication with Jake became less. Let's see, Jake hasn't talked to him in about two or three years now. Basically my wife had wrote a letter to reiterate what things he had said to her while he was in prison: you said you were going to be there for him because you didn't want him to be fatherless like you were. She kind of basically in that letter cut all lines of communication with his father, so now Jake considers me as his father, his only father.

Though I got the impression that the mother was initially prepared to foster a relationship between her son and his father, Emmit's steady presence in her life and his fondness for Jake made it much easier for her to write her letter to the father telling him that he had squandered his opportunity to be a father to their son.

Although plenty of stepfathers found themselves in family settings where they could easily represent an improvement over the biological father, several stepfathers spoke highly of their stepchild's father. Neal says of his eight-year-old stepson,

> He has a very good relationship with his father [Chris]. In my opinion he has a great dad. [Chris] . . . sees him over the summertime. And over that course of the number of weeks, as far as I know, he'll have things planned almost every day. Chris now has another fiancée that is there, and they'll plan and do activities, going on camps, fishing or something. Kinda keep it entertaining, but also, course he wants to go there already, Stanley wants to go. He really does make time for him. There's never a concern whether Chris will be there for Stanley at all. I don't think a lot of people have that.

By all accounts, especially when compared to Doug, Thomas, or Emmit's recollection of their stepchildren's fathers, Neal offers a glowing appraisal of Chris. Although he has briefly met Chris on a few occasions to transfer Stanley from one parent to the other, Neal's perceptions of Chris have been formed largely from what his partner and Stanley have said.

MOTHERS IN THE MIX

Obviously mothers play a major role in shaping men's experiences as they get involved and stay involved in their new families. Although stepfathers are the primary source of data for this study, I gained valuable insights from the thirteen interviews my research team did with men's partners. The subsample of women who volunteered to share their thoughts is distinctive because almost all faced serious difficulties in their family upbringing. In the population at large, lots of single mothers have had and continue to have wonderful relationships with their fathers. Nonetheless, the mothers in my sample tended to report that they had strained relationships with their fathers and stepfathers, and, in a few instances, that their fathers had died when the mothers were children. Most felt neglected, abandoned, mistreated, or abused by their fathers and stepfathers at some point in their lives. Many also felt their mothers had mistreated them.

These unfortunate experiences were compounded by the mothers' more recent troubles with the fathers and stepfathers of their own children. Few had any kind words to say about the men who were the biological fathers for their children or the men who subsequently acted like stepfathers prior to their current partner getting involved. Some of the men in these earlier relationships had been abusive to the mothers and most had shown little if any interest in being involved with the children in a positive way. Accumulating these negative family life experiences led many of the mothers to become cautious and cynical about bringing romantic partners into their children's lives. However, a few mothers, despite their difficult life experiences, or perhaps because of them, were eager to incorporate new men into their lives and their ongoing family dance.[13] These women tended to see individual men as assuming the role of a "rescuer" or "knight in shining armor" who enabled them to feel better about themselves as mothers and to grow more hopeful about their own and their children's future happiness. Now that the male parental figures had been integrated to some extent into the mothers' lives, most mothers felt pretty good about how their partners treated their children in a fatherly way. Though some of these mothers were a bit reluctant to get romantically involved, all but two appeared to feel that their involvement with their current partners was good for them and their children.[14] Stephanie clearly felt this way about her current husband, Thomas, and remembered why she had anticipated feeling this way while they were dating. She describes in an emotional voice how Thomas cared for her son when he had a 104-degree fever that would not break.

> I sat there and I watched Thomas take care of my child. We were only together six months. And he sat there and he loved that child. He took care of that child. He paced the floors at night, that night, over that child. Like it was his own child. And it was just so, so touching to see somebody do this for somebody else's child. [I: Right]
>
> And it's like, that's when you know that this man loves your children. And that's what you're looking for and hoping for in a stepfamily.

[I: Right] . . . I don't think anybody can love your child as much as you can. . . . But to come that close. . . . I mean, to watch somebody to worry and fret and six months into a relationship over your child, there is nothing more touching than that.

Unfortunately, I am limited in how far I can explore the psychological dimensions to mothers' lives and their consequences for stepfathers. However, it seems rather clear that some mothers were struggling with identity issues. For those who had not established their own identities separate from their children, introducing a man into their ongoing family dances became problematic. With two exceptions, these mothers currently held jobs outside the home and all of them had done so within the past few years. They were employed at jobs rather than careers and consequently few appeared to have strong personal convictions about the work they did outside the home. In other words, their work did not play a major role in defining who they were as individuals. Quite possibly, had my sample of birth mothers included more women whose identities were firmly rooted in their lives as workers, I probably could have explored whether these mothers had an easier time than less career-oriented women introducing stepfathers into their family dance. These mothers left me with the impression that when mothers are completely enmeshed with their children, men have a more difficult time developing a strong connection to the children. Though I can only speculate, when mothers have not achieved separate identities from their children, stepfathers may be less likely to forge their own stepfathering path. As a result, whatever relationships they have with their stepchildren are likely to be mediated to a large extent by the mothers. At the same time, though, men's own personality styles may influence whether they are content to follow the mother's lead. Some men simply insist on carving out their own agenda for relating to stepchildren irrespective of how mothers approach the situation. John provides a perfect example when he responds to my question, "What do you see as your future with Harmony [stepdaughter]?"

I'm always going to have her in my life; I'm always going to be a male role model for her; I'm always going to be someone [she] can talk to besides her mother. And even if Beth dies before me, I can still have a relationship with Harmony, and that's what's beautiful because what we've created is, I'm not talking to Harmony through Beth. . . . So since I bypassed her, I'm not always going through Beth, now I have a relationship with Harmony and it's a good relationship. And that's what I look forward to: is how she grows up, becomes a woman and gets married maybe or has kids. Then I'm in the picture over here. I feel like whatever happens here, I have a daughter.

Whatever mothers say or do, stepfathers still grapple with the ongoing family dance that a birth mother and her child or children have developed. For many, as mentioned earlier, the ongoing family dance they initially encounter will have at one time been influenced by a birth father. The vast majority of men have to deal with the single woman's family dance that was constructed without the birth father being present in the household. Sue, one of the women in my study, described at length how she was reluctant to introduce her kids to her current husband, Monty, and how the kids had a difficult time accepting Monty into their lives because of Sue's circumstances.

> At first I didn't want to because they were having a hard time dealing with, Beverly's [Sue's daughter] father was in jail, and had been for a year, so I was taking care of them and working, and I had a lot to do. And Mom was lonely and they didn't understand that, and they didn't want another man interfering with our world because I made them my world. When you have an abusive husband or addict you tend to, you have your own world so that you don't get involved with their world. And I protected the kids by keeping them away from him and we, they were my life. And I was theirs. And when I met Monty, they felt like he was interfering and taking mommy away, even the older ones did. Gail, the oldest one, she was sixteen at the time, she didn't like him at all from day one. He wasn't going to tell her what to do, you know, he wasn't her father and that was the way it was going to be. And she rebelled from the very beginning. And my son liked him, and my son played football for high school, and they related and Monty would show him different moves and help him out. They got along great until Brad raised his hand to me one time and that was the end of it. . . . Monty said, "Don't you ever do that to your mother or you'll find yourself picking yourself off the floor." Well, from there it just kind of went downhill between them.

As Sue described it, Monty faced an uphill battle from the start because she and her children had developed an exclusive, safe family unit as a way of coping with their abusive husband/father. Her story, and Monty's confirmation in a separate interview, revealed that it is sometimes next to impossible to reorganize a family system once it has become entrenched, particularly if a person is entering the picture as a threatening outsider.

The death of a spouse, though less common than a relationship breakup or divorce, can produce a difficult set of circumstances that a potential stepfather will have to face if he wishes to get romantically involved with the mother.[15] Paula was widowed in her mid-thirties and developed a romantic relationship with Stephen soon after her husband's death. Her husband's debilitating illness lasted more than five years, with the last four being particularly difficult. Although Paula described her deceased husband as her soulmate, she allowed herself to get on with her life much faster than her daughters felt was appropriate. She said that she had missed the physical company of a man for years because her former husband was not able to have sexual relations. Paula also reasoned that Stephen could help pull her out of her depression and lift her and her daughters out of poverty. Both she and Stephen recognized that he was entering a tricky situation because the man the twins knew as their father had died only a month before. In their first month of dating, Stephen began to spend the night and he moved in within a couple months. Paula became pregnant with her third daughter during this early period. Stephen had entered a unique family dance that was heavily influenced by Paula's and her daughters' sadness about the death of Paula's husband. Although he felt he had navigated this situation fairly well, his fourteen-year-old stepdaughter's description suggested that she and her twin sister continued to feel uncomfortable with Stephen's involvement in the family.

> For me, like when I was littler, it didn't really come to me that my dad had died and that this man was taking over. I really didn't think about that when I was six. I started like really actually thinking about it when I was like around eleven. . . . But like I did accept him when I was six years old. I felt like oh, he's so good, he's a really nice guy, but that was just like—he was nice like when we first met, and then like a year later he started like trying to act like my dad and all. . . . I know he doesn't think he can replace my dad. But sometimes I feel like he tries to, tries too hard sometimes. [I: What does it mean to say that he tried too hard?] . . . Like when my mom and me would talk about my dad, he'd get real mad. He said to me, he was like "I don't want you talking about your dad in front of me," and I was like what are you talking about? That's my dad, I should be able to talk about him wherever, wherever I am. He's like well—and then he later told my mom that he feels jealous because that I can't—that—he thinks I don't accept him. In a way, I kind of don't. But then there's really nothing I can do, so I kind of have to accept him, but he's like—he's brought a lot into our family [finances].

Men who try to get involved with single mothers like Lynn, who have been on their own for a long time, must also be prepared to go the extra mile if they wish to be invited to enter the mothers' preexisting families. Thirty-two-year-old Lynn described the past several years of her life as a single mom.

> I was not shopping for a daddy for him. I was—I had really gotten to the point where I was very happy to just be by myself. And if I was going to be by myself, a single parent, until Trevor was eighteen years old, and I never met somebody—that was okay. But if I did meet somebody, it was going to be good and it was going to be right and it was going to be done properly or it was not going to be. Because if it was something like—if it's best for Trevor or best for somebody else, then Trevor was going to win. Trevor took the cake. So it was going to be somebody who was good for him.

Lynn seldom dated prior to meeting Kevin, Trevor's current stepfather. When she began to date Kevin, she was curious about the way Kevin interacted with her son. She already respected Kevin as a single father who had half-time responsibility for his own young son, but she gained renewed respect for him as she watched him interact with her son. Both Lynn's and Kevin's separate descriptions of how they wove their lives together as they moved from a mindful dating experience to marriage depict a process that was guided by explicit discussions.

Obviously much of what occurs in dating relationships is not stated explicitly. In this vein, one important dating strategy that may creep into a couple's world includes how a man tries to gain favor with a single mother by being extra kind and attentive to her child. A man can manage the impression he gives to his partner as someone committed to her child's well-being. He may do this in a calculating way, fully aware of his intent to present himself as the caring, fatherly type. Melanie, in hindsight, seems aware of this pattern as she talks about how her partner's relationship with her daughters changed since they met.

> He was sweeter with them when we first got together. I think he—it was part of that trying to sweep me off my feet thing. You know what I mean? He was all about—oh man—he was hugging them all the time. They were great. Let's do everything with the kids! I love your kids! Your kids are great! Now it's like—we need to try and see if we can get a baby-sitter before we go out to dinner because I am not going to listen to them screaming in the restaurant all night.

Unfortunately, my research team and I did not ask men or their partners if they had any specific impressions of how men might have gone out of their way to impress a partner through their involvement with her child. Some men spoke of their understanding that the mother and her child or children were a package deal and that it was important for them to get along with the child. My impression was that they were sincere in their feelings. Some may have gone out of their way or stretched themselves to accept what they believed to be the appropriate attitude, but this was not apparent in the way they described their experiences. Lisa provides a mother's perspective on this matter when she recalls how her future husband, Ernest, put her mind at ease about having children. Reflecting back to a specific conversation she initiated with Ernest, she recalls that "He said to me 'I love you for who you are. I don't want to change anything.' And I asked him how did he feel about the fact that I had children. And he said, 'Well, they're a part of you. I'm going to have to accept the whole package, and just not pretend like they're not there.'" Asked when she first thought about Ernest's perceptions of being involved with her children, Lisa describes how she asked him to help her look for an apartment. At the time she was trying to leave her abusive husband. She told Ernest that she had to bring her kids with them; he had never met them. His easygoing attitude toward having the kids along and the way he volunteered to carry her daughter in his arms all day left her with the impression that he was "such a natural at it."

Lisa apparently found herself pretty relaxed with Ernest being involved in her children's lives from the beginning. Ultimately Lisa and other mothers act as gatekeepers by encouraging or restricting stepfathers' access to their children. They make decisions that affect how often, when, and the ways in which the stepfather interacts with the stepchild, during a relationship as well as after it ends. At the outer edges of this gatekeeping continuum we find situations involving men like Derek. When asked whether there were specific things that his fiancée did to help him be a father, he was quick to compare her favorably to the mothers of his biological children:

> She allows me to be a father. With my other kids, I have no say so whatsoever over, unless they're literally with me, then I say what they can and cannot have, but aside from that, I have no say so in their lives. . . . [The mothers] actually try to make me feel like I'm only in this child's life financially. They look at me as a paycheck. At first it used to bother me, now I look beyond their ignorance. I just won't let it bother me. . . . But Lily has allowed me to be a father. Even down to decision making. Not only is it what I say, not that it goes, but she listens to it unlike the others. Along with that, if there is a decision to be made, if it's not some-

thing small, but if it's a big decision, she won't make that decision without talking to me, or will I make it without talking to her.

Similarly, Brad has positive things to say about the way his girlfriend has allowed him to enter her daughter's life. "She's actually drawn me out and said no, it's okay you can if Sherry does something that bothers you, you can say 'Sherry, please don't do that. That bothers me.' Or if you want to give input, please do. . . . If anything, she wants me to be more, to go ahead and assume more of a role as times goes by. That part's been pretty easy." The partners of Derek and Brad have each opened the gates to their children, welcoming these men to express themselves in a fatherly way.

BEING EXPERIENCED

Experience matters, sometimes. One important factor that can influence how mothers react to men who may become stepfathers involves the type and amount of experience they have had being around and caring for children prior to their current relationship. The most obvious way for men to gain experience, of course, is to spend time with their own children. Nineteen of the men in my study had children prior to beginning their current relationship, although some had very little contact with them. Men also talked about other opportunities that gave them time to be around children, including spending time with nieces, nephews, friends' children, previous partners' children, and working with children as part of their recreational or professional jobs. Irrespective of the type of experience, it can be meaningful to stepdads as well as mothers. Men with experience are more likely to feel confident about their parenting abilities; this often translates into a desire to take a more assertive role in raising their stepchildren. Having experience does not, however, guarantee that men will feel more confident. If they feel that they have failed miserably in being fathers to their own children, they may feel insecure about their ability to be effective fathers to other men's children. But they may also channel their sense of failure and make a concerted effort to be a better father figure to their stepchild(ren).

Some mothers take men's previous experiences with children into account. Depending on the circumstances, men's prior experience may provide mothers with the incentive to loosen their parenting reins and allow stepdads to be more involved. A few women were impressed with the level and quality of men's involvement with their own children. This helped convince the mothers that their new partners were good fathers and family men. However, men's experiences as fathers might also intimidate mothers, making them more reluctant to share parenting responsibilities because they fear being marginalized with their own children.

Clearly, entering relationships with a personal history of living with and caring for one's own children can help legitimize men as parental figures in their partner's eyes. The mothers interviewed for this study sometimes remarked that they were willing to seek advice in raising their kids from their male partners who were fathers. In some instances, the men took on a parent educator role because they were perceived to have valuable insights about parenting, especially when it came to the types of discipline issues I discuss in chapter 4.

Another way to look at this situation is to consider how the presence or absence of experience shaped men's negotiating position on parenting issues. Not having children was sometimes a liability for stepdads. In addition, the children with whom these stepfathers were involved had typically always lived with their mothers so the men were at a distinct disadvantage of not knowing their personalities and patterns as well as the mothers did. Partners of those men who were not fathers appeared to have a more difficult time trusting men's judgment or compromising on significant parenting issues. Although the stepdads sometimes felt that the mothers overruled them irrespective of the men's own experience with children, those men without their own children were sometimes viewed as naive. This left men feeling detached from and out of step with the family dance.

Interviews with a forty-two-year-old mother, Beth, and her much younger twenty-seven-year-old husband, John, touched on these issues as the participants talked about John's assuming parental responsibilities three years ago for Beth's daughter, Harmony, who was fifteen at the time. When asked if John comes to her to get advice on how to handle issues involving Harmony, Beth says,

> He doesn't [do] that so much anymore because he knows more now. But in the beginning, he's never been a parent. He didn't know. So he would check with me because he would feel like something needed to be said but he didn't want to come on too hard. . . . he was very careful. And he did take a parental role from the start.

Beth offers that they talk about decisions affecting Harmony.

> I don't think we've ever had a situation where he's completely disagreed with what I did and I did it anyway. In the parenting, we really work together on that, but he does defer to me as kinda the final. I've done a

pretty good job with Harmony and I'm a lot older than him, and so, when he's making decisions or taking actions with her, he checks them out with me.

As with many relationships, John's account of his stepfamily experiences differs somewhat from Beth's. In John's eyes there were a few instances where Beth "pulls rank" on him. For example, when Harmony was having difficulty in school, John felt that she should be encouraged to stay at her school and work things out, whereas Beth decided to send her to another school. John uses this situation to illustrate those few times where Beth asserts herself as the birth mother. In his words, "I could say my piece but that was it, and I had to leave it alone. And ultimately it was what Beth wanted." Those situations are important to John because he feels as though he's left "out in the cold." He goes on to say that in situations like these he feels, "well it's kinda like its none of my business, so just stay out of it. Then I feel left out, and . . . that I will never truly be that father because when it comes down to certain things I don't have any say in what happens."

Consistent with his admiration for Beth, John balances these comments with others.

> She [Beth] gives me full freedom to be the stepfather. She gives me room to make mistakes, like I said, she will counsel me, she's far wiser than me, she can counsel me and help me to relate to Harmony. She knows Harmony better than me. She can help me in ways that I would never come up with. We, it's kinda like she's my coach.

John's situation highlights the reality that various factors may come into play along with a man's previous experience with caring for kids. Not only did John have to contend with not being a father, he also was fifteen years younger than his wife and only nine years older than her daughter. In addition, Harmony had spent a few years as a very young child with her biological father and then more than ten years with a stepfather. John therefore had to contend with Beth's and Harmony's history of interacting with other men in paternal roles.

The interview data in this study suggest that being a father prior to getting involved with stepchildren did not guarantee men an equal stake in parental decision making with stepchildren. Rodney, the biological father of two children who were four and five years younger than his two stepchildren, expressed his frustration with his current wife's approach to parenting in a stepfamily. He noted that he and his wife disagreed about discipline issues 90 percent of the time and that her decision was final 90 percent of the time. When asked how this made him feel, Rodney replied, "Like I'm not a permanent part of the family." He went on to say that his wife had structured their arrangement so that it was "her kids, me. Her kids and me." As Rodney's more extensive description reveals, he is annoyed with this arrangement where he feels he's being excluded from her separate relationship with her kids. She has her own family unit and then there's him. "It's led very close to a divorce on more than one occasion, because I don't agree with the way she restricts my right to be a parent within that household at this point." In his mind, "I should have the right to say whether or not the kids will do or will not do something, if they should come up and ask. And my voice be heard, not necessarily agreed, but at least heard and discussed before decisions finally are written in stone." When viewed in a larger context, Rodney's position is consistent with his belief that he has equal responsibilities toward both his biological and stepchildren. He feels he should treat both sets of kids equally in every way (love, affection, caring, financial).

Having their own kids was the most notable way men could demonstrate their competence without being tested in the child rearing trenches. But men were also able to draw on other resources to earn their partner's respect and trust. For example, fifty-year-old Randy had spent a number of years caring for two children in two previous relationships. He spent five years around the son of his best friend for thirty to forty hours a week. His friend had impregnated someone and then went into the service and ended up in Vietnam. Although Randy didn't sleep at the mom's house, he spent a great deal of time there. These experiences made Randy feel confident that he knew how to raise children.[16] In particular, he felt more self-assured when it came to assuming responsibility for Jamie, his stepson. Randy in some ways may perceive these earlier experiences as helping him establish a moral claim that enables him to feel knowledgeable despite his lack of a biological tie. Without hearing from his current wife, there's no way to confirm Randy's assessment of his competence, but his detailed knowledge of his stepson's life leads me to believe that he is indeed an active and caring stepfather.

Carl's involvement with his cousin's children gave him the opportunity to get hands-on experience with kids. These experiences were consistent with his view of himself as a "kid person" who likes to read children's books and be around children. Carl talks about wanting to devote more time to writing children's books in addition to reading at the local libraries and his stepdaughter's school.

Landen mentions that he was friends with a number of single mothers and couples with kids and that he went out of his way to form friendships with children. With a comical grin he shared a story to illustrate his ability to form ties with children. He recalled how one of his young friends who now lives in Texas responded to his mother's boyfriend telling him to stop doing something. The child said, "No. You're not momma. You're not nana. You're not papaw. And you're not Landen." When the boyfriend asked, "Who's Landen?" the child replied, "Landen's my friend."

Another way to gain experience came from coaching kids between four and sixteen years of age. As a swim instructor, Neal spent a lot of time thinking about how he could motivate his students to train harder. He took this knowledge and applied it to his everyday chores with his stepson, Stanley. Neal's motivational principles allowed him to work with Stanley on performing various household chores in a more pleasant fashion.

Although most men had some experience with kids, some had very little. Gerald was "pretty ignorant to the whole thing [parenting]." He had grown accustomed as a child to having lots of space and few people in his house. Kids were largely a "foreign subject for me." This orientation led Gerald to keep his distance from the children of his former cohabiting girlfriend. In his current relationship, he has learned to be more involved in the stepdaughter's life but he has had to force himself to do so.

Granted, the child care experiences men bring with them into their relationships may affect the way men and their partners relate to each other about the children, but what is likely to matter most is how men interact with the children. Men without children of their own can convince mothers in many instances that they can treat children in a kind and fatherly way. In many instances, how well men pass this test will influence the extent to which partners become "involved" with each other in a serious way.

4

OPENING DOORS, BEING INVOLVED

Once a man gets romantically involved with a single mom, important choices follow. He becomes implicated in decisions about how involvement is defined in terms of physical intimacy and commitment, whether a child is made aware that he is dating the mother, whether sleepovers or sex occur with a child in the house, and what types of rights and responsibilities he has vis-à-vis the child. Deciding on the man's type and level of involvement as an authority figure, as well as his contributions in other areas of family life, is particularly important. Some choices are made deliberately with considerable reflection. Others occur casually, as part of the seemingly natural evolution of a relationship, with little thought or effort. Thus individuals are assertive and decisive on occasion; other times they simply drift toward an implicit understanding of what works. Ultimately the decisions a man and woman make knowingly or unknowingly, together or separately, affect whether the man continues to get more involved or if the budding involvement dissolves.

Part of the "being involved" experience builds on how a man responds to the family dance that existed prior to his arrival on the scene. How a man deals with these family dynamics is likely to influence the partner's decisions about the romantic relationship and parenting. Central to this process is a man's attitudes about how seriously involved he wants to get with his partner and her child. At some point, a man and his partner will find themselves going public with their relationship, telling their friends, family, coworkers, neighbors, and child. When adults are concerned about introducing a child to a dating partner prematurely, a child may be the last to know about the dating relationship. As a relationship evolves, a stepfather and his partner make decisions about whether living together or marrying is a desirable option. Logistical concerns may arise related to money, religious beliefs, living arrangements, and where the couple will be spending time, thereby limiting how a stepfather organizes his life in practical terms. Clearly the involvement path for a man who dates a single mother is likely to be more complex than one where a child is not part of the equation.

If a man does get involved with his partner's child, the implications can be wide-ranging, from dramatic to insignificant, fantastic to horrific. What happens when a man takes care of another man's child? How does this experience affect the stepchild? The birth mother? How does a man assess what he has been doing and wants to do? Given the nature of my sample, and my primary interest in how a man experiences his life as a stepfather, most of the stories I heard (but by no means all) emphasize positive outcomes for the man and his stepchild.[1]

A stepfather's attempt to treat a child in a fatherly way can be affected by various factors. Social science research points to a stepfather's relationship with his stepchild being influenced by the child's age, gender, and personality.[2] The degree to which the biological father remains involved in his child's life and the qualities of the man's relationship with the child's mother are other conditions that can make a difference.[3] I interviewed a relatively small number of men who are involved with their partner's children of varying ages, and some have their own children. Consequently, few of the men face similar types of circumstances. To complicate matters, the stepdads came on the scene at various points during their stepchildren's lives, meaning that the men have been involved with their children for varying amounts of time. Consequently, I shy away from making sweeping statements about the impact stepfathering has on children or men within any particular stepfamily type, such as men who have young teenage sons with whom they have been involved since the kids were in preschool. On the upside, my sample diversity allows me to look at stepfathers in a wide range of circumstances. I can explore how they evaluate and what they feel about the influence their stepfathering efforts have on the kids.[4] An important part of stepfathers' evaluations is the social support they receive for their efforts.

RELATIONSHIP LOGISTICS

Among the married men I interviewed, 64 percent reported that they had lived with their partners before marrying.[5] Most of the unmarried participants are living with their partners, with a majority describing themselves as engaged to be married. Whether the men are married or cohabiting, they previously had to make practical decisions about how the new family was going to operate. The most obvious decision affected where everyone would live. For the subset of men who reported being financially strapped, their decisions often were tied to their financial survival, although financial considerations sometimes played a role for men who were not struggling. Other matters of convenience, such as who had the bigger place or who lived in the more desirable city, inspired some men's decisions about where they wanted to live. Many men realized that consolidating households made economic sense. In making the case to his stepchildren why they and their mother should all move to his house, Herman reasoned that "not only is this a good arrangement for us physically, but it's a good financial merger."

The consequences of limited financial resources were often more challenging when the couple had multiple children. Tim, for example, agreed to help Melanie three months after they started dating because she was having problems living with her mother. Melanie and two of her daughters moved in with Tim in his small two-bedroom apartment. Because Tim's two young sons also came to visit every other weekend, six people periodically lived in this "pretty packed little place." As Tim explains, "That was pretty chaotic too, because it's a smaller environment so everyone was together a lot more." Although living together in close physical quarters can be a trying experience for families where everyone is related, the complexities and politics of parenting four children five years of age and younger in such a space are likely to tax even the most patient, easygoing person.

Expecting to find that many men forming stepfamilies would have significant logistical and emotional concerns about living accommodations, I was surprised to find that this was not the case with my participants. Some of the men said they had few if any problems moving into homes where their partner's former spouse or partner had resided. In some cases, the men moved into houses that the biological father had owned for some time and returned to occasionally when picking up his kids. A fifty-two-year-old professional, Barry, describes how he felt when he moved into his wife's house, a place where she had lived with her ex-husband and kids. "It was a little awkward. I didn't really want to do it. . . . but now I've gotten comfortable there. It's a beautiful house and all that, but it was pretty awkward. It was particularly awkward when Domenick would come over. He had to pick up the kids or something and I'm there, here in this guy's house." Barry decided to move in with his wife because she had expressed her desire not to disrupt her "stability with the kids," which she associated with the house. Moving in was, relatively speaking, the option that required the least total effort by all involved. Barry's wife told him that he would get over his worries about making such a move, and he confessed that he did.

For others, like Jackson, moving into a house that had been lived in by his partner and her ex-husband was not an issue. He had no particular feelings about making this type of transition, even though his partner and her former husband had bought the house together. As he reasons, "I had never visited her at that house [with ex-husband present], so I had no mental or memory images of him being there. The only thing I had ever known of that house was Helena and Mason." Another man, Rodney, moved in with his girlfriend and her two kids about four months after he met her. The woman had "kicked out" her husband and there was an injunction against him to stay off the property because of spousal abuse. Rodney admits that he feels his moving in was a "tense situation, because I knew their divorce wasn't final." However, asked to reflect on how he felt about the "space" issue, of moving into someone else's home where another man had lived, he offers in a matter-of-fact way, "I don't think I gave it a whole lot of thought. I just moved my stuff in and it just seemed to work fine the way it was, without having to make any major changes for anybody."

Now on his third marriage, Eddie shares his easygoing approach to moving in with his fiancée and her five-year-old stepdaughter. He made this move several months before the wedding.

> Well, it was kind of one step at a time. I just couldn't go in and rush in and try to change everything. It was kind of relax and sit back, see how things go. I had to adjust. They didn't have to adjust. It was me coming in. I was the outsider, so I had to make all the adjustments to their ways. The emotions, to eating, comings and goings, activities. I had to adjust to all that. To me, if I could adjust to it before it becomes some drastic change, I will adjust to it, so I felt I had to adjust to it. It happened in a positive way. . . . Everything happened at the right time.

Eddie's comments reveal his heightened appreciation for the preexisting family dance and household rituals that were a part of his new living environment. He seems convinced that his willingness to ease his way into his new living arrangement kept him from developing unrealistic expectations that might have gone unfulfilled. As he portrays the experience, he was the one making the accommodations and he appears to have been a good sport about it.

The typical reality of these situations, of course, is that everyone living in the house makes concessions and accommodations. Gerald, who moved with his future wife into a house they bought together a few months before they were married, provides a look at what is probably the more typical way people try to balance and mesh their living styles.

> I think it was awkward. I mean, the house was roomy, but I just was not used to living with one woman, let alone two. I think she [stepdaughter] felt awkward too. Everybody felt a little awkward. Everybody was like on their best behavior in the beginning. You know how when relatives come to visit, you can put up with just about anything, you know. So I think everybody was trying to be on their best behavior and it was awkward for everybody, but not earth-shattering. And then just little by little by little, it just started to work itself out. Again, no big revelations came in at any point. Again, I spent a lot of time in the back room, my office. Big room, had my books, whatever, watched TV, had a place to escape. And I was there often. Then little by little [he began to spend more time in the main living areas].

For Gerald, the moving in together phase of his relationship differed from Eddie's in that Gerald moved into a new physical space, a house, that neither his fiancée, her child, nor he had occupied. True, whatever family dance his fiancée and her child had established in their own home could still find expression in the physical surroundings of the house, but moving into a house where none of the stepfamily had lived meant that there were opportunities to see their connections to physical spaces in fresh ways. Moreover, because Gerald and his partner had decided while they were dating that he would not spend the night at her place when the kids were at home (at the time another daughter was living at home), he could try to define his presence in the new living environment at various points in the day. This included staking a claim to the "office" space at the back of the room in the evening and at other times. Claiming a specific area as his own was probably easier in the new home because no one had already assigned symbolic meaning in a practical sense to the space. Because Gerald had valued his privacy throughout his life, having a secluded place for refuge was critical to his emotional well-being and successful adjustment to living in a stepfamily. He was able to move into a new stepfamily dance at a comfortable pace while protecting his individuality.

In general, those who ended up moving into their partner's house or apartment adapted fairly well to the symbolic meanings that could have been associated with the physical accommodations. This does not mean, however, that men did not feel better when moving into a place that they had a hand in selecting. In the course of talking about what it was like for him to move into his partner's house, Robby distinguishes between home and house while clarifying the symbolic meaning of different houses for him.

> I guess I didn't really think about it 'cause it was just hers; this house she didn't buy with her husband. She had moved out of the house that her and her husband had bought, and had bought this other home and was living there. And I had been staying there almost every night so, I guess it didn't really cross my mind very much. Actually I can tell you that, it didn't feel like my house. It didn't feel like, it was my home but it wasn't my house. *We* bought a new home last November and now it's our house, our home. And the feeling is a lot better.

Apparently Robby felt comfortable living with his partner and two children in their house, but he didn't feel that it was his house. Moving into a different house that he had a hand in picking made Robby feel more at ease. Still, he had to contend with his feelings about his thirteen-year-old daughter, Shelly, not having her own room in the new house. She lived out of state with her mother during the school year, but visited for an extended period during the summer and some holidays. During those visits she shared a room with Tracy, Robby's ten-year-old stepdaughter.

> I find myself aggravated at when I go into Tracy's room, I don't see any of Shelly's stuff. And when Shelly's there, we have a dresser full or matching dresser sets. And Shelly has her own dresser, and when Shelly leaves, Tracy kinda takes over [the] dresser. And I want to tell her that she can't use that, that's Shelly's dresser. There's no reason for you to be using it. Even when Shelly's there, and I walk in there, it's still all Tracy's stuff in there, and we don't have an extra room for Shelly. I don't like that; I think my own daughter should have her own room, just like they [stepchildren] have their own rooms all year around.

This case illustrates how a couple's financial standing can affect a stepfather's approach to the practical aspects of the transition to stepfamily living. Though I didn't ask specifically, I sensed that had Robby and his wife been wealthier, they would have purchased a home large enough for the two girls, as well as Robby's stepson, to have their own rooms. Perhaps money cannot buy happiness, but it can help some couples secure housing that reduces friction within the home.

It bears repeating that most cohabiting or married men participating in my study survived the initial transition period. Men who have a difficult time with their new living arrangements and responsibilities of sharing a joint household may simply leave their stepfamilies and move out, or have their partner and child find a new place to live.[6] Though the significance of these practical matters is unclear, I suspect that they contribute to interpersonal struggles in stepfamilies in various ways.

Some of the participants in my diverse sample are living apart from their partners, though most have expectations of living together someday. Decisions about making such a move can be quite complex because children are involved. For instance, Brad and his partner, Nannette, currently live apart. Because he is the father of two teenagers and she is the mother of three children living at home, they face the dilemma of finding an affordable house large enough to manage a family of seven. Unfortunately Brad has been struggling for two years to finalize his divorce. Brad summarizes how his circumstances have affected his thinking:

> It's still taking so long [divorce] and there's this little part of me that says "trial period," "trial period," you know. Move in together first and make sure everything does work out and then take the next step and get married. But at the same time, she's not the kind of person who wants to actually, officially live together unless we are married. But then she's had a lot more time to adjust. She's been divorced for ten years. So she's had a lot more time to go through all of that and have her period where she wasn't married and was completely on her own, that kind of thing.

When Brad contemplates the possibility of moving in with Nannette, he imagines that they would need to sit down and establish clear ground rules. From Brad's perspective, one of the conditions would be that "Brad's word, just like mom's, goes. If Brad says you have to do something, then you're going to have to do it. Basically, full parental role and responsibility." Brad quickly adds that the "flip side" of this claim to parental authority involves the typical set of parental obligations.

Looking at Brad's complete interview, I sense that Nannette would probably be more willing to live together outside of marriage if children were not involved. This case illustrates how the presence of children discourages some people from living together without getting married. I suspect, though, that some may feel even more compelled to have a trial period if children are involved in order to protect themselves and their children from the emotional trauma of a painful divorce.

For Brad and Nannette, the presence of children, Brad's in particular, limits the way they spend their time together as dating partners. When Brad has his children, he often takes them to dinner at Nannette's, where they have a dinner for seven. Because he is concerned about doing anything that would delay or damage the divorce process, Brad always brings his children back to his place to spend the night. The logistics of finding a place for everyone to sleep is an obstacle as well. When he doesn't have the children, he often spends the night at Nannette's.

The men who had their partner and her children move in with them had to alter their physical space to make room for them. Like men who moved in with their partner, they seldom voiced any significant concerns about their partner and the children coming to live with them. They seemed happy about this change for the most part.

DISCIPLINE AND RESPONSIBILITY

In addition to practical decisions about spending time together and living accommodations, important choices will be made regarding the kind of role a new man will have as an authority figure in the emerging stepfamily. Critical decisions will be made, or patterns will evolve in an unremarkable fashion, at various points during the evolution of the relationship and in numerous ways. Irrespective of how the process unfolds, the possibility of the mother asserting a gatekeeping role, especially in terms of discipline, is a defining feature of the process affecting stepfathers' involvement in a stepfamily.

The men who feel they have affected their stepchildren in a significant way are most likely to say that they have brought more discipline and responsibility into their stepchildren's lives, or at least see this as included in their mission.[7] Part of this effort involves encouraging children to be more accountable for their actions and responsive to adults' requests to do things such as chores. The other aspect is actually administering discipline to children who do not act appropriately. Research and anecdotal experiences have shown that there is a great deal of ambiguity about whether and how parental figures should discipline children who are not their offspring. The ambiguity surrounding stepparenting is one aspect of the larger set of uncertainties often associated with stepfamilies.[8] About twenty-five years ago, Andrew Cherlin, a sociologist, aptly labeled remarriage and stepfamilies an "incomplete institution" because the normative structure for this family arrangement is not well defined.[9] Not much has changed in this regard; considerable confusion still exists about what norms should guide stepfamily life.

In light of this ambiguity, I was curious to learn more about how men transition from being friends and dating partners without any role in their partner's children's upbringing, to taking authority to discipline the women's children. The process by which the men and other stepfamily members come to see stepfathers in a different light can unfold in a variety of ways. Only a few men discipline kids more or less from the outset. The more common pattern is for the men to gradually slide into the role. Some lack a clear understanding of how they came to take on discipline responsibilities; for others, the transition is more deliberate. Men who follow the latter path are more conscious of their awkward standing in regard to their partner's children and ease into being an agent of child care and discipline who deserves children's respect. Those who drift into a disciplinarian role voice their recollection in various ways.

> I don't know how it got to be where I discipline them 'cause I actually discipline them more than Jamie does. I don't know how it got to be; I didn't ask for the job; I just got it. [Robby, thirty-four-year-old with eight-year-old stepson, ten-year-old stepdaughter]

> I think I was always kind of in that role. I mean, we both do the discipline but I think because, like I said, I have a little rug rat [nine-year-old son] running around, with the experience of doing that I was just always kind of that way as far as to verbally discipline them anyway. . . . I just kind of evolved into that position. [Brandon, thirty-year-old, with stepsons two and five years old]

> About a year after we were married it really became that I was the primary disciplinarian in the family. I'm a big guy, you know. . . . I think I just assumed that role, as part of being the father figure. My dad was the disciplinarian in our house. [Keith, forty-five-year-old, with stepdaughters twelve and ten years old]

In some instances men's partners play a pivotal role helping the stepfathers and children make the transition that enables stepfathers to take a more active role in directing and disciplining children. Kristen supported her husband Calvin's parental role with her ten-year-old daughter. She describes herself as "laid back" and Calvin as being more "consistent and firm" when it comes to her daughter's behavior and discipline. Kristen explains further:

> He tries very hard to get me to give her [daughter] rules, because sometimes she won't listen to him. I just tell her, "What did he tell you to do? That's what you need to be doing." I know one time we sat down and we had a talk and I said, "You know, Calvin's your father, Calvin's

your daddy and is that something you would say to your daddy?" And she's like, "no," so you wanted him to be your daddy, he's your daddy, so you need to give him that respect and you need to do what he says and don't come and ask me.

By talking to her daughter in this way, Kristen tries to convince her that Calvin is a legitimate member of the family with certain rights and responsibilities as a father figure. Kristen is eager to remind her daughter that she asked for Calvin to be her daddy; now she needs to accept him and let him do his job.

Part of Calvin's job, as he sees it, is to pass on the messages of "responsibility and independence." He has a strong desire to impress on Rebecca that she has "incredible control" over her life—even at age ten. Calvin wants her to become more aware that she has the chance to make important decisions for herself, ones that she shouldn't pass on to others. He also wants her to develop self-discipline. When asked specifically, Calvin states that he and Kristen have similar goals for Rebecca but they may differ in the "process" by which they pursue their objectives. Having thought about this issue prior to the interview, Calvin quickly says, "I'm less flexible, but not necessarily in a bad way, but I think maybe less pliable and— but I think I'm more reasonable, where she's more flexible but sets more— she has high—she sets more, higher expectations but is more willing to compromise on them. I'll set more reasonable expectations and try and stick to them."

Like Kristen, William's fiancée, Chandra, clarifies that she wants William to assume a more active and legitimate disciplinary role in her son's life. As William recalls, "I have had to spank Deon [ten-year-old stepson] before and I think that, along with the fact that it was with his mother's approval, has set into his mind that okay, this is the man. He is going to be dad. . . . He's not my father but he will be daddy." William first spanked Deon because Chandra asked him. She felt Deon needed to be punished with a spanking but she didn't feel comfortable doing it herself. According to William, her reluctance was rooted in her own difficult childhood, hinting that she had witnessed or experienced physical violence. He enthusiastically welcomed Chandra's request and describes his sentiments this way. "Here I come to save the day! I mean, that's what I'm here for. We're going to set this program up and we're going to run it." Earning Chandra's trust and being invited to take on this important task pleased William.

At the time, he interpreted this gesture to mean that he was going to play a significant role in his emerging family while making a difference in the children's lives. The role is also consistent with his traditional child-rearing philosophy: "I strictly believe that discipline should be enforced. Be it sitting in your room, sitting alone, quiet time for an hour, no video games, or if a spanking is called for, a spanking is due. . . . I believe a child should be raised with a stiff rod. Spare the rod and spoil the child." Speaking candidly, Robby provides an additional voice to show how a man might believe that his partner has helped him be the kind of father he would like to be to his stepchildren.

> She doesn't bitch about anything; she doesn't, she very rarely corrects me. She doesn't step in when I say something; I don't step in when she says something. I think that's what, I think that's why we got a strong relationship cause we don't correct each other. If she tells the kids to do something, or if she doesn't make them do something, I'll ask her why, and she'll tell me and okay no problem. And if I tell the kids to do something, she don't say a word about it. She'll just let me be the adult to the kids; the father to the kids. Or the stepfather to the kids I should say.

Although Robby never uses the word "team" to refer to the way he and his wife, Jamie, coordinate their parenting styles, he seems comfortable knowing that he and Jamie have developed an understanding of their roles in their coparenting project. By allowing Robby to exert control over the kids without interference, Jamie enables Robby to feel that he has a legitimate paternal role with the accompanying rights. Thus he is free to make a difference in the children's lives.

What we've heard from Calvin, William, and Robby highlights how the coparental trajectory is often an important aspect of men's experiences as stepfathers. Each birth mother played a prominent role in how the men eventually defined themselves as stepfathers. Thus men's experiences as stepfathers are intimately tied to the ways the birth mother allows them to participate in a fatherly way with the stepchild.

Researchers who have studied children's adjustment to a stepfather generally conclude that positive outcomes are most likely to occur when stepfathers do not prematurely attempt to assert their authority in stepfamilies.[10] Studies show that in remarriages that occur prior to the children's adolescent years, the relationships between stepfathers and their children are healthier when stepfathers support the birth mother's efforts to discipline, work at developing a close relationship with the stepchildren, and gradually try to assert themselves as authority figures. Surprisingly, some research also finds that when remarriages involve adolescent children, more immediate attempts to be an authoritative parent are related to better outcomes for stepchildren and stepchildren's greater acceptance of their stepfathers.[11]

Although there are no guarantees that a child will accept a stepfather's approach to discipline, an understanding, patient stepfather is more likely to navigate the murky waters of stepfamily life successfully while maintaining a healthy relationship with the child. A stepfather with this mentality is apt to be mindful of his standing in the birth mother's family dance. Brad portrays himself in this manner as he talks about his relationship with his girlfriend's sixteen-year-old daughter and thirteen-year-old son, whom he assumes will become his formal stepchildren once he marries their mother. Speaking specifically about his relationship with Sherry, the daughter, Brad says,

> Sometimes Sherry just gets to me and I just—"Go Away!" It's frustrating because I can't really—I'm at that tentative stage where you can't really discipline, but at the same time you have to interact and you have to suffer the consequences. But you have to put up with a lot and sometimes I pride myself on maintaining, constantly maintaining control with everything. Every once in a while she really pushes you to the limits— "enough, enough!" I'll finally work up and I'll get fed up with it and I'll actually yell back at her, which—yelling for me is a foreign concept. And so I get mad at myself if I ever get to that point.

By referring to his place in the stepfamily-building process as the "tentative stage," Brad implicitly acknowledges that he does not have the same parental authority with Sherry (and her brother) that he would have if he were the father. He knows the feeling of parental authority because he has three children of his own whom he sees regularly. One distinctive aspect of Brad's stepfathering in this transitional period is being sensitive to his role in his partner's family dance and making a concerted effort to monitor his emotional reactions in a manner that does not affect his partner's children directly. At this point, he simply wants to get by without jeopardizing his relationship with Sherry.

Some stepdads in my study came to view their disciplinary role as important. This is to be expected because some describe their stepchildren as being undisciplined when they first met them. Much can be learned by looking more closely at how several of these men characterize their experiences. Recalling the beginning of his eighteen-month relationship with his fiancée, Melanie, and her daughters, Tim comments that Monica, his three-year-old stepdaughter, was "really not disciplined at all. None. . . . There would be no time out, no, none of that stuff. Monica basically did whatever she wanted to. . . . Melanie would get mad at her but there was no real discipline." Given Monica's unruly behavior, Tim describes how he felt "kind of bad" and awkward in the beginning when he would "get after her" for misbehavior. But he felt obligated to say something because "no one else was doing anything." Despite its importance in his life, he had a hard time recalling precisely how he assumed this daddy role involving discipline. For him it "just kind of evolved." He did recall that it grew to a point where he felt as though he had become the "bad guy"—the person mom called in to put the fire out and bring order to the girls. When Tim became more aware of what Melanie was doing, he urged Melanie to realize that they needed to discipline the children together.

The circumstances Harry faced were significantly less complicated when he first got involved with his future stepdaughter (he had no children of his own and she was his only stepchild). Despite these differences, Harry voices concerns similar to Tim's about what he was up against when he entered his four-year-old stepdaughter's life.

> The first thing I had to do with Kelly was discipline her; the kid had no discipline. The grandparents who were pseudo-parent figures did not discipline her, and when Jennifer [Harry's wife] did it was never consistent and she'd let it go so long and it would blow up at her. . . . Kelly was damaged goods when she came along, she had that hurt look to her, and she needed some support, she needed some discipline.

Harry describes Kelly as "damaged goods" because her father had not been involved in her life. He feels that she, as well as her mother, was struggling with feeling "abandoned." Despite this characterization, Harry portrays Kelly as a "pretty good kid." Harry believes he assumed an important disciplinarian role for Kelly during her preadolescent and early adolescent years. His opportunity to be involved with Kelly in this way was fostered by his wife, Jennifer. She explains why she let Harry get so involved: "I allowed it because if he was going to be a part of our life it just couldn't be me. She [Kelly] had to realize there were two people here, and she just couldn't run to mom and say save me." Even though Jennifer's perspective helped open the door for Harry to be involved in disciplining Kelly, Harry acknowledges that he has never developed a truly close relationship with Kelly.

That Harry, unlike Tim, had no children of his own when he got involved with his wife raises an important issue about the familial context of stepfather discipline. A family or household situation in which both the man and the woman have children from previous relationships, particularly minor children who spend time in the household, is likely to foster a more complicated set of circumstances and parental concerns than if only the mother has children. A situation of this kind is likely to evoke comparisons from adults and children alike focusing on whether children are treated differently and fairly by the birth and stepparents within the home. Concerns about fairness in discipline and privileges head the list of issues typically involved in these comparisons.

Another potential implication of blended family arrangements is illustrated by Mark's circumstances. In his case, his stepchildren's primary residence is his household whereas his biological children only visit on alternating weekends. Mark is aware of how this set of circumstances has shaped his approach to discipline and rule setting. Asked about how he disciplines all four kids when they are together at his house, Mark replies,

> It's a tough one; it's a real tough one. Her kids and I know I hold her kids to a higher standard—there's no doubt about it. And I justify it by saying that her kids are there a lot; her kids know the rules of that house really well; her kids have heard it a lot over and over and over and over. My kids know the rules of the house because they've heard it but not nearly as much, so they haven't had, they don't have near as much experience with the rules of the house as her kids. . . . I would get more frustrated . . . if her kids did something versus my kids doing something cause I would expect her kids to know better.

Although he adds that he would get after any of the kids if they didn't do something they were supposed to, he suggests that he is willing to be less rigid with his own children when they step outside the lines. Mark clearly reacts to his stepchildren and own kids differently, but it is less clear if Mark's influence on his stepchildren has been significantly altered because at times he nurtures them alongside his own children.

Even though Harry and Mark may not have ideal relationships with their stepchildren, they far exceed the experiences of some stepfathers, such as Monty and Ron. Of the men I interviewed, these two are the most distraught and frustrated about their involvement with their partner's children. Discipline issues are central to their troubled relationships with both their stepchildren and romantic partners. They are the poster boys for the stereotypical, negative images of what stepfamily life can be like.

Monty has experienced an uphill struggle with his four stepchildren who are currently ages twelve, nineteen, twenty, and twenty-two. Although his relationships with a couple of the kids have improved since they moved out of the house, much of their life together was riddled by tension. He's been involved with them for about six years.

Unlike Tim and Harry, Monty tried to lie low in the beginning and let his partner, Sue, do the disciplining. "At first I wasn't bossy or anything like that—didn't really try to get into their business a whole lot. I just wanted to be their friend, and that's exactly what I told them. . . . then after a while [about eighteen months] I just decided that this is my house, I'm paying most of the bills and everything, and I'm going to have a say in something whether they like it or not." At that point Monty tried to assert his views on what the kids should or shouldn't do. This led to a major confrontation with his stepson, Brad, who was fifteen at the time. Monty went against what Sue had allowed her son to do in the past and decided that Brad couldn't sleep over at his girlfriend's house. According to Monty, his decision caused Brad to revolt and their relationship never recovered. Comparable situations arose with the other kids and he quickly found himself at odds with the entire family, including his wife.

When asked in a separate interview to comment on Monty's role in disciplining her children, Sue put a different slant on things. Listening to Monty and Sue talk about their experiences brought up images of the classic notion of "his" and "her" marriages.[12] They clearly have different images of why their family life evolved the way it did. Sue's recollection, similar to Monty's, is that he got along fairly well with all of the kids when they were first dating and before they moved into Monty's place. At some point, when they were all living under the same roof, she feels his attitude changed and her role did as well. "That's when I became the mediator. That's what I call it, I'm the mediator. I'm the go-between. He would not tell them to do anything, or not to do anything. It's always been me. I'm the meanie."

Continuing, Sue explains that Monty had done nothing to deserve or earn her children's respect. "If he wants them to respect him, he has to put forth an effort, to act like he deserves respect. Tell them not to do something, tell them that they can't talk on the phone for thirty minutes, you have a ten-minute limit. Instead of when I walk in the door, jump on me to jump on them." Without knowing what Monty was saying in his interview, she challenges Monty's assertions that her children didn't respect her. Although she admits "I lacked in disciplining my children for a long time," she feels that her kids have given her a loose kind of respect consistent with her parenting style as a single, working mother with four kids. Identifying herself with single moms and their struggles, she says, "Sometimes single moms let kids get away with, we're not consistent: one day it's a no, and the next day the same question could have a yes answer cause we're tired, we're tired of saying no." When all is said and done, she feels that her kids feel comfortable with her and she has a negative view of how Monty has affected her children. In her mind, Monty was "not made to be a father." But from Monty's perspective, it is Sue's kids and her parenting style that prevent him from being a more supportive, healthy adult figure for the children. He feels that, despite his efforts, he ultimately fell victim to circumstances beyond his control.

Unlike Monty, who had a grace period after he first got involved with his wife—feeling reasonably comfortable with his partner's children—Ron began to experience problems much more quickly. His unique story is worth describing in some detail. At the time we spoke, Ron, age twenty-two, and his thirty-one-year-old cohabiting partner, Gayle, whom he referred to as his "wife," had been dating for about two years. Five months earlier Ron and Gayle, along with Gayle's two kids, moved from out of state to north central Florida. Throughout our interview, Ron expressed discomfort about the way the two kids treat him. Neither the kids nor Gayle accept him as an authority figure. The fact that their relationship is interracial adds to Ron's problems because he feels his stepson and his stepdaughter (to a lesser extent) are racist. They apparently have called him a "nigger" to his face. Their negative behavior was accentuated when everyone moved to Florida and they lived with Gayle's mother and brother, whom Ron saw as rednecks. According to Ron, the kids became more unruly and defiant toward him because their grandmother and uncle disapproved of Gayle's involvement with a black man. The ill feeling escalated to the point where the uncle pulled a gun on Ron and Gayle. After that incident, Ron, Gayle, and the two kids moved out of the house, left the city, and eventually ended up living in homeless shelters in another city. To compound Ron's problems, the kids often use the stereotypical ploy of reminding Ron in a confrontational way that he is not their dad and that they do not have to listen to him. Ironically, their own separate biological fathers are almost completely absent from their lives.

Like Monty, Ron feels he is entitled to have some standing with the kids. He resents that the kids do not listen to him and that their mother takes their side in most disputes, often believing the kids' descriptions of conflicts they have with Ron rather than Ron's version of the events. After describing several examples of how Gayle has dismissed him and sided with her kids, Ron comments, "I don't mind being a father figure. All I can do is try my best to help the kids do the right thing. But if she don't allow me to do that, all I can do is look at them do the wrong thing. And just sit there and watch them grow bad habits that way. Just because I can't tell them to do the right thing."

The social ecology influencing Ron's involvement with his partner and her kids works against his being perceived as a legitimate parental figure in many respects. He is significantly younger than Gayle, has never been a father, must confront the racial stigma directed at him by Gayle's racist relatives and her kids, and is currently poor; in addition, his partner is taking medication for a mental illness. To this list of hurdles add the fact that Gayle grew accustomed to dating older men who took care of her financially and allowed her to stay at home without being employed. Ron rejects being a traditional male breadwinner, particularly because the kids are not his. He expresses his discomfort with the idea of investing too much in the kids—especially in light of how poorly they treat him. Ron's situation illustrates that children's personalities and behavior can either facilitate or, as in this case, hinder men from developing a father identity and feeling comfortable disciplining their partner's kids.

Ron confides that he recently adopted a new strategy of indifference toward the kids out of his increasing frustration with his rather limited, powerless role. If they mess up, then so be it, but he isn't going to try to discipline them because he will hear Gayle's "static" about his behavior. At least for the time being, he has committed himself to the tactic of ignoring Gayle's kids. He plans to let her deal with any situations that arise.

Both Monty and Ron are immersed in adverse situations. They and their partners have never established a sense of being a parental team. Each feels excluded from the family core and neither has been able to integrate himself into a new and healthy stepfamily dance. These men understand how difficult it is to navigate the terrain of being a stepfather if neither the mother nor the kids are willing to recognize them as a legitimate authority figure. Once the downward spiral in their relationship with the kids began, they were unable to find a way to make things better. Eventually they both threw their hands in the air and began to ignore the kids, becoming increasingly indifferent. They simply resigned themselves to believe that they were not going to have much of an impact on them. These couples' prospects for staying together are far less promising than those of many of the other couples I interviewed.

Not surprisingly, friction over discipline issues is one of the more important negative factors affecting the quality of life in stepfamilies. This point is illustrated aptly by Gerald's telling comments about how his experiences with discipline in a previous stepfamily contributed to its demise.

I didn't want to be a father. It was—I had two little kids. It was a load. I was supposed to share the responsibilities but yet I wasn't really allowed to discipline them. A lot of contradictions. Messy rooms, clean them up. Mom said we don't have to. Well okay, screw all you people. I never really gave it my all. I wasn't in with both feet in the relationship. I was more interested in Emily [the mother]. The kids were—well—along with that relationship. But that's probably the one thing that led to the breakup was—I just didn't like, with the kids—I just was uncomfortable. I didn't want a marriage. I didn't want a family. I wanted Emily, and I just found it difficult.

Continuing, Gerald emphasizes how he and Emily had a fundamental difference of opinion about his role as a stepfather.

If I was going to take the parental role, then I needed to be treated like the parent. And Emily always seemed to want to do it her way. "Don't discipline the girls. Don't do this, don't do that." Well, I got the responsibilities—I got to feed 'em, but I can't yell at them? She would make comments like, "Well, you don't love them like I do." No kidding. They're your kids. I mean, I can't, I never will. I don't think a biological father feels the same way as a biological mother. It's just different. You know. You pretty much create them. So that was always a problem.

When a stepfather wants to be with the woman romantically but does not want to be part of a family, discipline issues are likely to take center stage. Add to this troubling equation a mother who is protective of her parenting turf and the man's belief that a biological father, let alone a stepfather, cannot love his children as much as a mother does, and you end up with a disaster.[13] Perhaps if the child is incredibly well behaved, requires little attention, and responds quickly and efficiently to the stepfather's requests, then the man may have a slight chance of cruising in his romantic relationship while remaining largely oblivious to the "unwanted" child. However, if a child acts more like a typical child who requires supervision, authoritative direction, prodding, and discipline, the stepfather who doesn't want to be in a family is likely to find the stepfamily arrangement untenable. He will have little desire to make a lasting and positive impression on the child because he sees the child as a distraction and undesirable appendage.

In my sample, the stories of Monty, Ron, and Gerald, though powerful, are the exception; most of the men feel as though they have and will make a difference in their stepchildren's lives. Some are assertive, making sure that the stepchildren are clear about the men's position as an adult authority figure in the household. For example, Herman, an outspoken, authoritative stepfather of three, laid out his agenda as head of the household to his stepchildren and their mother, Anna, before the marriage. His views on gender shaped how he approached his new stepfamily. When he met Anna, she was a single mom raising her two teenage sons and a daughter. It didn't take him long to realize that she was struggling with her sons who were, according to him, taking advantage of her. After watching these teenage males mistreat their mother over a period of months, Herman decided he needed to assert himself as the only "silverback in the tribe," alluding to males' struggle to gain dominance in small groups. One way he did this was to inform the kids on numerous occasions that when they relocated from their mother's house in the city to his country home there was going to be a new set of family and household rules. Herman felt compelled to assert himself in this way because he anticipated that Anna's teenage sons would challenge him. They apparently had already started to do "little man things. Staying out late at night and one of them on the phone all the time." Herman had a clear sense of how the household should be run; he was going to be calling the shots along with Anna. "I'm going to have to be the one that's going to have to keep a lid on things. Because I want them to understand that even though they're welcome here they're not going to run this [household]." From his perspective, if the boys wouldn't abide by the new rules they would need to find alternative places to live—which they eventually did. Although Herman directs these comments at his stepsons, he displays a similar style of tough love and firm discipline with his biological son.

Anna has acquiesced to Herman's demands that neither of her sons be allowed to take advantage of them, though she is emotionally distraught because her sons are not living with her. Herman seems to have leverage in this situation because Anna believes he has good intentions. He has always expressed a strong commitment to her kids and is especially involved with her fourteen-year-old daughter, who is living with them and doing well with the new arrangement. Even though Anna isn't completely happy with the decisions Herman persuaded her to accept, she believes he loves her children and wants to help them as best he can while keeping the peace at home. Anna sees, for example, how much Herman encourages her daughter to excel at school, get involved with her band activities, and stay in contact with her biological father.

Whereas Herman exemplifies the assertive stepfather who assumes a major role in matters of discipline, Barry represents the laid-back stepfather who lets the mother handle these issues: "I never punished them once for anything." Although he never confronted his two stepchildren directly, he admits to talking to his wife privately on several occasions about her decisions regarding punishments. If Barry has had an impact, it has been indirect and based on his decision to remain in the background when discipline decisions were being made. Concerned for a long time about his wife's rather lax approach to discipline, he believes, in retrospect, that he did the right thing by not challenging her parenting style. "Her philosophy has always been all you can do is kind of set an example. Lay the groundwork. You can't be with them all the time. You can't be on their backs all the time or they're going to wind up hating you. I kind of ended up agreeing with that." As he sees it, the wisdom of his decision to follow his wife's lead is reflected in how well he feels the kids have developed into responsible young adults who love to spend time with their mother and him.

Some stepfathers and mothers are more comparably assertive. These stepfathers mention their occasional struggles to follow through with discipline efforts. In these instances, the women take on a gatekeeper role by monitoring how their male partners respond to their children.[14] The implications of this gatekeeping are apparent in the remarks of Emmit, the twenty-eight-year-old stepfather whose stepson, Jake, is almost six. He is Jake's only active father figure because Jake's biological father lost touch with him. Within three or four months of dating, Jake's mother told Emmit to discipline and correct Jake if he saw him doing something wrong. At this early stage, Emmit was reluctant to say or do too much, fearing he might offend his partner and inadvertently end the relationship. However, after working his way into a father figure role, Emmit grew more comfortable asserting himself and disciplining Jake. Emmit is upset, though, that his wife handcuffs his parental authority at times by giving him mixed signals. On the one hand, she has given Emmit her blessing to handle her son when he misbehaves. On the other hand, she wants to dictate the terms of the punishment. Consequently, Emmit questions whether he can be a "full father" to Jake if his wife "pulls rank" on him.

A similar story came through in Landen's description of his involvement with his girlfriend, who has three children. He describes how his partner

> sometimes wants me to discipline them, but then she'll undercut me on it. I'll tell them, "No, no you didn't clean your room so you're not having any TV tonight." She'll go, "But they can, they can just watch for a little while." Or she'll, she wouldn't tell me, she'll just go tell them, "Oh, you can watch it for an hour."

The struggles that Emmit and Landen describe are not unique to stepfamilies. Parents in households with two birth parents often undermine each other's parental roles, but stepfathers (or stepmothers) have a more difficult time dealing with these types of mixed signals because their legitimacy as authority figures can be challenged more easily. They can't fall back on their genetic bond and say, "I'm your father, you need to listen to me." Unless they have formally adopted their stepchildren, most stepfathers don't even have legal rights to buttress their authority. Under these circumstances, the birth mothers have the upper hand and are in a position to call the shots. Whether they are perceived as "pulling rank" or not can influence stepfathers' perceptions of how they want to create and perform their stepfathering roles.

On the other hand, a birth mother's long-standing connection to her child and willingness to offer a stepfather constructive criticism in a non-confrontational way can help a stepfather develop a deeper understanding of the child while learning how to make a positive contribution to the child's development. Of course, the stepfather has to be willing to listen and adjust his involvement in the stepfamily dance in an effective way. In separate interviews, Kevin and Lynn describe in considerable detail the circumstances surrounding Kevin's initial experiences with spanking Lynn's son and their subsequent discussions about why he should relinquish that role. They also explain how Lynn made a concerted effort to sensitize Kevin to Trevor's mind-set as a child who had lived with a single mother for most of his life. Kevin begins, "One of the difficult things for me was recognizing that Trevor's whole life he's had his mom as the authority, so I would tell him to do something and a lot of times he would go appeal to his mom or 'But my mom says'. . . This used to frustrate me. 'Listen, you know, I am your stepdad, or your dad, I'm in charge of you.'" Kevin recalls that at one point Lynn told him in private to "be the adult, recognize that he [Trevor] has only seen me [Lynn] as an authority for five years in his life and he hasn't seen you as that and it's going to take time." From that point on, Kevin made a conscious effort to remain calm when Trevor tested his patience and authority. Kevin's ability to do this has been fostered by Lynn's support throughout their relationship. He describes Lynn as

> really conscientious about making sure that he [Trevor] respects my authority too. If she disagrees with something I've done, she'll tell me privately. She'll say honey . . . give me the look. The old "you come talk to me right now, I don't like what you're doing." So I'll go talk to her and sometimes it takes me a while to see things from her point of view.

Sometimes I don't, but with matters of Trevor I try and defer to her, because she knows him a lot better than I do. She's been around him a lot longer.

This mentality was useful when he first assumed the responsibility of spanking Trevor, with Lynn's blessings, in hopes of encouraging him to do his schoolwork, which he repeatedly refused to complete. Later, Kevin's role evolved so that he was administering occasional spankings when Trevor misbehaved in other ways. This changed after one particular incident that left Trevor "screaming bloody murder." Kevin remembers being taken aside by Lynn who said, "I don't want you to spank him anymore . . . with me, Trevor knows, trusts my love for him. I don't want—I want the foundation of your relationship with him to not be this punishment." Trusting Lynn's judgment, Kevin handed the discipline reins back to her. His willingness to defer grew out of their ongoing communication about discipline and their mutual trust.

For her part, Lynn recognized that she needed to be mindful in how she dealt with Trevor once Kevin started playing a role in administering discipline. Lynn mentions, "I didn't want to undermine Kevin, so that was the real period of negotiation. When I thought he was handling something wrong, not jumping in front of Trevor, which I had done several times and saying, 'I'll take care of this.' Marginalizing him, basically, and pushing him off the scene and then managing it myself." It took time and courage for Lynn to make the difficult decision to step back and trust that Kevin's relationship with Trevor would be okay. As she puts it, "Trevor is so mine, and I've always had him to myself. It's very difficult for me not to micro-manage the relationship too." But Lynn learned to share her feelings and preferences with Kevin in private. Because Trevor's personality makes him a challenge to raise, Lynn's and Kevin's ability to have frequent, candid, and calm discussions about parenting have proven essential. Building on the foundation he established with Lynn, along with the frequent time he and Trevor spend together without Lynn being present, Kevin has earned Trevor's trust. As a result, Kevin has placed himself in a comfortable position to shape Trevor's development in a positive way. Things have actually progressed to the point where a few weeks prior to the interview Lynn suggested that Kevin step back into the role of handing out spankings when needed.

In families with kids who are easier to parent, the mother's role in helping the father negotiate the terrain of stepfathering is less important. As I've alluded to throughout, some stepfathers feel their stepchildren are a delight to be around and are easy to manage. For example, Keith summarizes his situation with his stepdaughters by saying, "We're blessed. They're both fine young ladies. They don't give me lots of cause to discipline them for anything." These fortunate stepfathers are not as dependent on their partner's cooperation. Consequently, their options for making a difference in their stepchildren's lives often involve areas other than those dealing with discipline issues. The mother's role may be less significant in some of these areas, but her parenting style can still have implications for the stepfather. In chapter 3, I briefly described some of the dynamics associated with mothers introducing a potential stepfather into their family dance. Mothers can continue to play an important role in orchestrating a man's relationship and emotional ties with his stepchild throughout the course of a stepfamily's life together. The tone and style of parenting that mothers establish early on may be important in this regard; however, it is not necessarily fixed in stone. In short, with or without taking the birth mother into account, concerns about how stepfathers participate in discipline are vitally important but should not obscure the many other ways stepfathers can influence a stepchild.

OTHER WAYS TO BE INVOLVED

Stepfathers, just like biological fathers, can be involved with children in a variety of ways that don't involve discipline or instilling responsibility. Tim, for example, is conscious of his desire to go beyond his role as disciplinarian. One of his responsibilities to his stepchildren, as he sees it, is to recognize that "they need to know and see that, men, specifically, are not just about discipline and this is the way it should be, you know. I feel like I need to be more open to them and more responsive as far as emotionally goes. . . . I feel that that's probably an area that I haven't done so well, and I don't know exactly why that is." Elaborating on his concerns, Tim adds that perhaps he has been less emotionally involved with his stepchildren because "they're not really my kids." His partner, Melanie, has noticed and brought this to his attention as well, a point I elaborate on in chapter 7. Robby, another stepdad responsible for multiple kids, describes how he has encouraged his stepchildren to be more playful since coming on the scene.

> My ability to bring myself down to their level, that's my strongest point.
> I tease and joke and the same way and they give it right back to me. I

think it's, they let some of my humor in. 'Cause before they were pretty much uptight; it was just their mom and them, and they were uptight. Now I always got them laughing, and being silly. They enjoy me being around. I think I've helped them quite a bit.

Although Robby defines himself as playing a significant role disciplining his stepchildren, he feels he's also made a big contribution to his stepchildren's lives by helping them to be lighthearted and to have fun. It is often easier for a stepfather to become the family clown than the disciplinarian. Becoming both suggests that a stepfather has made a concerted effort to be involved with his stepchild in an active and healthy way.

One critical way a stepfather can focus his energies is to promote his stepchild's formal and informal education. A number of the stepfathers in my study have played a significant role in their stepchildren's schooling and have done so in various ways. As I discuss in the next chapter in connection with social capital, sometimes this means having discussions with the school personnel responsible for a stepchild's education. For now, I simply mention a couple of exemplary cases to show how stepfathers can demonstrate a strong commitment to their stepchild's education. At the top of the list is Ernest's year-long experience a few years ago with homeschooling his stepson, Scott. After dealing with Scott's mediocre grades and a fighting incident on the school bus, Ernest and his wife decided to give homeschooling a shot. Ernest spearheaded this venture and established a routine of coming home after working the nightshift and getting Scott involved in the program first thing in the morning. Although Ernest describes the program as relatively self-directing, he was responsible for supervising Scott's work, answering his questions, and testing him several times a week. A family move out of state, in addition to a joint parental decision that it would be in Scott's best interest to interact with other students and friends on a daily basis, meant that the homeschooling experiment lasted for only a year. Nonetheless, Ernest's willingness to take on this significant responsibility speaks volumes for his commitment to be a supportive and instructional force for his stepchild.

Carl expresses a similar commitment as he professes, "I feel [I] have a responsibility for education." He supports his contention by saying that he and his wife send his eight-year-old stepdaughter to a private school. "That's a big thing for me because I'm into education myself." In addition to his money, Carl contributes time, apparently lots of it, to reading to his stepdaughter. Offering a self-appraisal and speaking from the perspective of being part of a coparental team, Carl explains,

If I could quit my job and become a career student I probably would. We read to her a lot, and that's only because I grew up reading myself. . . . And even before Vicky could learn to read, or could read, we read to her, usually a little bit at night and things that she could grasp, with lots of pictures, and then we moved more toward word books. I think we're on, we're halfway through book three of *Harry Potter* now. We've done the first two books and we're working on book three. . . . she reads on her own. In a lot of cases she'll pick up a book herself and we'll read it. She's advanced for her age in reading, so a lot of that has probably helped.

Carl takes pride in knowing that he has helped Vicky acquire his love for reading. As Calvin and Carl illustrate, a stepfather can be a powerful force in a stepchild's life, especially if the birth mother paves the way for his involvement.

Stepfathers, not unlike biological fathers, sometimes take a stab at providing spiritual guidance to a child.[15] Though I did not regularly ask the stepfathers to talk about their role in this regard, a few brought it up themselves. Doug, for instance, appears to take pride in his efforts to mold Sammy, the boy whom he helped raise for the past sixteen years, into a Christian man. "I have literally, from the time he was old enough to understand, tried to teach him to believe in the Bible, and I've tried my best to keep him in church and everything. I guess literally, what I'm trying to say is, I've tried to teach him to be, grow up and be the best man he can be." I did not talk to Sammy, so I cannot confirm how successful Doug was in his efforts, but the familial circumstances were in his favor. In addition to his wife's support for his Christian philosophy, Doug has not had to deal with the biological father interfering in any way because he gave up custody rights and has been out of the picture for most of the time Doug has known Sammy. Though it wasn't an issue that surfaced in my interviews, I suspect that some stepfathers and involved fathers butt heads over how a child should be raised from a religious perspective. When this occurs, a stepfather's ability to affect his stepchild's religious upbringing may sometimes be limited.

Finally, stepfathers, birth mothers, and even children generally express an understanding that the stepfathers brought additional financial resources into the children's lives. Although I did not systematically explore what kind of effect the stepfathers' financial contributions had on the children's lives, some participants indicate that it has been significant.[16] My interviews with the men left me with the impression that they generally feel comfortable spending their money on their stepchildren, even when they have financial responsibilities toward their own children. Some stepfathers feel their obligations are lessened in a practical sense because the biological father is making a financial contribution, but a number of stepfathers and birth mothers point out that the biological father is either not involved financially or only to a limited extent. In Harry's situation, the biological father hasn't been involved. But Jennifer, Harry's wife, firmly believes that Harry has provided much more for her daughter than she could have provided by herself.

> Oh he's given her things I could have never given her 'cause I worked a full-time job. I mean, I was a secretary but we lived comfortably in a two-bedroom apartment and I had a car. I know I could have never, well he didn't give her the car his mother did, but all the things I couldn't have done. The costumes for dance; he's given her the things in life I could have never given her. Just 'cause he makes good money.

I expected to hear a bit more from the stepfathers about their concerns regarding the money they were spending on their stepchildren.[17] A few complaints surfaced but were rare and seldom came from men who expressed having a reasonably good relationship with their stepchild. In some middle-class couples, like Lisa and Ernest, the birth mother is less eager to spend money on her kids than the stepfather. Lisa summarizes her philosophy: "I had things the hard way and I just think it made me a better person and, not that I'm saying I want to make it difficult for the kids, but I don't want to pamper them." She adds, by role-playing how Ernest talks to her when she raises her concerns about spoiling the kids, "Well, we've learned a lot going through the hard times we have, and we don't want the children to go through that. Why not make it easier for them?" To which she responds, "I go, 'at what point do they learn how to fend for themselves?'"

That few of the stepfathers expressed any serious reservations about sharing their financial assets with their stepchildren is consistent with the idea that, despite the emergence of the "nurturant" and "care-giving" model of fatherhood, the breadwinner role remains an important dimension for contemporary images of fatherhood in the United States.[18] When men enter the world of symbolically creating their own family, they expose themselves to a life domain in which traditional emblems of masculinity abound. A man's ability to contribute to the support of his family members, whether they are genetically related to him or not, is an attribute closely linked with self-images of manhood for most men. A man who shares financial resources with a stepchild reaffirms his commitment to his romantic partner, thereby acknowledging his investment in the "package deal" of mother and child. Thus it is not surprising to find that men who are at least reasonably content with their romantic partnerships are also comfortable sharing their money with their partner's child. However, I suspect that this family man mentality may not be as strong for men in conflict-ridden stepfamilies. Had I interviewed more men who were frustrated with their stepfamily circumstances, I probably would have encountered more men like Ron who were willing to voice their reservations about financially supporting stepchildren.

PERCEPTIONS OF INVOLVEMENT

The stepfathers' descriptions of their involvement with their stepchildren, and how they have influenced or would like to influence them, are connected in some ways to how they think about their performance as parental or father figures. In turn, how stepfathers judge themselves often involves comparing themselves to certain types of persons. Men's perceptions about their own fatherly experiences—whether real or hypothetical—are sometimes influenced by their childhood experiences, as I discuss more fully in chapter 8. Men, in a sense, compare themselves to their own parents, most frequently their father. Stepfathers' comments describing how they have actually affected their stepchildren are intertwined with their method for evaluating their contribution as stepfathers. Stepfathers look to the birth mother, biological father, or a more general and amorphous type of generic standard to determine how successful they have been in acting in a fatherly way.[19] In addition, they may look at themselves to appraise their current experiences with a stepchild. They can do this by reflecting on their earlier experiences raising their own child or a stepchild, or they can consider their current experiences with their own child. The stepdads at times explicitly compare themselves to a person and/or standard but on other occasions they are less focused in their self-assessment. What they typically don't do, however, is compare themselves to other stepfathers.

Although a number of stepfathers apparently are at ease comparing their experiences as a stepfather with those as a biological father, not all stepfathers feel confident in doing so. As Tim begins to respond to my request for him to evaluate himself as a stepfather and a father, he offers, "I think I'm doing worse as a stepparent, because, the reason why I think that is I think that I'm not, umm, patient with the girls as I am with my sons. And I'm not exactly sure why. . . . I try to figure out why and I think maybe it's just because they're not my own kids." As he continues to clarify his thinking on this matter on the spot, it becomes clear that he has doubts about his ability to put his finger on why he is less patient with his stepdaughters. He adds that with his stepdaughters he gets "upset quicker" and doesn't "tolerate as much of whatever kind of thing it is." Immediately upon saying this, he questions whether his perceptions may have more to do with the fact that his stepdaughters are girls and younger than his sons. Tim's struggle for clarity is a reminder that men may not always find it easy to understand exactly why they treat their biological and stepchildren differently.

When asked how they felt they had affected their stepchildren, the stepfathers did not volunteer that their involvement had produced any negative outcomes. Consequently, the men's descriptions of their impact is essentially synonymous with either a favorable or inconsequential evaluation of how they believe their involvement has mattered. That said, most of the men admit that they are not perfect; most are reluctant to give themselves the highest praise, although several do. Instead, most characterize their involvement along these lines: I have been trying pretty hard and have done rather well, but I can do some things better. Those feeling this way tend to emphasize that they want to be more available for their stepchild in an active, time-intensive way.

When considering discipline issues, men often use the mother as the point of comparison because she is at the center of the family dance. As I described earlier, men often, but not always, think the mother is too lax in how she treats her child. The stepfathers therefore have a tendency to feel that they have made, and are making, a valuable contribution to the stepchild's life by compensating for the mother, who is a pushover. In short, they sometimes feel that they are doing something the birth mother should have been doing all along.

The men's concerns with how children should be disciplined sometimes extend into other areas. For example, comparing his involvement in parenting to that of his cohabiting girlfriend, Landen says, "I put more effort into it. And she feels like I've got more knowledge. From what she's told me." He prides himself on providing the children with options, giving them choices at a young age so they can learn to make decisions on their own. Landen believes he's more attentive to the children, a difference that accentuates how his parenting philosophy differs from his partner's. Fortunately for Landen, he feels that he reaps the benefits of being more attentive to his stepchildren because even though the kids see him as the "big, bad Landen," he's also the one they go to rather than their mother because he's the "one that will show them what they want to see. Or, take them where they want to go." Though Landen seems to have his own standards for how he can best treat the kids in a fatherly way, those times when he sees that he does things differently from his partner bolster his sense of how well he is doing with the kids.

Stepfathers also measure their fatherly contribution by comparing themselves to what the biological father has done or is doing for the child. In some cases, the father is an easy mark because he has not been involved at all. Under these circumstances, it is almost impossible for the stepfathers to feel that they have not brought something positive into their stepchild's life. Almost anything is better than nothing. Similarly, stepfathers who think the biological father has been or is only remotely involved with his child are inclined to feel that they have made a meaningful contribution. For example, Thomas supported his stepson Danny during his time of need several years ago. Danny's father left town unexpectedly, reducing Danny to brokenhearted tears, a story that I'll return to later. At that time, Thomas told him that he would love him like a father. Now Thomas knows that for the past seven years he has been there in a constructive and fatherly way for Danny and his brother, day after day after day. Because the biological father has been off somewhere else and largely uninvolved in his sons' lives, Thomas has had a clear comparative advantage leaving him feeling pretty good about his fatherly input, a sentiment Danny and his brother reinforce.

Terry, too, doesn't pull any punches, concluding that the way of life he and his wife lead, and his approach to fathering, are much more beneficial for his stepson, Zack, than what the father has to offer. After describing how he and his wife are doing well professionally and are "very proeducation," he portrays the environment Zack experiences when he visits his father.

> It's a completely different world up there in [name of state]. They're in the woods. They live in a trailer. They smoke 59,000 packs of cigarettes a day in the trailer. They drink beer. They—not that I don't mind drinking beer, but I mean, they drink a lot. There's always fighting and cursing going on. He [father] has a different girlfriend every time he's around him. It's just a completely unsavory environment from what we try to foster down here. We curtail television channels, the music he listens to. We go to church a couple times a week. He's really involved in different productive groups. And then he goes up there and for weeks when he comes back, it's "yeah this," and—his speech patterns have to be corrected. His behaviors have to be corrected. It's a complete disruption in his life. And it's hard because he's only a little guy and this is

his biological father. While he's up there they spoil him to death because they only have him for a month. All he knows is that it's really cool and he falls right into this good old boy behavior up there. It's not what we have planned for him. We'd like something—he's enrolled in the Florida One Program, hoping he'll get a baseball scholarship, and if he doesn't college is paid for. We have a lot more plans for him than to drive a truck. That's where his father is, up there.

Terry's comments speak to many intriguing issues that can affect how a stepfather assesses the quality of his fatherly efforts. One of the more prominent ones deals with the question of social class. Given Terry's commitment to education, a professional career, and a middle-class lifestyle, he is quick to suggest that he and his wife are in a better position to provide Zack with the type of environment that will enable him to aspire to and achieve more in life than being a truck driver. Terry also draws attention to other value-laden subjects involving relationships and religion. As a happily married, churchgoing man, Terry believes that he, as a stepfather, can provide a healthier environment for Zack than his biological father, who has a history of active dating, excessive drinking, and foul language. Although Terry espouses the belief that it is fine for Zack to have two fathers, as noted previously, he feels that he is in a much better position to help Zack develop into a responsible young man.

Making a more subtle observation, Brad comments that he sees himself as having a "role model position with Bobby because I am also male." Bobby's biological father, who suffered serious brain damage in a car accident a few years ago, lives out of state and is unable to visit with Bobby on his own. With these circumstances in mind, Brad says, "I feel a little bit sorry for him because he hasn't had an active influence from his father for several years. . . . So I want to take that role and sometimes he's very accepting of that and sometimes he's kind of like 'oh God, here's another one telling me what to do. It's bad enough Mom tells me what to do, now Brad's telling me what to do.'" Even though Brad feels he's willing and capable of providing that male role model he thinks Bobby is lacking, he recognizes that he needs to be careful about being too aggressive in trying to be a paternal figure alongside the mother. Because Bobby is a thirteen-year-old boy, Brad is more concerned about being a role model for him than for Bobby's sixteen-year-old sister, whom he describes as already having an "incredibly strong personality. . . . She's really her own person." In describing how he tries to reinforce the mother's ideas about what Bobby should or shouldn't be doing, Brad shares a telling example of the way Bobby sometimes responds: "'Yeah, yeah I'm getting away with something mom told me not to do.' Occasionally he even looks at me like 'Hey, you're a guy. Why are you giving me a hard time?'" Brad's remark highlights the potential significance a stepfather's gender can have for a stepson. Bobby seemingly expects to connect at times with Brad because they're both males. This kind of gendered expectation may help motivate some boys to be open to, perhaps even reach out to, a man other than their father. At the same time, the gendered competition surrounding much male interaction may make it more difficult for some boys to feel comfortable with a man who replaced his father as his mother's romantic partner.

As already noted, how others respond to a stepfather can influence how he perceives his fatherly roles and contributions to a child's well-being. Thus a stepfather's self-evaluation can be reinforced or challenged by others, most notably the mother. In addition to this type of feedback, a stepfather is free to compare himself to the mother, the biological father, his father, the "typical" father or parent, or some combination of reference points.

Just as a stepfather can compare his fatherly efforts to different sources, he can use various subjective standards to determine how satisfied he is with his performance and contribution to his stepchild's well-being. Interestingly, whether it is the stepfather evaluating himself or someone else judging him, the standard used to judge a man's competence as a stepfather is probably lower than it is for biological fathers. Consequently, without the genetic tie to establish the baseline for an expected degree of commitment or investment, stepfathers have more latitude in assigning meaning to and enacting their fatherly roles. However, some men, like Doug, who do not have a genetic tie to a specific child, may still evaluate themselves and feel comfortable being judged according to a measure of success generally associated with biological fathers. This is particularly true for men who have formally adopted a child.

For many people, the normal scheme for interpreting parental behavior is knowingly or unknowingly altered when stepfathers (or stepmothers) enter the picture. Stepfathers' minor accomplishments may be given greater weight and viewed as remarkable signs of love and devotion. Likewise, others, especially those outside the stepfamily, may view displays of impatience, indifference, or limited involvement as not unexpected or awful but an understandable pattern given the circumstances. Some feel that stepfathers, compared to biological fathers, have a more legitimate excuse for being less committed to and active with their partner's child.

Mark's candid analysis of his current life and philosophy as a stepfather, compared to his fathering experiences in his earlier marriage, provides a

useful illustration. While contemplating some of the reasons why his previous marriage ended in divorce, he is quick to note that he had a tendency
to spend his time doing a variety of work and recreational activities away
from his former wife and kids. He notes that he is much more aware now
of time management and priority issues when it comes to how someone
might assess him as a father or stepfather, but his present stepfamily circumstances provide a very different kind of context for judging him as a father and husband.

> I realize that when I describe the way I am with her [current wife] girls,
> it's not a whole lot different than I was with my own kids. Now it's a
> lot more acceptable, this now, because they aren't my children. If they
> were, if her girls were there all the time, it probably would be different,
> but my wife gets lots of breaks. My ex-wife told me, why didn't you
> take the kids away for the day and give me a break, you know? Because
> I was too selfish or whatever, but today, I don't carry that because they
> go away. They go away for the whole weekend. They go away for a
> Wednesday night, so she gets all these breaks. She gets all this down-
> time. It's very different the dynamics. It almost fits in perfect to my be-
> havior. 'Cause you know, if I go play tennis tonight, sure go play ten-
> nis. She doesn't care; she knows she'll be doing homework with her
> girls. Beats the heck out of me sitting, standing there, walking around
> the house going, what's going on? Well in the old days it would be like,
> why are you playing tennis? . . . You are ignoring your children.

The "downtime" that Mark refers to is produced when his stepdaughters stay with their father. Essentially, the father functions as a nanny,
a convenience Mark never had with his previous wife and kids. The father's
involvement in his daughters' lives in a practical sense limits the chances for
tension to arise between Mark and his current wife over Mark's desire to
spend lots of time doing things that take him away from home. As Mark
notes, things would probably be different if his stepdaughters spent every
day and night at his house. Another practical arrangement in Mark's favor
is that when his own kids come to visit, they usually do so when his stepdaughters are also there. As a result, he and his wife still have free time once
a week and every other weekend when there are no children at home. After confirming that he has thought about all of these things prior to our interview, he shares more about how he sees his current life as a stepfather.

> Sometimes I think I have it made; . . . in spite of having been divorced.
> . . . I am free every night to do whatever I want to do, within reason.
> I'm not going out with my buddies and partying and doing that kind of

stuff. I'm not chasing girls; you know, I'm not doing anything wrong. It's more, work stuff or sports stuff. But I can do whatever I want; I don't have to worry, I don't have to worry. As long as I'm respectful; I don't have to worry about being around all the time. Although I try not to abuse it. . . . I just can't blow them off the whole night; I mean, I've got [to] let them know what I'm going to do.

From this description it is clear that, much to Mark's delight, he recognizes that his performance as a husband and stepfather is being evaluated by his current wife and stepchildren from a significantly different perspective than was the case in his previous marriage.

Perceptions of stepfathers may vary, of course, depending on whether people view a man as a stepfather or biological father. Some people seeing a man with a child in different settings may simply assume that he is the child's father. For instance, Robby learned from his own father how the father's mechanic had incorrectly perceived him. The mechanic, who happened to live down the street from Robby, commented to Robby's father that he saw Robby "down with his kids all the time." After being told by Robby's father that the kids weren't Robby's, the mechanic responded surprisingly, "you're kidding me 'cause he treats them just like they're his." This exchange makes Robby's father laugh. It also implicitly suggests, from the mechanic's perspective, that Robby deserves even more adulation for his fatherly behavior because he is interacting with children who are not even "his." At the same time, this type of misunderstanding—where others define a man as a biological father because they have no reason to believe otherwise—means that their perceptions and judgments of the stepfather will be based on a higher standard typically reserved for biological fathers. Unless a stepfather is aware of others' misperceptions of him as a "father," it may not matter much from his point of view, although it may still affect what the others have to say or how they react to him.

Some of the men are distinctly aware that people perceive them as having fatherly roles. For Carl, this means that he is able to gain a more objective perspective on his contribution to his stepdaughter's development. He initially sums up his feeling about the impact he has had this way:

I sometimes step back and look at her from a nonfather point of view and she just does so well compared to when I first met her. You can see a progression over time. Like when I first met her she was scared of things or scared of the light not being on or the hallway and sleeping in her mom's bed a lot or coming in in the middle of the night when we were living together and sleeping with us, things like that. That's all slowly gone away and all those fears and things like that have all smoothed away because there's somebody [Carl] else there.

Carl weighs in decisively with the idea that his presence in Vicky's life has eased her worries and significantly changed her. But Carl has not formulated his self-perception in a vacuum. His wife's friend, for example, helped him to appreciate his role more fully. Speaking of this friend,

> [she] said to me at one point, just after Lani and I got married, that she had seen a remarkable change [in Vicky]. . . . you kind of have an inkling of what's going on, that you're making a part in her life or making things happen in her life, but until somebody points it out really and sits you down and says hey, this is cool, this is happening that you really get a sense of being able to look at it from a different point of view.

This "different point of view" can be a valuable resource if it enables men to gain some perspective on their involvement in a stepchild's life. The mirror that people hold up to stepfathers can play a vital role in shaping men's self-evaluations. Though they may differ in how important others are for their self-validation, stepfathers are likely to be influenced to some extent by what some people think and say. What people think and share with the stepfather probably reflects general impressions about the stepfather's involvement and the stepchild's disposition and behavior. Although impressions probably tend to focus on matters of discipline, affection, recreation, and financial contributions, men can get feedback from others on a much wider range of experiences.

5

OVERLOOKED ASPECTS
OF STEPFATHERING

When we think about the everyday issues and implications associated with stepfathering, our attention likely drifts to obvious activities like discipline, supervision, financial support, and playing.[1] How assertive is the stepfather in defining the house rules or looking after his partner's child? Does he help pay for the child's food, clothes, and activities? If the mother works, does the stepdad take on the role of babysitter when she's away from home? Does he spend time doing fun things with the child?

We seldom reflect on the indirect ways a stepfather can influence a stepchild's life. Without this broader view, though, much goes unnoticed about how the complex and often ambiguous nature of stepfamily dynamics provides the stepfather with unique opportunities to make a difference in a child's life. A stepfather, just like a biological father, can influence a child's well-being in many ways, some direct, others indirect. The stepfathers' stories in my study shed light on two key indirect avenues for making a difference: contributions to building social capital and efforts to support the biological father, or, as I put it, to be the father's ally.

Another dimension of stepfathering that often flies beneath the radar is that the experience of stepfathering, like fathering, is not a one-way street. A man's willingness to get involved with his partner's child in a fatherly way means that he too may be changed by the experience. The stepfather who is mindful of how he makes a difference in a stepchild's life, as well as how he develops because of his involvement, is likely to have a much deeper understanding of what stepfamily life means to him.

SOCIAL CAPITAL

Under the right circumstances, a father, either biological or step, can contribute to his child's well-being indirectly by providing the child with what
sociologists call social capital.[2] This type of contribution goes beyond the
typical cognitive and financial resources a parent can provide a child. In this
study, it refers to the stepfather's contributions to either family-based or
community-based relations that can affect a child's cognitive, emotional,
and physical well-being. In terms of family relations, it captures a stepfather's relations with his child, the extent of his positive involvement and
support. It also focuses on the extent to which a stepfather maintains a relationship with the mother based on trust, mutual respect, and a sense of
loyalty. Does the stepfather share similar parenting values and conflict res-
olution strategies with the child's birth mother? To what extent and in
what ways is the stepfather supportive of the birth mother, especially in
ways that the child can notice? Is the stepfather an integral part of a coparenting team with the birth mother in which they routinely share with each
other information about the child, a practice that allows each to know what
is taking place in the child's life from day to day?

The other domain in which social capital comes into play involves the
stepfather's set of relations with individuals and organizations directly involved with the stepchild. The individuals either interact with the child or
are in a position to provide resources and opportunities if needed. Included
among them are teachers, coaches, ministers, camp counselors, medical personnel, neighbors, and the child's friends, as well as the friends' parents. Individuals who presently are not involved with the child can also be viewed
as part of this potential network if the stepfather has the option of bringing
them into the picture to benefit the child (an acquaintance of the stepfather
who hires the child for a summer job).

Taken together, these two general forms of social capital are meaningful because they enable a stepfather to expose a child to a healthy model
of adult interaction, bring about closure in the child's social networks so
that people important to the child can share vital information about him or
her, and act as a liaison to valuable community resources for the child. If
persons in the community share the stepfather's interests in helping the
child, they can provide an important source of supervision while reinforcing or sanctioning the child's behavior. Similarly, if the stepfather is integrated into a larger network or community where mutual obligations, expectations, and trustworthiness prevail, the child will be exposed to social
capital. Focusing on these types of connections and fatherly contributions

reminds us that the stepfamily (or family) is a social system embedded in a larger social ecology replete with neighborhood, school, and peer contexts.[3] How then can a stepfather, given the ambiguous norms often associated with stepfamily life, contribute to a child's social capital and thereby affect the child's quality of life? Because the norms and arrangements associated with stepfamily life are sometimes unclear to family members[4] and are often muddled in the public eye,[5] a stepfather may be forced to work harder than a biological father if he wishes to develop social capital on behalf of a child.

When stepfathers describe their parenting circumstances, they often emphasize their desire to be part of a team. As already noted, some are more successful in achieving this arrangement than others. The "team" mentality that some of the stepfathers experience can be thought of as part of the family-based social capital they contribute to their stepchildren. This is one form of social capital that requires the birth mother's cooperation. The men's efforts to promote a team approach can sometimes be viewed as part of their general attempt to provide social support for the birth mother. When men take an active role in the hands-on parenting of stepchildren with the mother's blessing, her life becomes easier.

By definition, for a stepfather to produce community-based social capital, persons and organizations outside the family must be involved. The public face of stepfathering is relevant because a stepfather's ability to build social capital depends in part on how others foster his ability to act in a fatherly way. Yes, the stepfather must be motivated if he is to secure knowledge and connections necessary to make use of the larger social network within which his stepchild operates. Ultimately, though, motivation is not sufficient; a stepfather's ability to develop social capital depends on the cooperation of others. Put simply, if others do not respect a stepfather's desire to have a fatherly presence in the stepchild's life, he is likely to be handicapped in the type and amount of social capital he can provide. If the stepfather is not included in the network of people and organizations that are integrated into a system where obligations, expectations, and a sense of trustworthiness are shared regarding the care of children, he will be less effective in transmitting social capital to his stepchild.[6]

From a practical standpoint, opportunities to create community-based social capital are more readily available for men with school-age children who are involved in school and other activities outside the home. Because a number of the men I interviewed were involved with stepchildren who were still quite young and had little exposure to the world beyond their home, my sample is a bit limited in the breadth and depth of insights it can generate on this topic. Nevertheless, a third of the stepfathers in my sample met the target stepchild when he or she was at least seven years old, and two-thirds were currently involved with a stepchild who had reached school age. The stepfather's experiences with school-age children highlight several points germane to the development of social capital.

Several of the stepfathers spoke about how they took it upon themselves to have discussions with teachers and other child care professionals in order to understand their stepchild better and to intervene on his or her behalf. Some of these kids had been diagnosed with a learning disability or behavioral problem (for example, ADHD—attention deficit hyperactive disorder) and/or were having problems at school. Although they varied in how they went about getting involved, a number of the stepdads took their roles quite seriously. Randy, for example, describes his experience with his wife, Molly, and her son Jamie. Talking about how he and his wife responded to a teacher's suggestion that Jamie probably had ADHD, Randy says, "We were able to get him tested early and have a firm handle on all the problems, before he got into public schools. So we have in some ways been really tight with all his teachers." Continuing, "We interact with the teachers. And basically we have to because if anything happens to Jamie, Molly's going to be in somebody's face about it. So I've got to be right there to make sure she doesn't overdo the 'in the face' stuff, . . . we're kind of a good cop, bad cop team, when it comes to Jamie." By using "we" and "team" to characterize his involvement, Randy apparently sees his role in Jamie's life from a coparenting perspective. His consistent use of these words illustrates that he perceives himself as playing a critical role alongside his wife in looking out for Jamie and developing social capital to serve the child's best interests.

Brad similarly describes his initial contribution to a coparenting approach to developing social capital and being involved with his stepson Bobby, diagnosed with ADHD. He entered the picture at a time when Bobby was struggling at school and his mother was distraught over what she could do to help him improve. She had been particularly upset over one teacher's treatment of her son, while being generally dissatisfied with the response she was receiving from school personnel. Given this awkward context, Brad's initial involvement in confronting school representatives meant that he was jumping into an already volatile situation. Referring to this first meeting, Brad says, "I went basically to try and help her keep her temper, help keep the discussion at a level that was rational and not just angry at the, expressing anger to the teachers. I failed miserably." Although Brad does not view his initial experience as a success, he recognizes that he has made a difference since then.

Like Randy, Brad felt that he was part of a parental team, with his specific role being to bring a calm and sober perspective to the meetings with school personnel. Presumably, both these men, as well as their partners, assumed that they could provide this perspective because, compared to the birth mother, they did not have the same history with and investments in the child. However, these men still saw themselves as having a vested interest in looking out for their respective stepchildren, but they implicitly recognized that their best shot at building social capital and helping the child was to monitor the birth mother. They wanted to help her make her case while building social capital, instead of antagonizing school officials to the point that it might be detrimental for the child. Each situation shows how a "crisis" in a child's life can offer a stepfather the opportunity to prove his commitment to the child and the birth mother. Although these heated situations may create tension and push partners away from each other, they can also solidify their mutual commitment as they jointly struggle to find a solution to a child's problem.

The same sort of paternal commitment is expressed by Doug as he talks about how he became very active in his nonbiological son Sammy's academic life a few years ago, when the boy was in his senior year of high school. Doug differs from Randy and Brad in that he assumes a more proactive and independent role. He describes at length a situation in which Sammy (who had on his own stopped taking the drug Ritalin earlier in the year) announced near the end of the academic year that he was probably not going to graduate with his class. On hearing the news, Doug immediately called the school principal and arranged a joint meeting the next day with a few of Sammy's teachers, the principal, Sammy, and himself. As Doug describes it, it was an intense meeting where he confronted both the teachers and Sammy about Sammy's predicament. He recalls telling the school officials: "I am here on behalf of my son. . . . he's what matters to me. . . . he's going to graduate." During that meeting, Doug negotiated an arrangement whereby the teachers agreed to tutor Sammy and Sammy agreed to resume taking Ritalin. Doug proudly finishes the story by noting that Sammy graduated on time that spring, adding "had it been let go the way it was; Sammy would not have graduated." Although Doug's wife supported his intervention on Sammy's behalf, she did so from a distance. It was Doug who made the phone calls, arranged the meeting, attended the intense session and spoke on Sammy's behalf, and forged an agreement with both the school personnel and Sammy about how they could work together to ensure that Sammy graduated with his class. Doug acted like and was received as Sammy's father, which he was legally because he had adopted Sammy about fifteen years ago.

Among the men in my study, Doug was not alone in taking the initiative to make calls to teachers and principals on behalf of their nonbiological children. For some of the men, like Doug, their heightened involvement came on the heels of a situation they believed demanded immediate, decisive action. In Harry's case, his involvement with Kelly intensified after agreeing with some of his personal friends who worked in his stepdaughter's school to have her placed in an eighth-grade enrichment program at the beginning of the school year. Much to his surprise, he was told the third week of class that Kelly technically was not in the enrichment program. This news "really torqued" Harry because he felt it would "disrupt her entire schedule" and "stigmatize" her as well. After inquiring further, he learned that the school officials had initially placed her in the program because the school received more state money for teachers who taught enrichment and the school had been short a few students. When state officials reviewed and questioned the program, school personnel tried to drop her from it. Learning this, Harry threatened to take the story to the local news station. This threat apparently prompted school officials to have Kelly tested officially, ultimately leading them to retain her in the enrichment program because she received a high enough score. Although Harry had been involved in establishing social capital for Kelly before this incident, his fatherly involvement at this time punctuated his willingness to invest time and energy into confronting the network of adults responsible for shaping Kelly's life. In a separate interview, his wife confirms his strong commitment to her daughter's educational and emotional well-being.

Although situations like those described above are noteworthy in their own right, a stepfather can experience plenty of less dramatic, more pleasant opportunities to build social capital for a child. Under the right circumstances, a stepfather, like a biological father, can volunteer to participate in various school activities, affording him a chance to build relations with persons who may have contact with or be in a position to monitor his stepchild. This rings true for Calvin. While talking about his experiences at the charter school his stepdaughter Rebecca attends, he mentions that parents are required to volunteer for a certain amount of time. For his part, Calvin has stuffed packets, participated in an area cleanup, taken charge of selling candy for the safety patrol, and managed a listserv—a newsgroup for the parents. He also describes himself as having "positive interactions with the teachers." Many of these interactions occur spontaneously while he's waiting to pick Rebecca up from school. "I'll see them and talk to them at that time. There are three or four of them that were there last year and I've kind of gotten to know. . . . I'll talk to them about whatever's going on and if there's a problem. And Rebecca is usually good in school, but if there's a problem I'll talk to them about that." Calvin's last comment highlights the opportunities parents have to develop social capital stemming from their children's needs and experiences. Both minor and more serious kinds of needs can provide an impetus for parental action. When children struggle in some way, parents are often compelled to contact members of the child's network outside the family. Building social capital for a child who has not experienced significant problems may help some parents prevent specific problems from ever occurring.

Let's stay with Calvin's story to illustrate another example of how social capital can be developed, while interpreting social capital broadly. Calvin stresses how he and his wife, Kristin, need to talk more about helping Rebecca in school because in his opinion, he and Kristen "haven't really gotten on the same page" yet. Prompted by his concerns for Rebecca's behavior, he went to a community-sponsored "parenting fair" a few days prior to the interview with Rebecca in tow. The listserv he manages came in handy because he learned about the program from one of the parents who posted information on the listserv about it. One of the workshops he attended dealt with children's problem behaviors and how to help children build self-esteem. Calvin plans to talk to Kristin about what he learned when they have some free time. This example is useful because it depicts how a stepfather, under the right set of circumstances, can serve as a liaison between the community and his family. In Calvin's case, he brought his own commitment to education with him when he got involved in Kristin's and Rebecca's lives. Consequently, he became active in promoting Rebecca's school performance, which entailed his getting involved in school-related activities, including developing a listserv for the parents. From this resource he then learned about the parent fair that he attended, prompting him to think about strengthening his family-based social capital by improving his communication with Kristen about Rebecca. Calvin's desire to participate in Rebecca's life in a fatherly way extends to his wanting to share with Kristen his knowledge about parenting, some of which he learned while at the fair. Thus his efforts to build social capital are tied to both his stepfather–child and coparenting trajectories.

Just as a biological mother and father may possess different philosophies about creating and sustaining social capital, so too parental figures in stepfamily arrangements may disagree. Some parents feel that it is reasonable and useful to share family "secrets"[7] or information about their offspring or stepchildren with persons outside the family. Others, particularly when it comes to certain issues and specific people, are reluctant to talk about family issues with those whom they do not define as family. This message comes across vividly when Rodney talks about his stepson Gary's involvement in the Boy Scouts. Asked if he ever has conversations with the scout masters about Gary, Rodney says,

> Yeah, I do talk to them. I keep them informed on the good as well as the bad in his life, because when I'm not with them, when Gary's with them at scouts, they're responsible, they need to know what his behavior has been, what they might keep an eye on, you know. I want them to know as much information as possible to make sure he doesn't make the same mistakes.

Rodney is clearly comfortable building social capital through his interactions with the scout masters. In his eyes, it makes perfect sense for adults with a stake in promoting a child's well-being to share information; doing so helps them coordinate their efforts to guide the child. This approach calls to mind the popular culture images that it takes a village to raise a child.[8] But what works for Rodney apparently doesn't sit well with the birth mother. According to Rodney, "She doesn't like me telling them anything about what Gary has done." Although Rodney and I did not explore the implications of his viewing this situation differently than his wife, these kinds of disagreements can cause relationship friction between a birth mother and stepfather, and perhaps between child and stepfather too. What's more, this type of situation may lead a birth mother to call upon her privileged status as the biological parent. Asserting her parental rights, she may try to dissuade the stepfather from pursuing his more open approach to sharing information about family members. Such a move might not be surprising in Rodney's stepfamily because he is frustrated with his wife's tendency to sometimes make unilateral decisions regarding her kids without even consulting him.

Sometimes individuals intentionally try to build social capital mindful of serving a child's best interests. If others are supportive, they may be inclined to continue their efforts. Some social capital is initially accumulated through a person's connections with friends, community leaders, work opportunities, and so on, that have nothing to do with the child originally. At the appropriate time, these connections can be called upon to help a child.

Whether or not social capital is intentionally developed, a stepfather's opportunities and approach to building social capital for his stepchild may be affected by the nature of the biological father's presence in his child's life. When a biological father is not involved or only remotely involved in his child's life, a stepfather is likely to have more opportunities and a stronger desire to build social capital. If the father is involved, he may tap into his own social capital resources to assist his child, thereby minimizing the need for the stepfather to do the same.

The biological father also enters the picture through the relationships he has with the birth mother and the stepfather. One relatively rare form of social capital that is likely to be developed intentionally, if it is developed at all, involves a stepfather's relationship with the biological father. Viewed through the eyes of the child, this relationship can represent an important form of social capital that may be generated by the stepfather, father, or both. Of course only in situations where a biological father is involved, or is willing to get involved, in his child's life is the stepfather potentially faced with the prospects of having some type of relationship with the father. Developing social capital with the biological father is moot if he is absent from the child's life. Irrespective of whether the stepfather has established a meaningful relationship or information exchange with the biological father, a stepfather can still indirectly affect his stepchild's life through the way he handles issues involving the father. Whether it makes sense to label the stepfather's contribution to his stepchild's life in particular kinds of arrangements as social capital or something else may not always be clear. But it is worthwhile to consider in general terms how a stepfather's approach to dealing with the father can influence a child's life.

FATHER ALLY

One of the indirect ways stepdads can leave their mark on their stepchildren that goes largely unnoticed in the literature about stepfamilies is how stepdads relate to biological fathers.[9] Do stepfathers make it easier or more difficult for biological fathers to maintain contact and a close relationship with children with whom they do not live?

Some stepdads have little or nothing to do with biological fathers because these fathers have either walked away or been pushed away from their children, sometimes completely. A significant minority of the men who participated in my study describes the biological fathers as being out of the picture. In a small number of cases, the biological fathers may not even be aware that they have fathered a child. But most of the stepdads are directly or indirectly aware of the biological father's presence in the children's lives as well as his interaction with the children's mother. Not surprisingly, a number of the stepdads are accustomed to dealing with the biological father's continued involvement with his children. In some cases, the biological fathers are even involved on a limited basis with the children and mother together. Some of the stepdads find it eye opening, being nonresident fathers themselves, because they sometimes develop a more well-rounded view of stepfamily arrangements when they have contact with men serving as stepfathers to their own children. This allows certain stepdads to relate more easily to issues involving the intersection between their roles and those of the biological father.

As my participants clearly illustrate, stepdads face a range of possible stepfamily scenarios. These scenarios differ in the frequency, type, and quality of biological father's involvement with the children.[10] Though many of the patterns are stable over an extended period of time, they are not etched in stone. A scenario familiar today may be gone tomorrow as biological fathers get more involved or distance themselves from their children. Biological fathers may also change how they're involved. A sudden job loss may result in a father not being able to pay child support, but he may have more free time to spend with his child. Or a father may get involved, perhaps marry a woman who has her own child and begin to invest time, energy, and money in this new family. Given this type of uncertainty within stepfamilies, stepdads may, over time, face differing stepfamily scenarios where the biological father's role varies considerably.

When dealing with a biological father who is at least moderately involved in a hands-on way, a stepdad is likely to be concerned with how his own involvement will be supported or challenged. Will a biological father try to undermine the stepdad's household authority or will he encourage his child to respect the stepfather? By paying child support, being consistent with scheduled visits, speaking respectfully to the child and mother about the stepdad, and treating the stepfather cordially, a father has plenty of opportunities to ease the stepfather's transition into his various familial roles. The father can also help the stepfather thrive in the new roles. Additionally, the biological father who interacts with a stepdad in supportive ways can often improve his chances of having the stepdad act on his behalf in return. Along these lines, William, a twenty-seven-year-old man who was acting as a stepfather for his fiancée's two young boys, knew the boys' father before he became involved with the kids. William recalls having a conversation with the father during the early phases of becoming involved with the boys. He said the father "was just telling me that he was sorry that he wasn't there, but since I was there and he knows what kind of person I am, he said he felt that his kids were in competent hands. He told me that to my face." Hearing the father's sentiments made William "feel pretty good" about himself. It also helped reinforce his willingness not to say anything negative about the father in front of the kids.

The biological father who wants to remain involved in his child's life, even though he is no longer romantically involved with the child's mother, is likely to be concerned with how the stepdad affects his ability to retain his fatherly roles. A father may feel this way irrespective of the custody or residency arrangement. In many situations, the father's and stepfather's perceptions and actions can influence each other, even though they may not be conscious of their effect or acknowledge it directly. The old adage "scratch my back and I'll scratch yours" captures the experiences of many men with children as they try to settle on new ways of organizing their family roles, rights, and responsibilities in a wide range of different family settings. Although this agreement is often left unspoken, it exists nonetheless. This kind of arrangement eventually unfolded between Barry and his stepchildren's father, Sam, who had known and disliked Barry for some time before Barry got involved with his ex-wife (Lucy) and children. In Barry's words:

> I would hear back from the kids and from other people that he overcame his dislike of me, so to speak, because he felt I was being so nice to the kids and I wasn't trying to replace him, that I was in fact saying positive things about him and trying to encourage Lucy not to be bitter. He really encouraged that. In fact, I was getting Christmas presents from them [biological father and his current wife] and a birthday present, things like that. He'd call me up. But we never sat down and said oh, you're a great guy, I love what you're doing.

One distinct pattern that emerged from my interviews with the stepdads was that many acted in ways that had the effect of helping the father remain active in a positive way in his child's life. From the stepfather's perspective, this activity sometimes enabled the biological father to strengthen his emotional ties with his child. Some stepfathers' efforts were intended and obvious, while others were much more subtle. If the term "ally" is used loosely, some stepdads acted like an ally to the father because they helped prevent problems or smooth over ones that probably would have tainted the father's relationship with his child had they gone unattended. For instance, a number of the stepfathers said they encouraged mothers not to say anything negative about the father in front of the children. Those who took this position thought it was counterproductive to "bad-mouth" a father in a child's presence, even though some mothers might have found this to be an effective short-term strategy to release stress. A few stepfathers, like Barry, even took it a step further. "I encouraged Lucy to try and get over her bitterness toward Sam's new wife [woman who had adulterous relationship with Sam during Lucy's marriage to him]. . . . And I never ever said anything about Sam in front of them [the kids]. In fact, I would say good things, even though I didn't always think it sometimes."

Stepdads who had kids of their own living elsewhere appeared to be the most sensitive to giving the biological father a fair shake in the step-family household. From their own experience, they knew how they would like to be represented to their children when they were absent. However, as Emmit illustrates, even stepdads who don't have their own children living elsewhere can develop empathy for a nonresident father. Although Emmit never met his five-year-old stepson's biological father, he explains why he told his wife that it was fine for her to give the father their phone number when she and her child moved in with Emmit. "I said yeah, because I'm all for him having communication with his father. I mean, he knows that I'm not his biological father and I wouldn't want to cut that tie, because I know how it is. I mean now like having my own, from my blood." Even before Emmit became a father to his own baby, he was of the mind that he should not try to restrict a biological father's relationship with his son. Apparently his perspective was reinforced once he felt for himself what it was like to have a biological child.

Some stepdads made a point of taking their own advice by going out of their way not to say anything negative about the biological father around the kids. A variation on this theme involved those who had something less than favorable to say. If they did have something to say, they did so diplomatically. Brad, a thirty-eight-year-old informal stepfather to two teenage kids, one a thirteen-year-old boy named Bobby, has endured a rather unique situation with Bobby's father, Len, who lives out of state. As mentioned previously, after experiencing severe brain damage from a car accident, Len was unable to fly his kids to see him because he lives in a group home. Brad's partner, Len's former wife, graciously makes arrangements for Len to stay at her house three times a year for a week at a time. During these visits, Brad goes over to the house and witnesses Len interacting with Bobby. Recently Brad has even taken to spending the nights. He describes how he delicately navigates the difficult situations when he feels that Len is filling Bobby's mind with unhealthy ideas.

> If I see Len demonstrating one of his more egregious behaviors, I will tell Bobby, "That's not the way all men think. That's not—I don't believe that's correct. I know he's your dad and you love him but you need to understand that there are other ways to think about that." So—I don't want to countermand him [biological father], but at the same

time, sometimes it's just so out there that you feel like it needs to be—Bobby needs to understand—he's at that very impressionable age and he needs to understand that yes, your dad feels that way but not all men feel that way. That's not necessarily the way you need to think about that situation or whatever. And unfortunately it's mostly how he [biological father] feels about women.

In situations like Brad's, it may be a stretch to refer to stepdads as being an ally to the father. However, even though Brad is tempted to be critical of Len, he refrains from doing so partly out of respect for the father–son bond Len shares with Bobby. Because he cuts the father some slack, Brad can be viewed as an ally—loosely defined—who is willing to encourage Bobby to sustain his relationship with his father.

A stepdad has various opportunities to be an ally to a father by how he speaks to or interacts with the child directly. He might, for instance, make a point of saying nice things about the father, jump in to defend the father if circumstances call for it, or give advice on how to communicate with the father. Without being in the home himself, the nonresident father has a more difficult time speaking on his own behalf and explaining his behavior in a convenient and timely manner. One stepfather, Eddie, recalls several times when he consoled his stepdaughter Melissa on being disappointed by her father's irresponsible behavior. Asked if his efforts minimized Melissa's pain, and in the process helped the father's relationship with her, Eddie replies:

> Well, the damage is when he does it—the damage is already done. I'm just trying to make her feel a little bit better. I guess you can say, because if he does something—if he don't call or he don't pick her up when he says he's going to pick her up, then I guess I kind of smooth things over for him. I guess you can say that. I mean—I try to make him—he's not bad. I try to make him, when he do bad things, whether he do it intentionally or not—I try to make him look like he—it's a mistake, nobody's perfect. Dad is going to make mistakes. It's okay for dad to make mistakes. He's human. It's going to be all right. He'll call you the next time. I think that—she loves her dad. When I think—if I really didn't soften the blow for her . . . I think she'd be a little ticked off at him at the time. She'd be a little mad at him. And trust me, when she gets mad she can make it hard on you.

As his comments indicate, Eddie acknowledges that he probably helps minimize his stepdaughter's disappointment and anger with her father. But when I asked Eddie specifically if he feels comfortable with the language of being called the father's "ally," he said he felt a bit uneasy with the label. Apparently Eddie has difficulty thinking of himself as the father's ally because "he [father] doesn't know half the times I cleaned up his mess." For Eddie, thinking of himself as an ally seems to necessitate an explicit agreement between the two men. It seems reasonable to conclude that Eddie acts like an ally in a functional sense, even if he does not clearly see himself as doing so and if the father is unaware of his efforts. The bottom line is that he does things as a stepdad that help the father maintain the quality of his relationship with his daughter.

Eddie's experience highlights two distinctions relevant to situations in which a stepdad acts like an ally to the father. First, does the stepfather do his work behind the scenes away from the father's view or does he actively work with the father, telling him what he is trying to accomplish? Eddie is essentially a "secret" ally because the father remains in the dark about much of what he does. A selective few, however, are more direct in making their approach and intentions known. The second distinction involves the stepfather's motivation for doing the things that are intended to enhance the father's relationship with his child. Is the stepfather making this effort because of his concern for the child, the father, or both? The driving force behind Eddie's efforts is his desire to look out for his stepdaughter's feelings. He is not particularly concerned about the father's dilemmas or feelings. In some instances, though, the stepdad empathizes with a father and goes out of his way to help him. Sometimes the stepfather may choose to play this role because he wants to be treated similarly.

Herman, a gregarious forty-two-year-old man we have already heard from, provides a detailed account of what it means to be an active and open father ally. In addition, he expresses his interest in helping both his stepdaughter and her father. He goes to considerable lengths to describe how he tries to keep the biological father of his three stepchildren involved in their lives. A self-described "initiator" when it comes to conversations, Herman explains that he once talked to the father on the phone and candidly told him that "you need to spend time with your kids." Compared to many stepfathers, Herman has gone the extra mile to reach out to the father and develop his own line of communication with him. Seeing the father in the stands at a high school football game, for example, Herman made a point of introducing himself to him and his current wife. Herman clarifies his assertiveness by explaining his line of thinking. "We don't have a reason not to be civil because—it's four different lives now [Herman and his wife, the father and his wife]. . . . There's no reason for us not to be civil together. Plus, we need to be civil for the kids anyhow." According to Herman, the father eventually embraced this view and they had subsequent conversations.

In addition to talking to the father directly, Herman talks frankly and forcefully to his stepchildren. He is particularly eager to have his fourteen-year-old stepdaughter, Annette, maintain contact with her father. In one instance, after Herman convinced Annette to rejoin the band, he asked her if she had told her father that she was involved in a jamfest at one of the universities in the region. As he explains,

> See, what I'm doing is, I'm pushing her up to do it, because I don't want it to seem—granted, like I told him on the phone—look man, I don't have a problem with you calling my house. I don't have a problem with you coming to my house. She's my wife now. I'm not insecure about that. I'm not insecure about anything. I want you to spend time with your children, because they're your children.

Herman also makes a point of asking Annette if her father knows about her other school and recreational functions as they approach. In his words, "I make sure that she initiates with her father, let him know what's happening. . . . One day he's going to need you [Annette]."

Herman offers other astute comments that reveal how he believes Annette is growing closer to him over time because they live together. He worries about this and reflects on how his own fathering experiences with his son, who lives elsewhere with his mother, enable him to empathize with Annette's father.

> She's coming more to my side because I'm with her all the time. . . . he's going to be distanced but—and that's the thing that concerns me, that after awhile I'll take on the persona of being her father and her father will be just a memory. I don't want that to be. I want him to actually be in her life. Because I'm going to be there. . . . But he'll be missing the growing up stages in her life. She'll end up getting married and he'll miss that. Like with my son, I miss stuff. He's eleven years old now. Out of his entire life I think I've—if you put all the time that we've spent together, I've had two years, maybe three years of his life. . . . My son's got his own life now. It hurts because I've missed . . . ten years of his life that I don't even know what happened to him. I don't even know when he was sick. Did he cry? I taught him how to ride a bike. I bought him stuff. But then I miss days in the wintertime coming home, sitting out in the yard and he coming out there and sitting in the yard or helping me mow the yard. Well, I got a few days of that. So, I don't want this guy to miss that. He's got a girl. She's going to give him

grandchildren. . . . She's going to go to the prom. I'm going to be there. Okay, I'm going to enjoy that because she's in the house with me, but that's one of his privileges. . . . Who's going to be there on her first date? I'm going to be the one scrutinizing this rookie coming up. Where you from, son? Okay. Tell me about yourself. He's going to miss that. You see? It's just not a good thing. I mean, it's a good thing for me, but I'm sure he should be in on that. She's his daughter. But now she's my daughter. I'm going to take responsibility for her. I have taken responsibility . . . everything I would do with my child, she gets the same.

Listening to Herman's thought-provoking, emotional description of his efforts, it is clear that he takes pride as a proactive, nurturing, and protective father in overseeing Annette's life. In a separate interview, Herman's wife attests to his commitment to Annette. Unlike some stepfathers, Herman has a sense of security in his relationships with both his wife and Annette that provide him with the confidence necessary to incorporate the father more fully into the network of adults who have an interest in supporting Annette's transition through her teen years. In addition, the intense frustration and pain he has experienced as a nonresident father provide him a reservoir of feelings enabling him to relate to and empathize with Annette's father. As suggested previously, Herman's compassionate approach seems motivated by a genuine concern for both Annette's and her father's emotional and psychological well-being.

Vern, a forty-eight-year-old stepdad who got involved with two boys in their late teens, provides another example of how a stepfather indirectly can be an ally to a father. Neal, his eighteen-year-old stepson, lived with him for three weeks after living with his father. During this time he mentioned that he wanted to move in with his mother and Vern, and his father became very upset with him. Vern recalls stepping in to offer advice to Neal after the teenager discussed his dilemma with him and the mother. While it took some time, Vern was able to help Neal by offering him suggestions on how to approach his father and manage his emotions. As the father of three teenage boys himself, Vern is experienced in managing paternal relationships with boys. Even though Vern's motivation was to help Neal manage a difficult situation, he indirectly helped Neal's father minimize the damage he might have caused to his relationship with his son.

Yet another practical example of how stepdads can act as a father ally comes by way of Landen's experience with his four-and-a-half-year-old stepdaughter. Landen remembers one occasion when he suggested to his cohabiting partner that they program her daughter's personal bedroom phone so that one of the memory buttons would be assigned to the father's telephone number. His rationale was to make sure that she "can call him whenever she wants." This simple suggestion illustrates how a stepdad can be mindful of the little ways in which he can foster a positive relationship between his stepchild and the father. Offering this type of suggestion, however, requires that the stepfather be willing to acknowledge that the father is part of the child's life, talk about him to the mother and perhaps the child, and foster a practical way for the child to maintain a private and personal relationship with the father. These tasks may seem commonsensical and reasonable to many, but some stepfathers have difficulty following through with one or more of them. Sometimes the stepfather's difficulty is due to a personal jealousy or insecurity, other times the problem stems from the birth mother's poor relationship with the father.

Another way a stepdad can be a father ally involves his approach to being in the same physical location as the father, primarily when the stepchild is also present. This might involve the time when the kid is participating in recreational or school events, being shuffled from one parental home to another, or perhaps when parents are attending an open house or teacher-parent meeting (though children are seldom present for these meetings). These situations give a stepdad various chances to assist or hinder a father as he tries to remain actively involved with his child. Similarly, the father can do and say things that either distance or embrace the stepfather as a parental figure.

A stepdad's motivation for behaving in a way that benefits the father is not always altruistic. Mark, a forty-two-year-old stepdad, provides a useful example by talking about how "uncomfortable" he feels at public events where his eleven- and eight-year-old stepdaughters are participating and their father is present. Before describing how he manages situations with his stepdaughters, Mark reflects on his presence at events where his biological children are involved.

> There's some anxiety of knowing, my ex-wife is remarried and it bugs the hell out of me when I go to some event and he's [ex-wife's husband] there; I'm the father. What the hell's he doing there? And I hate to hear about him parenting, and him acting like a dad type of thing. So, I purposely don't do that; I mean, I make it clear that I'm not their [step-daughters'] father and they have a father. I make that very clear. I just, only because I know the effect it has on me. . . . So when we go to some event, like open houses last night, my wife went and I stayed home with her girls. And their father went. Well I've been to those before. I've gone with my wife. I probably would have gone with her had the kids were with him that night; I probably would have gone. And I've been

there and there he is, and I'm just sitting there kinda like the, you know, the stepdad. The odd one, who is just kinda hanging out. When they're done [performing] I don't go up and hug them—when the kid gets off the stage, you go up and hug them, well I don't do that. I just kind of hang out.

Asked if he does things differently when the father is at the performance, Mark replies that he does. "If he [father] wasn't there, I would probably be right there with her [wife]. You know, give them a little hug, and say you did great or something like that." But if the girls' father is present, Mark adds, "I purposely let him be the dad—just because I see what it's like." Thus, based on his firsthand experience with his own children, Mark has learned to act in this deferential way. He has built his philosophy from the ground up; as a nonresident father he participated in his own children's events such as "recitals, plays, and open houses where you typically look up to your parents." So, from where he sits, the biological parent should assume the privileged position with the kids and the stepparent should be a "nice fairly stable person, and not too involved with kids."

Although most of the stepdads are aware of some awkwardness when the biological father is present and playing his parental roles, some are remarkably comfortable with these moments. Take for instance thirty-four-year-old Robby who is involved with a ten-year-old stepdaughter and an eight-year-old stepson. He has been good friends for more than fifteen years with the father of these children, Brett, and has dealt with an unusual set of circumstances because of their long-standing friendship. Robby once confronted the matter head-on by telling Brett:

We've been friends ever since high school. We were friends before you and Jamie got married. We were friends after you and Jamie got separated. And I said, "I don't see any reason why we can't be friends now." But when we're together we don't bring up Jamie; we don't bring up the kids. There's just no reason to, unless there's a problem with one of the kids. Most of the times I let Jamie handle it because she's the mom and he's the dad. We have a pretty good relationship, not bad at all.

In addition to this encounter, Robby mentions that he and his wife, along with Brett and his wife, have sat down together and talked about how they should not bicker in front of the kids. It appears that Robby's willingness to deal with issues directly in this case has probably made it easier for the father to share the same physical space with Robby when they are at the boy's football games. Robby is currently his stepson's football coach and has been for the past three years. Because many people don't know that Robby is a stepfather, some of the other coaches, players, and people in the stands verbally refer to him as the stepson's father in a way that Brett overhears. Robby excels at the tricky task of being committed to his stepkids as though they are his but then backing off to allow Brett the space to increase his role in his kids' lives. He stresses his disappointment that Brett does not invest more time and effort being involved with his kids. Robby was therefore delighted when Brett showed up to his daughter's open house at school. Explaining why he felt comfortable leaving the school when Brett made an appearance, Robby says, "Brett needed to be more involved, so him showing up was awesome; it was great you know, going in to see your teacher. I thought mom and dad was there, I didn't need to be there at that time."

Given the overall context of Robby's comments about his participation in his stepchildren's lives, he gives the impression that his willingness to leave the meeting was an act of deference to the father. For sure, Robby is highly involved with his stepchildren. In some respects he views them as his own. Robby's account provides an example of the types of situations a stepdad can run into as he tries to develop and sustain relationships with a child whose father still plays an active role in his or her life. Although most stepdads and biological fathers do not play golf together, as Robby and Brett do, the types of relationships these different father figures maintain is quite varied. Many are asked to adjust on the fly to their mixed feelings and ill-defined situations when the father is either physically present or the subject of a conversation.

Fortunately, most stepdads, like Robby, only have to deal with one biological father. However, some find themselves facing a more complicated set of circumstances. These men either encounter multiple father figures for the same child (biological father and previous stepdad) or separate fathers for their partner's different children. John, twenty-seven, married a forty-three-year-old woman, Beth, and found himself three years ago assuming some of the roles of a stepdad to a fifteen-year-old girl, Harmony, who maintained relations with both her biological father and a previous stepfather. When John first met Beth, Harmony had been living with her mom and former stepdad for thirteen years. Beth eventually left her previous husband and moved in with John; Harmony followed in a month or so. John mentions that he talks to both of these men directly and he also chats with Harmony about them "all the time," especially the biological father. Although the father moved away recently, John offers that "I'm real good friends with her real father. We became real close. When he left town

I gave him a hug, so we [Harmony and John] talk about him all the time. When he calls, we talk on the phone. It's real comfortable." Juggling these different relationships proves to be challenging at times for John, especially because the former stepdad was abusive to Beth, but he feels he has made a concerted effort to provide Harmony with the type of support she needs to sustain her relationships with these two other father figures.

Only a handful of the men in my sample had to deal with multiple fathers for their stepchildren, but these situations are clearly a part of the social demography of stepfamilies.[11] These types of situations illustrate the point I made in chapter 2 about men having relationships with multiple children. A stepdad's unique relationships with particular stepchildren can be accentuated if they have to deal with different biological fathers for the respective children. If the biological fathers relate differently to their various children within the stepfamily, this may help explain potential discrepancies in how a stepdad connects to specific stepchildren in the household. A highly involved father may minimize a stepdad's opportunity to bond with a particular child, whereas a less involved or completely absent father may contribute to a set of circumstances that lead a child to open up more easily to the stepdad.

Although it is a bit of a stretch to talk about a stepdad being a father ally to a biological father who is dead, looking at this issue through a child's eyes can be revealing. Viewed from this vantage point, a deceased father can still be instrumental to the child's feelings and sense of identity. In a couple of instances, stepdads spoke about their roles in stepfamilies where the fathers were dead. My research team also spoke with the wife and stepchild of one of these men. The nature of the father ally concept is obviously different in these cases because the stepdad cannot interact with the deceased father. However, a stepdad can try to squelch or sustain a living memory of the father in the mind of the child. When a stepdad is open to discussions of the father or representations of his existence being displayed in the household (for example, photographs, memorabilia), he fosters opportunities for the child to keep active memories of his or her father. If the father were alive to express his opinion, he presumably would appreciate the gesture. Thus a stepdad who is not willing to listen to stories about a deceased father can be seen as a negative case example of the father ally concept, as was the case with Stephen in chapter 3. Competing with the image of a deceased father can prove challenging, especially if a stepfather doubts the stepchild's commitment to him as he witnesses the kid's unwavering bond to the memory of the father.

As was the case with this stepdad, not all stepfathers are willing to assume an ally role toward the father. Some may resist this supportive role early on but open up to it over time as they grow increasingly secure with their place in the lives of their partner and stepchild. Recall how Herman portrayed himself as being secure with the biological father maintaining contact with his daughter and former wife. Being an ally, especially early on in a relationship, can sometimes carry certain risks and is connected to a stepdad's trust in his partner. A man may inadvertently make it easier for the biological father and his former partner to rekindle their romantic relationship if their squabbles about coparenting are minimized. Compared to Herman, William was a bit more curious and nervous, especially early on, about the biological father's intentions of hanging around the house where William was living with the father's former partner and kids. He suspected that the father might be trying to work his way back into his former partner's life as a romantic partner. With time, William worked through his concerns and was willing to support the father's involvement, although it eventually became a moot point because the father was spending so much time in jail.

By showcasing some stepfathers' interest in furthering the relationship between the biological father and his child, the previous sampling of comments reveals the potential complexity of stepfamilies. It should be clear that understanding the nuances of stepfamilies requires us to go beyond stepfathers' crucial support of the birth mother. Although it may not be easy to capture precisely how the stepfather's support of the biological father translates into positive experiences for the stepchild, the impact of these efforts is likely to be real, and potentially significant, in numerous cases. Similarly, how a biological father responds to his child and the child's efforts to enlist his loyalty when dealing with the stepfather can indirectly affect the child, a topic I explore in chapter 10.[12]

KIDS MAKING A DIFFERENCE

Sometimes a stepfather's active involvement with a child leads him to make fundamental changes in the way he lives and sets his priorities. He may gain insights about himself, others, and life in general. When a stepfather seizes these opportunities, he often feels differently about himself.[13]

The stories the men tell about how they have been affected by being involved with stepchildren are similar in many ways to those typically shared by biological fathers. Unlike many biological fathers who make a conscious decision to have a child with their partner, most stepfathers become active with children because they get romantically involved with a woman who happens to be a mother. Concerns about how being involved with stepchildren may affect their lives may not fully register with stepfathers. They may not plan for or anticipate these consequences prior to getting seriously involved with the mother. But whether the consequences of their involvement with the kids are expected or not, some men are aware after the fact that their experiences as stepfathers have affected them.

Not surprisingly, some of the men comment on how involvement with stepchildren helped them develop a sense of purpose, become more responsible, and feel grounded. Among these men, Keith, Carl, Eddie, and Ray provide excellent examples of how being an active stepfather can affect men's lives. Keith, a stepfather of two young adolescent girls, says with conviction, "I have purpose now. That's something to do besides work and take care of Keith. That seems to be very important to me. I don't know why though. I need to have something to turn around and look back on, that's more than me, I guess." Keith's reference to being able to "look back on" his stepdaughters captures his feelings about helping others grow. These feelings are not new to Keith because he spent a number of years in a previous marriage helping raise a stepson who is now thirty years old. His long-standing and strong relationship with his stepson enabled him to feel comfortable about the prospects of devoting himself to raising children who are not biologically related to him. He anticipates that they will remain a part of his life forever.

Carl, the married stepfather of eight-year-old Vicky, shares Keith's sentiment about feeling connected to and responsible for others. Speaking of Vicky, Carl remarks,

> She's made me more responsible. I always was fairly responsible, at least I see myself as that, but she's made me more responsible, in terms of knowing that I have people to take care of and knowing that the things that I'm doing with my life are making a difference in not just my life, but in two other people's lives. Things that I do as far as education and stuff are only going to make the opportunities for Vicky that much more, and the opportunities for us to be a family that much more.

Carl's comments, here and elsewhere during the interview, reflect his strong commitment to care for his stepdaughter as if she were his own. This kind of sentiment apparently motivates Carl to take his work and education more seriously than if he did not have a child in his life.

Eddie identifies only one way in which being a stepfather for eight-year-old Rhendy has changed him, but he feels it is significant.

> My sense is I know I have to work harder. . . . it's the extra stuff that
> she wants, so I figure I'll go out, I'll sacrifice my time for a little extra.
> Why not? You only live once. If I didn't get it when I was little, and
> my kids want it, by golly I'm going to go out and work and make sure
> they have it. . . . I've had to work harder just to make her happy, her
> life comfortable.

Eddie's willingness to work longer hours relates partly to his interest in
providing financially for his three biological children, but he focuses his
remarks primarily on his current responsibilities for Rhendy. Consistent
with his traditional view of men's fatherly responsibilities, Eddie takes his
financial provider role quite seriously. Thus Eddie's desire to make
Rhendy happy has led him to deepen his commitment to being a family
man who expresses himself through his financial contribution to the
family.

For Ray, being a stepfather and biological father helps him feel
"grounded." Being involved in a fatherly way with his two stepchildren
and one biological child gives him a "good feeling" about the "responsibility angle" of raising kids. "I like responsibility. To see that well, hey, I'm
not a scared little child. I'm actually doing this. I'm actually taking care of
this. This feels good. I feel strong. I feel powerful. I feel confident. That's
a good deal." Ray conveys the idea that the kids in his life provide him
with opportunities to perform certain adult, fatherly roles that in turn give
him a sense of empowerment. Although most might find it a little odd that
Ray, at age forty-two, refers to his contentment with being able to avoid
the "scared little child" role, Ray's comments apparently reflect his sincere
feelings about his contribution to his kids.

In some respects, Keith, Carl, and Eddie represent men who have become more future oriented because of their involvement with stepchildren.
The men have a heightened sense that they need to provide for their stepkids now, as well as plan for the future. But for some of the stepfathers,
their experiences with children actually encourage them to slow down and
pay more attention to the present. This is what happened with Jackson, an
introspective thirty-nine-year-old man who decided that he wanted to
have a child with his former wife several years ago and was disappointed
when he realized that she was unwilling to do so. His desire for a child was
so strong that he divorced his first wife and pursued a new relationship with
a longtime friend who has a small son. Jackson, who is now living his dream
of being involved with a child, has found new inspiration by being around
his five-year-old stepson, Mason.

He really got me to slow down from the—I guess I lived for quite a long time in future-oriented goals and trying to achieve something that's tomorrow, tomorrow, tomorrow. It's really pulled me into the present more, because just answering the questions of someone who's trying to define the world and is working very hard to define the world is—it takes a lot of energy so I can't be as future-oriented or as worry about tomorrow and the next day, so that's one way, I've slowed down. And he's given me remarkable opportunities to be introspective, to think about what's important to me. . . . He says something like well, light reflects—we've got colors because light reflects off of the surface and—as he's learning these things and repeating different, very basic concepts that I have just taken for granted for most of my life, it's kind of wondrous. It makes me realize that, well, as corny as it sounds, this is really a precious thing we have. And it's very easy to get lost chasing the goals that we think are important when we're twenty or twenty-five that don't really mean that much later in life.

Here, and in other portions of his interview, Jackson emphasizes that Mason has affected his outlook on life. Jackson thinks less about promoting his business and acquiring the material symbols of success. He is more inspired by the beauty of life, nature, and being a family man. Mason has brought Jackson back to the present and into a world where he values his personal connections to others much more.

Although Mason's personality and behaviors have helped Jackson reprioritize his life, the impact was filtered by Jackson's sensitivity to children that he had begun to cultivate prior to becoming involved with Mason. Jackson recalls a situation that occurred when he was married to his first wife that indicated to him that he was becoming more attuned to children's needs. He distinctly remembers one occasion when Mason and his mother, Helena, a person he had been friends with since high school, were visiting him and his ex-wife over the Christmas holiday. When Mason woke up crying one morning, Jackson found himself "wondering what's wrong? I wonder why Mason's crying. My ex-wife said I wish he'd stop crying. There's just a very subtle difference there. She wanted him to stop crying. I wondered why he was crying. I was kind of concerned." When stepfathers are open to children in this way, they are probably more susceptible to having children affect their lives than if they remain aloof and detached.

Just as Jackson spoke about the ways Mason gets him to think about things that he hasn't thought about since he was a kid, other men comment on how being with their stepchildren helped them remain young. Carl, for instance, mentions that Vicky "just done wonders for me as far as making sure that I stay with my kid-self, staying with being able to read children's books and seeing it from a kid's point of view and seeing all the wonderful things that I remember as a kid, that you forget when you get into the workplace and you, the day-in-day out drudgery of paperwork." Similarly, Rodney offers that his two teenage stepchildren are responsible for making "me stay on my toes and I think they're helping me think younger than I would if I didn't have kids their age." A stepfather may not initially seek experiences such as these when he gets involved with a woman who is a mother, but they can nonetheless become powerful experiences over time.

For stepfathers who assume their place in a stepfamily without ever having kids of their own, being involved with stepchildren can offer them a unique opportunity to become less ego-centered. Gerald, even though he lived with a woman who had kids for several years, had for the most part lived the bachelor life, growing accustomed to having his living space to himself. Becoming a stepfather and living with his thirteen-year-old step-daughter Sabrina has given Gerald a chance to expand his perspective. In his words, Sabrina

> caused me, forced me, allowed me to just open my heart a little bit more than maybe I normally would. Just learning to live with somebody makes changes in an individual. I'm probably less spoiled than I was. You live with a kid you can't be—even if you want to be, you've gotta set a good example. . . . when you have kids, you have to give and take. . . . You can't necessarily show your true self.

Throughout the interview Gerald describes himself as "pissy," so his involvement with Sabrina has allowed him to change his personality while learning how to "chill a bit." Presumably, when Gerald talks about not showing his "true self" he means that he wants to shelter Sabrina from the less congenial aspects of his personality. Although he still enjoys his alone time, I got the sense that Sabrina has been drawing him out a bit from his self-centered ways, encouraging him to think of others more. Sabrina is basically helping Gerald mature.

Along similar lines, Randy, a stepfather who is unemployed because of serious physical disabilities that confine him to a wheelchair, feels that his nine-year-old stepson has made him a "better person" and forced him to think of others more. Since becoming a stepfather, Randy has become more concerned with presenting his genuine self. "He's made me realize that I got to be more truthful with myself and I can't like tell him to do something and then not really do it myself." By pretending to talk to his stepson, Randy makes the point that his stepson is likely to model his behavior: "'Take your bath and don't back talk your mama.' Well, I better take my bath and don't back talk his mama too." He adds, "I take pride in what he does. I mean more so than I do with what I would do. . . . He's made me have to live my life for somebody else, more so than I think than just if Molly [mother] and I were married." This became apparent when Randy faced serious surgery and was asked to sign a bank form in case he died. "I wasn't just worried about me. I was worried about other people and what happened to me. Now if I get sick it affects two other people, so I damn well better take care of myself. I better listen to the doctor." Randy's appreciation for his stepson is perhaps best captured in a simple statement he made: "He has given me tons more than I think I've given him."

For men who were fathers prior to getting involved with their current partner who was a single mother, becoming a stepfather meant that they were in most cases spending more time with children than they had in the recent past or, in some cases, ever. Because some of the men miss living with their children and seeing them as much as they once did, getting involved in their stepchildren's lives gives some a chance to fulfill their desires to be around children. This reality hits close to home when I think about why I became so attached to Alli and Josh at a time when I had not lived full-time for the past seven years with my own eleven-year-old son. I enjoyed sharing the fun times of going swimming, building bonfires, playing catch and board games, having meals together, reading bedtime stories, watching their school and athletic performances, and so on. And I found it exciting to be with them as part of an emerging stepfamily spiced up by their mother's affectionate and upbeat personality. Unfortunately, I had not been able to duplicate this more complex "nuclear" family dynamic when I was with my son since his mother and I divorced. I probably was not fully aware at the time of what I felt I was missing, but in retrospect I can say that incorporating a mother into my experience of "fathering" broadened how I related to children. In addition, Alli extended my appreciation for some of the gendered aspects of parenting: being involved with a girl in a fatherly way allowed me to learn from and teach a young girl. Importantly, she was much more keenly aware of other people's feelings than either her younger brother or my son. I distinctly recall how wonderful I felt when Alli would ask me how my day had been—and really wanted to hear about it. Having a child display this kind of interest in my life and well-being was foreign to me, and it drew me deeper into my evolving stepfathering roles.

Turning back to what the men in my study have to say about their stepchildren, Robby, father of a thirteen-year-old daughter who now lives on the West Coast, talks fondly of his time with his two stepchildren. Reflecting back to when he was dating his current wife, he mentions how difficult it was for him when his daughter and his former wife left the area and moved across the country. During this transition Robby missed his daughter a great deal. Consequently, he says his stepkids "were kinda replacements for my daughter not being there. It kinda helped me, and they needed a father figure." Later he adds, "Those two kids have helped me as much as probably I've helped them. I don't have my daughter here all the time. I don't want to call them substitutes, but they're right up there." Similarly, Barry reasons that he loves his stepchildren "because I had such a strained relationship with my own children, which I had a real bitter divorce. It's still bitter. It's still going on and I'm estranged from my two kids who live here in town. . . . I got to have the children that I kind of missed out on."

A subtle variation on the substitute or replacement theme can be detected in Derek's comments about his toddler stepson, Elkin. Derek has four biological children, two to one mother, one to another, and then one more to his current partner, Elkin's mother. As he reflects on his relationships with the three children he had prior to getting involved with his current partner, Derek notes that Elkin is going through a stage where he says, "I'm proud of you, Daddy." Hearing Elkin use phrases like this touches his heart.

> It makes me feel good about myself. I mean my other kids do when they're with me, but he's with me on a daily basis. Whereas okay, they make me feel great Friday, Saturday, and Sunday, but then Monday through Thursday, I'm kinda dangling. That's when the subconscious mind talks down to me, "If you were a real man you would be with your kids; what are you doing wrong?" All you do is beat yourself up; whereas I'm not permitted to do that anymore because I have this kid who won't let me. I think he's helped me more than I've helped him.

Derek emphasizes the value of having Elkin around every day. Elkin's daily presence limits Derek's inclination to sulk about not receiving the emotional energy and joy that comes from being around loving children. In a way, then, Elkin serves as a substitute because he is able to bring a sense of continuity to Derek's life as a father figure throughout the entire week.

Elkin also makes a difference in Derek's life by enabling him to see himself in a different light as a father. Because Elkin is with Derek on a daily basis, Derek feels he is in a better position to take credit for Elkin's development—the good and the bad. He shares a story in which someone told him that Elkin was "well-mannered." On hearing the compliment, Derek recalls feeling

> proud because I honestly feel like I did that. Whereas with my other kids, I can't actually say that. I mean, okay, your daughter really loves you, but their actions have very little to do with me because they spend very little time with me, so all the things they do that I don't like, I just have to deal with it. Because that's what they are permitted to do in their mother's house. Whereas with Elkin, if it's something about his actions that I don't like, I blame myself because that means I'm doing something wrong. And I have an opportunity to change it.

Derek's comments highlight how a stepfather and stepchild can mutually benefit from their relationship. He pinpoints how a man can take pride and joy in raising a child in a productive manner. This accomplishment allows the man to feel more fulfilled, especially when he can echo Derek's comment about Elkin: "He's actually becoming a better young man, not really a man, but young man because he has a male role model to look up to." Investing time and energy in raising Elkin, and seeing the results of his labors of love, causes Derek to feel that he's making a significant difference in a child's life, even if the child is not his biological offspring.

The stories I use to capture the nature and significance of the impact stepfathers and children have on each other come from the minds, hearts, and mouths of stepfathers, and to a lesser extent the birth mothers. A more complete portrait of this impact awaits future research incorporating children's voices directly. For now, we glimpse the power a child's perspective can bring to the story of stepfatherhood by turning to Danny, one of the two fourteen-year-olds I interviewed and discussed earlier in connection with his stepfather, Thomas. After I asked him what letter grade he would assign to his stepfather, Danny was quick to reply, "I would give him an A plus. Because he's just the best thing that has happened to me. So, it's like I really appreciate what he's done and how he's affected my life and helped me get through my father leaving me and stuff." Later, while discussing different aspects of his relationship with his stepfather, Danny talks about the pride his stepfather takes in him. At one point he says, "He's like very quick to tell people how smart I am and how good grades I get and stuff. It's like, he really likes to tell people how good I am and stuff." [I: "And what does that do for you or how does that make you . . ."] "It just makes me feel proud, it's like . . . makes me feel proud of what I'm doing and it kind of encourages me to do more." Danny's heartfelt, thoughtful analysis pinpoints the value of parental support, whether it's from a biological father or stepfather. In this case, it is Danny's stepfather who lets him know that he is appreciated for who he is and what he does. In a number of cases, this sense of pride can be heard in the stepfathers' voices as they glowingly talk about their stepchildren. A sampling of these comments:

> He's intrinsically a really good boy. He has a good heart. He's very sensitive. . . . I someday see him being a really good father himself because he's just got a good soul, he's got a kind heart. . . . He's nine years old and he's already, I mean he plays with kids that are two, three years old and genuinely play with 'em and keeps 'em company and has a good time with them. [Terry, 41]

> They're both great kids. They're fabulous kids. [Barry, 52]

> She has an incredible voice, a beautiful singing voice. She's really very naturally talented. [Brad, 38]

> She's a great kid. She's smart and she's added a whole new dimension to my life. [Calvin, 38]

> When you see her contemporaries acting certain ways. It made me appreciate even more what a good kid she is. I mean, she's not a typical thirteen-year-old. I think she's more sensitive. . . . She does not get into any trouble. . . . she really does occupy her time quite productively. [Gerald, 44]

Not all the stepfathers, of course, praise their stepchildren, as shown by Monty's and Ron's comments presented earlier. However, most feel at least reasonably content with their stepchildren's character. Most of the stepfathers also tend to think that they have lent a helping hand in shaping these kids. Once again, we must keep in mind that the sample of stepfathers who volunteered to be in my study probably does not fully tap the men who are struggling in their stepfathering roles or those who walked away from them. That said, the overriding impression I formed from my interviews is that most of the stepfathers are proud to be around their stepchildren and delighted to have others see them together.

Kids, like their stepfathers, come with all types of personalities and dispositions, some much more pleasant than others. The dynamics associated with the family dance that predates the stepfather's introduction into the stepfamily mix, as well as those that emerge after the stepfather gets involved, can affect how a child reacts to the stepfather and how the stepfather perceives the child.

6

THE NAME GAME

Feeling connected to someone or something is a sensation that appeals to us all, stepfathers included. Admittedly, some stepfathers may only truly wish to be connected to their romantic partner; any children she brings into the relationship may be seen as an unwelcome, though tolerable, appendage. But others, like most of the men I interviewed, embrace their chance to feel bonded to not only their romantic partner but her children as well.

As comments included in the previous chapters have shown, stepfathers can play a pragmatic role in sustaining relationships and making varied contributions to the stepfamily dance. However, men's relationships with their stepchildren, and their role in shaping the stepfamily dance, can be far more than just a practical exercise in familial maintenance. The symbolic and emotional dimensions to stepfathers' experiences are potentially quite powerful, illustrating poignantly people's desire for group belonging. This desire may grow not only in the hearts of stepchildren but also in the hearts of the men who enter their lives as their mother's boyfriend. Consequently, a complete picture of stepfathering must account for these two interrelated aspects of the stepfather–stepchild relationship: the symbolic and emotional. They are intriguing because of the ambiguity often associated with how stepfamily life evolves and is managed. Everything, or almost everything, seems to be negotiated, especially during the early months and years. Everyday routines and decisions are often complicated by the uncertainties of family norms and unstable alliances between the various members. For sure, stepfathers and other members of the stepfamily can sometimes find a smooth and unobstructed path with little conscious effort or distress, though those situations are likely to be in the minority.

Of the many insights stepfathers share, perhaps the most profound speak to a few of the ways a stepfather is implicated in the symbolic and emotional life of his stepfamily. The power of labels to signify a sense of family belonging, and the significance of a stepfather's degree of passion to nurture, protect, and provide for a stepchild as his own, are issues relevant to understanding stepfathers' experiences. Exploring two of the key symbolic and emotionally laden areas that offer men chances for leaving a mark on the nature of the stepfamily and stepfather–stepchild relationship broadens our outlook on stepfatherhood. I explore the "name game" here while devoting the next chapter to men's experiences with claiming children as their own and bonding with them.

NEGOTIATING LABELS

In the beginning of this book, I emphasized how people typically are affected by the words "daddy" and "dad," as well as terms that convey the notion of "step" father or "step" child. These words, along with the other labels that help identify players in the family dance (son, daughter, brother, sister, mom, similar surnames), remind us that language helps shape social experience but personal experiences help bring life to language. Put simply, people's identities and relations in stepfamilies are often tied to how people use and feel about labels that define identities and roles.[1] Having glanced at this fascinating terrain in chapter 1, we now return to take a closer look at how men and others negotiate the use of labels, especially "daddy," "dad," and the "step" prefix attached to words like "dad," "father," "parent," and "child." The markers that convey family ties affect how people negotiate their identities within this evolving dance. They are intimately tied to the politics of the family dance as it evolves over time and speak to people's efforts to claim others as their own. By using particular words, people hint at whether or not they feel obligated or entitled to have certain sentiments toward others. Words also tap into the emotional core of how people experience their sense of belonging to a family.

The timing of when these language issues become meaningful for partners and children varies considerably. Sometimes the importance of the words signifying certain types of family relationships is brought to the forefront almost immediately. In other situations these concerns don't surface until decisions about marriage, living together, or adoption are made. These words become a part of the discussion at different times, and people express widely different levels of concern about whether particular words are used.

Early on, when a man—father or stepfather—first hears the "daddy" and "dad" labels directed at him, he is likely to view these experiences as memorable moments. With the passing of time, however, the emotional power of these labels wanes for many. As we'll see shortly, for some men those words still carry great weight a few years after they were first spoken—perhaps in part because of the innocent young voices that breathe life into them. Even when the label is taken for granted, though, its symbolic power in a larger context remains real. Whether we are a dad, mom, son, or daughter, we long to feel wanted. We want to be needed. We want to feel connected to others. And we want others to look at us as though we matter to them. Being called daddy or dad, or using those terms to capture someone else's attention and paint them with meaning, is a common reminder of our basic psychological and emotional needs.

With these basic images in mind, I sought to learn more about the meaning of the "dad/daddy" label by offering my participants an opportunity to talk about their own experiences with this emotionally laden aspect of the family dance. These labels provide a window for viewing the politics of the family dance as well as men's relationships to children. Although some men began to talk about these labels on their own, I led most down this path by asking them what their stepchildren called them, when and how any references to "dad" where used, how they felt about the labels kids applied, and what types of discussions, if any, they had with their partners and stepchildren about the labels. The men usually found this to be a worthwhile topic and were eager to share their stories. I had anticipated that this topic would strike a responsive cord with many of the men because I could still recall, even fifteen years removed, how emotional I was when Alli playfully started to refer to me as "daddy." Though this period of time was short-lived because my relationship with her mother ended, hearing her say those words at age eleven or twelve affected me deeply then and leave a lasting impression to this day.

Whereas some stepdads raised the topic of labels with their partners prior to the kids saying anything, many first dealt with it after children broached the subject by either referring to them as "dad" or after the children asked the men or the mother what label they should use. As expected, the stepdads who entered their stepchildren's lives when the kids were older were less likely to be called "dad." Asked if he felt comfortable with his stepdaughter Harmony calling him by his first name, John says, "I'm cool with that. Yeah, coming into a girl's life at fourteen [mother referred to her as fifteen], I'm not really expecting a miracle. I would like for her to call me father cause I really love her, but I get along with her so well. But truth be told she has two fathers already, and it was kind of rocky sometimes, so she isn't really going to jump on that bandwagon." Because Harmony interacts with her biological father, as well as a stepfather who raised her for about thirteen years, John has had to work extra hard to establish himself as a father figure. His relatively young age, twenty-seven, has also contributed to his struggles, although it appears he has made considerable headway forging a meaningful relationship with Harmony.

When stepdads come into younger children's lives, various circumstances can pave the way for children to experiment with using the "dad/daddy" label. One stepfather described his stepchild who experimented with using "dad" for about a week after leaving the West Coast where his father lived. The child and his divorced mother moved in with her boyfriend in Florida. The five-year-old child found himself in a new school environment where kids were bringing their fathers to school, but his father was thousands of miles away. He became good friends with another boy who called his stepfather "dad." Apparently he longed to fit in and feel that he had familial connections similar to his friends so he started calling his mother's boyfriend "dad." The mother and stepfather convinced the child to call the stepfather by his first name and retain "dad" for his biological father, who was still active in his life, despite living far away.

Some children parroted the language of the stepfather's own children. Two-year-old Elkin learned to talk while under the care of a stepfather who had his own children with him at times. In other instances, preschool or elementary school children were exposed to the language used by a stepfather's child. In the case of seven-year-old Trevor, the man he eventually came to identify as his father had a nine-year-old son, Matthew, who spent a lot of time with them. After Kevin adopted Trevor, Trevor started calling him "dad." Kevin describes some of the interpersonal dynamics the naming issue has created for him and his two sons.

> It's a little weird sounding just because he's called me Kevin for so long, but I like it. I am dad. I am daddy, so—and that's what Matthew calls me. I noticed Trevor sometimes kind of seems to emphasize, to overdo it when Matthew is around. I don't know if that's payback, because Matthew pulled a little bit of "I'm the son and you're not." Jockeying a little bit. We had to deal with that. Matthew just about, being sensitive to Trevor's feelings and just the sort of thing you tell a son, that that's not nice to try and push that in his face, and reassure him, Matthew you're my firstborn son and you're special in a way Trevor isn't special to me. So that's been one of the things I've been also kind of paying attention to, is just making sure that Matthew knows he's still

my number one son, I guess you could say, in my eyes—and he still is my number one son. And Trevor knows that too, but I want Trevor to know that he's special to me and he's my son as well. So with Trevor, I've told him, you know, Trevor, if you'd been born to me, you'd still be the number two son. And then you'd still be special, but the first kid you have, it's just that there's a different thing with the first kid and the second kid and so on and so forth.

Kevin's description of the circumstances surrounding Trevor's transition illustrates how the "daddy/dad" label can be manipulated to foster feelings of inclusion or exclusion. Trevor, perhaps in a slightly taunting way, appears eager to alter his feelings of being marginalized by Matthew by asserting that his claim on Kevin as his dad is now comparable to Matthew's.

The power of language to elevate or marginalize can also be seen in how some children feel about their last name. In several instances, children made clear requests that they wanted to have the same last name as their stepfather, a gesture tied to the "claiming" process I discuss later.[2] According to Calvin, his ten-year-old stepdaughter Kristen had initially asked her mother if she could start calling Calvin "daddy" about a year after he and her mother started dating. Shortly after they got married, Kristen started to use Calvin's last name when writing her full name, often at school. Calvin summarizes his feelings about Kristen's newfound ritual: "I felt good. . . . That was another acknowledgment that I'm doing something right. And she's persistent about it too." Kristen is also steadfast in her feelings about the distinction between father and stepfather, dad and stepdad. An experience at the dinner table one night stuck in Calvin's mind. Kristen, her mother, and Calvin were talking about some aspect of stepfatherhood and Kristen "said something like if they [persons outside the family] called me stepfather she would inflict bodily harm or something like that." Calvin found this response "surprising." He adds, "I think partially because it was pretty clear that she understood exactly what that meant and she also felt an attachment that was I guess greater than [one] would assume she would have with a stepfather."

Other children who wanted to have their stepfather's last name did so for various reasons. One boy made his request when he learned that his sister, who was yet to be born, would have his stepfather's last name. A few children apparently didn't want to be the only one in the household with a different last name once their mother married and changed her name. The pressure seemed to be even greater if the man had a biological child with the same last name who lived with him much of the time. Whether the issue was the use of "daddy/dad" or the adoption of a stepfather's last name, some children were sensitive to wanting to feel connected to those who were part of their household family. In their minds, as well as the minds of others, the various men who might claim a fatherly presence in their life were not perceived or treated as equals.[3]

Although some adults found it important to correct children when they called their stepfathers "dad/daddy," this only seemed to matter if the children had some connection with their biological father. Melanie reasons, referring to her two-year-old daughter,

> I'm not going to sit Teresa down when she's a baby and explain to her why Tim's not her daddy and I'm not going to do that. I don't feel like it's appropriate. When she gets older, I can try to explain it to her and, you know, try to explain that "you have a daddy and you know, Tim's not your real dad, but he's your stepdaddy and I mean, it's okay if you want to call him daddy." Nat [biological father] doesn't care. He wants to give them up for adoption. He wants Tim to adopt them.

Melanie's concern for Teresa's developmental stage, her perception that Tim is the only father Teresa has ever known, and her sense that Tim cares about Teresa, gives her peace of mind that it's okay for Teresa to call Tim "daddy" now. Moreover, Tim never asked Teresa or her sister to call him "daddy," so Teresa's "decision" to refer to him in this way grew out of the natural process of Tim being a welcome fatherly presence in her family as she knew it.

Melanie and Tim, like numerous other couples, discussed the benefits and potential risks associated with a child using the "daddy/dad" label with a stepfather. Encouraging or allowing a child to use this label is likely to intensify his or her feelings for and attachment to a stepfather. Although this approach may be quite rewarding for everyone involved, children (and stepfathers) risk more emotional pain if the romantic relationship ends after they have used language to construct and solidify their symbolic father–child relationship. Carl and Lani faced this dilemma about six months after they started dating. Up to that point Lani's daughter, Vicky, had called Carl by his first name. But seemingly overnight, with no prompting from Carl or Lani, Vicky, who was three at the time, started calling Carl "daddy." Carl's recollection of how Lani felt when she learned that Vicky was calling him daddy was that she

> was happy about that too, I think. We talked about it afterwards. I told her how excited I was. She seemed that same way. We talked a little bit

about it and at that point it was—we were unsure because we were not married. . . . we weren't sure whether to tell her—no I'm not your daddy yet—to give her false impressions, so we just ended up letting her move into that transition. It was a tough decision because if there was a point where Lani and I didn't get along, stopping her calling me daddy or me not being there after a certain point. . . . We talked about it and we decided it would be a fine thing to do that and . . . we started having—I started, at least, having marriage-type feelings about Lani. . . . It all came into play and came together at that point.

Though married at the time, Juan and his wife had a similar talk after Juan's stepson, Ivan, "out of the blue" called him "dad." "I told her that we should keep things very clear for him and like telling him that his dad is where he is [in his native country] and I love him as much as any person can do but I am not his real dad, and I like it when he call me that [dad]. I think that I am trying to keep things clear. Not messing with his head." Asked about his wife's thoughts regarding this issue, Juan adds, "I think she love it. She love the way I am trying to keep things with him and accepting the role."

For both Carl and Juan, the impetus for talking to their partners about what labels the stepchildren should use when referring to them stemmed from kids using the "daddy/dad" label. These conversations can also be initiated when one or both of the partners feels awkward with the stepfather being addressed by his first name. William, for example, is basically okay with having his cohabiting fiancée's two sons, ages nine and eleven, call him by his first name for now. But he expects that to change. "When we decided we were going to get married, we addressed that. We decided that once we get married, 'William' wouldn't be appropriate any more. So we're going to have to—I think we're all going to sit down and we're going to pick a name for daddy. It doesn't have to be daddy, but it won't be 'William.'" Asked about how it makes him feel for the boys to call him "William" and their mother "Mom" William offers:

I was kind of uneasy. . . . I was raised that a child shouldn't address an adult on a first-name basis. That's only to show that respect that's due from a child to an adult. . . . Once we decided we was going to get married and stuff and I said okay, I'll accept this for now, but once we're married, then the name has to change. We're not going to be on a first-name basis then. . . . We're going to keep the camaraderie, but that respect, just that little, slight level of respect—will be issues in some form. Be it some kind of nickname or whatever. It won't be William.

Although William does not know what the family will decide to call him, he anticipates that the issue will be resolved easily. On a few occasions the boys have already called him "Daddy William." The first time this occurred the family was at the grandmother's house where one of the boys, who regularly refers to his great grandfather as "Daddy Jay," jokingly said "Daddy Jay, Daddy William" as he addressed them both. William feels this would work because "it won't be just plain William."

William's comments, focusing as they do on two young boys, emphasize the power that naming can have in conferring respect to others. In one sense, William is speaking more about not being called by his first name than he is about being called "dad." But because he is living in a family situation, acting in a fatherly way toward these two children, he is reluctant to be called either by his first name because it is too friendly or by "Mr." because it is too formal.

Stepfathers who had a biological child living elsewhere were in a position to develop a unique perspective on the naming process. Not wanting to imagine their own child calling someone else "dad," they were often reluctant to have their stepchild call them "dad," especially if the biological father was at least moderately involved in the child's life. There were exceptions, though.

EMOTIONS

Why do some men seem to place so much weight on using a simple label? Anecdotal evidence from people's everyday lives beyond this study illustrates several points about the emotional tenor of family language. We are all aware that when uttered with the innocence of a young child's voice, "daddy" can elicit a tender response from a man. Said playfully, it can raise the corners of a man's mouth in delight. Shouted as a frightened plea for help, it can propel a man, heart pounding, to search for and protect a young, vulnerable life. With time, "daddy" is likely to be replaced with "dad" as most kids mark their advancing years by leaving their "childish" talk behind. "Dad, can I have some money?" "Can you pick me up from soccer practice, dad?" "Are we there yet, dad?" "This is my dad." "Dad, I love you." Though the short version, "dad," lacks the tangible cuteness of "daddy," it can still carry a big punch, moving a man and others to feel deeply.

Many of my participants who heard stepchildren refer to them as father figures of some sort recalled having a number of positive emotions.

Several comments illustrate how most men felt when they first heard a child not their own refer to them as "dad."

> I was just ecstatic. . . . It was like seeing her walk, which I never got to see. But it was kind of that same type of experience. . . . It was just neat. [Carl, 30]

> I thought good, he's taking to me, we're getting along good. It's just, I don't know, if just felt natural that he was, it kinda told me well you can't be that bad of a father because if he feels comfortable to call me that. [Doug, 44]

> Really good. That's hard to describe. Words are inadequate. [Ray, 42]

> That made me feel good cause I don't have any kids, and I wasn't really trying to have no kids 'cause I'm still young. [Alan, 26]

A number of men recalled in vivid detail the exact circumstances surrounding this important moment. Others, though they had trouble honing in on the exact moment, could recollect clearly how it made them feel. Some men experienced this moment in the company of their romantic partners, the children's mothers; several reported sharing smiles of joy and relief with their partner as they acknowledged that their relationship with a child was moving in the right direction. Terry, for example, recalls "looking over at my wife [in the car] smiling and she was real happy to hear that too, because I'm sure it felt good to her." Juan was caught off guard when his stepson, Ivan, in the company of the mother, called him "dad" the first time, a month after Juan married Ivan's mother. While in the company of friends, he shared a smile with his wife but remembers purposively trying to prevent Ivan from noticing that he and his mother were communicating about something he said. Juan says, "I just hug him or give him a kiss or something like that." Partners assumed that if children felt comfortable enough to use this type of language, things must be good.

Some stepfathers commented on how their stepchild's continued use of "dad/daddy" gave them great pleasure. Gloating in a good-natured way about his two-year-old stepson's attachment to him, Derek says, "He prefers me over any one else in the world. In his eyes, I can't do anything wrong at all. He sees me and he has this big smile that comes over his face, and he starts yelling, 'Daddy, Daddy!' There's no feeling like that. Even if you don't like kids, he'll force you to love him." Similarly, Emmit comments on his initial reaction to being called "dad" by offering, "It made me feel good." Then he adds, "Because every time he calls me dad I feel like I'm somebody important to him. Even to this day, if I have to go out to the school and talk to his teacher or something like that, he'll, when I come through the door, he'll start smiling and he'll come grab me." These stepfathers, as well as others, were moved by the symbolism of the "daddy/dad" label, connecting it with a lasting, deep interpersonal bond.

As mentioned earlier, many men did not experience being called "dad" by a child who was not biologically related to them. Keith's stepdaughters, for example, have not called him "dad" during the six years they have known him. Although Keith downplays how this makes him feel, hearing that word probably would have brightened his day, as it did when a stepchild from a previous relationship called him dad and continues to do so. Asked what his biggest struggles have been as a stepfather to his two stepdaughters, Keith says,

> I always kind of wished they'd call me dad. But I don't think that's going to happen. But I don't dwell on that. I truly believe that I am that role for them. When they need to go to the doctor, I take them. They go on my medical insurance. They live in my home, so it would be nice if they called me dad instead of Keith. That'd be the biggest issue, but I don't dwell on that, because that's not important. It's how they give me a kiss every night before they go to bed and how they tell me to have a good day before I go to work. I pack their lunches every morning. Little things like that. Letting me know what I am, which is their dad. I think when they get older there may come a day when they do do that, but I won't ask them to do it. I think that's something they have to do on their own. I didn't ask Charles [stepson from previous relationship] to do it. It just happened. We've never discussed whether they should call me that or not. It might have come up, I think, at some point and I said, well, if you're ready to some day that would be fine but if not, then Keith's fine.

According to Keith, the overriding issue is not what his stepdaughters call him, but how they treat him. He is content to perceive himself as having a fatherly presence without the title. What his stepdaughters call him may indeed be secondary, but the potential exists for it to become highly meaningful.

In addition to eliciting positive and practical emotions, the use of "daddy" or "dad" can stir jealousy or anger in a man (or woman) if applied "improperly." For example, feelings of betrayal may surface if a child uses this term to refer to someone whom another man deems undeserving of the title. This "undeserving" recipient is usually a stepfather. Several of the stepfathers who also had a child of their own shared poignant thoughts on this matter. The thoughts typically surfaced when the men contemplated the "dad" label after their stepchildren initially used it. Robby described how he was opposed to using the "dad" term to refer to stepfathers.

> 'Cause it's come up because when my daughter [stepdaughter, Tracy] would call me daddy. And one time when we were sitting at dinner and Tracy looked at me and said daddy, and I stopped and said, "Tracy, I'm not your daddy. Your daddy is Brad." I don't want my daughter calling anybody else daddy and I know Brad must feel the same way; he doesn't want his kids calling anybody else daddy and I don't blame him.

Although Robby never directly talked to Brad about this issue, he assumed that Brad would feel this way. Buried in Robby's reaction appears to be a sense that a father's sacred claim to his children will be violated if the words used to identify this position are used broadly. Ironically, Robby's glowing descriptions of his stepchildren revealed that he was totally committed to being involved in their lives; he was just not prepared to have them call him dad. He was, for instance, comfortable talking about how he created an opportunity to bond with his stepson. "I like the bond that I have with me and Tony. I went out and bought Tony his own little lawnmower. And he can get out there, and it's kinda fun having a son around. Now I know how my dad feels." Similar to Keith, the emotional connection Robby has with Tony is enough; he doesn't need the label to confirm it.

Tim and Brandon, both biological fathers, also shared their thoughts while emphasizing their mixed feelings. Tim, a stepfather for three preadolescent girls, two of whom live with him and his fiancée, recalls that it made him feel "good" to have one of his stepdaughters call him "daddy" for the first time. He describes this good feeling as well as his conflict about it.

> That tingly kind of feeling you get . . . it was a kind of combination, though. I felt that because it was like "Wow, she really loves me," I really mean something to her and she thinks a lot of me. . . . And then the other thing was because I thought of it from being the other dad's point of view and I was like oh, wait, that's not—you know, kind of bad.

Notwithstanding these mixed emotions, Tim ultimately allowed his stepdaughters to call him "daddy" because their mother reassured Tim that the girls' biological father had not been actively involved in their lives. There was no paternal bond to be violated. This explanation appears to have made it easier for Tim to accept the "daddy" label because he felt he was providing his stepdaughters with a hands-on relationship with a father that they didn't have already. If the father had been involved in his daughters' lives, Tim might have chosen to discourage the girls from calling him "daddy."

Brandon, a biological father of a nine-year-old son, also described his conflicted feelings about hearing his five-year-old stepson call him "dad." "I thought it was pretty neat, but I know how I would feel if I saw my son call somebody else "dad." It would kind of hurt me, I think, although I know it's not that big of a deal." Unlike Tim, Brandon added that he and his stepson's mother talked to the boy to clarify for him that he had an involved father who was committed to him. They wanted to make sure the boy wasn't "confused with the two-dads situation." After doing this, Brandon encouraged the boy to continue to call him by his first name. In his mind, had Brandon allowed his stepson to call him "dad," he would have been treading on the biological father's turf because the father was clearly making an effort to treat his son in a fatherly way.

Jackson, a man who had never had children, offered a thought-provoking example of how hearing "daddy" provided another set of mixed emotions. In the words of this reflective thirty-nine-year-old man:

> [I felt] very glad and warm to hear it, but there was a surprising bit of fright to it because I was realizing the responsibility that was coming with that. If he was going to place that name into my world, then I needed to meet up to that. Which actually did help, because it helped me to realize a little bit more what I was accepting in my life, that I was moving into the world of parenting and away from the world of the visiting uncle or whatever, which is about as close to any type of child contact as I'd had.

Here we see how language can shape people's experiences. Jackson heard a lot more than a word when Mason called him "daddy" from time to time during a three-week holiday travel adventure he took with Mason and Mason's mother. With that word came a host of images about parental roles and responsibilities that had not been a part of Jackson's everyday life. For some time he had hoped and dreamed about becoming a family man while he was with his previous wife, but those dreams never materialized because she was not interested in having children. So it was with his new partner and her son that he got his hands "dirty" and started to feel like a father. Even though the boy's use of "daddy" was only one piece of Jackson's transitional experience of becoming a stepdad, and Mason has since reverted back to calling Jackson by his first name, it was notable nonetheless.

Decisions about how to refer to stepdads are affected by many factors, some of which revolve around biological fathers' involvement in their children's lives. The "two-dads situation" to which Brandon refers is an important part of this context. People perceive and manage the presence of multiple father figures for children in various ways. Terry, the stepfather discussed at length in chapter 1, was open to helping his nine-year-old stepson Zack recognize a few years ago that it was okay to have two dads. This topic surfaced when emotions grew particularly hot and heavy one summer when Zack was visiting his birth father in another state. After Zack used the phrase "my dad in Gainesville" in a conversation he was having with his biological father, the father, according to Terry, "lost it." Terry describes the biological father as a "very ugly person, and [he] called up threatening me and very demonstrative towards Zack and telling him he can't call me dad, I'm not his dad." Terry adds that he tried to encourage the biological father during this phone conversation to think about what was best for Zack, but he was unsuccessful in winning his support. Later that summer, after Zack came home, Terry and Zack's mother talked with Zack. Terry recalls telling Zack something like,

> "Look, it's okay to have two dads. You have a couple sets of grandparents and whatever. It's okay to have two different fathers. I'm the one that's here with you all the time and he's the one up there. If he gets more involved in your life, then great! If he doesn't, nothing changes. I'm still here. I'm the one that's going to be here every day." So I said, "Don't be afraid to call me whatever you want to call me."

For Terry and his wife, the notion of Zack, or anyone for that matter, having two dads was seemingly not a big deal. It reflected many people's everyday reality; why not acknowledge and work with it in a mature fashion? Terry's eagerness to have Zack call him "dad" was also fueled in part by his desire to have Zack feel comfortable around the future siblings he would have eventually. He discussed this with his wife.

> I said we're going to be having more kids and our kids are all going to be calling me dad. I said he's going to feel like an outsider if he's not— you know, I mean, we go places together and if the kids are calling me Dad and he's calling me Terry—kids don't miss a beat, with other kids in the neighborhood and families that we're around. I think it would be putting him in an awkward position.

This conversation builds on Terry's earlier comments (presented in chapter 1) in which he stressed the importance of making sure that everyone experiences a sense of belonging in a particular family. For him there was no room for "step" fathers, mothers, or siblings. All family members should feel that they fully belong to the family and be comfortable with their respective roles in it.

Although Zack's biological father challenged Terry's position in Zack's life, these kinds of accusations can be directed at biological fathers as well. A biological father may be cast in a negative light if he is thought to have neglected or abused a child. Ironically, a "devoted" stepfather may be at the head of the line trying to discredit the abusive or neglectful father. The process of discrediting the biological father seldom focuses on the inappropriateness of a particular child literally using the "dad" label, although sometimes it may. In some instances the terms that are used or not used may seem secondary to how close or distant a stepfather feels toward children.

For Monty, the thirty-three-year-old disgruntled stepfather involved with his wife's eleven-year-old daughter, Beverly, his outrage was tied less to how or when this teenage girl used the term "dad" and more to her feelings for him and her biological father. Monty was deeply hurt by how Beverly had treated him compared to her biological father, who he felt had neglected and mistreated her.

> I never really understood what I was to her; I still don't. I felt, I've always felt like I should have been her father, but I never was, and I never will be. . . . I was always there for her in positive ways, and he never was; I mean, never. When she lived with him, he was mean to her; he would stay out all night and never call her and tell her that he wasn't coming home. She was eight years old living with him, alone in the house all night because she didn't know where her own father was. . . . So, that made me resent him even more and that just added to the whole thing I couldn't understand—her father hurt her so much yet she still loves him so much. I just don't understand that.

I asked him several minutes later if he ever hoped that she would call him "dad."

> Well, not really. Whether she called me dad or not didn't matter that much to me. But whether she was close to me, like you know had a father-daughter relationship, that was important to me, and that never happened. Which is why I'm so bitter now. It's like I'm punishing her for being, for liking her father basically. To me it's like a slap in the face. I'm always there; I'm always providing for her, and at one point was

willing to listen and be a father figure. And he never did any of that, and he got all the credit and I got nothing. I just couldn't stand that; I still can't stand it.

Apparently, from Monty's perspective, what matters most is not the title of "dad" but the closeness of a father–daughter relationship. Although I can only speculate, I was left with the impression, after hearing Monty repeatedly express his bitterness throughout the interview, that he would have felt at least a bit better if Beverly had simply called him "dad." It is not clear whether her verbal recognition of Monty's position in her life would have affected the way he saw and treated her to any significant degree. Nor is it clear whether Monty would have been more accepting of Beverly's unconditional love for her biological father. Perhaps. It seems reasonable to assume, though, that had Beverly clearly identified Monty as a "dad" with her everyday language, this might have helped buffer Monty's resentment and drawn him into her life. As a result, he might have developed a stronger sense of having a father identity despite his negative feelings about Beverly's commitment to her father.

The extent to which a stepdad's identity as a father is influenced by the stepchild's use of "daddy" terms may be influenced by the way he interprets a stepchild's reasons for using those words. If a stepdad feels that these words are coming from the child's heart, he may be more inclined to embrace the label and its associated roles. This was an issue that surfaced for Rodney when he was engaged to his stepchildren's mother. Recalling the first time his stepson called him "dad," Rodney describes the situation this way.

He said, "Dad, can I do this?" Or "can I go do this?" I looked at him and said, "Sure, son." It warmed my heart and made me feel good, but I was wondering also inside, is he being told by Judith [the boy's mother] to call me that or is he doing that on his own? But I never asked her whether or not she had told him . . . because I want to think that it came from him, and as long as I don't ask, that's what I'm going to believe.

Ignorance is bliss for Rodney on this matter because he appears to enjoy feeling as though both of his stepchildren see him as a father figure, an issue that has apparently taken on greater importance since the death of the children's biological father several years ago.

In my sample, there was clearly a mix of men who were called "dad" and others who were mostly called by their first name. Coming into a stepfamily setting with older children appears to limit a man's chances of being called dad or father. But even among those who had very small children, the likelihood that children would call the new man in their life "dad" appeared to be related to the nonresident father's level and type of involvement.

Though rare some men have difficulties with terms like "dad," regardless of whether they are applied to biological fathers or stepfathers. Landon, a pensive twenty-seven-year-old stepdad and father, describes in detail why he felt uncomfortable with his live-in girlfriend's children, as well as his own son, calling him dad. With his girlfriend's children he felt it was inappropriate because he wasn't their father. He made a point of telling one of the girls that she should not call him dad because her father lives in Virginia. Although he admits to feeling good when this girl calls him "dad," because this shows that she likes him, he forcefully points out,

> Their dad should be their dad, and I should be . . . their friend, and someone that they can look up to. . . . I want to be someone that they want to be in their life, not someone that they feel like they need in their life. . . . I want to be someone that they would choose to have in their life, not someone that they feel they need, because they don't have a dad.

Part of Landon's reasoning goes beyond his concern that the biological father should be acknowledged as the dad, even though he has done a poor job of being involved with his children. He uses his own son as a way to illustrate his belief that the terms "father" and "dad" are inappropriate because they reflect a system of ownership for claiming kids. Landon has his son call him by his first name. He explains,

> I come from an abusive household that's, to me the whole title [dad] kind of goes along with ownership and I don't feel that you own your children. If anything, your children should own you. So, I don't want my son to call me dad or father or anything until he really understands what it means and says, I want to call you dad.

CONTEXTS

Another way to tap into children's use of "dad" is to consider how children's usage may vary within different contexts. Several obvious distinctions may occur when a man is with his own family members versus with people outside his family and then those situations where these two camps overlap. This distinction can be seen in the way Randy's nine-year-old stepson relates to him. "Very rarely does he outright call me dad. But he uses dad as, you know, 'I have to ask my dad. I have to do this.' 'This is my dad.' So I'm still Randy, but now I'm Randy his dad." In this kind of scenario, stepdads can have their identities as father figures reinforced, even though it is done indirectly. A man who hears a stepson or stepdaughter refer to him as "dad" in front of other kids, family, or strangers may have an easier time internalizing his sense of being involved with a child in a fatherly way. It does not, however, provide a stepdad with what is likely to be the ultimate chance to see himself as a father based on his child's use of titles. That privilege is reserved for the man whose stepchild freely refers to him as "dad" to his face. "Hey Dad, can I go to Carsten's house?"

Children have lots of options at their disposal to let a man know that they see him as a father figure. Although many children rely on the obvious terms like "dad" and "daddy," others are more creative. Take, for instance, eight-year-old Rhendy's approach with her stepdad, Eddie. Based on Eddie's account, Rhendy had been talking to someone a few months ago and said "that's my steppy-dad" while referring to Eddie. He recalls saying "Your steppy-dad? What kind of name is that? Your steppy-dad?" Rhendy replied, "Yep, you're my steppy-dad" to which Eddie countered, "Okay, I'm your steppy-dad." The effects of that innocent exchange have persisted for the past two or three months because Eddie has adopted the label of "steppy-dad," a label that has been reinforced repeatedly by Rhendy and her mother. Eddie appears to appreciate how this term has solidified his role in Rhendy's life and provides him with a "good feeling." The symbolic meaning of this affectionate term gives Rhendy and Eddie an endearing way to locate themselves within their relatively new familial arrangement.

In fourteen-year-old Danny's stepfamily, he and his brother initially called their stepdad "Thomas." With time, they began to call him "DT" to distinguish him from their biological father. They made it clear that these initials stood for "Daddy Thomas." Later, they began to use the full label "Daddy Thomas." Ultimately, the boys began to call their stepdad "daddy." Danny, the eldest boy, even went so far as to start calling his biological father by his first name because he feels that the father abandoned him. With the clever use of language, this boy claimed a man to be his new father while marginalizing his biological father at the same time.

Labels for stepfamily members can sometimes capture a child's connection with a man even if the labels do not expressly confer father status. Herman's experience with his fourteen-year-old stepdaughter Annette illustrates this point.

[She] calls me dude. Hey dude! She calls me mister sometimes. Where she got the mister from I don't know. And she calls me Herman. I just recently noticed that she started calling me Herman. So I guess she's starting to loosen up a little bit. . . . Like I said in the beginning, I don't expect her to call me dad. If she does down the line, I'll accept it. I have no problem with that. But when she met me, she met me as—they [Annette and her brothers] met me as Mr. Herman. But I'm like—hmm— I don't like that too much. It makes me too standoffish. Mister. I noticed today she was calling me Herman. So it's like okay. Whatever she wants to call me, I'm comfortable with it.

Annette, whose biological father remains a part of her life, appears to be working through the process of getting comfortable with having Herman's fatherly presence in her life. As Annette experiments with different ways of referring to Herman, she seems to be searching for ways to express her evolving sense of being connected to Herman.

Just as Herman's and Annette's approach to language is affected by their practical circumstances and personality traits, other stepfathers and stepchildren face their own realities. Obviously the symbolic power of language is an active force in the lives of many stepfamily members. However, the name game is of little or no importance for some stepfamilies. A more pervasive aspect of stepfamily life involves the bonding process, a process sometimes linked to stepfathers' feelings about claiming stepchildren as their own.

7

CLAIMING AND BONDING

A man, woman, or child who clarifies family relationships by using particular labels implicitly says something about his or her sense of belonging
and entitlement. The discussion in chapter 6 about naming is tied to this pattern, but managing names is only a small part of a person's efforts to establish
an identity and make sense of relationship issues within a stepfamily.

In chapter 1, I described how Terry negotiated with his fiancée how
he wanted to be involved in his future stepson's life once he and she were
married. Terry spoke forcefully about his need to have the moral authority
to act in a fatherly way toward his stepson. I now expand that initial discussion about the "claiming" process where a man attempts to establish his
rights and responsibilities toward a particular child. As part of this process,
an adult man is looking to solidify his place in a child's life, sometimes trying to negotiate a legitimate place within the family, whereas the child is
looking more for a sense of belonging and support. Key to this process of
claiming is how a man and a child develop a sense that they are bonded or
connected to each other as part of a family, or that they are in a relationship that seems familylike.

DEGREE OF CONVICTION

A man can establish a foothold in a stepchild's life as part of a natural process
that unfolds casually over time, or he can be more deliberate with specific
objectives in mind. Among the men I interviewed, most felt a reasonably
strong connection to their stepchildren and felt as though they were responsible for them in numerous ways. With the perception of responsibility
came men's tendency to see and treat the stepchildren as their own.

145

However, the men varied considerably in how willing they were to lay claim to children in this way.[1]

Among the many factors that appear to contribute to the stepdads' inclination to see their stepchildren as their own, the biological father's role in the children's lives is one of the more important ones. On occasion, a stepfather can feel as though he has claimed a child even if the child's father is actively involved with the child. Eddie found himself in this situation with his eight-year-old stepdaughter.

> Sometimes I feel like I'm on the outside looking in because—sometimes I wish she was mine. I guess because we're just that close. Sometime we can just have that right chemistry. We just . . . smooth. That's the time when—that's the time I'm actually—that kin, that father, just right, because she's happy, I'm happy, everybody's happy. When everybody's happy, everybody is doing their job. I'm doing the job as a father, doing the job as a stepfather, and my wife's doing a job as mother—everybody's happy. . . . I sometimes, you know—in my heart, I feel like I'm her father. In my heart. I know in reality, I'm not but, I'm going to give her all the benefit that a father should. I'm going to make sure she gets those benefits. Even though her dad is giving them to her, she is given a little extra and I figure that extra go a long way. That holds a lot of truth.

Though Eddie recognizes that his stepdaughter is not his biologically, he has a deep emotional connection to her; he feels like a father. Interestingly, although he acknowledges that her dad provides her with benefits, Eddie feels he can supplement the father's contributions. In this type of situation, the child is likely to accrue significant benefits because the biological father is active and the stepfather respects the father's place in the child's life while simultaneously making a concerted effort to help the child as well.

Listening to Eddie talk reminded me of how I felt about my experiences with Alli and her father many years ago. I had grown to wish that Alli were my own child, though I fully recognized that her father was actively involved in her life and committed to sustaining his relationship with her. Unfortunately the on-again, off-again relationship I had with her mother limited to months the amount of time I was able to feel as though I was becoming another father figure to Alli. Nonetheless, I was awash in my commitment to express fatherly love even though Alli had an involved father who lived a few miles away. I committed myself to being there for her and her brother in all the ways typical of an involved and nurturing father.

Not surprisingly, when fathers are not around or play only a minor role, stepfathers are more likely to assert a stronger claim to their partner's child. They feel more compelled to step in and fill the void. Listen to Carl describe how he initially got involved with his stepdaughter Vicky when she was almost three.

> I just kind of let it flow as much as possible and just tried to be a person that was there, being there for Vicky and spending as much time and involving her with us as much as possible, so that she got the sense that I wasn't replacing someone or I wasn't taking her mom away, but rather adding to her life or adding something that wasn't there before or—I mean, she didn't know her dad before, so it was—I don't want to say it was an easier situation, but not knowing her dad and not knowing that she had someone there at the stage when I met Lani was—it was a little bit more easy to have Vicky come around, I guess, in our relationship together, because I think it might have been more difficult having a father there.

Carl clearly sees that his ability to connect with Vicky was fostered in part by the father's absence. Being careful not to upset Vicky by having her think that he was taking her mother away from her, Carl was able to move into Vicky's life without competing with another man for her time or loyalty.

As briefly discussed in chapter 4, Thomas dealt with his stepson's biological father, who had been largely absent from the boys' lives for a number of years until he agreed to allow his eldest son, Danny, to live with him. Thomas describes a painful experience he had with Danny several years ago during the time Danny was living at his father's house. After dropping Danny off for a weekend visit with his mom and Thomas, the father was supposed to pick up Danny on a Sunday evening and take him back to his house. However, unknown to Danny or Thomas, the biological father moved out of state over the weekend without telling anyone that he would not have Danny live with him anymore. Shortly after learning what happened from the biological father's parents (Danny's grandparents), Thomas went to Danny's room to console him and found him surrounded with family photos. As Thomas remembers, "he had hundreds of pictures, and all I could do is just talk with him. Just tell him, 'look, I know I'm not your dad. I can never fill his shoes. But if you'll allow me to be a part of your life, I'll love you like it.' And from that we have progressed to where we are today."

This was a dramatic turning point experience for Danny, as well as the rest of the family. Let's listen to the emotional account of this experience from Danny's mother's perspective.

And here's this little boy who's expecting his father to come back for him. And just up and leaves the state and doesn't even tell him. Doesn't say good-bye. Doesn't, none of that. So here's little Danny. He gets all the pictures of his real dad and he spreads them out all over his bed. And he's sitting there looking at the pictures of his real dad and boo-hoo crying. I mean, it was heartbreaking. And, I mean, I cry now just thinking of it. . . . (pause—crying) So I had to comfort him. [I: Right.] The best that I could. And then Thomas was trying to comfort him the best that he could, but here's a seven, eight-year-old little boy has basically just been abandoned by his father. No good-bye, no "I love you, son." No nothing. (crying) [I: Right.] That's very difficult. So . . . yes, he, he's had to comfort him and hug him and love him and he told him, "I know I'm not your real father, but I will love you to the best of my ability like a real father."

Asked how she felt when Thomas said this to her son, the mother reveals that it "made me love him more." So, the bonding process between Thomas and Danny that was set in motion by this unfortunate chain of events extended beyond these two and accelerated a sense of solidarity for the entire stepfamily.

In his comments about how Danny's father was largely absent from Danny's and his brother's lives, Thomas describes how he claims the boys as his own.

They're my kids. I look at them like they're my boys. I tell everybody, they're my boys. And I don't want to take nothing away from his [Danny's] dad, but I've raised them for so long now, I mean . . . you have a child in your home for the amount of time that I have, you feed them and long enough, they'll start acting and looking just like you, you know what I'm saying? They just do. They just call me, call me "dad."

Thomas's description reveals that the kids have started to take on some of his personal characteristics because they've been together so long. This type of modeling can help solidify a man's perceptions of his stepchild because he will be able to see more of himself in his child, reinforcing his identification with the child. This has been happening for Derek, who proudly shares that his two-year-old stepson Elkin "imitates everything I do, to the T. . . . His actions let me know that, one he looks up to me, and I guess he would want to be like me because of that, I think just off his actions, Elkin forces you to love him." Derek is aware that Elkin has grown more attached to him than he has to either his mother or grandmother. Consequently, this type of bonding has reinforced Derek's desire to claim Elkin as his own son.

When stepfathers notice similarities between themselves and the stepchildren, the bonds between them are often solidified. A few men mentioned similarities in their personalities and leisure interests. Kevin offers this assessment of this stepson.

> As I've gotten to know Trevor it's amazing how much he's like me, for not being my own child. We're of a kindred spirit. We're both talkative. We both have rich imaginations. I daydream when I'm bored. . . . I'll imagine something that I've been thinking about or something that would be cool or something that sparked my interest. . . . He does the same thing. That's what's causing him problems in school.

Because Kevin has come to know Trevor better over time, he is able to understand him more clearly and identify with him. This makes it much easier for Kevin to empathize with Trevor and accept him. Other men found that they related to stepchildren, primarily boys, because of their mutual love of sports. Terry, an avid multisport athlete since he was a child, describes how he and his stepson Zack "immediately hit it off" because Zack is "a little jock, very very sports-athletic." Their mutual interest in sports, especially baseball, was a convenient way for them to bond ever since Terry first started to visit Zack's mother. Their love of sports has provided them with countless opportunities to be together and solidify their bond. Talking about how he incorporated himself into Zack's life early on, Terry says, "Just kind of going out and playing ball, playing basketball, playing baseball. He always had a ball in his hand. He still does. It was very easy for me because I did too growing up. Lived with one, slept with one. It was really easy to just come over and have a few minutes and go out and shoot some basketballs, throw some baseballs—then come in and say okay, I'm going to spend some time with mom now. He'd be cool with it."

Terry's description of his involvement with Zack these past four years represents an ideal case in which a man and a boy click almost immediately. Their relationship has continued to deepen without experiencing any significant detours. All stepfathers would like to be lucky enough to share a story similar to Terry's about the first time he spent the night with Zack's mother.

> I didn't know how he was going to deal with it. The next morning he came in and climbed into bed with me with a cup of coffee. He handed me a cup of coffee and then wrapped his arms around me and hugged me. That was the first morning. I was like—wow! Wow! So it couldn't have been any smoother of a transition than you could ever

ask for. There was no competition. I didn't know if he was going to be jealous over me, with his mom—stealing her from him or whatever. It was nothing like that. He just wanted a father figure and I guess he saw me as one, as a potential one for him, because I worked for him. I fit.

The stepfathers' personalities appear to play a role in the way they orient themselves toward stepchildren. Herman provides a useful example. I learned from my lengthy interview with him that he is a self-proclaimed "take-charge" kind of guy who has traditional views about a man's place in a household and is committed to helping children lead healthy lives. When it comes to his stepdaughter's life, he makes it clear that he wants to take, and has taken, an active role in parenting her. Herman, reenacting what he has told his stepdaughter on one occasion, says,

> I expect something from you now. I'm not saying everybody else didn't expect something from you before, but I have expectations and I expect good grades, good behavior, and I expect a future out of you, because *you belong to me now.* So at this point, we're going to start doing everything that we should in order to get you to where you need to be.

Obviously Herman's choice of words, "you belong to me now," signals a strong paternalistic approach: Herman sees himself as being in charge of his new family. The content of the interview, as well as my observations of Herman's interactions with his stepdaughter thereafter, indicated that he had assumed responsibility for this child and that she was at ease with him. With his own words he conveys the notion that he is invested in this young girl's life in a fatherly way.

> I've got to admit, I love her, man, you know. She's my daughter. When I introduce her, I don't introduce her as my stepdaughter, because I didn't step on her. You see what I'm saying? I introduce her "This is my daughter." . . . So it's not like she's not a part of me, just because she's not a part of me. She's a part of me. I'd go crazy if something happened to her. Even though we've only been married for six months, we've been together for umpteen years [actually four]. I'm proud of the little girl. I want the best for her, because I don't have a daughter [he has one son], and I don't plan on making any more kids, either. You see? I want the best for her and I want her to have—see my son lives with his mother.

COMPARING CHILDREN

Just as Herman has a biological son of his own who provides him with a benchmark to judge his paternal commitments, Derek compares his relationship with his resident stepson with his biological children, who live elsewhere with two different mothers. He asserts that he has a closer bond with his stepson, Elkin, than his own children because he has been with Elkin on a daily basis. This contact provides Derek with more opportunities to experience the feelings of being a proud father. He finds it easier to take the credit or the blame for Elkin's behavior because he feels he plays a bigger role in shaping his behavior. Even though he goes to great lengths to clarify that he loves all of his children, he is willing to acknowledge that his bond is stronger with Elkin because of the daily contact and a sense of being held accountable for his behavior.

Brandon and Robby provide further evidence that some stepfathers can feel as close to their stepchildren as they do their own children.[2] Again, having kids of their own gives these men a practical way to measure the intensity of their feelings.[3] Asked if he feels differently toward his two stepchildren than his own child, Brandon replies,

> I really don't. I mean, I thought initially when we first, we all moved in together that maybe—I was a little worried, how am I going to feel toward them? But now I've—I mean, I consider them my kids even though I'm not the biological father. I don't really try to step in to take—for them to call me dad or anything like that—but I don't really see them as any different. I mean . . . I'll do my best to protect them and treat them fairly. I don't really see a difference.

He adds that he feels he can "love" his stepchildren as well as his son in all aspects. Meanwhile, Robby begins to describe his involvement with and feelings for his stepchildren by comparing the way he treats them to how he is with his own daughter.

> If they need a new pair of shoes, we [he and his wife] go out and buy them a new pair of shoes, I mean, I know they need clothes on their back, they need school supplies, you know this, that, I buy them things if I have five dollars in my pocket and Tony wants to stop by McDonald's, we'll stop and I'll buy him lunch or whatever. I don't . . . if it was my own daughter, I'd do her the same way and, I mean, I don't, I spare no expense, it's like having my own kids. To me, they are mine, when they're with me they are mine. So I, I treat them just like I would my

own daughter, buying them things and whatever. If I don't feel they need that, then no they're not going to get that.

Like Brandon, Robby also describes the intensity of his feelings for his stepchildren by comparing them to how he feels toward his own child.

> I know, biologically they are not mine. But I feel, I love those two kids just like I love my biological daughter. And I would do anything for them. . . . I am the father figure in their life. Other people around us will tell you that I am the father figure in their life. . . . In the back of my mind I know that I am not their dad. But when Brett's [biological father] around and he says something to them, I don't say a word because I know that's their dad. I want to see them do well; I know they're great kids; they are very smart. I know they need discipline like every kid does. I know it's my job to be there at their school functions; whatever they got going on, I know it's my job to be there. And I enjoy being there for the kids. I love these two little kids, and I would not trade them for anything. We got a great relationship.

Although some of the stepfathers have strong convictions that they are able to love and bond with stepchildren in a manner similar to what they experience with their own kids, some feel this is not the case. Of particular interest is the subtle difference that a few men speak about. By all accounts, forty-two-year-old Ray presents himself as someone who dearly loves his two stepdaughters and biological daughter. Despite his insistence that he loves them each dearly, he admits that the

> only difference is that deep, deep, deep empathetic communication. The telepathy. I can feel what my daughter—whatever she's doing, even if she's in the next room. I can feel what's going through her mind. Lindsey [four-year-old stepchild] I can see, but like I said, it's just not that easy with stepchildren. There is like a little bit of a tension. They know. They're aware. There's questions. I know because I was adopted, so I understand there's just a certain separation that's there.

Thus Ray relies on his firsthand experience as an adopted child to form his understanding of what he believes to be a real, though not particularly significant, difference in how he relates to his stepchildren and biological child.

In my interview with Rodney, the thirty-seven-year-old stepfather of two, I pointedly asked him if he had ever thought about whether he could love his stepchildren as much as his biological children. His reply, "Yes and no. Yes I can—well physically and emotionally yes, but there's another kind of love that's—I call it blood love, that goes beyond a stepchild situation. So there is a difference from my point of view, but it's not something that can be displayed." With both Ray and Rodney, there is something extra that goes along with having a biological child that can't be duplicated with a stepchild. In a practical sense, the fact that it cannot be duplicated may not mean much. As Rodney suggests, it's not something that is "displayed." In some ways it may not be present in the way a stepfather, at least Rodney, interacts with his children—biological or step. For Ray, the telepathy he feels he has with his biological daughter is not necessarily something that has much, if any, impact on the way he treats his children either. It's just something that's part of a communication link that resides "deep, deep, deep" inside.

Though it was not always apparent, it seems that how a mother feels about and treats the stepfather's biological child influences his tendency to feel as strongly about a stepchild as he does a biological child. Not surprisingly, a stepfather who sees his partner acting lovingly toward his child may consciously or unconsciously reciprocate and open himself up to her child. As was the case with some of my participants, when partners each have one or more children they can commit themselves to treat all the children the same. This works fine in many instances, but practical difficulties arise when a stepfather's child spends only short periods of time with him and the man's stepfamily. Add to this the fairly consistent finding documented in other research that stepmothers, when compared to stepfathers, struggle more with their relationships with stepchildren.[4]

Whereas some stepdads can use their own children as a point of reference for their feelings toward stepchildren, many stepdads do not have this option. Although he is not a father, Carl, age thirty, is quick to assert his powerful feelings for his stepchild.

> I wanted a child biologically, but now it just seems that there's no need for it because I have everything I want and could ever possibly imagine having in a nonbiological child. I don't see Vicky as anything but my child. I don't classify her as my blood or not my blood. I see her as my child without that kind of classification.

Similarly, fifty-year-old Randy, another stepdad who has no children of his own, explains his relationship to his stepson this way.

> I don't think I can love Jamie any more if I really was his father, than I do right now. And maybe in some ways, maybe even more because ours is simply based on trust. I don't have any stickers all over him—you're

my son. . . . It's basically, hey, we're together and if you want to stick around, I'll stick with you type of thing. In some ways—like I said, I got to earn it every day.

Randy highlights a key aspect of evaluating stepdads' voluntary involvement with their children. Because most stepdads have no legal claim to their stepchildren, they must rely on others to grant them permission to be involved. From Randy's point of view as a stepdad, he has to "earn" his place in his stepson's heart. Nothing is given, as is often thought to be the case with birth parents. Randy, and others like him, develops his sense of being in the mix of a child's life through his everyday involvement.

Understanding the scope and depth of their feelings is probably easier for men if they have children of their own, especially children with whom they've been involved. Having biological children living in the house or visiting on a regular basis may also enhance men's ability to develop a clearer sense of whether the stepchildren view them as fathers. Vern, a forty-eight-year-old father of three teenage sons, was such a man. He was an involved father while he was married and worked to stay active with his boys after his divorce. In the past few years he has remarried and has taken on the responsibility of being a stepfather to two teenage boys. He feels his experiences have taught him a lot.

> My understanding of stepparenting has been, first of all—you have no standing as you come into this, you know, with your biological children you're father, from the get-go. You have standing. But with stepchildren you have no standing. You have to earn all your merits with them. . . . I think that the partner who brings the children into the relationship has to have a very clear sense of who we all are here. My guess is that there are a lot who don't. I would think that to be successful at it, it has to be very clearly and very specifically negotiated as to who gets what and who says what. . . . But I think the single most important thing to realize is that a stepparent comes into that particular kind of relationship having to earn the stripes, having to—nothing is given. I don't know—that's with the older ones. When they're little, I'm sure it would be very different.

Vern concludes his remarks with an important observation about the ages of the stepchildren when the stepfather enters their lives. Although older kids are more likely to require their stepfathers to "earn the stripes," children who are at least two years of age can make these kinds of demands on stepfathers. But, generally speaking, stepfathers are likely to have a better chance of having children develop an emotional attachment to them if the children are infants or toddlers when they first get involved, especially if the biological father has little or no influence.[5] This attachment will pave the way for stepchildren to accept stepfathers as having a legitimate role as an authority figure in their lives. Mothers, meanwhile, can require stepfathers to prove themselves regardless of the children's ages.

ADOPTION

A relatively small percentage of stepfathers solidify their sense of ownership by institutionalizing it through the legal system.[6] Men who adopt their stepchildren have another resource to help them feel that a child belongs to them. This legal ritual can clarify and solidify men's feelings for their stepchildren. In some cases, men may not view the children as stepchildren at all. Doug, for example, adopted his wife's son when the boy was about three. Like a few of my participants, Doug placed a stipulation on his marriage. In his words:

> I told her, I'll marry you, but that's my son legally. No step involved, nothing like that. That's my son. She said, "Fine; I don't see anything wrong with that." So that's when she went back to him [biological father] and said she don't want any alimony, child support, nothing. Just want you out of the picture. He signed the papers; he said no problem. I won't cause any trouble. So when the papers came back, they just simply read my name, didn't say stepfather or nothing else.

Doug's aversion toward being perceived as a stepfather stemmed from his own negative childhood experience growing up in a stepfamily where he felt uncomfortable with his stepmother and stepsiblings. Though the other men appeared to be less uncomfortable using the "stepfather" term during the interview than Doug was, some clearly did not base their self-perception on it, especially those who had formally adopted a child or children. "Stepfather" may be the term of choice that captures men's experiences accurately for a period of time, but some men's feelings evolve to the point where it does not adequately capture their current sentiments even though it may make sense from a sociological point of view.

Another man who became a stepdad through marriage, thirty-two-year-old Kevin, officially adopted his seven-year-old stepson just a couple of months prior to the interview. Thus the powerful images of how this process affected him were fresh in his mind.

> I don't know why, but I did notice a change when the adoption went through. But just a genuine affection I felt for him really for the first time, it seems like. Not for the first time, not affection—but just a real natural love feeling for him, like he was mine, my own. . . . I don't know what it was. Just something changed—it became—it's hard to explain why—I've thought about it since then—just why—and maybe it was there and it didn't dawn on me at the time, but that day, in fact, that night after everybody was gone, Trevor was still getting used to calling me dad. I mean, he's called me Kevin since we met and the last month, the last two weeks really, I don't think he's called me Kevin once. He's called me dad and daddy.

As Kevin describes it, there was a link between the adoption and Trevor calling him "dad." Prior to the adoption, Trevor had been calling him by his first name. Apparently the adoption experience helped Kevin see Trevor more along the lines that he saw his own son. With pleasure I watched Kevin and Trevor interact for about thirty minutes while they waited for Trevor's mother to complete her interview in another room. It seemed clear to me that both had defined their relationship as father–son and were comfortable with the arrangement.

Whereas Kevin had already experienced the adoption process, Derek was actively considering how he could adopt his partner's two-year-old boy. He wanted to ensure that the boy would be entitled to an inheritance from the businesses he planned on launching in the next several months.

> I would like to sit down and talk to his father. I would like to get custody of him, and adopt him, so he would have to sign over his parental rights. But I would also let him know that he is always welcome to see Elkin. The only reason I'm doing it is because of my businesses that I'm starting, I'm leaving them with my kids. Elkin is my child in my eyes. So I wouldn't want to leave him out, so he would have my last name.

Derek's interest in claiming his stepson as his own is tied to his financial considerations. The issue relevant to Derek's concerns will become increasingly important as more and more children are raised in households with stepparents. Figuring out who is entitled to what resources when parents die will become increasingly complex as stepfamilies proliferate.

IDENTITY TRANSITIONS

Claiming a particular child as his own often becomes an established part of a man's sense of self, at least while he is romantically involved with the child's mother. However, a man's certainty about claiming a stepchild may fluctuate while he is still involved with the mother. Listen to one mother describe her husband Stephen's occasionally shifting role in the life of her fourteen-year-old twins.

> Only a few times has he said, when he's really gotten mad and he's really mad at them—is like, they're not even my daughters! They're your daughters, you go handle it. So I'm just like . . . don't let them hear you say that. So I don't know why the stepparent has to feel that way. Like in the sense, with Robert [her first husband], he knew he was the stepparent but he took over as the father image and the father role. I am the father. Stephen I don't think has totally done that with Danielle and Chrissy.

Clearly men's views on claiming their children are in many ways tied to their sense of feeling connected to them. The men commented frequently about their feelings of being bonded to their stepchildren and the circumstances that affected their feelings.[7] Although most did not recognize specific turning points[8] in their relationships with their stepchildren, a few stepdads highlighted specific instances when they realized that they had a strong connection to their stepchildren. Doug, for instance, recalls how he responded a number of years ago when he thought that his young stepson was drowning in a river. Despite Doug's extreme fear of being in water above his neck, he rushed to the edge and was prepared to get into the deep water, when he learned that it was only a prank. Doug has vivid memories of turning and walking up the riverbank, where he "lost it" and began to cry. At that point he realized that he had established a bond with the boy, whether it was reciprocated or not.

For Randy, the key moment occurred one afternoon shortly after he picked up his partner's child from day care. As Randy was driving he came upon a car accident. He describes the experience this way.

> I pulled my car across traffic so you know, people wouldn't be running into the people lying in the streets. And the next thing I know we're surrounded by fire trucks and police cars and stuff like this. We're more or less caught in this situation. And at first this is exciting. But then it gets scary. And up to that point, it'd been more like, that [I] was okay

to play with, but I wasn't okay for, if he wanted comforting or he wanted to feel secure—it was, that still mama's ballpark, you know. And it still is for a lot of—but he, that day, decided it was okay to crawl in my arms and be okay. And that was, in a way, was a big, big point.

With this experience, Randy feels that the small boy he had grown to see in a fatherly way had suddenly taken a huge step forward in being able to seek and accept his fatherly love. Though different in many ways, the turning points Randy and Doug experienced were both prompted by a crisis situation.

Some turning points result from less dramatic events. For example, Eddie recalls the first time he went to pick up his stepdaughter from school because her mother was working late. Eddie's fears about how she was going to feel seeing him at the school were put to rest when she said, "Oh goody!" on learning that he was there to pick her up. After spending quality one-on-one time with her as they went home, Eddie came to realize how exciting it was for him to see her and to know that she enjoyed spending time with him. His thoughts at the time were "it's going to be all right."

Although some of my participants can point to specific events as turning point experiences, most feel that their relationship with their stepchildren simply evolved over time. By spending time with their stepchildren and learning about them, most of the stepfathers came to appreciate and grow fond of them. Of course, the kids' response to them, as well as the mother's involvement, can move this process along or slow it down. Kevin, for example, prior to adopting his stepson struggled to teach himself to be patient with Trevor's "stubborn" personality. It took Kevin a while, particularly because Trevor was different from his other son, but he eventually came to realize that Trevor's being "tenacious" was a good quality that could be "molded and pushed in the right direction." Once Kevin became more accepting of Trevor's unique personality, he was able to feel more attached to him. Trevor's mother played a significant role in getting Kevin to realize that Trevor was different from his own son and needed to be dealt with accordingly.

Most of the men commented on ways that remind them how connected they feel to their stepchildren. Tim talks about the "day-to-day type of living" experiences that highlight his feelings. He mentions how it is "cool" that the kids have begun to feel more comfortable holding his hand and that on some occasions they reach out for his hand when they're out in public. Another wonderful experience for him is being dropped off at work and having his stepdaughters kiss him good-bye and ask for a hug. "I mean it's amazing the power a child has over your feelings in something like that, and it really makes a big difference." In his case, the big difference is that it helps him feel as though he wants to treat these young girls in a fatherly way even though he is not their biological father. Despite his apparent fondness for his stepdaughters, his fiancée, Melanie, struggles with what she perceives to be his limited connection to them. "I wonder on a constant, not constant, but on a daily basis if he's ever going to feel as close to them as I do. Because you can see that there's something, there's an emotion there that you get from being a child's birth parent, I guess. It's more there with Teresa, because he was around from the time she was a baby." Melanie's concerns illustrate that partners may see the depth of a stepfather–stepchild relationship from different vantage points. Tim admits that the connection may not be as strong as he would like, but Melanie seems to view it as being less than it really is. In addition, she draws attention to the potential significance of bonding with a child at a very young age. Melanie reasons that if a stepfather gets involved with a stepchild as a baby, there's a better chance for him to bond to the child as his own.

MINDFULNESS

One sign that is often a powerful indicator of a man's immersion in his identity as a stepfather is his mindfulness of his stepchild.[9] This mindfulness, both in degree and type, captures a stepfather's attentiveness to a child's likes, dislikes, moods, needs, and the times they've shared together. Although being aware of the stepchild means that a man must have relevant ideas lodged in his long-term memory, mindfulness in a practical sense refers to the man's active consciousness at specific times. A stepfather may have images about his stepchild packed away in his mind but not think much about the child from day to day, whereas another stepfather may think constantly about his stepchild even when the two are not together. Other dimensions of this mental imaging include what kind of thoughts a stepfather has about his stepchild, the impetus and circumstances associated with those thoughts, and the depth and accuracy of men's reflections. One reason to pay attention to this kind of imaging is that it offers clues about how involved a stepfather is in his stepchild's life and the extent to which he has claimed the child as his own.

Even though this mental imagining can occur with or without the child's presence, thinking frequently about a child in the child's absence probably indicates that the stepfather is attentive to the child when they are together. In the course of my interviews, I often asked the stepfathers what kinds of thoughts they had about their stepchild when they were away from each other and how often they had them. Though some men seldom think about their stepchild outside his or her company, some indicate that they spend a lot of time in this type of thinking.

> I would say pretty much hourly at least. . . . He's pretty much there right when I'm thinking about people I'm thinking about Mason. [Jackson, 39]

> Quite a bit. Like, especially if I'm out someplace. [Landen, 27]

> I really do think about them a lot. I call during the day, if I'm working late . . . and see what they're doing. [Brandon, 30]

> I think about him a lot. It's like when I come to work every day, I'm wondering what he's doing in school, how he's doing in school? It's kind of like worry, worry, worry. [Emmit, 28]

The kinds of thoughts stepfathers have about their stepchildren are similar to those of biological fathers: what they're doing or feeling at the moment, what types of toys they might like, what can be done to improve a behavior or school problem, memories of playful activities, and visions of future experiences. As I was winding down one of my interviews with Eddie, a stepfather who thought about his eight-year-old stepdaughter "all the time," I learned about his heartwarming concern for his stepdaughter's emotional state. His mission for the day: think about how he can cheer her up.

> Right now she had a bad day because it was supposed to be a mothers–daughters day. . . . I'm the only one got the truck, so my wife had to take the time off. She volunteered to take time off to help the kids' grandmother move her stuff out of their house, so it was supposed to be a mommy–daughter day so I've got to think of some kind of way to, you know, not make her [stepdaughter] feel so bad. I'll take her a little bunch of flowers home. She'll like that.

Based on my entire interview with Eddie, my impression is that Eddie's sentiment is not an isolated expression. His comment is consistent with his more general sensitivity to his stepdaughter's moods. Eddie asserts that he is able to "tell when she's sad or if she don't get enough sleep." This type of awareness is essential for a stepfather to develop and sustain a meaningful bond with his stepchild based on a nurturing model of fathering.

Sustaining active mental images of a stepchild is sometimes tied to a practical strategy. For example, Carl, despite his demanding job, makes a conscious effort to think about his stepdaughter while at work. Asked about how often he thinks about Vicky when he's not with her, Carl replies,

> I have a lot of pictures of her on my desk. As much as I can. It's hard when you're in the middle of work and people are asking you and telling you that your computer's down and you're focusing on those problems and issues. But I try and think of her as much as possible. . . . It's going to be all that much more because we just got a digital camera. . . . I put them up on a web page [that he built].

Carl's technical computer skills and resources provide him with the means to stay grounded in his family life and strengthen his bond with Vicky by allowing her to become a vital part of his everyday life. Although fathers and stepfathers alike may become more active in the area of keeping family albums now that this process is tied to the computer age, the impetus for thinking about a child need not be tied to photographs and computer files. Ray, for example, keeps it simple, saying, "I have a whole giant warehouse of stored tapes in my mind of experiences that I can pull out and play any time and watch, or I can pull her face up in my head and I can see her and her little . . . funny, mischievous smile."

Carl's and Ray's comments highlight the value of stepfathers developing shared and pleasant memories involving their stepchildren. The emotional bonds that emerge from these encounters can strengthen men's sense of being involved with stepchildren in a fatherly way and provide them with a unique opportunity for building cultural capital.[10] Over time, as stepfathers accumulate memories of their stepchildren, they will have more events to recall. Even memories of unpleasant events can pave the way for stepfathers to spend more time pondering their stepchildren. Whether it's thoughts about fixing problems, addressing needs, or reminiscing about wonderful adventures, stepfathers have the means to reflect on their stepchildren in ways that either reflect or affect the kind of bond they have with them.

SEXUALITY AND GENDER

Arriving at that mental and emotional space of feeling comfortable with a stepfather identity is part of a process often subject to ebbs and flows. My participants describe events, discussions, or moments where they sometimes become keenly aware that they are not biologically related to a particular child. Because many of these experiences can be interpreted in the context of men fathering in a private or public context, I talk about these issues more fully in the next chapter. For now, I focus on sexuality issues because numerous stepfathers grapple with concerns related to this topic when they interact with teenage girls. Using Herman's own words, I have already portrayed his strong fatherly commitment to his fourteen-year-old stepdaughter Annette. I turn again to Herman, this time to provide an intimate account of how he struggles to express physical affection to Annette precisely because she is a teenage girl. His comments speak volumes about the difficulties stepfathers often face, as men, when they try to bond with teenage stepdaughters, especially those whom they did not know as young children. Prefacing his comments about sexuality with a sample of conversations he has with himself, he attempts to figure out the borders of how he should interact with Annette.

> Now, Herman, don't forget now. Don't forget, she's not really your daughter. But she is your daughter. So I have to catch myself. How do I handle this? . . . She doesn't know it, but she's teaching me a lot. . . . I'm dealing with—well, if it was my daughter. . . . I'm afraid and I don't think she'll ever do this, but I'm afraid that she could say something, whether it's true or not, and there I am. Whew! And I don't want that. [I: Have you ever talked to Anna [Annette's mother]?] About my fear? [I: Yes.] I haven't said anything to Anna about it. But it's not my fear of Annette, it's my fear of society, encompassing Annette. You see? So I do have a fear. I've got to admit that, and I'm like—and I'm sure if I ever, whenever I get over that, I'm going to feel—you see, I feel uneasy hugging her in public. When it comes down on me, man, it's like—look over there, aren't you proud of her? And I'm like yeah—I want to show love but it's like—nahhh—don't do that. And I'm sure we'll both benefit from it because I'll get the pleasure of holding her, and she'll get the pleasure of being held. I'm like, nahhh—don't do that. You know what I'm saying? Because I look around and I see people and it's like—oooh, look at him over there hugging that young girl, like—I mean, we're a sick society of people. We never think of the positive things that come out, we always think of the negative, and it's not a good thing.

Herman's sensitivity to these kinds of issues, as well as his desire to figure out the borders of what is acceptable, is heightened by his experiences with his nieces, as well as the young girls he used to interact with in his previous job as an adolescent counselor for juveniles. Speaking of the young girls he dealt with as a counselor, he says:

> They could come to me and they could sit there. And I didn't know
> they wanted me to hug them. I'm not talking physically, sexually hug.
> They wanted an adult-to-child hug, a male-to-female, adult-to-child
> hug—they wanted to be loved. Man, I could feel that. They just—man
> I could just feel them longing for a positive adult in their lives. A posi-
> tive male adult that would just hug them.

Given his work experience and his interpretation of young girls' needs,
Herman is particularly mindful of his involvement with Annette. Despite
his genuine interest in providing Annette with a strong but nurturing male
adult presence in her life, Herman continues to feel frustrated by the difficulty of accomplishing that through physical display. Although he admits
that he is now "starting to hug her and kiss on her," he's still "a little
squeamish about it." And apparently he is not showing that type of physical affection in public.

Though I only spoke with a few men who entered the lives of stepdaughters when the girls were teenagers, my impression is that Herman is
not alone in his struggle to navigate the awkwardness of expressing physical intimacy with a stepdaughter.[11] It is here, in the relationship a stepfather
has with his teenage stepdaughter, that the gendered nature of stepparenting is most visible for a man. Prevailing social expectations and suspicions
about male sexuality means that individual stepfathers are likely to face
unique challenges.

Some face these challenges in silence, others do not. Unlike Herman,
John made a point of speaking with the mother of his teenage stepdaughter fairly early on about how he could manage any awkwardness or tension
related to physical intimacy. John and his wife both acknowledge that those
conversations were helpful in laying the foundation for John to have a
warm relationship, including hugs, with his stepdaughter, Harmony. John
also discussed these matters later on with Harmony, saying in effect, "I
don't want you to be creeped out with me hugging you. But I want more
of the relationship. I don't want to be just the guy that married your
mother."

Throughout the three years they've known one another, John has
taken the time to reflect on and wrestle with these matters in his own mind.
He continues to be vigilant about sustaining an affectionate relationship that
has "enough distance." His thoughts have been shaped considerably from
what he learned about his father pulling away from John's sister when she
was a teenager, and the pain she felt as a result. Johns summarizes his take
on his situation with Harmony.

But even though Harmony is my stepdaughter, I didn't want to exclude her from my life because she had sexuality or other people would think. But I do know there is an appropriate way to hug a girl that age whether in public or in the house. I don't touch her anywhere but on the shoulder blades, a real nice hug. I don't get, I don't pet her or anything; I don't do any stimulating physical action. So that's one thing. And I do take that to heart because I don't want her to think I'm a weirdo or a sicko. And when I've kissed her it's only been on the forehead or the cheek; it's never kissed her on the mouth or anything. And I don't think it's appropriate. She's not my real daughter so I don't think that's appropriate. Maybe if it was my real daughter, a light kiss maybe.

John's detailed analysis shows that he appreciates the subtle details of how his interactions with Harmony can affect her perceptions of him and her ability to feel comfortable with him. He's also aware of how his relatively young age affected Harmony's initial reaction to having him hug her. "She said that originally she didn't give me hugs because I was so young. There were guys my age hitting on her. She said that it felt a little weird because it wasn't like hugging her dad." With time, Harmony grew increasingly comfortable with John's affectionate overtures, allowing them to establish a safe place to express their fondness for each other.

Ironically, one of the "oddest thing[s]" for John having to do with Harmony and sexuality has been figuring out how to discourage her from wearing revealing clothes in public. Though he struggled with this a great deal before, the evolution of his relationship with Harmony has enabled him to feel more comfortable asking her to change her clothes when he feels she's wearing something inappropriate.

Although concerns about sexuality issues may be most visible when adolescent stepchildren are involved, issues also may arise with younger girls. For example, Melanie, a mother of three preadolescent girls, hints that she worries a bit because she sees her fiancée Tim looking at "twelve-year-old girls" who wear revealing clothes. Mimicking what she says to him, Melanie shares, "'You're raising my baby girls and you're looking at these teenage girls—what is wrong with you?'" She tries to make sense of his behavior by noting, "but I think that's kind of, I think that's a guy thing. I think they all do that. . . . But it just—sometimes that bothers me. You know, he's raising my baby girls and he's looking at these girls that look like eighteen years old and—I don't know. That kind of bothers me and I'm afraid that or worry sometimes that I might not be good enough and not be pretty enough and whatever." So, in addition to her concerns that Tim's proclivity to look at young girls as sexual objects might somehow spill over into his interactions with her daughters, Melanie is concerned about what Tim's behavior says about his level of interest in her.

Gender, and its role in the way men parent, may be most obvious for stepfathers interacting with young stepdaughters, but gendered aspects of parenting can also surface when stepfathers interact with stepsons. In one scenario, the issue is not inappropriate sexual touching but the homophobic norms that often guide men's interactions with one another. William implicitly picks up on this point as he responds to my question about whether he and his stepsons show affection to one another. "Oh yeah. There's a genuine love there. But I don't, it's just hard for guys to, I don't know to express that kind of love to one another. It's just hard. But we know it's there. It's a common felt feeling." William's understanding that it's "hard for guys" to "express that kind of love" is implicitly grounded in the prevailing gendered belief that interpersonal physical intimacy between males is undesirable and suggests homosexual tendencies. This view, as it relates to stepsons or sons, is probably more entrenched among stepfathers than biological fathers for two main reasons. First, stepfathers typically enter a stepson's life after he has already moved beyond the toddler years when spontaneous physical affection is common and accepted even among men with traditional views of masculinity. Second, stepfathers lack the genetic tie to their stepson that would help legitimize physical affection in some instances, even among older children. Stepfathers can, of course, find a way to become physically affectionate with a stepson, but to do so they will often travel down a path other than the one of least resistance.

STEPCHILD'S ROLE

Some of the stepfathers are more reserved in how they look at stepchildren as their own because the stepchildren have resisted; they have not opened up to them fully.[12] This reluctance affected some stepfathers and curtailed how deeply they could internalize their identity of a man acting in a fatherly way toward specific stepchildren. Despite their desire to act in a fatherly way, some stepfathers were keenly aware of a child's effort to sustain borders, making sure that stepfathers never felt like a real father. These efforts had the effect of accentuating the stepfathers' ambiguous and sometimes precarious place in a child's life. For instance, Harry is fully aware that he has struggled with his stepdaughter Kelly who, he feels, "never really opened up" despite his efforts to make her feel comfortable. A product of a stepfamily himself, Harry describes his sensitivity to the issues of having stepparents and how he has tried to reach out to Kelly. As he describes the situation, "Kelly has never been very close with me and it's not at all like my two other children [more recent biological children to Kelly's mother]. She likes the idea of having a dad, but she doesn't really want the personal relationship that comes with it. It's a matter of appearance I think more than anything else for her." For Kelly, then, it has been important to fit in with her friends and having a dad has allowed her to do this more easily. But it is apparent, from both Harry's comments and his wife's separate comments, that Kelly has held back. By not investing fully in her role as daughter, Kelly has reinforced Harry's awareness of the borders restricting his ability to feel a deeper bond to Kelly as her stepfather.

Mason, the five-year-old son of Jackson's fiancée, provides another example of how a child, a boy in this case, manages the ways and extent to which he identifies a man as having a fatherly presence in his life. Although Mason experimented with calling Jackson "daddy" for several weeks a number of months ago, he has not used that language recently. Nonetheless, Mason's unique play behavior with Jackson suggests that he may be trying to feel more secure about having Jackson in his life, perhaps as a father figure. According to Jackson, Mason

> does a lot of play games where "Jackson, you're the daddy, I'm the honey and mommy is the whatever." He puts us all into little roles and then he acts out a play game that way. He does actually have a very interesting recurring play game where he is a puppy at a pet store and I'm the person who's going to buy the puppy. And he does this eight days a week, anywhere we are. He says "Jackson, let's play Mitten," which is what he names his puppy, so let's do that. First time I did that I wasn't sure what was going on, where he was going with it, but as he's repeated it, it's just a little bit—I think it's a security thing and hoping that—it's a fun thing too for him, obviously. He loves to play it. But that's one of the more interesting recurring games that he and I play together.

At the time of the interview, Mason had not yet spontaneously said anything about how his life would change when his mother and Jackson married the following month. But the couple has talked to Mason in order to help him understand that there are different types of families.

> One thing we did do, is we read to him a book on various types of families. Some families have one daddy, some families have one mommy, some families have two mommies, some families have two daddies, some families have a grandma and a mommy, or a grandpa and a

mommy. Then we went into the stepfather thing. And about a week later, Helena said yeah, Jackson's like a stepdaddy to you, when he was asking about other types of families, and Mason says, "No, he's not a stepdaddy yet. You have to wait until you're married." So he had already put that in order. He's not a stepdaddy yet. I don't know what that really means in his mind.

Though his perceptions may not be crystal clear, Mason appears to have some sense of the importance of marriage as a way of defining people's roles. I assumed that once Jackson married Mason's mother, Mason would feel that Jackson had carved out a more permanent place in his family circle. When I contacted Jackson about eleven months after we first spoke (ten months after Jackson married Mason's mom) to ask him to review what I had written about him, he shared, "The puppy game has changed! It's now a game of partnership—I'm Rally, the dog who can do anything." It seems that Mason is indeed growing more comfortable with his new life and Jackson's role in it.

The situations that Harry and Kelly, as well as Jackson and Mason, find themselves in are vivid reminders that the implications of stepfathering do not begin and end with stepfathers. Stepdads' experiences are intimately connected to children, birth mothers, and others outside the family dance. In addition, stepfathers are not born, they are made. Consequently, to understand stepfathering we must consider men's evolving life histories while recognizing the stepfathering experience as being part of a larger, multifaceted familial and social process.

8

FATHERING VISIONS, PHILOSOPHY, AND CONTEXT

When a stepdad develops ownership feelings toward a stepchild, when he bonds with a stepchild, and when he invests time and energy into acting in a fatherly way, he does so as a person in process. In other words, his life has a past, present, and future dimension to it. When pieced together, these dimensions affect the way he sees and presents himself in relation to a stepchild. How he reflects and assigns meanings to his past experiences, makes sense of and negotiates his current situation, and anticipates what lies ahead are dynamic aspects of a man's life journey and experiences with stepfatherhood.

To gain this view of men, it is useful to consider how their lives are colored by their life histories as men who are husbands, boyfriends, sons, fathers, stepfathers, and uncles. These family and relationship experiences often prompt men to consider if they want to have children of their own or are willing to be involved with someone else's children in a fatherly way.

Throughout their lives, as they move through adolescence to young adulthood and then beyond, men develop feelings and opinions about the way they were raised. Some men are disappointed, some grateful, and some have mixed reactions. Whatever their perceptions, men's feelings about their upbringing can affect their desire to have their own children. Recollections about their childhood can also shape men's ideas about how they want to raise their own children. They may ask themselves: Do I want to duplicate the way my parents raised me? How can I modify their parenting style? These questions may surface whether men are involved with their own offspring or dealing with the opportunities and challenges associated with parenting stepchildren.

Thinking about a stepfather's life as being in process suggests the three fathering trajectories introduced in chapter 2. These include a man's personal sentiments about being a father, his hands-on experiences with particular children, and his relationship with a child's mother. Each of these often overlapping and dynamic paths is relevant to a man's life as a stepfather. Some of the activity associated with these paths occurs inside a stepfather's mind as he contemplates aspects of fathering in a general way, independent of any specific child. A lot also unfolds as the man interacts with and thinks about a specific child and the child's mother—the man's romantic partner. Friends, relatives, coworkers, and others outside the family dance can shape a man's journey along any of these three paths. A man's intention to procreate and his desire to be involved with his own child or stepchild can fluctuate over time due to changes in a man's relationships, work, health, legal standing, religious beliefs, and other circumstances that affect his self-image, perspective on life, and access to key resources.[1]

Men who enact stepfather roles represent a diverse set of life histories and experiences. Once stepfathers arrive on the scene, there are numerous types of arrangements they may have to manage in order to develop and sustain relationships with their partner's children. These arrangements will depend on various factors: the number of stepchildren, the ages of the stepchildren, whether the biological father is active or inactive, and whether the stepchildren have different fathers. Family members' personalities and legal arrangements associated with child custody, visitation, and child support will also shape the way stepfathers perceive the challenges and opportunities associated with stepfamilies. Circumstances associated with the stepfamily, in combination with the unique aspects of men's life histories, are likely to shape men's experiences, attitudes, and sentiments in connection with stepfamily living.

CREATING VISIONS

Most of the men I interviewed say that when they were younger they assumed that they eventually would have children.[2] Some knew this when they were in high school whereas others acknowledged it in their early twenties. Most wanted to postpone the transition to fatherhood until they were in their late twenties or early thirties.[3] One exception to this pattern was Stephen, currently a stepfather of two children who had raised a stepson in a previous relationship. "I don't ever remember really having a huge urge to have my own offspring. . . . I don't ever remember feeling like I had to have, pass down my genes so to speak. That wasn't real critical."

In the process of sharing their thoughts about their desire to have children, some men reflect on what they thought years ago, some focus on what they have been thinking recently, some cast their sights on the future, and some share comments relevant to different time frames. Not surprisingly, men have a variety of things to say about becoming fathers and, in some cases, talk about how their views changed over time.

Robby and Neal provide revealing examples of the types of things men say about their youthful perspectives on fatherhood. With Robby, now thirty-four, we hear from a man who married at age twenty and became a father in thirteen months. Ten years later, he remarried and assumed responsibility for two stepchildren ages eight and ten. Asked whether he thought about being a father before his child was born, Robby places his thoughts in a larger context.

> I've always been great with kids. I love kids. I think they are the greatest, and they're going to rule this world later on in life. And I want them to be nice to me. . . . I was your typical teenager; I didn't think about getting married or having kids or anything like that. Mainly because my older brother was twenty-four with three kids. When he was twenty he had his first. . . . I was just graduating high school. . . . Watching him because he was struggling, had the new baby, and I definitely didn't want all that. He actually had two kids before I had one. I probably should have waited a little bit longer to have the kid, but it turned out right. We got to the point where, well if you got pregnant you got pregnant. It wasn't one of the most important things in my life to do, to just be a father, but I'm very happy to be a dad.

From Robby's point of view, his brother represented a negative role model who indirectly dissuaded him from developing the desire to have children in his late teens. However, by twenty-one, Robby became a father soon after getting married. As he describes it, he and his wife more or less drifted into parenthood because they became indifferent to whether she became pregnant then or not. In a sense, it just happened. Robby grew more willing to explore the world of fatherhood with this wife at a relatively young age despite the unplanned pregnancy. Subsequently, his love for kids and his positive experience with his own child enabled him to feel comfortable getting seriously involved with his second wife's children in his early thirties.

Unlike Robby, Neal had less time and experience to get himself ready for the challenges of life as an informal stepfather.[4] Recall that Neal is the twenty-two-year-old whose partner has an eight-year-old son, Stanley, and was about to have another baby by a different father in a few weeks. Though not a father himself, Neal shares some of his thinking over the past few years regarding the prospects of becoming a father.

Being a teenager, I was more concerned about doing well in surf contests and at swim meets, and I think, yeah, I want to be a father. I want to be like my dad, I want to kind of have the things that he has, or has had. I won't be disappointed if it, if I don't. Because I'm not a father, I think, I don't know what I'm missing, so I don't know. But I can tell you yeah, I mean the desire is there to eventually have children but I'm not in a hurry.

Neal describes his views of becoming a father in very general terms. Although he presents his thoughts in broad terms without connecting them to his girlfriend or anyone in particular, it was his relationship with his girlfriend and her son that led him to think seriously about fatherhood issues. Now he finds himself using his father as a positive role model when he tries to figure out how to treat Stanley in a fatherly way.

These two accounts of how men venture into the realm of fathering and stepfathering are two among many. They are useful because they draw attention to some of the sources that affect how men develop their initial perspectives about fathering. For instance, some men's initial and subsequent views are, to varying degrees, tied to their involvement in a romantic relationship. Girlfriends seem to be an important impetus for many men to develop their first clear sense of wanting to be a father. Likewise, relationships can provide a context for men to envision what kind of father they would like to be. Men are also quite capable of developing paternity intentions and views about fathering without relying on a romantic partner's input. We can see this with Monty who, while being married to Sue, the mother of five children (four of whom she raised), apparently changed his mind during his early thirties about having his first child. Monty describes his situation as it existed immediately prior to Sue becoming pregnant with his son a year and a half ago. "I just made the comment that if it happened now, I was more ready for it than ever in my life and probably made the statement that I hoped it happened. That I didn't want to grow up without having at least one child. Prior to that I was real specific you know, I don't want any kids." Sue's comments reveal that she was definitely not encouraging Monty to have a child. "He didn't want kids and he was thirty-two when we got pregnant, so it was a big, it was a big surprise for both of us. I didn't want another child at forty years old. . . . I was done." In recalling their discussions prior to the pregnancy, Sue does not mention Monty's apparent shift in openness to having a child. She captures her take on the situation by stating that "we agreed that we didn't want children, other than the ones I already had."

The girlfriend factor played a role in changing Rodney's life as a father. Having spent four years in the marines right out of high school, Rodney never had a serious relationship until he left the service. At that point he developed a relationship with a woman who became his first wife and the mother of his two biological children. Rodney remarked that while he was dating her he saw her as someone who could be the mother of his children. "She was patient. She had a soft, gentle voice. I guess the qualities that my mom had. So yeah, I think I saw some things in her that made me want to have children with her." For Rodney, developing a fairly well-defined desire to have children grew out of his relationship with his first wife. Still, as he points out, "It wasn't planned. I didn't have any grand plans on being a father. It's just the way nature went." Part of what Rodney labels "nature" involved his relationship with his first wife. Later Rodney divorced and remarried. For the past seven years he's learned about the new responsibilities of being a stepfather for two more children. Ironically, though not having any "grand plans" in his early twenties to be a father, Rodney has become, at age thirty-seven, an involved father figure to four children.

Rodney, like Robby, was introduced to the world of fathering by first becoming a biological father and developing the emotional bonds that typically go along with a father–child relationship. With this foundation of firsthand experience, both men subsequently learned how to develop strong ties with children who were not of their own flesh and blood. Neal, on the other hand, had to learn how to develop strong ties and act in a fatherly way toward his partner's child without ever experiencing the emotions and lessons of being a biological father. Stepfathering for him entailed a whole new set of responsibilities.

Each man had a fairly clear sense of becoming a father someday even though fulfilling the related roles came a bit sooner than expected. This vision stands in stark contrast to how some men orient to this issue. Jackson, the thirty-nine-year-old I have already described, provides such a contrast. For many years Jackson devoted all of his time and energy to expanding his personal business. By his own admission, he was too busy accumulating material possessions to think about starting a family. Consequently, neither he nor his wife at the time thought seriously about wanting or having children. It was when he reached his thirties that Jackson began to yearn to have a child. Unfortunately for Jackson, his former wife was not interested in the least. Ironically, it was his involvement in two aspects of his wife's life that he believes led to his change of heart about having children. First, he describes how he spent a great deal of time and energy supporting her struggle to overcome her anxiety attacks. In his words, "I guess I became more nurturing, this is in retrospect, in trying to support her for what she needed actually made me aware of the things that I found valuable in life." Second, Jackson discusses how he helped his wife, who had begun to raise dairy goats. Because she was unable to manage some difficult tasks such as removing a dead offspring from a goat's body, Jackson pitched in with this chore and also got involved in "raising the goat kids." This in turn helped awaken Jackson's desire to have a nurturing relationship with a child. Jackson's experience with the goats reveals that life-changing events come in many unexpected forms.

After several frustrating years, he realized that his desire for a child was incompatible with his wife's life philosophy.[5] Jackson shares how he began to make the transition from being indifferent toward children to being more sensitive to them.

> It used to be when a child was crying or upset, this is years ago, that the first instinct was to go as far away from that child as I could. If there's somebody crying and screaming it was like no, I want to be away from here. But as, I guess beginning about a year and a half ago is—more I heard crying children and it was like—what's going on over there?

Jackson's transition is somewhat remarkable because of the psychological distance he traveled from being focused on self, work, and an ex-wife to expressing himself as an attentive, nurturing man who is deeply committed to being a fatherly presence in Mason's life. He is now at a point where he can say, "I think it took about four months or so [after living together] before I started to make that transition from 'man with someone else's child' to 'man with his child.'"

Jackson's experience of developing the desire to be a father and then getting involved with a stepchild raises another set of issues involving what happens to a man's paternal desires once he enters a new relationship with a woman who has a child.[6] Will a man be content to be a stepfather or will he want to have his own biological child with his new partner? The desire to procreate may be highest for the man in his twenties or thirties, or someone who has never had a child. But an older man, or someone who has already fathered a child, may also have this desire. A few studies show that American men tend to report that the most important reason for having children is wanting to have someone to love.[7] Should we assume that this reason for having children is not restricted to men having only one child or having children with only one mother? I think so. Men may place increasing weight on other factors when considering the value of having more children with new partners (wanting a child of a different gender), but the fundamental importance of wanting children to love is likely to remain unchanged.

A man's feelings for a stepchild as well as the child's mother can affect how he thinks about having his own child. Now that Jackson, during the past eighteen months, has developed a close relationship with both his fiancée and her five-year-old son, Mason, his life has changed dramatically. After listening to him talk in glowing terms about Mason, I asked him if his involvement in Mason's life affected his thinking about becoming a biological father.

> Yes, oh yeah, that actually—it just pretty much confirmed that that would be a very wonderful experience for me. It's a peak-and-valley thing too, because there are times when I think that just being a stepfather to Mason would be enough. Actually I realize that now. That's more than I could have ever hoped for, just being a stepfather. If I never became a biological father I would still be a very happy and fortunate person. But there are also moments where I'm thinking—there would be nothing more amazing to me than to go the next step and actually have a child. Have a child with Helena that would be our child. That's kind of an odd thing because I hadn't ever really felt that, that deep an emotion until a year and a half ago, nothing remotely close to that.

Jackson's day-to-day experiences with being a stepfather have given him a taste of what it's like to raise a child. Being a father figure to Mason has clearly helped satiate Jackson's craving for the opportunity to play a nurturing role in a child's life. Ironically, while the wonderful bond he has developed with Mason accentuates Jackson's desire to have his own child, the bond has forced Jackson to consider how bringing another child into the family might adversely affect his fiancée and his ability to "provide the degree of nurturing that Mason is used to and wants." Ultimately, practical concerns related to limited time and money, as well as his fiancée's biological clock, may preclude Jackson from having a biological child. Even so, his experience with Mason has reinforced his ideal vision of having a child, particularly with someone he loves and who presumably wants to have his child.

Carl voices similar concerns about his stepdaughter's welfare if he were to push to have his own child.

> Having an extra child would not allow us to do some of the things that we do for Vicky now, private school and some of the shopping and things like that. . . . One is enough because we can have all of the things that you have with children, the joys and all of the different things that you go through as parents, without having to be strapped financially and have to worry about clothes and food and what are we going to do about two college educations and planning for all of that.

Like Jackson, Carl has no child of his own. But, as mentioned earlier in connection with stepdads claiming their stepchildren, Carl feels that his eight-year-old stepdaughter, Vicky, is his. Legally she is his daughter because he adopted her a few years ago. His connection to her is further strengthened because her biological father is completely out of the picture. Carl's comments here and elsewhere in the interview reveal that he is satisfied with his current fathering roles and does not sense any need to procreate and raise his own biological child. His remarks about making plans for Vicky's college education, some nine or ten years down the road, suggest that he has a long-range vision of himself as a father.

Jackson's and Carl's mindfulness of their stepchild's needs, and the welfare of any additional child who might be born, can be contrasted to Alan's more ego-centered approach to the paternity question. Possessing only modest financial means, Alan expresses no concern about how having his own child might influence the standard of living issue for his seven-year-old stepson.

> I'm married so I'm tryin' to have a kid—it's hard. Real hard. And she [wife] say, she like to say, 'cause I always be tellin' her you know, you got to get pregnant but I want a little girl. That's what I really want. Well you don't love Danny [stepson]. Yeah I love Danny. But I also want something I made. She's like, we be tryin' but I don't know what it is, but it ain't happening. That kinda upsets me you know 'cause when she was pregnant I used to tell her take it easy, and don't be tryin' to go and do all this. And the doctor said from her tryin' to do so much is how she lost the baby. Sometimes in my own mind I don't tell her, but in my mind I kinda think like, I figured she didn't really want the baby anyway. That's what I think sometimes, but I've never mentioned it to her.

Not only does Alan desperately want his own child, he feels that his wife secretly opposes the idea and may have been irresponsible when she was pregnant with his child less than a year ago. The fact that Alan already has a stepson, whom he appears to love very much, has in no way curtailed his desire to have his own child. Alan convincingly verifies his love for Danny by claiming that he resisted the temptation on at least one occasion to leave his wife because he couldn't bear to leave Danny behind. Less clear is whether Alan's sense of urgency to have his own child is heightened by Danny's presence in the home. However, Alan's comments seem to show that he wants to have a biological child to satisfy his personal needs; he says nothing about having a child as a shared experience that would bring him and his wife closer together.

Brad's unique story about reuniting at thirty-five with his childhood sweetheart directly illustrates how a man can see paternity as a way to solidify a romantic connection, in this case with someone who would be the second woman to bear his child.[8] As the author of his own romantic tale, Brad told me that he dated his current partner, Nannette, when he was twelve and thirteen years of age, then again in high school and a little in college before they went their separate ways. They stayed in sporadic contact over the years and were aware that each married and had children. After many years of not having contact, they ran into each other while they were picking up their kids at a summer camp. Brad, who at the time was having a difficult time in his marriage, recalled immediately feeling that he wanted to rekindle his romance with Nannette, who was now divorced. As luck would have it, they eventually ended up living in the same city and started dating. By this time, Brad had separated from his wife and had begun a divorce process that turned into a long ordeal, one that was still unresolved at the time of the interview, two years afterward. At one point during Brad's storytelling, I asked him if he and Nannette had "seriously talked about the possibility of having a child together."

> We have, and given our history—the roots go way back—she always wanted to have my child and actually I always would have liked to have her have my child. And so we're both kind of excited about the possibilities of that. At the same time, God, I'm going to be forty in another—well, I'm going to be thirty-nine in December, so forty in a year. I think about being sixty with a twenty-year-old kid—and I guess that's not so bad, especially nowadays. . . . and that's one of the greatest sources of her frustration at the length of time my divorce is taking, is because her biological clock is ticking away. The longer the divorce drags out, the less opportunity. The window is closing.

Listening to Brad, I got the sense that if he never had a child with Nannette he would be disheartened but not devastated. He already had three children with his soon-to-be ex-wife and Nannette had two kids of her own, whom

Brad likes. Nonetheless, I got the impression from the way Brad talked throughout the interview about his long-standing affection for Nannette that he would cherish the chance to go through a pregnancy and have a child with her. Brad's situation illustrates again how men's procreative desires can be affected by their feelings for and involvement with particular women.

In addition to his feelings for his stepchild and the mother, a man's perceptions of how well he is doing as a stepfather may motivate him to desire his own child. This may be particularly true for men who do not have their own children. Kristen illustrates this point when she talks about her husband Carl's enthusiasm about the prospects of their having a child together. Asked if they ever talked about having children, Kristen replies:

> He always said whatever I wanted. . . . It didn't matter to him one way or another. But we started about—we talked about—yes, I want to have another baby—let's try. So he's been the one feeding my [me] vitamins every morning and making sure I eat all the vegetables I need to eat and getting up every morning and saying "Are you pregnant yet?" He's really—he just seems way more excited than I expected him to be about the whole thing. I think that's probably due to the fact that he sees he can be a good father. And I think this child will probably be even better off than Rebecca [Calvin's stepdaughter], because Rebecca doesn't—Rebecca has ten years of her mama kind of formed and shaped her and—you know, without Calvin.

From Calvin's side, he says that prior to meeting Kristen he thought he might not ever get married or have children. He had begun to resign himself to living a single life. With his marriage and active involvement in Rebecca's life, Calvin has experienced a dramatic turn of events, the most recent being his eagerness to have a child of his own.

Just as Jackson's and Mason's story illustrates how the experience of being close to a child may inspire a man to want to father a child of his own, being away from a child may have the same effect. The man who is estranged from his own child for one reason or another may be inspired to have another. He may long to develop the type of connection with a child that he never had or sustained with his own child. The most common reason for the father–child relationship weakening is that the man's relationship with the child's mother ends, often meaning that he has to live apart from his child.

Looked at from a different perspective, a man who has experienced the frustration associated with being cut off from his young child may be reluctant to risk growing attached to a child again. He may fear the prospects of reliving the emotional pain of having his relationship with his child suffer if his romantic relationship with the mother ends. This fear can also touch the man who grew close to a stepchild in the past and then, lacking any legal standing as a stepfather, had that relationship severed when his involvement with the mother ended. This situation can factor prominently into both a stepfather's life history and his perceptions of future relationships where a child is involved.

This stepfathering reality, especially the informal variety where a marriage has not yet occurred, is all too familiar to me personally. After my relationship with Alli's mother ended, she was instrumental in preventing me from seeing Alli and her brother. This experience sensitized me to the risks I would be taking, irrespective of my good intentions, if I allowed myself to become emotionally attached to another single mother's child. If the relationship with the mother ended, I might be forced to forgo my involvement with the child as well.

Sometimes a man may be selective by only getting or remaining seriously involved with a mother who is willing to provide him with his own child or a woman who is childless. In the former case, the man may not feel that having a stepchild as a "substitute" is sufficient. He may want his own. A man without kids may tend to take a stronger stand on this issue. In addition, a man with a child, especially one not living with him, may find comfort in interacting with a stepchild. William, for example, feels that he has been a "terrible father."

> And that's another reason I'm trying to make amends just within myself, even though I know it doesn't do my children any good. But for me to be there for her and her children, I feel like it will maybe balance out some kind of way. But as far as my own children, the only two that I've really ever spent any time around would be the last two, but the sixteen-year-old daughter, I don't even know her. I'm a biological father. That's about it.

William entered his current relationship knowing that he has weak relationships with four of his own children, two he admits to barely knowing. Thus he has been comfortable with allowing himself to get close to his partner's two sons while enjoying their fondness for him. Apparently enjoying his new opportunity to "make amends" for his lack of involvement in his own children's lives, William does not mention anything about wanting any more biological children.

Several men talked about their strong convictions at a relatively young age that they wanted to have children and be family men. Most did so because they were in relationships where questions or thoughts about having children together were more likely to surface. Unless they were in a relationship where their partner had children already, men tended not to think much about being stepfathers.

For example, Brandon apparently knew before he had his son at age twenty-one that he wanted to be a family man. "I definitely saw myself as being the kind of guy just to hang out with the kids and have fun, doing similar things like my dad did with me. Throwing a football, having cookouts on the weekends, just everybody coming over and hanging out with us and the kids and stuff like that." The significance of wanting a genetic paternal link had been self-evident for the forty-two-year-old Ray since he was in his twenties. "Being that I'm adopted I always felt this empty, hollow feeling inside me. That's the best I can describe it. I just didn't feel like I was attached to anything. And I thought, I'll start a family of my own." Ray was quick to express that having a child was important to him and was on his mind before he became a father. "I can remember like playing with little kids and fantasizing that I was the dad. It fills you with a lot of pride." Not surprisingly, after Ray got involved with and married a woman who already had a child, he went on to have his own daughter with his wife.

In contrast, Gerald was one in the minority of men who didn't want to have children. During his first marriage, when he was in his twenties, he recalled that "when I looked ahead [and thought] where will I be?—I didn't see myself as a father with a big family. I just didn't. It never came to me. . . . I was too childish to think about having a child." By appraising his maturity level, Gerald had decided that having kids wasn't a part of his life plan, at least not then. Since that period of his life, he has lived with two different women, including his current wife, each of whom has children from previous relationships. Gerald's lack of interest in wanting to be around children probably adversely affected his earlier relationship, and his lack of interest in having children of his own enabled him to pursue each of his last two relationships without having any expectations that his partners would provide him with his own child.

A man's desire to have a child may represent a potential stumbling block for a romantic relationship. Ron and Gayle, who have been together for two years, were vocal in their separate interviews about their frustrations and worries about Ron not having his own children. Responding to a question about how important it was for him to have his own biological children someday, Ron provides this emotional response:

For a long time it really is, it was important to me. I might not be think-ing about it now, having biological children, but she can't have no more kids. . . . If me and her lasts. I say that it might hit my mind a couple times, but I'm not going to plan on doing nothing behind her back. It was im-portant to me in my lifetime. I'm only twenty-two years old, but by the time I hit thirty, I'm not going to be gettin' no younger. . . . I might want kids. I'm not going to lie to you the fact that she can't have none, that does hurt. Sometimes I feel like I'm going to be raising somebody else's kids. . . . I know when I got into the relationship she had kids, but I didn't know they acted like this [disrespectful]. Sometimes I feel like, she went out there and had the fun, and had two marriages, and the fathers aren't around to do nothing. All they do is pay child support and that's it.

Ron describes juggling his current fertility desires, the possibility that his desire for his own children may grow over time, his feelings about his stepchildren's behavior, and his resentment about being saddled with re-sponsibility for children who are not his. Given his poor relationship with the two stepchildren and his rocky relationship with their mother, it is easy to imagine that Ron's desire to have his own children will present a seri-ous problem sometime down the road.

Now let's consider what Ron's thirty-one-year-old partner, Gayle, had to say. After expressing disappointment that she was unable to have any more children unless she had a $16,000 operation (which she could not af-ford), Gayle comments on how Ron feels about her situation.

He told me, it's not a big deal; I don't care. I wanted three but two's enough—this is how he puts it. Just like they're his [Gayle's children]. But it still bothers me in the back of my head because I know he's only twenty-two and he'll grow. I feel that at some point, if we go ahead with marriage, or are together six years or seven years, at some point when he gets to his thirties he going to realize, I don't have any offspring of my own. And I'm scared at that point, that far off, people do start venturing 'cause they're bored with the relationship. He might not leave me, but he might do something to get that baby. He says though that he loves me and that it doesn't matter to him, but when other people talk to him about having more kids, he's like I wanted to have three of my own, but I have two now so it would be cool to have one more, but Gayle can't have any kids. I'll catch him in conversations like that, and I think, oh God if I ever make him real mad what the heck will he do? Would it push him away?

Gayle's comments reveal that she has scrutinized Ron's comments about kids. Despite Ron's reassurances, Gayle feels that their different life stages, Ron's young age and his not having children, may make them incompatible. Fearing that Ron will become restless about having his own kids in the years ahead, Gayle remains skeptical of their long-term potential as a couple. Thus their differences in age and fertility status are the seeds of a rocky relationship, one that has been negatively affected by Ron's poor relationship with Gayle's children.

Another couple in an age-discrepant relationship, John and Beth, also came face-to-face with John not being a father and Beth being unable to have any more children. Twenty-seven-year-old John describes the ordeal he experienced as he contemplated his involvement with a woman sixteen years his senior.

> I had asked her to marry me. I really wanted to marry her but I just kept thinking, she's older and she cannot have another kid. It's like, I had to make this decision. Was I going to get rid of her, go on with my life so I could have kids with another woman, or was I going to embrace this? And this was a big, big up thing. I had all this stuff, said some pretty dumb things to her, ended up leaving—not for long, but for a night. But I went for a couple of hours. Went to talk to my father. I had to get some kind of clarification because I was like, this is a big mistake. And my dad just spelled it out for me, you know, what life is really like. I had to make the decision: was I willing to go into this relationship knowing that I probably would never have a kid of my own, or was I going to go to her and tell her to bugger off. Of course I chose to stay, marry her. Sometimes in our early marriage, I would talk about having a kid with her, and we thought about maybe getting some kind of surgery where she can get her tubes back or whatever. But it was $5,000, not even in our price range. And then the other thing, this is what is really cool, my sister's got four kids, and they come to visit. And after four hours, I'm like, get them out of here. So I think, maybe I don't have the patience for a kid; maybe it worked out the way it was supposed to. I would say it's only been a year since I really stopped wanting a kid. Even in our first two years of marriage, this is our second year, even in the first year of marriage, I still had desires for a kid.

I was curious about the advice John's father gave him that convinced John to marry Beth and asked him to share that conversation with me.

> You know I don't remember word for word what he said, but the gist of it was, we don't make life, life is handed to us and we have to accept what we want or don't want, or what is right for us. And he was saying that sometimes God gave us something that we don't really want, but

it's what we really need, and so we have to get over our selfishness, self-centeredness of wanting and really take what's handed to us in life, and deal with it that way. 'Cause you know my dad didn't want a kid, he had a kid and then my sister, and then he had to go a certain way, and that's what was dealt him. Sometimes life is not always what you want it [to be], but sometimes it's exactly the way it should be. That's the gist of what he was saying, and so I took that to heart and decided that, I prayed about it and decided what is the right way for me to go and I chose what I thought was the right way.

John struggled with what he perceived to be a difficult choice. He was mindful enough to look into the future and make a decision for the present that would have implications for him and Beth later on. Taking his dad's advice to heart, John appears to have concluded that his desire to father his own child was in a sense a form of "selfishness and self-centeredness" that he should overcome. John therefore willed himself to appreciate what had been handed to him in this life and has worked ever since to make the most out of his relationship with Beth and her fifteen-year-old daughter.

Slightly more than half of the men in my study began their current romantic relationship after they had already fathered a child. These men describe their paternity in a variety of ways. Some men portray themselves as devoted fathers who had been and remain committed, involved fathers. Though they are in the minority, several men have their children living with them. As discussed earlier in connection with how men's previous experiences with children affect their partner's view of them, men's experiences with their own children typically help frame their outlook on being involved with a woman who is a mother.

At the other extreme are the men who see very little of their children. William, introduced earlier, has not been an active father to his four children. Responding to a question about whether he sees himself as someone who wanted to have kids before he had his first son, William replies, "Not really. I was out there, young and learning and thought I had all the answers. No, I wasn't family oriented at all." Continuing with his explanation of what happened with the birth of his first child, William adds:

Well I wasn't a big part of his life. When his mother got pregnant, and at the time of her pregnancy, I joined the Service. After that we pretty much lost contact, but then—I would say he was about six months old before I actually met him. I had to go home on leave. I went home and I met him on leave. By the time I got back home, she was with someone else. So I've never really been a big part of his life. Then I would see him off and on, here and there. That was pretty much the way I started with this children, being family oriented type style.

Later William took a bigger step into the world of being "family oriented" with another woman. His perception of his involvement with his ex-wife and children is captured in his response to my question about how he felt when that relationship ended.

> Devastated. I thought it was my whole world. I was really set into doing the family thing. By then I thought I had it all figured out, because I had these other two children, I wasn't a part of their life—here I am now with a woman I love and she has my two beautiful children. I'm the man of the house. I'm the husband. The father. I was doing the family thing. So when it ended, I was devastated.

William provides an excellent example of a man whose complex life history, especially the part of it involving his relationships with his children and their mothers, comes into play in the way he approaches his new role as a stepfather. Drawing on his most recent divorce, as well as his largely nonexistent relationships with his two oldest children, William is determined to be an active father to his two stepsons.

Although numerous men had not fathered a child prior to getting involved with their current partners, most wanted to have this experience someday. Some had clear intentions of wanting to have children with the women to whom they were currently dating or married. This was the case for Terry, whose story I presented at length in chapter 1. Prior to getting married, he had clear visions of having children of his own with his wife. These visions apparently solidified his sentiments toward stepfathering as well as his views about some of the practical aspects of managing a stepfamily and raising a stepson in a family with other children who are his half siblings.

LOOKING BACK TO DAD AND MOM

Whatever visions a man holds about becoming and being a father, they are likely to be affected somehow by his experiences with his own parents and guardians. However, the realities of what is involved in being a stepfather are seldom depicted in the visions a man has when he is younger. Being a stepfather is a demanding experience that requires a man to figure out how to navigate the muddled terrain of stepfamily life with little guidance. Although few individuals, either as children or adults, receive formal training on how to be a good parent, even fewer receive training of any sort on how to be a stepfather. Aside from rare popular books like Carl Pickhardt's *Keys to Successful Step-Fathering* or the many general books on stepfamily life, a man is left to improvise with his partner's and stepchild's assistance. The stepfather, like the biological father, can develop his approach to fathering in numerous ways.

Some qualitative research on biological fathers has shown that fathers tend to create their fatherhood models by looking at different individuals and selectively focusing on certain aspects that seem useful.[9] In essence, they pick and choose appealing features of good parenting from different men or women they know or from images they see in the media. Some try to emulate a particular person, but this appears to be more the exception than the rule. Other men identify particular behavioral traits or specific fathers as negative examples that illustrate how they do not want to behave. Stepfathers are likely to follow these same patterns to some extent as they make sense of and forge their relationships with stepchildren. Tim is aware, for example, of how he felt "intimidated" by his father when he was growing up. Now, looking to the future with his stepchildren, he explains, "I wouldn't want to come forward with that. I think that's kind of like another reason why I want to get out of the adversarial role with the kids, because that's not going to be productive to them coming forward later, if they have a question or problem they may go to someone else, or whatever."

In general, when men look to their own upbringing for guidance, they either emulate or compensate for how their fathers treated them. Not surprisingly, the stepdads I interviewed seldom tried to identify unique parenting styles their own fathers used that pertained to stepfathering per se. Rather, they sought to cull from their fathers more basic lessons about fathering or general messages about guiding children. They then try to apply these to their stepchildren.

A few men, though, were in a position to draw on their childhood experiences with their own stepfathers or stepmothers. Reflecting on their personal experiences gave them a child's perspective on what it was like to interact with stepparents and live in a stepfamily. Bringing this perspective to their own situations as stepfathers, some men could empathize more directly with some of their stepchildren's dilemmas. Recall Harry's situation described in chapter 3. He provides a useful illustration because he, despite his willingness to develop a deeper relationship with his seventeen-year-old stepdaughter Kelly, whom he had known for thirteen years, had to grapple with her tendency to keep her emotional and physical distance. Though frustrated and disappointed for many years, Harry did not pressure Kelly to do or say things that didn't come naturally to her. He chose this stance, in part, because of the rocky relationship he began at the age of twelve with his own stepfather, a relationship that remained rocky for thirty-two years. During high school, Harry had heated arguments with his stepfather, who sometimes became violent. But Kelly does not have a violent stepfather, and Harry is sensitive to why children sometimes feel reserved around stepparents. By empathizing in this way, he attempts to understand Kelly's reluctance to call him "dad" to his face even though he is the only father figure she has ever known, and her mother and Harry have had two other children who call him "dad" regularly.

Similarly, Ernest does not push his stepson to call him "dad" because Ernest recalls what it was like to be raised by a stepfather. Ernest had a fifteen-year relationship with his stepfather before he passed away. For an extended period of time Ernest referred to his stepfather as Uncle Jake. However, after coaxing from his mother and other family members, Ernest agreed to call him "pop." Because Ernest was coached into calling his own stepfather "pop," he is reluctant to have his stepson call him anything that doesn't come naturally to him. Ernest is perfectly comfortable with Scott calling him by his first name. He resists his brother's pressure to get his stepson to call him "dad," something his brother has persuaded his own stepson to do.

Several men learned from previous relationships what it was like to be involved with women who already had children. These men entered their current relationships having firsthand experience with children not their own. Nevertheless, their new situations were often different enough that they were still learning on the fly how to respond to their unconventional circumstances. John, for example, was married to a much older woman whose daughter was fifteen years old when she met him. John came into this relationship with some reservations because of his earlier unsuccessful experience living with a woman who had three children ages four, five, and seven, each of whom had a different father. Despite his reservations, John quickly learned that there were few similarities in these two women and their circumstances. In addition to the obvious difference in the number and ages of their children, the women had very different approaches to parenting.

Several stepfathers praise their fathers for how their fathers raised them, a sentiment reflected in the strength of their current relationships. Listen to how several describe their fathers, each emphasizing different qualities.

The greatest man I've ever known was my dad. He was my best man at my first wedding. He's a great guy and I'll never be able to live up to him, in my opinion. He was [a] good, fair, caring, loving father. He disciplined me when I needed it, explained to me why I was being punished, teaching me the difference between right and wrong. [Monty, 33]

When he got home [from work] we [father and sons] used to go rake yards. He said that was our extra money. . . . We had to buy our school clothes with it. It was that thing of responsibility. I respect him for that today, because that's me, I always believe in, if I want it bad enough, I'll work hard enough for it. That was a good thing to learn, as in disciplining us, you can't discipline kids like it used to be. . . . He's good. I love him to death. [Eddie, 35]

He was always building a relationship. . . . If I did something wrong and my father got all bent out of shape, at the end of the day or I'm in my room crying because my dad got all mad at me, he'd come in and apologize for raising his voice at me, and he'd just talk to me. . . . If there was something between us, we had to work it out. We couldn't go on and on, day after day without talking to each other about what we did wrong. [John, 27]

I have a great father who was always there for our family. Dad and Mom have always gotten along. I've never seen them fight or anything like that. So I grew up in a really stable, good household. [Jesse, 20]

A quick glimpse of how these men characterize the important efforts their fathers made reveals that they learned about discipline, a sense of responsibility, a desire to build meaningful relationships and resolve issues in a peaceful manner, reliability, and the value of parents sustaining a harmonious relationship with each other. These and other men also emphasize the time their fathers devoted to hanging out with them going fishing, playing sports, doing chores, and so on. These are significant aspects of fathering that some of the stepfathers highlight when they talk about their role in their stepchildren's lives. They see these lessons as being important irrespective of whether children are their own offspring or stepchildren. Lessons learned by observing their own father are important, yes, but they are not the only lessons stepfathers consider. As Jesse observes, "There's aspects that I'm going to take from my dad and there's aspects that I'm going to take from other people that I know that I've seen and I guess blend them altogether into what I think would be a good dad."

Not all of the men have fond memories of how their fathers treated them while they were children. Some feel that they still have poor relationships with their fathers. The bitterness is apparent in Alan's voice as he tries to summon memories of his father from his childhood: "Going to prison, that's about it." Continuing, he mentions that his father has "changed his whole life around" since the time Alan was six or seven. Alan has called him and visited him at his home, but he gets emotional telling me how hurt he was when his father, who lives only forty-three miles away, didn't bother to come to his wedding in the past year. Talking about his father's absence from the wedding, Alan says, "When I was little my grandma used to always tell me, 'you gonna be just like your daddy ain't no good.' You know I heard that all growing up. So that kinda made me want to do better, you know learn on my own."

Doug's long-standing bitterness is also palpable as he describes his feelings about his unhappy teenage years after his divorced father got involved with another woman who had children. Focusing his attention on the stepmother, Doug says, "That woman was always out to get me into trouble so I just told him [father], I can't handle this. She finally got him to kick me out, so I started fending for myself at fourteen. And I made up my mind at that point, my son or daughter would never face that situation." Although Doug directs his strongest hostility toward his former stepmother, he clearly remains angry with his father, whom he holds responsible for letting the situation develop.

With few exceptions, those who have negative comments about their fathers balance their remarks about these shortcomings by highlighting their fathers' redeeming qualities. As the following comments suggest, several men are disappointed with their fathers because of the way they abused alcohol and lost control of their temper.

> My relationship with my own father was distant at best. My father was an alcoholic among many other more serious problems. And he was abusive to both me and my sister. [Larry, 54]

> My father was a moonshining alcoholic; he was abusive. I'm not ashamed of it. Because you know, later on down the line, he broke that, but I always said, I said I'll never grow up to be—I'll never grow up to do that. I told myself . . . I won't get drunk and beat up a woman. [Herman, 42]

> My father, when I was a teenager, I recall my father drinking too much; being verbally abusive to my sister and my mother. Still treating me with respect—being nice to me. [Mark, 42]

The stepfathers who developed negative perceptions of the men who raised them talk about how they are trying to compensate for what they went through. This pattern is similar to how men in other studies talk about the way they treat their biological children.[10]

An implicit message embedded in the three previous quotes is that these men are aware of the importance of providing their stepchildren with a positive image of men and women relating to each other. Treating the stepchildren's mothers with respect took on considerable importance for these men. Alan, for example, reflects on how he has been left with a negative impression of how his mother used to fight with men. Consequently, he told his wife early on that he did not want her four-year-old son to see them fighting. Alan is concerned that if his wife's son sees them fighting he will grow up to "argue with women." Another stepfather, who has been involved with his eighteen and twenty-one-year-old stepchildren for the past eleven years, finds great satisfaction in how he has treated the children's mother and been a role model for the kids. Offering his stepchildren's comments as confirmation of his efforts, Barry says, "Robert tells me the way I treat his mother is the way he would like to be able to treat his wife. Linda tells me that she hopes to marry somebody like me someday, that treats her the same way." In a similar vein, Mark mentions how important it is for him to show his wife affection in front of her kids.

> I go out of my way to show emotion towards their mother. Even, I purposely will do something—will give her a hug or give her a kiss, or sit in her lap. Something so they see love. I know when two parents divorce it's like you know it can really affect you. So I want them to realize that two people can be happy and I'm trying to provide a good role model there. I try to provide them a good role model for an adult male.

The stepfathers, while harboring measured criticisms of their fathers, sometimes sought to improve on how their fathers treated them in select ways. Randy, a disabled stepfather confined to a wheelchair comments,

> I try to be there more for Jamie than I think my dad was there for me. . . . because when my dad was there, my dad was good. He just wasn't always there when you thought you needed him. . . . When I had to go back on disability, in some ways I lucked out because I got to be home all the time. I still got paid. So I'm here all the time, which is sometimes, it's a drag but the truth is, I enjoy what I do with Jamie. I like being Mr. Mom and taking care of him.

Although Randy places a premium on time, it also matters what he does as a father during those times when he is available. Again, building on the lessons he learned from the way his father treated him, Randy describes how he tries to interact with his nine-year-old stepson in a different manner.

> I try to be more practical. I try to do things at Jamie's level. And I try to wait for Jamie. I don't try to make Jamie come up—I was always raised with these great expectations that—they'd always, in lip service, "If you just want to be a truck driver it's okay." But in reality that wasn't okay. It was like—nobody else has ever graduated from the university. . . . I've tried to do things on Jamie's level instead of trying to bring Jamie up to a level that I would understand better, and I don't think my dad did that. My dad expected me to come up and try to meet his level. Now it's not to say that I don't expect Jamie to improve himself, but I'm not as demanding. . . . And if Jamie wants to do something, he's going to do it. I'm going to back him a hundred percent and give him everything there is, too. There's going to be none of this, "You want to be a truck driver? Fine. But we really want you to go to college and do this." If Jamie wants to be a truck driver, fine. He's going to be a good truck driver.

The image that Randy creates is one that shows him entering Jamie's world and trying to understand and work with him on his own terms. Randy can still provide guidance, but he will pay closer attention to Jamie's preferences and developmental capabilities. In contrast, Randy's father was more reserved and appealed to Randy to raise his standards and dreams in order to achieve some type of prestigious adult status. This appeal came from a father immersed in his adult world. Randy would rather be the "practical" father, the guy who spends lots of hands-on time with his kid in a way that his kid fully understands. Although he is not able to capitalize on the physical opportunities available to able-bodied men, Randy emphasizes how he can verbally support Jamie in whatever he decides to do. Being practical in this sense requires Randy to defer the larger or more abstract goals he may have for Jamie while focusing on what Jamie wants to do.

FINDING A WAY

The preceding discussion aptly illustrates that the experiences, resources, and perspectives men bring with them when they enter the land of stepfatherhood take many forms. As they enter this unmapped territory, they do so with varying hopes, dreams, and reservations about relationships, children, and family. Some have been married or cohabitated before, others not. Some have fathered their own children, though many are without offspring. Among the fathers, some have been active whereas others do not know their kids or barely know them. The active fathers sometimes share a home with their kids, but many do not. Some men come to their new family with intentions to have their first child or another child with their seed; for others it is the furthest thing from their mind. Some carry fond memories of their own upbringing; others feel wounded by a parent's mistreatment or neglect. Whatever their experience, whatever their reaction, men who become stepfathers bring a life history to their new relationships and families. That history, the source for often complex and sometimes unresolved personal issues, provides the material from which men shape their self-image as adult men, images that affect whether and how their identities are linked to fatherhood roles.

At some point during the stepfather's involvement in his romantic relationship, his personal history influences how he orients himself to his everyday realities—the emerging and evolving aspects of being a real-life stepdad. In turn, this meshing of his personal history with the practical realities of stepfathering affects how the man sees his future identity as a family man and stepfather.

One aspect of life connected to a stepfather's personal history involves the "self-as-father" path he experiences. Recall that this path refers to a man's self-images, feelings, and visions about the prospects of fathering that are not directly tied to any specific relationship he might have with a child. Although these perceptions and feelings can be thought of as existing on their own, they can be influenced by others throughout a man's life. In my study, the stepfather's romantic partner, the woman who was a mother when they met and remains a mother to at least one child who lives with her, can affect his general sense of self-as-father.

Part of the reshaping of the man's self-as-father comes from his hands-on involvement with specific stepchildren and the way he interprets those experiences. The experiences reflect his individual relationship with a specific stepchild, perhaps multiple stepchildren. Drawing on his experience with his own stepdaughter, Eddie cautions that a stepfather–stepchild relationship does not gel over night. If it happens at all, it usually takes time and patience. He suggests that it's critical for a stepfather to make himself available, to be ready if and when the child reaches out and asks to spend time together. Moreover, in developing this one-on-one relationship the stepfather needs to adapt to the child's desires. "Coloring. I'm too big to color, but if that's going to strengthen our relationship, you better believe I'm going to be coloring. I may not like it, but I'm going to act like I like it. At the same time I'm gaining her confidence. I'm building a foundation." Thus, when a man like Eddie makes the effort to get involved actively with a stepchild, whatever general ideas he had about himself as a father or potential father are likely to be colored by his experiential sense of being fatherly.

Being a stepfather to Jamie has opened Randy's eyes to an important philosophy of life that transcends any specific relationship Randy might have with a child. Social scientists refer to this notion as "generativity"— the adult developmental need to nurture and teach the younger generation.[11] Randy vividly captures how his stepfathering experience raised his mindfulness about his need. "I guess I was a late bloomer, father-wise. . . . All of a sudden, being with Jamie I realized—gee, how important it was that you took a piece of yourself—and not necessarily physically a piece of yourself, but you took who you were and you passed some of that along."

Thrown into this mix, of course, are the man's efforts to negotiate his way into or out of the coparental path. From the man's perspective, he is interested in the extent to which and how the mother fosters an arrangement where the stepchild is perceived to be the mother's and his child and their responsibility, rather than her child and her responsibility. Do the man and the mother form a parental team of sorts? Or does the man find himself outside the mother's family dance, with little or no parental authority?

Eddie is quick to point out that learning how to be sensitive to the mother's preferences is an important skill for a stepfather to possess. Part of his take on the coparenting issue is that the stepfather, especially early on, should look to the mother for guidance and be careful not to upset her.

> You got to make some sacrifices. You got to see how mom is feeling. You got to know what buttons to push, what line you can't cross, what line you can cross before you even feel mom out. That's the key. If you say something and mom back you up, that's a point for you, but if you say something and mom doesn't back you up, you don't let that happen again.

Eddie's approach resembles a coparenting "lite" where he, as the man pursuing a path that is likely to lead to having greater presence in the stepchild's life, is willing to defer to the mother and hopes to earn her support.

Unlike the case of the more abstract self-as-father path, the man experiences the father–child and coparental paths in the trenches. How a man processes these experiences and relates them to one another will be framed by the visions, expectations, and experiences he brings with him. He will be influenced too by aspects of the fathering context and the types of exchanges he has with persons outside his immediate stepfamily. Becoming the father figure in the eyes of family, friends, neighbors, school personnel, coworkers, and even strangers can reinforce the stepfather's identity.

FATHERING CONTEXT: PRIVATE AND PUBLIC SCENARIOS

Scenarios where stepfathers could potentially act in a fatherly way can be thought of as being either private or public, to varying degrees and in various ways. This private–public scheme for categorizing stepfathering scenarios has physical as well as social dimensions.

The home and, for a select few, personal work space outside the home represent a common physical site for much of what a man does as a stepfather or father. It is here that a stepfather negotiates the terms of his day-to-day living with his stepchild and participates in family rituals. The stepfather changes diapers, cooks, helps with homework, disciplines, watches TV, plays, and argues with his stepchild. He also gets involved in activities with implications for stepfathering that require him to act on and immerse himself in his personal physical surroundings, including furniture, tools, clothes, food, telephone, cars, computer, garden/yard, and so on. We must keep in mind, though, that a stepfather's involvement with his stepchild, indeed any parent's involvement in general, is not restricted to the home or personal office space. Many activities occur in public physical space, such as shopping malls, grocery stores, soccer fields, schools, playgrounds, day care facilities, and other locations that are not perceived to be a person's own physical space.

On a more abstract level, the social dimension to stepfathering scenarios refers to the degree and type of interpersonal privacy a stepfather has when he is with his stepchild. From a social perspective, being alone with one stepchild represents the most private, personal type of scenario for a stepfather. In this situation a stepdad can focus on his stepchild without help or interference from others. The same holds true for the stepchild who can, in theory, direct his or her undivided attention toward the stepfather. Of course, the physical absence of others in a particular setting does not mean that the stepfather or the stepchild will not be thinking about what others might feel, say, or do if they were actually there in person. In some instances, the mental images a stepdad and stepchild have of others will make a difference and will influence their decisions even though they are alone with each other. Despite their significance, such thoughts are ultimately just mental images. Consequently, they usually do not carry the same weight as the other person being there in person.

The solo stepfather–stepchild scenario becomes less private and intimate when other members of the immediate family are present. The dynamics of intimacy, and a stepfather's perception of being in charge or having a particular sense of his fatherly way in this type of setting, may depend on which additional family members are present. For instance, having other stepchildren present may change the dynamics very little. However, having his own biological child present may accentuate a stepfather's tendency to see himself as acting in a fatherly way. If the mother is present, she may drastically change the stepfather's perception of privacy and cause him to feel less secure about his role. He may sense that his claim to authority is undermined when the mother is present and consequently feel less like a father.[12]

Looked at from a different perspective, the perception of stepfathering taking place in a private venue may remain largely intact so long as only immediate (step)family members are present. Even though they may not all share the same bloodline, they may feel part of a family unit, enjoying their own family dance in the confines of their own home. In this setting, a stepfather may feel at ease with his claim to a fatherly status not being challenged. He may sense a connection to his stepchildren and feel as though his private stepfathering scenario includes the entire stepfamily. However, to the extent that persons outside the family are introduced into or are already present in the scenario, it is likely that the stepfathering experience will become increasingly more public, from a social perspective. The home will become a public place where a stepfather is on display to those who may or may not view him as a father figure to the stepchild in question. Grandparents, aunts, uncles, friends of the mother or stepchildren, neighbors, and even the biological father himself may, under certain circumstances, give a stepfather reason to pause and consider, perhaps publicly defend, the nature of his relationship to his stepchild.

Interestingly, the combination of the physical and social dimensions of the context for stepfathering can provide individuals with various types of experiences that speak to the private–public faces of stepfathering. For example, the public face of stepfathering, referring here to the social dimension, can be experienced at home when the stepchild brings his or her friends over to hang out. Here, in the privacy of his own home, a stepfather may be addressed by others as the domestic father figure. This personal and private physical space can now be transformed into a domain for a kind of public stepfathering. Members outside these families can come inside the home and see for themselves how the stepdad interacts with his stepchild. While there, they are free to comment on, judge, challenge, support, or be indifferent to any signs or symbols of parenting. After the friends leave, the stepfather can reassert his private stepfathering face in the privacy of his own home—assuming he is now alone with the stepchild. Sometime later, the same stepfather may take his stepchild out to a more public setting, say, a playground. If other kids are playing there, especially if they are interacting with or clearly observing the stepfather with his stepchild, the stepfather will now find himself wearing the public face of stepfathering in both a physical and social sense. He will be away from the security of his home and he will be in the presence of others who can observe him interact with his stepchild. Of course, some may have no idea that he is a stepfather. A man's concerns about the legitimacy or nature of his stepfather identity may affect the extent to which he pays attention to other people's perceptions of him. If he wonders about what others might think, then he will alter his behavior accordingly. Herman, for example, talks about how he has been reluctant to hug his fourteen-year-old stepdaughter in public for fear that others might wonder about his sexual motives and see him as a "pervert." Although Herman does not have his own teenage daughter to make a comparison, I suspect that if he did he would feel less inhibited about being affectionate toward her in public. He would be less self-conscious of his father identity.

If the physical surroundings of the hypothetical playground were the same but no one else was around, then the stepfather could present his public stepfather face while experiencing the privacy of stepfathering in a social sense. Of course, a man may not be mindful of these types of differences unless he is confronted with an event that draws his attention to this private/public distinction in his stepfathering experience. In addition, a man's initial encounter with his stepchild in public is likely to occur before he develops a firm sense of having a fatherly identity. Thus a man's experience is likely to vary over time as he becomes more involved with his stepchild.

Why make this distinction between private and public faces of stepfathering? Simply put, it highlights important contexts for why and how a man works at managing his identity as a stepfather.[13] A stepfather may be fortunate and never find himself in situations where he or others question his relationship with his stepchild. The overriding perception is that he assumes a fatherly role in all settings. His fatherly ways and stepfather identity are never seriously challenged or negotiated. He is a dad or at least a stepdad, pure and simple.

Not all stepfathers are so lucky. Many go to great lengths to secure their position and roles as stepfather. They negotiate, debate, plead, and generally struggle to have others see them in a particular light, as a father figure of some sort. Their status as stepfathers or authority figures is contested on some level, sometimes on a regular basis. The biggest category of men probably fall somewhere between these two extremes. These are the guys who are typically seen as stepfathers, but in novel situations with people they don't know they may be forced to manage their identities to help others understand who they are in relation to the stepchild. For many men, these situations are no big deal, but for others, depending on the circumstances, the process of negotiating their identity and roles may provide them with anxious moments.

Public introductions are one of the more obvious sites where men and children have to negotiate the terrain of family language and, implicitly, relationship identities. How do particular stepdads introduce their stepchildren to others? In turn, how do children introduce the men in their lives who are treating them in a fatherly way? The conscious and unconscious distinctions individuals make between father and stepfather, dad and stepdad, son and stepson, and daughter and stepdaughter provide a context for thinking about how individuals define others.[14]

Juan, for example, describes how he was with his five-year-old stepson, Ivan, at a church when he ran into a "friend of a friend."

> We were talking and Ivan was there and he [the friend of a friend] ask me and "He is yours?" That was his question. I told him yes. . . . That's the way I react in the short term. If I have a longer talk, a longer communication with someone, maybe if the issue comes or we talk about it, I'm going to explain. But I really don't feel that it's something that people have to know about or have to—it's something between us, it's not something that other people should care about. It's totally personal. The last thing I want is Ivan listening to me explaining that—because it could be not very good for him.

This scenario shows how Juan, as a stepfather, is conscious of different aspects of his settings and negotiates his identity, and indirectly his stepson's, accordingly. In the type of situation he describes here, Juan is reluctant to divulge to others the "personal" information about his relationship with Ivan. On this occasion, he treats the information like a family secret. Because he perceives the conversation at the church to be a brief encounter, and Ivan is standing close enough to hear what Juan has to say, Juan makes a calculated decision to give a convenient, though not totally accurate, reply describing Ivan as his son. By doing so, he implicitly acknowledges that the public image conveyed by the word "stepson" is not as appealing as "son."

"People would come up to me and say like oh, is this your son? I would tell them no, he's my wife's child. Even though I kind of wanted to say yes, but we were kind of dating so I had no right of saying that was my son." This is how Emmit starts to describe his experiences in public with his five-year-old stepson, Jake, before he married the child's mother. It was common for people to tell Emmit that he and the child looked alike and even joke around with him, asking him whether he was sure he wasn't the father because of the physical resemblance. These comments would often lead Jake to look at Emmit and start laughing. With a sheepish grin, Emmit recalls a specific and more recent instance where Jake finally put him on the spot while Emmit was chatting with some of his parents' friends in a store during a trip back to his hometown. With Jake by his side, Emmit replied to their question about whether Jake was his son. "This is my stepson, this is my wife's son." On hearing that, Jake looked up and said, "No, I'm your son." Ever since that day Emmit has always called Jake his son.

Some men are quick to pick up on the meaning of "step" and avoid it completely before its use can ever become a problem. Herman's perspective on introductions conveys his sense of how labels can signal different meanings about the claims people make about claiming children and taking responsibility for them. As mentioned in chapter 7, Herman professes not to introduce his fourteen-year-old "step" daughter as his stepdaughter, but rather as "my daughter." Herman is rather emphatic about seeing and calling this young girl his daughter. In Herman's eyes the social element of a familial bond is as significant as the genetic tie.

Public introductions have also come into play with John, his wife, and his stepdaughter Harmony. When they run into Harmony's friends, she apparently doesn't always know whether to call John her father or stepfather. As John recalls, "She pauses, and I'm no dummy so I just put my hand out and say, 'I'm John, how you doing?' I don't want her to feel uncomfortable; she's still kinda, it's still building. We're still working on each other." John is sensitive to Harmony's predicament, which she captures by saying things to him like, "I don't know what to call you; I've got three dads." They have talked about introductions and the larger issues of her having different men in her life who have treated her like their daughter. That they are becoming more comfortable with their situation underscores the notion that families who can discuss these matters openly and frankly are likely to have the best chance of minimizing any potential awkwardness about introductions for stepdads.

Taken from the stepdad's perspective, he also has the option of using phrases that allow him to skirt the distinction between saying "children" versus "stepchildren," or "son" versus "stepson," or "daughter" versus "stepdaughter." Several men typically refer to their stepchildren in public introductions or discussions as "my boy(s)" or "my girl(s)." This convenient vernacular provides the men an opportunity to convey an intimate connection to the children while not having to worry about the awkwardness or impreciseness that may result if they were to use more common labels that are tied to "sons" or "daughters."

Other public instances where a stepdad can respond to the naming issues include situations where people refer to him or his stepchildren in a manner signifying assumptions are being made about the relationship status. Perceptions may be that two people are father and daughter, or stepfather and stepson, and so on. As a stepdad spends more time in a particular stepfamily, the chances increase that he will confront these situations. Forty-two-year-old Mark noted that the language of "dad" was not important anymore when people in public refer to his stepdaughters as his daughters. He simply lets it go and responds as if no clarification is needed.

Mark's experience shows that a stepdad and others must sometimes negotiate their roles and identities on the fly when circumstances dictate. A stepdad and his stepchild may arrive at a common understanding of how they plan to relate to each other, but this is not always the case. A child's willingness to buy into the idea that an adult man other than the biological father has a legitimate right to interact with him or her as a father figure, as well as the man's willingness to accept this status, help provide each with ready-made definitions to guide their perceptions and actions. Talking about and arriving at this understanding can ease the transitions a man and stepchild make when they move from private to public displays of their relationship. The extent to which these issues can be discussed in a comfortable and effective fashion will depend on various factors, including the age of the child and the extent to which the mother supports the stepfather's having a meaningful relationship with her child.

Negotiations focused on the meaning of a stepfather's involvement with a stepchild in private and public scenarios can also occur without the child being present. A man does not have to be with a child to express his stepfather identity. He can enter this mental space by discussing his stepchild with teachers, coaches, neighbors, friends, grandparents, or other kids. The private discussions he has with the mother could be seen as part of this public venue, though it probably makes more sense to use the family unit as the reference point and interpret the discussions as being private.

Whether in private or public, a man's commitment to and style of fathering may be influenced by immediate and extended family members. When the stepfathers in my study comment on how their family and their partner's family treat them in their roles as stepfathers, they generally say that they feel okay about it. For example, Jesse increasingly has received positive signs from his partner's family as well as his own for his involvement with his girlfriend's child, Shaun. Jesse parrots what Shaun's biological grandmother said to make a point about how she feels toward Jesse: "You know, ever since you first started hanging out with Shaun, I've thought that you were a super good guy and that you would be a good quality father for Shaun." The support is equally positive on his side of the family. Reflecting on the way his parents have taken a liking to Shaun, Jesse details how they have made a place for him in their home—where Jesse lives as well.

> It's kind of strange. You see all our furniture and then there's a football-shaped toybox and like how did that get here? And it's like my parents adjusted. There's apple juice in the fridge and baby yogurt and stuff like that. . . . My parents really like having him around and so it's not awkward at my house.

Carl remembers that his parents "had no problems with me having a small three-year-old tagging along and doing things." They eventually adopted the roles of "Gram" and "Gramps" to his stepdaughter Vicky, whom they first met five years ago. Likewise, he has felt at ease with the biological grandmother. Talking about the grandmother, he makes the point that "we've always both had Vicky's best interests in mind. We've always gotten along with how those interests were to be doled out and there's never a sense when I go there that I'm not important as part of taking care of Vicky's life. . . . I'm not superceded by the matriarch position of the grandmother." For Carl, things apparently have worked out well with all the grandparents because they have accepted Carl's strong commitment to Vicky and her mother from the beginning.

Although most of the stepfathers in my study feel supported by family in this way (or at the very least they have not been aggressively challenged or harassed), a few express serious concerns about how their family or their partner's family has treated them. Involved in one of the most unpleasant situations is Thomas, his wife, Stephanie, her two teenage boys, and a four-year-old daughter they had together. In a frustrated tone, Stephanie describes how she and Thomas have been infuriated by the way his parents have treated her and handled the stepfamily arrangement. She first mentions how Thomas's family members would introduce them to people they didn't know. "'This is Thomas and his wife, Stephanie, and these are her boys, Danny and Keith.' But this is their daughter. I mean, they would always distinguish and differentiate whose was, this is hers and this is theirs." Stephanie continues, saying that Thomas confronted his family after the tension got unbearable: "'This is my wife. And I love her very much. Those aren't my boys, but they are my boys.'" He would always say, "'They aren't mine, but they are mine. And I love them very much too. And unless you can treat them like family, then we just don't need to be around each other.'" Thomas apparently has been true to his word, remaining estranged from his biological family because he feels they do not embrace his wife and stepchildren as family. For Thomas, the blood tie was not as strong as the love tie.

One site some of the stepfathers talked about involved their participation in parent–teacher conferences at school. Although some stepfathers left that responsibility up to their partner and sometimes the biological father, a number of stepfathers went to these meetings. On the whole, these men offered a range of responses to how they were treated by the teachers during the meetings. Some felt that they had been taken seriously and treated like an important adult figure in their stepchild's life; some were treated as the father. A few felt more alienated from the process and marginalized.[15]

Plenty of places other than the school environment give the stepfathers opportunities to be observed and judged as they interact with a stepchild. In some cases, those doing the watching know for sure that a child is not biologically related to the stepfather but in other situations they probably assume the kid is his. One set of circumstances that can lead people in public to question a stepfather's relationship to a child involves the stepfather whose racial background differs from that of the birth mother and, most importantly, the children. Stepfather Eddie is African American, and his wife and eight-year-old stepdaughter, Rhendy, are white. Eddie describes how he interacts with his stepchild by saying,

> When we're out in public she's a kid, so I drop to a kid's level. I'll put them in the buggy and I'll run around the store with them. Or I'll hide somewhere and they'll try to find me. We'll hug. I mean, I'll pick her up, I'll carry her. I'll let her ride on my back. It's just if—like I say, if it was me looking at me, I would say the only reason they would separate us is that she's white and I'm black. That's the only way. If we were both white, they would think I was her father. Stepfather wouldn't even cross their minds. It's just, this is how I am in public, I mean. I don't try to hide anything because her feelings are more important than everybody else's.

Eddie realizes that his racial background raises a red flag for others who will automatically assume that he is not the biological father. This does not appear to faze him much because he is content with the fun-loving relationship he has with Rhendy. Ron, a stepfather of African American and Puerto Rican heritage, is more upset with how others treat him as part of an interracial couple involving white children. "And every time we sit in a restaurant together, everybody looks at us because we are a black and white couple. . . . I might as well not even be here [restaurant] because I don't even get responded to like I'm their dad." Asked how it makes him feel, Ron is quick to reply, "It makes me feel like shit of course." I got the sense that Ron felt marginalized as a father figure in a variety of ways and found it difficult to assume a full-fledged identity as a stepfather because others were not supportive.

For some of the stepfathers, feeling as though others see and treat them in public (and private) as the father is rewarding. William, for example, responds to a question I ask about how he feels when he's out with his stepsons and fiancée, and how he believes others perceive him. "I feel good about it, even though I know it's not totally accurate, it makes me feel good. To be able to walk out among people and they look and they don't see mother, son, son, stepfather. They see father, mother, son, son. It makes me feel good." Having others see and treat him as the father is important to William, particularly when he's with his new family. Although he did not use any of these words explicitly, his demeanor and story suggests that he does not want to be perceived as an outsider, an intruder, or an appendage. By placing himself at the head of the list of "father, mother, son, and son," William suggests that he would much rather see himself as the head of a nuclear family.

Whether the stepfathers were acting fatherly in the privacy of their homes or in public, alone with a stepchild or in the company of others, with the support of the mother or not, they were somehow involved with their stepchildren. As we saw earlier, an important facet of the larger story about stepfathers, from their perspective, is how they view the nature and impact of their involvement.

From an outsider's perspective, it is also important to realize that relations between a stepfather and child do not occur in a vacuum completely isolated from other family members, most notably mothers. Similarly, people outside the family often affect these relationships. Consequently, if we are to help stepfathers transition smoothly into stepfamilies and contribute to them in healthy ways, research and program initiatives must provide insights and resources that take into account the individual, interpersonal, and community contexts affecting the multilayered process of stepfathering.

9

LAYERS OF STEPFATHERING

At this point, it is time to take stock of the stories that have given life to my analysis of men's complex, dynamic lives as stepfathers. I now show how these stories relate to the personal, familial, and cultural layers of stepfathering.

My recruitment strategy, and the decisions I made to orient my participants to think and talk about their lives during the interviews, narrowed the scope of my research to one kind of social fathering. The voices I represent belong to an eclectic sample of men from many walks of life; men with diverse economic and social backgrounds, life histories, relationships, and personalities who face a wide range of circumstances in their everyday lives. Their romantic partnership with the mother of another man's young child is the common thread that has brought them into my sights.[1] My primary mission has been to shed light on men's experiences as they get involved and stay involved in a romantic relationship where they can act in a fatherly way, speaking broadly, toward the mother's child. Some of the nuances of stepfathering are best revealed by looking closely at how individuals identify, navigate, sustain, challenge, modify, and accept the various boundaries, spoken and unspoken, that define the stepfathers' interactions and relationships with stepchildren. The lens through which I study the men clarifies their subjective worlds while drawing attention to the three interrelated trajectories or paths of fathering I describe: self-as-father, father–child, and coparental.

As I've shown, various aspects define the private and public settings in which men act in a fatherly way. Thinking of both the physical and social dimensions to these scenarios reminds us that much of what resembles fathering occurs within particular sites, physical locations imbued with symbolic meanings (home, school, extended family homes, neighborhoods).

These experiences occur in settings: without an audience, with a select familial audience, or with one of many different types of mixed audiences including family, friends, coworkers, neighbors, strangers, and professionals who work with kids.[2] Because of ambiguous stepfathering norms, much can be learned by studying how men and others manage their relationships with stepchildren in different settings, and move back and forth from one site to another.

Although my lens allows me to capture a great deal about stepfatherhood, an important piece of the stepfathering puzzle remains largely outside my view. My sampling strategy had me interviewing men currently engaged in some form of stepfathering. It essentially excluded those who had once been stepfathers but were no longer. Surely, important questions can be asked about the many men who once acted as stepfathers, but whose romantic involvements with single mothers ended. Unfortunately, answering these questions is beyond my reach here. Finally, notwithstanding a few notable exceptions, the insights gleaned from my study are based not only on men who are currently involved with women who have children, but these men, for the most part, perceive themselves as doing rather well in their stepfamilies.

My research approach and the larger story I craft using the men's in-depth stories and comments is but one of many possibilities for considering men's lives in this domain. One way to assess the value of my efforts is to consider whether the stories I've shared, and my interpretation of them, resonate with stepparents and, to a lesser extent, the persons who work with them. The candid interviews help illustrate the diversity of men's experience as stepfathers, though I make no claim to cover the entire gamut of possibilities.[3] I focus primarily on stepfamily success stories (at least they appear that way for the time being), so I do little to explore the darker side of stepfamilies. Notwithstanding their rather positive focus, the stories also foster a richer, deeper understanding of a number of concepts relevant to stepfathers' experiences, such as the family dance, anticipatory socialization, claiming, social capital, and the father ally role (see appendix A for a complete list). Last, to appreciate fully what these men have to say we need to consider them within the larger cultural, social, and legal context that defines families, parenthood, and more specifically fatherhood in the United States today. The unique and collective wisdom the stories generate makes it easier to imagine strategies at the individual, familial, community, and institutional level that might enhance stepfathers' ability to be involved in children's lives in a way that benefits all parties.

One of the major products of my interviews is that I have been able to reveal much of the immense diversity associated with stepfathering. Men's experiences are far from being monolithic. Just as biological fathers think about and express themselves as fathers in various ways, so do stepfathers. In fact, I suspect that the ambiguity associated with stepfamilies ensures that individual stepfathers, on average, have a much more varied collage of personal experiences than biological fathers. When entering a romantic relationship with a single mother, stepfathers must negotiate the terms of that arrangement while dealing with coparental issues involving the mother's child and perhaps the men's kids as well. To complicate matters, some negotiations eventually incorporate the biological father. In addition, managing individual relationships with the stepchildren typically includes a more complex set of overlapping social processes than is the case for men who become biological fathers. As men work at negotiating their roles with others, they often experience their own identity transitions. Men who learn in a personal way to see themselves as having a fatherly presence with someone else's child do so within a social ecology including relationships with a partner and child, a family dance(s), a neighborhood, community organizations, and a larger cultural and legal context.

How men experience and present their private and public faces as stepfathers is intertwined with this larger social ecology. By revisiting the rich personal stories I have shared, I can illuminate the various layers of stepfathering and the significance of its individual and interpersonal dimensions. Many of these stories are laced with expressions of love, hope, and the desire to repair individuals' feelings and family circumstances. Mixed in with the voices of hope are those reminding us of the friction and frustration that runs deep in many stepfamilies. That a higher percentage of remarriages end in divorce than first marriages, especially those with children, documents that adults in stepfamilies often struggle to the point of calling it quits.[4] My participants' stories, filled with intimate descriptions of their emotions and experiences, bring to light key social and familial processes: cooperation, competition, emotional support, negotiation, distancing, boundary maintenance, and monitoring (supervision). These processes represent the nuts and bolts of the men's attempts to navigate their way within a stepfamily system and adjust to their new roles.[5]

Discussing participants' everyday life experiences before commenting on the institutional context is somewhat arbitrary because these two layers of social life are intertwined. One advantage of this sequence is that it moves us quickly into a discussion of what sociologists call "human agency"—individuals' ability to act in an autonomous, empowered fashion in their everyday lives. To show how people's actions and the larger soci-

ety are interwoven, I'll return to the human agency theme in the concluding chapter after discussing aspects of the larger context affecting stepfathers
and stepfamilies.

Although we all face obstacles in our lives that are rooted in the larger
culture, social structures, and historical conditions surrounding us, we still
have the ability to assign meaning to aspects of our personal existence. We
have the option, too, of making a wide range of choices. Consequently, individuals entering or immersed in stepfamily life can learn to develop a state
of mindfulness while monitoring their emotions. At the same time, they
can modify their personal perceptions while honing their communication
skills and coping strategies. People, for the most part, can make these decisions by themselves. However, it is not easy to change deeply engrained aspects of the larger culture and social structure that impinge upon how stepfamilies and their members are defined and treated. Though critical, it is
likely to be a time consuming and arduous task requiring the collective will
and effort of many people.

IDENTITY TRANSITIONS

A key question guiding my study of stepfatherhood is, How do men's identities as social fathers, stepfathers in particular, evolve? In almost all instances
the men in my sample either quickly or gradually developed an identity
where they saw themselves, and had others see them, as some sort of father
or stepfather figure. The precise meaning of that identity varies considerably among the men,[6] but they all recognize in their own way that they
have developed or are in the process of developing an important connection to someone else's child that extends beyond a typical friendship. Even
the youngest men who are not living with their partner perceive that they
play a significant role in the life of the partner's child. Though the identities for these few men have not yet crystallized in the sense of being a stepfather per se, they have thought about the prospects of being viewed in a
fatherly way and anticipate that this is likely to happen. On a practical level,
they have been doing the types of things with or for their partner's child
that fathers typically do. Similarly, they have begun to develop an emotional bond toward the child that reinforces their connection.

In some cases, even after the men embrace a stepfather identity, subsequent events and reflection can deepen their identity or lead them to become more conscious of it as they negotiate its meaning. Kevin, for instance, had already come to see himself as a stepfather when he developed

a stronger sense of being connected to his stepson by adopting him officially. Specific circumstances, many involving the biological father, also can lead men to reflect on and perhaps redefine the parameters of their identity after they have already incorporated a fatherly sense of self into their larger self concept. The events can lead stepfathers to either intensify or weaken their perspective and associated feelings.

For most men, transitioning to a deeper, more intense sense of having a fatherly identity occurred over time, often in an almost imperceptible way. However, several men comment on specific experiences that gave them fresh insight into how they saw themselves and how they felt others thought of them. Whether we look at Doug's emotional experience when he feared he was about to witness his partner's son drown in a river or Randy's sense of how his frightened stepson bonded with him when they encountered the traffic accident, men sometimes experience turning points that alter fundamentally their identities as stepfathers. However, the general tendency is for men to experience a more gradual shift in their identity.

Knowing something about men's state of mind immediately prior to their getting involved with a woman who is a mother to someone else's child sheds light on how the men move into and adjust to getting involved seriously with the woman and her child. In my sample, the men's life histories prior to their current romantic relationships, and the paths they took in changing their identities, varied greatly. Men like Terry, the happy stepfather presented at the outset of this book, and many others I introduced along the way, including Herman, Jackson, John, Kevin, and Randy, were ready, and in some cases eager, to get more involved with their partner's child. Full of hope, a number of men embraced their new venture and found their journey to be relatively smooth sailing, all things considered. Having their own children prior to entering the world of stepfathering did not appear to influence significantly the men's enthusiasm, but having extensive experience with kids prior to interacting with their partner's child did provide men with added confidence when they assumed their new responsibilities.[7] Randy, for example, did not have children of his own when he met his wife. But his years of hands-on experience caring for two children on separate occasions earlier in his life helped him feel secure enough to seek out and nurture a relationship with his stepson. Thus, readied by his child-oriented mentality and experience in the trenches of daily child care, Randy was primed to play an instrumental role in a stepson's life.

Assuming an identity as a stepfather, or more generally a social father, is not something men are specifically trained to do. Two types of socialization processes, sometimes related to one another, can influence how a man develops an identity as a stepfather.[8] The first process involves young males' exposure to abstract cultural imagery about fathering and stepfathering. This imagery is set apart from men's own lived experience. Nonetheless, it leaves boys and young men with at least a vague sense of how the public at large depicts the ideal, typical, and bad father. For the most part, the messages stem from a biological model of fatherhood, but males may still be exposed to occasional cultural images of stepfathering. Some of the public images of this sort tend toward stereotypical representations of indifferent and abusive stepfathers, for example, the ruthless stepfather portrayed in John Travolta's 2002 movie *Domestic Disturbance* or the frequent news accounts of former President Clinton's alcoholic stepfather.[9] These negative images are, to some extent, offset by more positive images. An example is the fun-loving character, James, played by Travolta in the romantic comedy, *Look Who's Talking*. James, a cab driver, picks up a pregnant single woman and promptly proceeds to coach her through labor and then becomes a doting playmate and child care provider for the newborn, Mikey, winning the hearts of both Mikey and his mother in due time.

The second, more personal level of socialization provides males with direct, intimate knowledge about what it's like to be in a stepfather–stepchild relationship. Given current rates of divorce, out-of-wedlock pregnancy, cohabitation, and remarriage, growing numbers of kids are experiencing firsthand what it's like to have a stepdad, or in many instances multiple stepfathers, during their childhood and later years.[10] For these kids, establishing an image of stepfathers is achieved firsthand, usually on a regular, daily basis. They negotiate and mold their own identities as stepchildren while figuring out how their stepfather does or does not fit into their family dance. Sometimes they navigate this transition while their biological father remains squarely in the picture, interacting with them according to a flexible or preset schedule.[11] On too many occasions, though, kids will make this transition without having much, if any, contact with their biological father. Those not knowing their biological father will have fewer practical reasons to experience the juggling of different identities: being a man's biological child in one situation, adopting the mind-set of being a stepchild in another. They may only learn what it's like to be stepchild to a man, or if the circumstances allow, they may more or less take for granted that they are "essentially" a man's biological child, even though they know deep down that they are not. Though rare, they also may develop an identity as a man's biological child initially, then learn what it means to be a stepchild once they realize that the man they had come to know as father is in fact not their biological father.[12]

From the stepfather's side, several of the men in my study developed their initial perspective on the stepfather–stepchild relationship as children. Being raised by a stepfather gave a few men an insider's view of what it's like to be a child and have a stepfather. Their memories of these experiences, similar to men's experiences with their own fathers, left them with either positive or negative images of how they should treat their own stepchildren. Having this firsthand childhood experience may affect men in different ways—some good, others not so good; much is likely to depend on what their life was like as a stepchild and their reaction to it over the years.

Those men without the childhood experience of being raised by a stepfather received their baptism into stepfamily life some time later during their adult years.[13] The men have their first direct contact with stepfamily dynamics when they get involved with a woman who has a child from a previous relationship. Thus their first taste of stepfamily life comes as they negotiate the transition to being a more significant adult in the life of someone else's child. This transition is marked by a changing view of the self as an adult authority figure for a child. However, unlike the men who experience stepfamily life as a child, their perception of and adjustment to stepfamily life is completely new—unless they have seriously dated other women who had kids. They are not prepared by childhood memories and a perspective of what it's like to be involved in a stepfamily. Compared to those who are personally experienced in being a stepson, men who develop their stepfather identity without this childhood perspective are likely to go through a different kind of learning process. They also may have a more difficult time empathizing with a stepchild who now has a new adult male in his or her life.

Men's comfort level with being a stepfather is shaped by many factors. Their personal development and sense of readiness to assume the responsibilities associated with caring for another man's child are probably two of the more prominent ones. As when fathering their own children, many men do not anticipate the full breadth of implications associated with investing in a child's life. Stepfathers in particular, especially those without children of their own, may not recognize the breadth or depth of the circumstances they will face as the days, weeks, and years come and go. Among my stepfathers, Ron and Monty are clearly the most surprised with how their relationships have evolved with their partner's kids. Harry, too, has been disappointed that his stepdaughter has never accepted him into her life as fully as he hoped. Some men, like Rodney and Allen, feel they have gotten along fairly well with their stepchildren but struggle with the birth mother's parenting style and personality. Even though some of the other stepfathers voice relatively minor concerns about their adjustment to step-fatherhood, most of the men in my study seem to have dealt reasonably well with the situations they have encountered. Other than Ron and Monty, none have been overwhelmed with what they have encountered thus far and they seem to have relatively reasonable expectations of what is possible. Time may, of course, paint an entirely different picture as new and unpredictable situations arise.

Given the wide range of circumstances the men face, they have developed a wide variety of self-images about their relationships with their partner's child. Herman, for example, recognizes that his wife's children have a biological father who is involved to some extent in their lives. He fully understands that he's not the biological father, yet he sees himself as a father and feels uneasy about language that refers to Annette as his "step" daughter. Similar to Terry, who says it's okay for his stepson to have two dads, Herman adopts an identity that enables him to invest in his sense of self as a father to Annette irrespective of her relationship to her biological father. Just as a child can have an identity as a brother or sister to more than one sibling, so too Herman and Terry feel reasonably comfortable forging a father identity even though someone else previously claimed and has sustained a similar title due to his genetic tie to his child.

How these men, and other stepfathers, manage their identities on a daily basis is often influenced by the degree and type of contact the biological father has with members of the stepfamily. In Terry's case, because his stepson Zack's father lives out of state and Zack lives with Terry full-time during most of the year, visiting his biological father for a month or so in the summer, Terry seldom finds himself negotiating his role in Zack's life. The main exception occurs during the summer when Zack returns to Terry's home after visiting the biological father. Because Terry's lifestyle and parental philosophy are quite different from that of Zack's father, the adjustment period after Zack's summer visit prompts Terry to be more self-conscious about not being the only father figure in Zack's life. Aside from this summer period, though, the limited contact Zack has with his father provides Terry the space to drift into a daily consciousness of being the main man responsible for taking care of Zack's daily needs. Zack consistently referring to him as dad also reinforces Terry's state of mind as a "father."

Other stepfathers, like Herman and Robby, negotiate their identities as stepfathers while the biological fathers live nearby and have contact with their kids throughout the year. In both cases, these stepfathers encourage the fathers to stay in contact with their kids and are comfortable with being called by their first names. Compared to Terry or to stepfathers who are a part of a stepfamily in which the biological father is not involved in the children's lives at all, it appears that individuals like Herman and Robby are more likely to have moments throughout the year where they are reminded that another man is involved as a father. They appear to take these reminders in stride; their commitment to their identity does not waiver. Others, like Stephen, the man who entered a stepfamily shortly after the father died, frown on their stepchildren or the mother mentioning the father's name while the stepfathers are present. Though it is impossible to say for sure, I suspect that Stephen's willingness and ability to make the transition to seeing himself as a father in his stepfamily was enhanced because he was able to minimize the "presence" of the deceased father in the stepfamily dance. However, his "gain" appears to be his stepdaughter's loss because she resents Stephen for making this demand.

CONNECTING INDIVIDUALS, CONNECTING FAMILIES

From a practical standpoint, when men become a part of a stepfamily, they establish a connection to the members of that family. Sometimes they do this with ease and a smile, other times they struggle. The difficulties sometimes arise because the critical process of weaving lives together pulls people in from different families, linking people as well as families or parts of families.[14] Family theorists and therapists draw attention to this reality by referring to stepfamily systems and subsystems.

To be a stepfather, a man obviously has to develop some type of relationship with his partner's child. As I've shown in the previous chapters, stepfathers can engage in the same types of activities as biological fathers, and many do. Some of the activities involve one-on-one forms of involvement where they attempt to establish affinity or bond with them. They pursue leisure activities like playing games, taking them places, or reading to them. Many also take on disciplinary responsibilities. These experiences help to influence the father–child trajectory I've identified as one of the three paths of the fatherhood experience. In an early stage, this trajectory may resemble more of a friend interacting with a child or an adult male doing the same. As noted earlier, for the men in my sample, this trajectory moved in the direction of the man developing more fatherly ways with the child, especially when a fatherly presence is defined broadly. Men who have more than one stepchild develop a separate relationship with each; some of those relationships may be very similar, others not so.

On occasion stepfathers instigate opportunities to blend families, formally or informally, and they do so with varying degrees of involvement on the mother's part. Several of the men in my study went out of their way to incorporate their biological children into their stepchildren's lives, and Keith even made a point of introducing his thirty-year-old stepson from a previous relationship to his current wife's two teenage daughters. When stepfathers engage in this blending of biological and stepchildren, they are likely to alter the trajectory of their relationships with each. Having biological children present, for instance, may mean that the stepfathers spend more time with their stepchildren.[15]

The stepfathers' involvement with stepchildren is obviously fostered by the men's relationships with the mother. Thus, in addition to the self-as-father and father–child trajectories of fathering, coparenting is the third trajectory critical to the stepfamily building process. It matters, too, in how well the stepfamily grows. Throughout, I have explored various aspects of coparenting by sharing the stories of stepfathers and their partners. These stories illustrate that when a man enters a birth mother's family dance prior to forming a new stepfamily, he becomes entwined in a social process, one that eventually requires him to come to terms with his place in his partner's life and her child's. Many times this process also requires the stepfather to take into account the biological father and relatives. In short, the more a stepfather gets involved with a woman who is a mother, the more likely he is to think about and interact with an entirely new set of people.

Recently a great deal of scholarly and public attention has focused on devising strategies to promote healthy, or at least civil, communications between former spouses and partners who have children together. Divorce mediation, sometimes court mandated, and couple's therapy sessions have been the rage in the United States in the past few decades.[16] During this time, evidence has mounted showing that children whose parents split tend to fare best emotionally and otherwise when the parents are able to communicate effectively and avoid open, destructive conflict.[17]

When a relationship ends, most people eventually move on with their romantic lives and take on new partners; some actually find these partners before the previous relationship "officially" ends. Consequently, understanding how the newcomers fit into a family dance involving children is becoming an increasingly timely topic. Although research continues to shed light on many aspects of stepfamily life and the adjustments individuals make when faced with living in a new family,[18] precious little is known about how the biological parent outside the stepfamily and the new parental figure relate to each other. Similarly, there's little discussion about how to improve these relationships.

My interviews reveal, and my discussion emphasizes, how some step-fathers attempt to preserve and enhance the relationship between their stepchildren and the biological father. This type of activity speaks directly to an important connection between individuals, and in some sense ties be-tween families, which can prove critical to stepfamily adjustment. When stepfathers and biological fathers establish ties built on mutual respect as adults and a concern about the best interests of the child, stepfamily adjust-ment is likely to be enhanced. Before commenting on the stepfathers' re-marks that help illustrate their role as an ally for their stepchildren's biolog-ical father, it is inspiring to look at an insightful essay that appeared in *USA Today* a few days prior to Father's Day in 2001.[19] Tim Friend, a writer for this paper, and nonresident father to a fourteen-year-old daughter at the time, prepared this unusual letter as a testimonial to his daughter's stepfa-ther, Jerry, the man who married Tim's former wife and took over as the resident stepfather.[20] With refreshing candor and wit, Tim praises Jerry for his efforts as a stepfather while casting light on a topic seldom breached in an open forum. This nifty letter, significant for many reasons, may be most noteworthy for its attempt to engage a national audience to think more deeply about the relations between biological parents and stepparents, if even for a day. In this abridged version of Tim's letter, I seek to capture the spirit of his sentiment toward Jerry, his sense of what is in his daughter's best interest, and his mindful approach to being, essentially, a stepfather ally. He begins by playfully commenting on how his daughter's transition into the adolescent years, when kids often assume they have all the answers to life's many questions, sets the stage for her frustrations with adult authority.

And now her vastly superior intelligence has become the source of a growing level of impatience with adults—especially him, the stepfather. Her mantra—spoken in a clearly audible voice, usually when he's forced to be the disciplinarian: "You'renotmyrealdadIhateyou!" . . . Sometimes it appears to be a thankless job. So, with Father's Day around the cor-ner, I figure it's time the real dad—that's me—said thank you to Jerry, the stepdad who is on the front lines facing the pretty demon of adoles-cence and making the daily sacrifices that would have been my job, had I stayed married. I'm sure my daughter, his stepdaughter, will thank him one day for the good job he is doing, but if there's a way to make her appreciate him sooner, then her young life and ours will be that much happier and more relaxed. I have a simple plan to achieve this goal, which is to show him my appreciation and try to lift some of the disci-plinary burden from his shoulders. If I'm successful, my daughter, who thinks that I can do no wrong, will hate both of us equally. It seems only fair. . . . My respect for Jerry is immense. It struck me most recently when my daughter was complaining to me that he was grumpy and I was always nice. I thought about all of the days that he had to leave work early to make those soccer practices and teacher conferences. It didn't really occur to me at the time, but those were days that I—living as a single adult—could work late if I felt I needed to, or schedule a business dinner, or simply go home and toss my shoes on the floor and turn on the television. It isn't easy to admit that another guy may be doing a better job of being a dad, or at least is doing as good a job as you if you were still there. But it is absolutely necessary to appreciate his role if you want your children to do the same. . . . My daughter told me recently that she didn't like the idea of this kind of cooperation between me and Jerry. I had to smile because it made me think that we are on the right track.

When I first read Tim's letter, I was reminded of my lively interview with Herman, the man who was most vocal among the stepfathers about doing whatever he could to help his stepdaughter and her father strengthen their relationship. Tim offers the same kind of mindful, mature perspective on the stepfathering experience, in his case, from the point of view of the biological father. Together, these men demonstrate what is possible, though currently quite uncommon.

Their comments enable me to extend my thinking on the coparental path as it applies to scenarios involving a stepfather.[21] From a conceptual point of view, this path can be expanded to incorporate not only a stepfather's experiences with the child's mother, as is now the case, but also with the biological father. In those instances where a man reaches out to another man, or in some cases to a few men (different biological fathers for stepchildren in one family), his experience may influence how he perceives and presents his identity as a stepfather/father. Though meaningful contact is far from the norm these days, some men speak to each other and many at least think about the other man who is treating a child in a fatherly way. Perhaps a growing number will do so in the future as people become more familiar with stepfamilies and nonresident fathers become more involved with their children; they are clearly capable of pursing this path. However, developing these connections is not likely to become the common course or path of least resistance any time soon. With men's competitive tendencies being what they are, many will struggle with the prospects of developing an identity as a stepfather or father that is based, in part, on the assumption that paternal responsibilities and rights are being shared with another man. A close look at why some fathers and stepfathers resist a meaningful relationship with each other is likely to reveal insecurities about how the child symbolizes a previous or current romantic relationship between the child's mother and one of the men.

Tim's story is revealing because he expresses his desire to apply his mindfulness to his daughter so that she might appreciate her stepfather more. Of course, in dealing with his adolescent daughter's young mind, Tim runs the risk of inadvertently giving her a nudge that will lead her to distance herself from him and side more with Jerry. But Tim wants to focus on the larger picture while considering what is in his daughter's best interest, now and in the future. His empathy skills serve him well; his desire to assume a stronger disciplinary role, and take more of the heat from his daughter in the process, suggests that Tim is capable of seeing himself as part of a cofather team that extends beyond his joint responsibilities and privileges with his daughter's mother.

The message conveyed in Tim's letter, as well as the sentiments shared by many of my participants, reveal how identities are embedded in a social context. For the cofather team approach to work for everyone, the two men need to be on the same page, both in terms of what they perceive to be the best interests of the child and their desire to respect each other's roles in the child's life. Because many people harbor negative feelings about their former partners and the uncoupling process, plenty of people would rather not deal with their former partners. If children were not involved, many would choose to avoid each other altogether. This tension can seep into the lives of the new partners and make it difficult for the woman's new partner and the biological father to foster warm relations.

This tension increases the odds that a child will at some point try to manipulate his biological parents and stepparents, especially when it involves family rules and matters of discipline. As part of a conscious or unconscious ploy, the child will look to test the loyalties of the authority figures in his or her life while promoting personal self-interest. Along these lines, some scholars have suggested an intriguing possibility: "a stepfather's demand for conformity is likely to have the most [positive] effect on stepfather–stepchild relationship quality in cases where the biological father's parenting input is great but his interaction with his child is minimal."[22] Although the evidence currently supporting this idea is thin, it warrants discussion because it addresses important interpersonal and interfamily dynamics.

Let's break this proposition down into several more manageable parts. When we do, we are left to consider how a stepfather's relationship with his stepchild, and his expectations that the child listen to and respect him, may depend on two factors: the frequency of contact between the biological father and child and the extent to which the father has a voice in decisions affecting the child. How much the child and father interact is supposedly critical. The amount of input the father has vis-à-vis the mother about the child's life only affects the quality of the stepfather-stepchild relationship when the father interacts frequently with the child. Ironically, if the father feels he has a great deal of input in the key decisions affecting his child but has little contact with him, then stepfathers who expect their stepchild to conform to their own wishes have the best chance of having a high-quality relationship with the child. But when a biological father has a high level of input, as well as a lot of contact with his child, then the stepfather who wants this child (his stepchild) to conform is less likely to have a deep relationship with him or her.

Though intriguing, this empirical pattern is not particularly strong in the study that notes it, and it is unclear to what extent it does and will generalize to all stepfathers. The proposition and pattern are based on the assumption that in the future fathers and stepfathers will continue to hold the same kinds of beliefs and parenting styles that they do now, including the tendency for them to seldom communicate with each other. Ideally, with encouragement, fathers and stepfathers will begin to communicate more often, honestly, and respectfully, but the prospects for this occurring are unknown. If nonresident fathers begin to increase their level of involvement with their children, it may become more commonplace for biological and stepfathers to develop better communication with one another. For some, though, this greater involvement could mean more friction if the men and birth mother do not anticipate and handle the implications associated with it in a responsible fashion.

We should also distinguish between two ways of thinking about greater father involvement patterns. One represents a historical pattern in which a cohort of nonresident fathers, compared to earlier generations of fathers, may make a greater effort to be involved with their children immediately after a romantic partnership dissolves, and then continue to stay involved. The other more personal pattern involves individual fathers who may for a period of time have a relatively low level of involvement with their nonresident children, but then shift gears and make more of a concerted effort to be involved. In the latter instance, those stepfathers who have been shaping the stepfamily dance may be forced to adjust rather quickly to the way they relate to their stepchildren because the father has come back on the scene. Whereas stepfathers affected by the historical pattern have a chance to learn upfront what to expect and make decisions about whether they are comfortable with an existing set of circumstances, those who experience the second pattern are asked to integrate themselves into a stepfamily dance where the rhythm changes, perhaps significantly, during the dance. Some stepfathers are likely to find this challenging to say the least; the father's renewed interest in his child may lead the stepfather to feel more uncertainty about his place in the stepchild's life and the stepfamily more generally.

Concerns about the naming and claiming issues discussed in chapters 5 and 6 are sometimes central to how biological and stepfathers feel about and manage their relations with each other. Fathers who are involved with children who do not live with them full-time, and only visit occasionally if at all, must grapple with how much say they have in their children's lives. Some men are the father in name and genetics, but they may have little formal or informal control over what their children do. This set of circumstances can lead fathers to struggle with themselves and others over their place in their children's lives. Many, despite not living with their children full-time, retain a great deal of parental control and sustain their belief that the children are theirs on all accounts. The personal and interpersonal dynamics that shape how these fathers think about and treat their children are complex.

Part of the complexity is accentuated because stepfathers often enter the picture and then they, along with others in the household/family, negotiate and assign meaning to their lives within this stepfamily setting or "incomplete institution."[23] Defining the stepfather's place in the stepfamily, including what to call him and how to define his level of responsibility and authority, is a critical issue intrinsic to stepfamily life. Decisions about these matters must be worked out either implicitly or explicitly. Sometimes individuals resolve them with relative ease and no friction. In many instances, people are not so fortunate. Struggles about how the stepfather should be incorporated into the stepfamily often lead to tension, arguments, and hurt feelings. Notably, when tension does exist, it sometimes implicates the biological father in one way or another.

The men's stories indicate that "naming" is not a goal per se for many stepfathers, but it is definitely an issue for some. I showed how some deal with this issue and how it affects the way they frame their identities and interactions with others. For these men, claiming ownership of a stepchild is often an important element of their bonding experience, though that ownership can be expressed in different ways and to varying degrees. Herman's and Robby's comments imply a form of ownership, but one that is shared with the biological father. These two men, and others, express this shared reality in numerous ways, but many stepfathers are able to recognize that the biological father and they both have important roles to play. Thus stepfathers of this persuasion demonstrate that they can attain a fatherly presence without necessarily replacing the biological dad. But sometimes the biological father distances himself or is somehow displaced, leaving the stepfather in the position to develop a more prominent and unilateral kind of identity as a father figure. Still, some stepfathers may make a concerted effort to recognize the biological father's legitimacy and ensure that the child and birth mother respect him. Even among those who adopt this father ally role, however, some also feel they have claimed the child as theirs. Just as a mother and father can each lay claim to a child as "theirs" without suggesting that the other parent is excluded, so too some stepdads develop an identity where they lay claim to a child without suggesting that the biological father does not have paternal rights and responsibilities.

These patterns highlight the complex web of relationships, loyalties, and desires that affect stepfathers' efforts to navigate stepfamily life and develop a secure place within their stepfamily. As I've shown, the birth mothers are often instrumental in how men try to manage this space. Although I spent more time talking about how they mediate the stepfathers' relationships with the stepchildren, birth mothers also can affect how stepfathers relate to the biological father. On rare occasions, stepfathers may even find themselves facing loyalty conflicts involving their partner and the biological father. The birth mother may harbor resentment if she feels the stepfather is taking sides with the biological father. Some birth mothers expect the stepfather to be the loyal supporter who defends whatever position they take relative to the biological father. Although the stepfathers did challenge how the birth mothers in my study treated the biological father on occasion, the mothers never let on that these challenges led them to feel angry or disappointed.

Whatever the issue, and whether it implicates the biological father or not, a stepfather who has not established legal custody through adoption is in a precarious position. The man without legal custody may find himself on thin ice, knowing that the birth mother ultimately has the power to limit his involvement with the stepchild. Thus, compared to a biological father, it is more critical for a stepfather to maintain a civil relationship with the birth mother if he wishes to preserve a relationship with her children. But the stepfather's civility is no guarantee of his continued contact with the kids. From a legal perspective, and often a practical one, the stepfather's ability to sustain his relationship with minor stepchildren is dictated by the birth mother's preferences and goodwill.[24]

THE WORLD OUT THERE

In many ways, stepfathers, birth mothers, and stepchildren are able to make individual decisions that shape their stepfamily relationships and personal well-being. But the decisions they make do not occur in a vacuum. How stepfamily members think about themselves, and interact with others within their stepfamily and those intimately involved with it (biological father, relatives), is affected by the larger cultural context within which particular forms of step or social fathering take place.[25] The images, messages, resources, and constraints that emanate from this cultural context are connected to the norms and structures of key social institutions and organizations, such as the legal system, education, youth organizations, health care, religious groups, and social services.

Laws and social policies related to stepfamilies can be meaningful for stepfathers, and others, because they help reinforce what is normative and draw attention to family boundaries.[26] In the process, laws can give, reinforce, and take away stepparents' rights and obligations. Thus legal customs can either legitimize stepfathers' roles or contribute to stepfathers feeling excluded from an institutionally supported status with regard to their stepchildren. Currently, in the absence of formal adoption, stepfathers in the United States have few legal rights or obligations toward their stepchildren while they are together or after their romantic relationship with the mother ends. However, because some states have issued new family laws that permit third parties to file requests for postdivorce custody and visitation, stepparents have been given a chance, though admittedly poor, to make a legal case for their continued involvement with a stepchild.[27] In rare instances, stepfathers have been successful in making their case. For example, the California Supreme Court decided on June 7, 2002, to reverse a lower court decision and grant custody of a seven-year-old boy to Thomas, a man who is not the boy's biological father.[28] Thomas, who is listed as the father on the birth certificate, moved in with the mother of the child when the mother was three months pregnant by another man. In the end, he got the nudge for custody because the woman had her own set of issues: keeping a job, being homeless, and having a drug problem.

The legal and educational systems are noteworthy because they often shape the social interventions targeting people involved in stepfamilies or those likely to be involved in them in the future. Recently legal scholars, social scientists, and the public at large have turned their attention more squarely to considering how social policy and the legal system is relevant to stepfamily life as well as the meaning and practice of fatherhood.[29] Social policies can either directly or indirectly affect stepfamilies. My participants' stories underscore two principles some scholars believe should be the foundation for policies directly addressing stepfamily needs: stepfamilies are diverse and steprelationships, especially between a stepparent and stepchild, can be significant and valuable to both parties.[30]

Even though I did not include, to my knowledge, stepfamilies in which physical child abuse occurs, my participants are involved in a wide range of stepfamily types. The lives of Terry, Herman, Jackson, John, Kevin, Randy, Monty, and Ron show how diverse stepfamilies can be. They vary in marital and cohabiting status, quality of stepfamily adjustment, the presence or absence of the stepfather's biological children, the degree and quality of the biological father's involvement, the length of time together, custody status, and the gender and age composition of the children.[31] This diversity should alert policymakers and those who work with stepfamilies to the fact that stepfamily life is not amenable to a "one solution fits all" mentality. Whereas some stepfamilies may manage just fine by modeling themselves after the nuclear family ideal, this ideal model is not suitable for many stepfamilies. Many who insist on using the nuclear family as the baseline end up feeling frustrated, depressed, and often alone.

Among the men listed above, we also find evidence that stepfathers can have meaningful and enduring relationships with their stepchildren. In some cases those relationships are every bit as powerful as the relationships biological fathers have with their children. Stepchildren can, of course, flourish without their stepfather adopting a deeply rooted fatherly way and commitment to them. However, institutionalizing social and legal supports that give men and children the option of nurturing such a connection, if they want it, would be ideal.

A potential innovative policy, already law in England, involves granting resident stepparents the opportunity to establish a legal relationship with a stepchild without adopting the child.[32] The Children Act 1989, which became law in England in 1991, views children as the responsibility of parents, rather than their property. Following a divorce, both parents retain parental authority. A provision also allows stepparents to petition the court for a residency order if they have been married to the biological parent for at least two years. The orders are usually granted and cannot be overruled by the other biological parent. Under this arrangement the stepparent gains parental responsibility for the child for the duration of the order, typically until the child turns sixteen. Although stepparents do not have exactly the same rights as the biological parents, they are quite similar. All persons with parental responsibility, for instance, must agree on any name changes for the child and the child cannot be taken from the United Kingdom for more than four weeks without each adult's consent. It differs from adoption in that the biological parents retain their rights; consequently, the child can have a legal relationship with at least three adults.

How would a similar policy work if implemented in the United States? One commentary on the English policy provides an extensive list of potential advantages and disadvantages that should be considered.[33] If we focus for the moment only on stepfamilies where a stepfather is present, one possible benefit is the "enhanced stepfamily cohesion" that might occur because the biological parent(s) and stepfather are likely to have serious and revealing discussions prior to the residency order being issued. These discussions could help clarify the stepfather's parental roles. The formal recognition for the stepfather would also go a long way to legitimize the stepfather-stepchild relationship and, in the process, may strengthen the stepfather's and stepchild's commitment to their relationship. By reducing the ambiguity of the stepfather's place in the stepfamily, the residency order might enhance the stability of the birth mother's and stepfather's relationship and the stepfamily more generally.

Other scholars have also championed ideas consistent with the residency order approach by calling for a new legal parental category, the "de facto parent."[34] This category would

> legally recognize stepparents as parental authorities but not cut off the rights of nonresident biological parents and not continue indefinitely in the event of divorce. The concept of de facto parent is currently used loosely in the law with respect to those caring for children, but it has not taken on full form, with clearly delineated rights and responsibilities. Moreover, there is not consistency in the courts as to its use.

The de facto parent would have the same types of rights and obligations during the course of a marriage and they would continue for a period of time in the event of divorce or the death of the biological parent.[35]

Despite the potential advantages of the residency order, or the de facto parent proposal, introducing either of these changes might produce unwelcome consequences. Some fear that it could add another layer of bureaucracy to an already cumbersome array of child welfare organizations. If it is perceived as interfering with biological fathering, it could limit nonresident fathers' involvement with their children, causing some to become more distant. In addition, the added parental responsibilities and rights could prompt stepfathers to move too quickly into a disciplinary role. When stepfathers get involved prematurely in this way, it sometimes produces ill feelings between the stepfathers and the stepchildren. Finally, some stepfathers may come to see the residency order as more of an obligation than a choice. When this happens, men may grow reluctant to marry a woman who has a child from a previous relationship. Because men can still develop a loving cohabiting relationship, not all observers view men's reluctance to marry a woman with children as a problem. However, some men may avoid all forms of serious relationships with women who are mothers if the men feel as though they will be faced with unrealistic and undesirable parental expectations. Given some of the men's comments in my study, it is not only the children and mothers who might miss out on desirable opportunities, men would also forgo a chance to grow personally from their close relationship with and commitment to a child—in this case a child not biologically related to them.

As some policymakers slowly turn their attention to the ways law relates to stepfamilies, states and communities have begun to either mandate or encourage individuals to participate in programs for separated and divorced families. In some communities the programs are even extended to parents who are not married to one another and their children. Most of these programs are based on a model to help biological parents and their children adjust to the immediate change in their family arrangement. Although divorce mediation and parenting groups are fairly well received by adults and positively affect their adjustment and coparenting skills, research has yet to establish that these programs clearly have a significant and beneficial impact on the children.[36] Despite limited evidence that these interventions work, it seems that interventions focused on persons going through divorce or informal breakups have become a more normalized aspect of people's lives in the United States. This is a by-product of people becoming more familiar with families' diverse life histories. With this awareness people have also become more aware of the struggles single-parent families face, including coparenting among parents who are no longer romantically involved with each other.

As those in the legal and mental health professions continue to revise their approaches for dealing with separated, divorced, and uncoupled families, they have become much more inclined to see uncoupling as part of a continuing process. Family members in these situations and the professionals who work with them recognize the value of treating families that include minor children as being in a transitional state where the connections between two households or families typically need to be taken into account. This departs from seeing the uncoupled partners and parents as making a "clean break" from their earlier life together. Now they are encouraged to recognize what has been called the "extended family network"[37] or the "new extended family."[38] As this view takes hold, the need for programs with longer-term objectives will become more pressing.

It also is becoming increasingly important to consider how emerging stepfamily arrangements affect the original family members over time. Granted, it may not be appropriate to deal with stepfamily issues in the early phases of parenting programs targeting former lovers and spouses. However, issues associated with how the parents are likely to get involved with new partners and introduce them to their children is an essential component of educating parents to be effective "single parents" who coparent in a cooperative way. Ultimately, many will take up the project of being a biological parent in a stepfamily. In numerous cases they will become stepparents too. For obvious reasons, the future stepfathers (and stepmothers) are unlikely to be incorporated into programs dealing with family members' immediate concerns after a relationship dissolves. Nonetheless, it may become ever more important to include them in follow-up programs that deal with the long-term formation of the "his" and "her" family and separate households. Effective initiatives must be developed to help individuals handle the potential sexual jealousy, animosity, and competition that underlie many coparenting situations where the ex-partners are at odds with each other and are having problems accepting their former partner's new lover/spouse. Addressing these frictions in a mature fashion is often critical to establishing the mutual respect necessary to coparent across two households/families while enabling stepfathers to feel comfortable with their roles.

Our schools represent another key social institution that can influence stepfathers' self-image and involvement with their stepchildren, as well as stepchildren's academic, psychological, and emotional well-being. Unfortunately, schools have been slow to adapt to stepfamilies' needs. Scholars have recently identified a series of practical steps professionals working in schools can use to enable students and their stepparents to feel more comfortable with their family circumstances.[39] Although much of the literature focuses on interventions with stepchildren and child outcomes, it is also important to focus attention on the stepparents. Enhancing stepfathers' level of interest in their stepchild's educational achievements may produce dividends for the stepchild as well as the stepfather. This may be especially true for stepfathers who already demonstrate a willingness to be involved in their stepchild's schooling.

Some of the stepfathers in my study took an active interest in their stepchild's schoolwork. For the most part, those who attended planned or special parent–teacher meetings describe the teachers, and other school personnel, as treating them as an authority figure in the child's life. William's experience provides an excellent example of how one man was made to feel relevant. He begins by describing his feelings about a previous conference he attended.

> Well, I was interested. I wanted to know why was Deon having trouble in school. This was year before last. That's when the problem started. Like I said, his grades were dropping off. He wasn't doing his homework. He was being disrespectful. Now the teacher called us two weeks ago—no last week. She said it wasn't a big problem, but she could see where it could turn into a problem. He's starting to follow that same pattern. So now we've got this meeting set up to see what is going on and we're going to try to nip this in the bud.

I then asked, referring him back to his first experience, "Do you remember how you felt about how the teacher interacted with you?"

> Well, she treated me as though I actually was his father. So I didn't have any problems with it. I mean, she wanted to know what I had to say and listened. She made me feel that she was giving me full attention and she would take into consideration the things that I said.

Apparently William is motivated to stay on top of Deon's school behavior partly because the teacher in the first meeting validated William's role as a parental authority figure. He feels that with the teacher's help, he and his partner can get Deon back on track. Although there's no way of knowing for sure, had the teacher not treated William as she did, he may have been less interested in being involved the second time. So, the social capital that William established during his first meeting with the teacher established an effective bridge for communication that has sustained his commitment to be involved in Deon's schooling.

On the few occasions that stepfathers complained about how they were treated, they tended to see it as a reflection of the teacher's personality that wasn't related to them as a stepfather. Although I am sure that some stepfathers in the general population feel isolated or unimportant during their interactions with school personnel, the blatant biases against stepfamilies that have been documented in the literature have probably declined over time as teachers, and the rest of society, become more accustomed to dealing with diverse family structures.[40] Unfortunately, blatant and subtle biases persist. Thus there is still a need for workshops to provide teachers and other school personnel with practical ways to acknowledge and honor the diversity of family arrangements while enlisting the support of those stepfathers who are willing to be involved in their stepchild's school life.

In addition to the school personnel's perceptions, a number of other factors are likely to influence the dynamics of how stepfathers interact with school personnel and feel about it. The stepfather's personality, the mother's attitude and orientation to her partner's involvement, and the biological father's approach are potential contributing factors. Rodney, for example, describes how he feels when he goes with Judith, his wife, to parent–teacher conferences. "I felt like a bystander. Judith would do 99 percent of the talking for us. Part of that's probably my fault for just letting her do it, but it's her kid. [I: And that's how you felt at the time? You say that it's her kid.] Yeah. Well, it's at those times when it's her kid, is when she wants to take control and be the responsible one and make all the decisions." Later Rodney notes that he felt like he was treated as an "equal amongst the parents" by the teachers, but that he wasn't particularly comfortable with the experience. He feels better when he is able to go by himself to one of the meetings due to his wife working. When that happens, he says, "I put myself in a different position. The one that's being responsible, accountable or whatever you might want to call it." For Rodney, his wife's assertive personality and commitment to her children, along with his reserved demeanor, create a group dynamic where he finds himself drifting into the background as she deals with "her kid." He is quite willing, by his own admission, to take a more assertive role in a situation where he is the person in charge. Rodney's situation highlights the complex web of personal and interpersonal factors that can shape men's self-impressions as stepfathers within an institutional setting like a parent–teacher conference.

One way to enhance a stepfather's identity as an important figure in his stepchild's schooling career is for school personnel to acknowledge and encourage his involvement outside the parent–teacher meetings. This can involve such things as allowing a stepfather to sign permission slips for school events, addressing notices to both the birth mother and the stepfather, and releasing the child's student records to him. Not being allowed to sign permission slips struck a cord with Randy. While talking about how adopting his stepson would change his life, he comments, "It means I can start signing some of the papers instead of her. It's ridiculous now in some ways because I read the paper and tell her what it says and she says, 'Should I sign it or not?'" Historically, school officials' ability to validate the stepfather's authority role by providing him access to his stepchild's school records has been restricted by public policy. Now efforts are under way to change this practice. For example, on July 18, 2001, the Family Policy and

Compliance Office (FPCO) made an important ruling about the Family Educational Rights and Privacy Act (FERPA).[41] This ruling was prompted by a stepfather's complaint to the FPCO alleging that the district had denied him access to his stepchildren's school records. He argued that it was his responsibility to deal with his stepchildren's educational concerns because his wife's work schedule precluded her from being involved. In addition, he complained that he was not permitted to participate in parent–teacher conferences unless his wife was present and the superintendent had instructed school officials not to discuss educational issues with him. The FPCO ruled that "a stepparent has rights under FERPA when he or she is present on a day-to-day basis with the natural parent and child and the other parent is absent from the residential setting. In this case, it stated that the stepfather would have rights under FERPA because he was present in the home on each day with the child and the child's mother."

This stepfather's frustrating experience with his local school system underscores the importance of thinking creatively about what individuals and groups might do to make the larger social and cultural environment more responsive to stepfamilies' unique needs. When the multiple layers of stepfathering are accentuated, it's also clear that stepfathers and other stepfamily members can take effective action closer to home through their conscientious thoughts, feelings, and deeds.

10

TAKING ACTION

One of the joys for me in doing this research was having a chance to hear men from diverse family backgrounds, with all sorts of relationship circumstances, talk excitedly about their involvement with their partner's children. The men serve as a reminder that despite negative public stereotypes,[1] as well as research showing that remarried couples and stepchildren tend to not fare as well as once-married, intact couples and their biological children,[2] many stepfathers are still able to express themselves in a positive, fatherly way in a healthy stepfamily. Many stepfathers and their families, however, do not do so well. So, what would it take for more men to experience the kind of well-adjusted stepfamily life described by many of the men with whom I spoke? Do adult men and women have the power to make changes in their own lives to improve their chances, and perhaps the chances of others, to create healthy stepfamilies? Can people shape their own worlds so that men can be effective in their roles as stepfathers, or are most people doomed to disappointment because stepfamilies tend to be too complicated and poorly defined? What about the chances for changing cultural stereotypes about stepfamilies? Will making significant changes in the way key institutions and organizations treat families create a backdrop that will improve stepfamily life for stepfathers? Can new social policies and laws make a difference, even a small one, in the way stepfathers and those close to them construct the meanings they apply to themselves and their involvements with stepfamily members?

CULTURAL DEFINITIONS

As with many family issues facing individuals today, there are both structural and personal approaches to improving people's lives. Legal scholar

Nancy Dowd reminds us to be leery about expecting the legal system to bring major changes to our lives in all cases. Speaking specifically about the need to revamp our cultural definition of fatherhood, she says, "If the change needed is cultural, then law cannot mandate it. It must come from below, from an individual and communal desire to reorient fatherhood, implemented by lived changes in men's lives."[3] But she does not write off the law's powerful role entirely. She continues, "The law not only reflects but also determines culture. Particularly when the law takes on the task of not only defining but also educating, it is explicitly used to create and mold culture." Dowd targets her remarks on definitions of fatherhood rather than stepfamilies, but they are relevant to my discussion about stepfatherhood as well. Just as the law may be of use in reshaping our definition of fatherhood, it can influence perceptions about the meaning and borders of families and stepfamilies as well as men's involvement in them.

Dowd goes to great length to show how cultural definitions of fatherhood and masculinity are intertwined in ways that have produced a legal definition of fatherhood in the United States fundamentally tied to biology, marriage, and economics. As I mentioned in chapter 2, she aspires to redefine fatherhood by elevating nurturance as the signature marker of social fathering.[4] To accomplish this she realizes that we must grapple with two destructive aspects of conventional masculinity: (1) the notion that males learn to define their manhood by distancing themselves from females and "feminine" traits and (2) the high premium attached to violence.

The first aspect is particularly relevant to stepfathering. Homophobic beliefs—concerns about being viewed as gay—are a well-established element of this gendered process. Males' homophobia encourages them to protect their masculine identity by managing their emotions and friendships with other men in a particular fashion.[5] Thus constructions of masculinity that breed homophobia will also lead some boys and men toward what has been called emotional illiteracy.[6] This may affect the extent to which men are willing to talk about and cooperate in cofathering. If true, men may be less likely than women to connect with their ex-partner's current romantic partner to serve their children's needs. I wonder, though, if this potential difference depends on the gender of the child. When men interact with one another as the biological and stepfather for a girl, as Tim and his daughter's stepfather described in the *USA Today* article, they may cooperate with each other more than when the child is a boy. Perhaps they will be more willing to acknowledge their helplessness and cooperate to parent a girl—a person whose gendered personality and perhaps interests are more foreign to them than what would typically be the case if the child were a boy. When the child is a boy, jealousy may simmer more freely. The biological father may be more inclined to identify with him and more likely to resent the fact that another male is trying to take his place as a male role model. Although purely speculative at this point, research could test my hypothesis.

Another consequence of these typical male friendship patterns built on homophobia and competition is that, compared to females, males face more of an uphill struggle to incorporate the ethic of nurturance into their personality and relationships. I raise these issues here because they can affect how men manage their identities and relationships within stepfamilies.

In recent years, we have witnessed significant changes in the gender order and the latitude of acceptable male behavior within and outside romantic relationships and families. However, our male-dominated culture and the images of masculinity associated with it have been firmly entrenched in our society for centuries, so it would be unrealistic to expect it to change radically overnight. Evidence on a number of fronts, though, indicates that the culture of fatherhood, and to a lesser extent the conduct of fathering, has changed along with some of the trappings of conventional masculinity.[7] Similarly, the public in recent decades has become more aware and tolerant of the diverse family forms that make up our social landscape, even though the nuclear family model remains the ideal.

No one can say for sure how the introduction of a residency order policy, or changes in how institutions and local organizations treat stepfamilies, might change what takes place in stepfamilies across the country. Widespread and serious initiatives to institutionalize and legitimize stepfamilies and stepparents' roles would most likely have some impact, but no foolproof formulas can be offered to ensure stepfathers' happiness. Similarly, there are no certainties about promoting fathers' well-being in traditional families where biological parents are together raising children. The additional complexity of stepfamilies makes the search for the magic formula to assist stepdads even more illusive.

ON THE PERSONAL FRONT

At the individual level, where men and women have the ability to manage their affairs, men should certainly take great care to contemplate what a serious romantic involvement would be like with a woman who has a young child from a previous relationship. Men are likely to improve their chances of making a wise decision if, prior to making a serious commitment, they anticipate, understand, and have a plan to deal with the interpersonal dynamics of stepfamily life.

For men to be more cautious they must learn to be more mindful of self, others, and the circumstances shaping their involvement with stepchildren. One practical step along these lines is for men to make a concerted effort to educate themselves about stepfamily life prior to immersing themselves in it. Drawing on his clinical experience, one therapist, Dr. Carl Pickhardt, offers a number of useful tips for men to mull over as they get involved with and manage their lives in a stepfamily with coresident stepchildren. His objective in writing *Keys to Successful Step-fathering* is to "help the stepfather keep his *choices constructive*, his *expectations realistic*, his *contributions significant*, and his *returns rewarding*."[8] The best way for a man to achieve these goals is to become more mindful and communicate with his partner and others about his feelings and experiences.

Although it is beyond my scope here to discuss Pickhardt's many practical suggestions in detail, it is instructive to comment on his recommendation that men should try to express "positive authority" with their stepchildren to establish a healthy relationship with them. Consistent with my comments throughout about the birth mother's important gatekeeping role, this type of authority depends on the mother providing opportunities for the stepfather to get involved. Pickhardt asserts that exhibiting positive authority can make five contributions to stepfather–stepchild relationships. He identifies numerous ways this can be accomplished.[9]

First, men can provide *positive influence* for their stepchildren by acting as their protector, interceding for them, and opening up opportunities. Doug did this exceptionally well when he confronted the principal and teacher about his adoptive son, Sammy. Like some of the other men who wanted to help their stepchild make academic progress, Doug demonstrated his willingness to come to his son's rescue immediately after Doug learned of Sammy's school difficulties and seemingly poor chance of graduating from high school on time. The opportunities that men can provide through their relations with others will sometimes provide their stepchildren with valuable social capital.

Second, being a *positive decision maker* can enable stepfathers to have a significant impact on their stepchild. They can do this by giving permission, making exceptions, and asserting leadership. By using this strategy, the stepfather allows the stepchild to see him as someone who can take charge of situations that involve the stepchild and offer him or her desirable outcomes (allowing the child to stay out later than normal for a special occasion). This strategy can be featured prominently when the mother is not available for several hours or longer because she intentionally removes herself from the setting or is absent because of her work schedule or other circumstances. When this happens, the stepfather has the opportunity to demonstrate that he is capable of making reasonable decisions that affect the stepchild. When the man gains his stepchild's trust without the mother being present, he can begin to establish his unique connection with the child. Several of the participants, both stepfathers and birth mothers, recalled the first time the man was left in charge of the kids without the mother being present. These first impressions, whether good or bad, can carry a lot of weight for the adults as well as the children because they set the tone for future interactions.

My own first experience of being "in charge" of Alli was a memorable one for us both and helped to solidify the mother's trust in me as a caretaker for her children. The occasion was Alli's eleventh birthday, and I knew several days in advance that her parents had professional commitments that would not allow them to spend the evening with her. Although I had not spent much time with Alli, I jumped at the chance to save the day, or evening as it were, by offering to take her out for a birthday dinner and movie. Alli was keen on the idea and I helped reduce the mother's nagging feelings of guilt. On the night of her birthday we went searching for a Mexican restaurant in a part of the county with which I was unfamiliar. I realized that, aside from taking my niece out to lunch one time a number of years before, this was the only time I had assumed the responsibility of entertaining a young girl. Because I was especially fond of both Alli's mother and Alli, I was nervous about making a good impression. Our special celebration of Alli's birthday proved to be a turning point in her recognizing that she could trust me and that we could have loads of fun together. Sharing the adventure of getting lost looking for the movie theater only added to our fun. The report Alli gave to her mother also reassured her that she had exercised good judgment in extending the kind of responsibility to me that she did.

Unfortunately, not all men make such wonderful first impressions with their future stepchildren and birth mothers. Gayle, for instance, vividly remembers with dismay the first time she gave Ron some parental authority to watch her kids while she was away from the house. "Well, the one day, the first day I tested him [Ron], I had to go do some errands. And I come home and he's sleeping. My son is down like two miles away from home. I don't even know what could have happened." Having explicitly told Ron that her kids were not allowed to leave the yard, she was quite annoyed to find her nine-year-old son two miles away and near the highway. Gayle's comments throughout the interview left little doubt that she had never learned to trust Ron fully with her kids.

Third, stepfathers can present themselves as persons capable of *controlling resources* in a productive manner. A number of the stepfathers provided the stepkids with money directly, helped out financially by supporting the stepchild's special interests, and gave them rides to school or other places. John recalls how important it was for his relationship with his stepdaughter, Harmony, to give her rides to school on a daily basis. This arrangement gave John ample occasion to be alone with Harmony and establish the foundation for his relationship with her. This experience reinforced for John the importance of establishing a separate line of communication and relationship with Harmony that was independent of the mother. Although the opportunity to be the stepdaughter's school chauffeur came about because the mother was unable to drive due to a physical disability, seizing opportunities such as these and actively creating others can have a profound impact on stepfather–stepchild relationships.

Fourth, passing on *positive knowledge* can demonstrate to stepchildren that their stepfather can provide valuable information about key topics. Stepfathers have the option of providing help, giving advice, and teaching their stepchildren. These experiences may often represent "affinity-seeking" gestures as the stepfather opens his heart to establish a connection with the stepchild.[10] Opportunities of this sort, where the stepfather tries to make himself likeable, may be valuable early on in men's interactions with their partner's child, though similar "affinity-maintaining" strategies can also be meaningful for those who have established some rapport with the stepchild previously. In fact, some stepfathers may be too quick to forget to sustain their affinity after they have established their initial rapport. Just as men may take their partners for granted, they may do the same with their stepchildren. Stepfathers also need to stand ready to respond to children's overtures to establish or sustain affinity when the kids ask for help, advice, and information. In some cases, stepfathers may have unique experiences or insights they can offer the stepchildren. A number of the stepfathers made the most out of their opportunities to befriend their partner's children by teaching them different things.

Fifth, *positive evaluation* is another way stepfathers can establish themselves in their stepchildren's eyes. For stepfathers, noticing the positive, giving praise, and rewarding the good behavior of their stepchildren are examples of how stepfathers can work toward earning their stepchildren's respect. Making these kinds of comments to the children while expressing the public face of fathering may be particularly important, though comments made in private can also leave a good impression. When stepfathers praise their stepchildren in the presence of their friends, family members, the stepfather's friends, and even complete strangers, they go a long way in reassuring the kids that their stepfather values them. Recall the profound effect Stephen's positive evaluations had on his stepson, Danny. We learned directly from Danny that it mattered a great deal to him that his stepfather told so many people that he was smart. It left him feeling proud and eager to try hard at his schoolwork. It also prompted Danny to feel closer to his stepfather.

Many men, as a matter of habit, may engage in activities exemplifying positive authority without fully appreciating what they are doing. Other men may be more self-aware as they reflect on how they might interact with their stepchild to produce a particular effect. When birth mothers, relatives, therapists, friends, and program directors encourage men to be more mindful of how and why they display positive authority with stepchildren, they can make a valuable contribution to stepfamily functioning. Men who express positive authority during the early phases of their relationships with their partner's children may help position themselves to engage in more effective coparenting with the birth mother and possibly explore chances to cofather with the biological father. Similarly, displaying positive authority may enable men to assume a more constructive disciplinary role later on.

Displaying positive authority rather than a more distinct version of a disciplinary role is likely to be valuable early on when stepchildren may be more receptive to having an adult friend in their life, rather than a father. As my interviews reveal, though, family circumstances and personalities vary widely enough to ensure that some kids are searching for a relationship with a father figure and are willing to accept a man as a disciplinary figure along with the positive authority. It seems, however, that children who are receptive to their mother's partner stepping into this disciplinary role do best when they are also exposed to the forms of positive authority mentioned above.

Positive authority, compared to the disciplinary role, also appears to be more closely associated with a kind of nurturing style of interacting with children. Those who practice it are not seeking to control children in a conventional sense. Rather, they are trying to provide children with a supportive environment where they will appreciate how an adult can be an asset to them. Men who have more androgynous personalities, appreciating both feminine and masculine traits, as well as those who are introspective, may be best suited for using the positive authority strategies. Those who are not eager to assume control in the traditional masculine sense may also be more likely to feel comfortable working with the mother, and even the biological father at times, as part of a coparenting team.

Jackson and John provide excellent examples of two men who, in my view, appeared to be both androgynous in their display of gender and introspective in their approach to thinking about their own needs and how they want to interact with their stepchild. Noteworthy is their desire to connect with their partner's child on terms that are comfortable to the child. Both are careful not to overstep their boundaries and each makes a concerted effort to respect the child's needs.

Men like Herman and Terry were in some ways more eager to assert control while demonstrating a distinct fatherly presence. Yet they forged their own approach to connect with their stepchildren in seemingly healthy ways. Herman tempered his take-charge attitude, and rather traditional masculine approach to family life, with his genuine empathy for kids. His perspective had been reinforced by his ten-year experience of working with troubled youth. Terry's work experience in a health care field that regularly exposes him to sick and disadvantaged children also helped to sensitize him to children's needs, including his own stepson's. Clearly, there are multiple paths to developing a nurturing style toward children.

GETTING ORGANIZED

The preceding discussion about the importance of men taking the initiative to be more mindful of their stepfathering begs the question: How might men be encouraged to adopt this approach? They may, for example, simply read a book like this one or Pickhardt's practical guide for helping men be successful stepfathers and begin to consider the relevant issues more seriously on their own. In addition to their self-reflection, they might instigate conversations with their partner and perhaps her child about their involvement in their lives.

Aside from these options, could stepfathers organize themselves to provide support for other men in similar situations? Biological fathers who are involved in father's rights groups have taken this approach.[11] Why not stepfathers? Most men I interviewed were eager to talk about their children and express their gratitude to me for making it possible to do so. With a few exceptions, the men agreed that I should contact them if I organized a future research project involving focus groups of six to eight men. This leads me to believe that many stepfathers would benefit from discussing their experiences and concerns within a group context.

We can get a sense of the men's feelings by listening to how Eddie, Derek, and Carl responded to the question I posed toward the end of the interview: "How have you felt talking about these issues today?"

Good. Actually, you know sometimes you get so caught up in life you don't actually take time out to think about things like this. Actually I'm glad I came today and talked about it, because you just don't get to sit down every day and discuss [stuff] like that. It's just, it happens and in the back of your mind—but there's nothing to trigger it, to make you think about it. You go on with everyday life. You've got to work. You go home. All these things you take for granted. You never do actually really sit down and think about it. [Eddie, 35]

It made me proud; I have no problems with it at all. [I: And when you say it made you proud, in what way?] I don't think about the effect that I have on Elkin's life, or the effect that he's had on my life, nor the other kids. It's like the sun; you take it for granted because it's there every day. So I take it for granted and I don't think about it or appreciate it. And after talking to you, and I have to think before I answer the question, I was listening to myself, it's like, wow, ok! It makes me feel good. [Derek, 26]

It's neat. It's one of the things that intrigued me about the ad [recruitment flyer] . . . it was kind of like I wanted to help your study from your ad. But it's also kind of given me a little more insight on how things have progressed over time and how—after speaking to you I'm probably going to go back and I'm probably going to reminisce about all the different things that have happened over time, remembering the picnic, the first time we went out with Vicky, things like that, and how she's changed over time and all that stuff. It will encourage me probably to take less school and take that more time that I've been talking about. [Carl, 30]

Eddie and Derek speak specifically to the point about mindfulness. Both mention that they take their lives as stepfathers for granted and don't make the time or have the opportunity to reflect on what is happening to them. They go through the motions, doing their jobs as stepdads, but they don't think about the bigger picture of what is happening and how they are affecting their stepchildren. Carl anticipates that he's going to take some time, think back, and cherish the wonderful moments he's had with Vicky. When he does, he expects that his feelings will lead him to alter his life so that he can spend more time with Vicky.

Talking to someone in a one-on-one interview setting, especially about an important, emotional topic that a man hasn't talked about that much, can be like a therapy session. I would be curious to see in what ways stepfathers might grow by speaking about their experiences and concerns in a supportive group setting.

To date, there have been few efforts to mobilize men who are stepfathers, although Internet technology has created a few opportunities and is likely to create others. The Fatherhood Alliance, for example, supports an Internet site with links to several sites relevant to stepfathers. At least one individually operated website dedicated to stepfatherhood was established in 1999, providing men a forum to discuss various issues and share information.[12] As proclaimed in its mission statement, *Stepdads.com* is intended to "help stepdads develop great relationships with the stepchildren, their wives, and other stepdads." The producer of this site appeals to stepfathers to develop a collective consciousness by adding, "This site will become a great community and resource for other stepdads, when we as stepdads, take ownership of the site's content."

Although stepfathers can surely become more invested collectively in addressing their concerns, their motivation to develop a sense of community or collective consciousness is unlikely to be as intense as it has been for those participating in the fathers' rights group. Whereas the nonresident fathers who belong to this latter group hold strong beliefs and feelings about allegedly being pushed away from their children, the motivation to establish a sense of community is unlikely to serve as a rallying cry for large numbers of stepfathers. Of course, men who once devoted themselves to being active stepfathers, but now find themselves without access to their stepchildren because they are no longer romantically involved with the mother, may feel compelled to work with others to change social policies and laws. As already mentioned, some men on their own have sought visitation and custody rights through the courts and a few have won.

Ironically, many of those participating in the fathers' rights movement may balk at embracing stepfathers in their movement because the former symbolically associate stepfathers with the birth mothers; they represent individuals who may weaken their own claims to play a more prominent role in their children's lives. The potential for an alliance between biological and stepfathers is fraught with complexity. The categories of nonresident biological fathers and stepfathers who either live with or are estranged from the children they helped raise are not mutually exclusive. As some of my participants indicated, some stepfathers are also nonresident fathers. Men in these two categories may not be eager to form an alliance with a formal, organizational component. An alliance built on a collective ideology to confront political injustice may not be in the cards because the two categories of men may not believe they have common interests. If they were to form an alliance, rather then compete with each other, they might find themselves at times in joint competition with birth mothers.

That individual men with a different paternity status relative to a child may find themselves competing with one another can be a serious issue. Several of my participants were eager to adopt their stepchildren and hoped that the biological father would not object. In my study, none of the biological fathers objected, but this is not always the case. When competition among men does occur, I suspect it tends to surface between the biological and stepfather at the family level, not between two different organizations of men with competing and vested interests. Interestingly, two women a few years ago organized a group called CoMamas with the expressed purpose of getting stepmothers and mothers to work together.[13] To my knowledge, the male counterpart to this organization has not been launched. If it does become a reality, I suspect it will not be as successful as CoMamas because men are less comfortable cooperating with other men about issues related to nurturance. Still, it may appeal to enough men to make it a worthwhile enterprise.

Several national organizations, Stepfamily Association of America and Stepfamily, Inc., founded in the mid-1970s, and the Stepfamily Network, established in 1998, currently operate websites providing general information and advice to stepfamilies. Although these organizations, and others like them, do little to target stepfathers directly, they can be a valuable resource for stepfathers.[14] Likewise, national initiatives focusing on fatherhood exist, but they have not yet dealt systematically with stepfatherhood issues.[15] Perhaps the most well-developed, and certainly one of the more politicized organizations addressing fatherhood issues is the National Fatherhood Initiative (NFI) begun in 1994. Launched in response to the organizers' concerns with the consequences of "father absence,"[16] it showcases biological fatherhood, ideally in the context of marriage. Though the coverage is limited, stepfathers searching for information and social support concerning the struggles and joys of stepfathering may find useful general information within these national stepfamily and fatherhood organizations. Several advice columns available through the NFI during the past few years address stepfathers' concerns about how to deal with various hurdles associated with stepfamilies. Stepfathers might also consider ways to use the infrastructure of these established organizations to draw more attention to stepfathers' special needs.

As of today, perhaps the quickest way for stepfathers to find immediate support is to take the initiative and organize collectively at the local level. Although I'm not aware of any informal, face-to-face support groups initiated by stepfathers themselves, men may have organized informally at the local level somewhere. I do know that some therapists, for a fee, offer multisession, separate support groups for stepmothers and stepfathers. So far, however, stepmothers have been much more eager than stepfathers to participate. Barbara Perlmutter, a therapist with the Stepfamily Consultation & Counseling group in Seattle, wrote to me that "men seem much more reluctant or unavailable to commit to a group. When we do workshops for couples, men are great participants. Ditto when I do classes. But support groups . . . no."

One promising approach might involve developing a community workshop on stepfathering. The organizers could coordinate it through a child-oriented group (day care center, school, boys and girls club), a religious organization, or a counseling center. Several speakers, including family therapists and professors from nearby universities interested in family studies, could be invited. Extending invitations to biological fathers whose children have a stepfather might also make sense. For men interested in participating in a small, informal support group, having a workshop could prove useful in establishing a network of similarly minded men. As previously noted, men are less likely than women to organize themselves in the way that CoMamas is doing. That said, a well-crafted workshop might inspire individual men to undertake something along these lines.

Some men may have a deep appreciation for being a father ally or stepfather ally. As alluded to earlier, men may have to overcome the birth mother's objections to the biological father and stepfather establishing closer ties. The mother's objections may be particularly strong when the father is perceived as having been abusive and/or untrustworthy. Thus careful thought should be given to finding productive ways to incorporate birth mothers into the target audience for a workshop on stepfathering.

Program interventions designed to work with stepfathers and their partners should review preexisting family life stepfamily programs[17] as well as couples group intervention projects that focus on biological parents' transition to parenthood.[18] The latter programs recognize that becoming a new parent can be a stressful experience, and the marital quality often suffers as a result. Although many of the dynamics of becoming a stepfather differ from those of becoming a biological father, lessons may be quite similar on how best to help partners improve their communication, develop clear expectations about what they might expect as new coparents, and become more sensitive to the gender patterns often associated with how men and women parent. Care must be taken to fashion programs for stepfathers and their partners that explicitly take into account the unique dynamics of stepfamilies.

One critical issue relevant to many stepfamilies involves how stepchildren adjust to their previous experience with their parents' marital or relationship disruption.[19] Because many children in stepfamilies have already gone through the trauma of seeing their parents' romantic relationship end, they may find relationship conflict between adults within a family frightening. They may associate it with divorce or uncoupling. These conditions call for stepfathers and their partners to be extra mindful about having heated arguments or open conflict in front of the children. Being mindful will be challenging to stepfathers in particular as they struggle with the uncertainties and friction associated with entering a birth mother's family dance. If stepfathers are able to express their most serious concerns to the birth mother in private, children's chances for feeling secure about themselves and their new stepfamily are likely to be higher.

A NEW VISION

If we expand our vision, there are other ways that men can collectively pursue changes that would enhance men's ability to be more effective stepfathers, as well as biological fathers who interact with stepfathers. In other books I discuss the significance of thinking more broadly about fatherhood as a concept and the interventions associated with it.[20] I emphasize the value of perceiving fatherhood as an experience that begins before a child is born, and in some cases conceived. I encourage men to think about fatherhood long before they become fathers and to develop ways of helping young men craft a better sense of what they want out of a romantic relationship and having a child. Although much of this discussion focuses on men's ability and experience with having their own offspring, the larger issue involves men's perceptions of creating and caring for human life.

The broad issue of men caring for children whom they have not created is critical for our purposes here. Some of this caring occurs outside of a romantic partnership; it involves men caring for children as part of their jobs as day care workers, school teachers, health care professionals, camp counselors, and the like. Other forms include men's volunteer experiences as coaches and leaders of kids participating in sports, Boy Scouts, 4-H clubs, and so on. Informal caring for children also takes place when men agree to baby-sit or spend time with the children of friends, neighbors, and relatives, as several participants mentioned doing prior to getting involved with their current partner's children. Although men often receive praise for their efforts with children, the pervasive cultural message too commonly associated with many of the occupations dealing with children is that it is "women's work." For example, despite its many permutations, the overriding masculine model that boys and men encounter discourages them from pursuing careers as primary school teachers and day care workers.[21] Given the ambiguity of norms and complex arrangements associated with stepfamilies, being an effective stepfather may require men to rely on specific interpersonal skills (patience, empathy, negotiation) more so than when they are biological fathers. Consequently, men's more limited exposure to children and nurturing styles of interaction may place them at a disadvantage as they enter a relationship where they have to negotiate stepfathering roles.[22]

As mentioned earlier, the value of spending lots of time around kids is evident in Herman's life; he had ten years of prior experience working as a counselor for juveniles. Though it is difficult to say to what extent this experience cultivated or reinforced his nurturing, protective outlook on children, the experience clearly affected Herman's views on adults' responsibilities to children. Throughout, I have illustrated how Herman expresses his commitment to his teenage stepdaughter, Annette, and his biological son. But his devotion to children goes well beyond his feelings for these two kids. Herman spoke of situations where he went out of his way to provide children with a helping hand and guidance. His description of what he experiences when spending time with his son and his "half" brother [from his former partner's subsequent relationship with another man] captures his openness to kids and his mindful approach to their needs.

> But like I said, when it came down to the kids—like her [former wife] other son, he's—my boy's eleven so her other son is about eight, something like that. And I always said that I was taking care of him. When I go down there to pick my son up, it's like man I hope he doesn't come to the door because I hate to tell him no, you know what I mean? Because he comes up there and his father doesn't come to see him and I'm like—I hope he doesn't come to the door because we've got a relationship, he and I have a relationship also. He knows he's my child too. . . . I had been allowing my son to make a decision about whether his brother went with us or not. For a while there it solved the problem for me. It was a cop-out but—it usually got some of the pressure off me because it was like it hurt me to tell him no. When nobody was actually, no positive male was doing anything positive in his life. They weren't playing with him. I'd go down there and throw the ball at my son, that football. . . . It feels good to have two of them to play with. I play with them, but when I want to spend some quality time with my son, it was hard to tell the other one no because I had started that. So I kind of copped out. Soon as I come to pick him up I'd go "you want your brother to go?" He was quick to say no. I'm like okay, okay, then that's

it. That's settled. But I still had to say, "Well, maybe we'll take him next time." Because I had to understand what my son was saying was—hey, you're my father. You come to see me. You want to spend some quality time with me. And I want to spend some quality time with you. So I had to learn to start telling the other one no. And it hurt me to tell him no because there he was—he'd go—my eyes are burning now— I'm not going to cry or anything—it hurt me to tell him no because there he was going back into the house and we were heading off and I'm like, what the hell—nobody's spending time with this kid. And all they're doing is getting shuffled around.

This sad tale reveals Herman's capacity to struggle with the sense of guilt he experiences as he tries to prioritize his commitments to the children in his life. By commenting about the boy, "He knows he's my child too," Herman provides yet another example of his willingness to make himself available for children who are not his own offspring, or the offspring of his current partner. Developing ways to encourage more men to embrace this sentiment is a worthy undertaking that would go a long way to enhance children's well-being.

The remaining context for men's caring of children, the kind I studied here, occurs within romantic relationships. Terry was one such man, among many, that we heard from in the preceding pages. He convincingly professes his love for his stepson Zack in countless ways. Although Terry loves Zack as though he were his own son, the reality is that he is not. He shares the social role with another man, one who ultimately has a more privileged position in the eyes of the law because he shares DNA with Zack. It should not be surprising, then, to learn of Terry's response when I asked him if there was anything that made it easy or difficult for him to be the kind of father he would like to be.

The only thing with Zack that I'm not going to have to experience with our other kids is I have this fear that you know he's going to, as I become more of a disciplinarian as he gets older, which is so important— you get into these tough issues that he's going to want to like go the easy route and "oh I want to go live with my other father" or one of those deals. I have that little gnaw in the back of my head that bothers me and I've talked about it with the pastor, one of the pastors I meet with, and he's reassured me that as long as I continue to love and support and be there for him, do the right thing, continue to do what I feel is necessary to be a good father and don't worry about it, in the long run he'll understand and he'll be there and it won't matter. So I have to keep the faith with that. I think that that's going to be true, but other than that, it's just normal life.

Recall Terry said that it was fine for Zack to have two dads. However, with two dads, there are two options. In Terry's case, he may feel as though he has more to offer Zack in terms of human, physical, and social capital, but Zack will have more of a say in where he lives when he gets older. The father might also use the law to intervene and gain custody of Zack if Terry and his wife divorced or Zack's mother died. These realities contribute to stepfathering being a uniquely precarious commitment with undertones that can affect how men perceive their future as family men.

Despite Terry's uncertainty about the decisions Zack might make someday, Terry anticipates having a wonderful future with Zack. As I wrapped up my interview with Terry I asked him: "What do you see in terms of your relationship with Zack, down the road, a couple of years, three years, ten years?"

> I see his whole life, you know. I see him doing well in high school. I see him going into college and finding a direction that he likes, I see him doing well in baseball, hopefully. . . . He's just, he's just a very neat boy and uh, he's going to make a really good dad one day and I really hope that I'm part of that and I hope that he includes me in his life afterwards, brings his kids home and lets me hold his kids and—you know—and looks at me like you know, you weren't my biological dad but you were my dad, you're the one that spent most of my life taking care of me and lookin' after me and doing what needed to be done because you loved me, and I'm hoping that that is the overriding factor that is going to prevail in the long run, over everything that's going to transpire down the road. God only knows.

With these closing remarks, we have journeyed the entire length of Terry's excursion into stepfathering to date and beyond. At the outset, we learned about the seemingly ideal path Terry walked as he grew closer to his current wife—then girlfriend—and son. His story has involved accepting Zack as his own, marrying the mother whom he loves very much, successfully negotiating the sometimes rocky road of being a loving stepfather who happens to dislike the biological father's influence on his son, bringing a biological son of his "own" and brother for Zack into the family, and now embracing an optimistic perspective on the future where he projects himself into the lives of Zack's children. Although Terry doesn't use the term "grandfather" to describe the future relationship he hopes to have with Zack's children, I have no doubt Terry will wholeheartedly take on the grandpa role should Zack become a father. Terry has made it clear that for him, family is not about the blood, or lack thereof; it is about love and hope. He has plenty of both for Zack.

Terry, and some of the other men whose lives I represent here, belong to the crème de le crème of stepfathers. Listening to their stories provides some balance to the negative stereotypes of stepfathers that we so often encounter. Many men clearly do play an instrumental role in being with children in a fatherly way within the context of a formal or informal stepfamily. Their path is often cluttered though with challenges, some residing within themselves, some linked to the family dynamics of their stepfamilies, and some prompted by the outside world.

The message the men reinforce through their stories about their diverse experiences is how stepfathers can define stepfamily situations and address their challenges in many ways. Some pursue a path more or less identical to what might be expected of a biological father whereas others make their contributions in a less fatherly way, but vital nonetheless. Being an involved, supportive adult friend with some trace of authority can be just what a child needs. The prospects of being successful in the stepfamily arena, regardless of the specific roles the man "chooses" to develop, are enhanced when he approaches his relationships and family life mindfully and with an appreciation for a child's best interests. This approach is essential in a context where clear social guidelines are lacking and norms are constructed and negotiated in a more fluid, fly-by-the-seat-of-the-pants fashion.

The bottom line is that a society can do much good by encouraging men, both informally and formally, to be respectful in their romantic partnerships and to apply the ethic of nurturance in their care for children. Some of the men's comments signal their awareness of both of these objectives; some do not. In a society where such a high percentage of children live part of their childhood in a stepfamily, improving individual men's chances of having a personally enriching experience as a stepfather makes a lot of sense. One aspect of this task will be to improve stepfathers' relationships with the birth mother. In addition, men's ability to cooperate with other men in raising children is likely to become an increasingly important skill if nonresident fathers get more involved with their kids than has been the case in previous generations. Creating a social and legal environment flexible enough to accommodate the various ways men are involved in stepchildren's lives, and the reality that many of the romantic partnerships between parents and stepparents will end, is a complex task. The balancing of rights and obligations is challenging, and some would argue that it is inappropriate to even talk about rights—we should perceive of parents as trustees for their children.[23] What is clear is that more needs to be done to help stepfathers and their partners navigate the muddled terrain of stepfamily life. If this happens, the children living in those environments are likely to reap the benefits. Men, in turn, will be in a better position to experience the personal growth associated with raising children.

My personal growth was surely enhanced when I crossed paths with Alli many years ago. Even though our time in each other's lives was far too short, and I never realized my dream to become an everyday stepfather to Alli, the engaging, playful, and tender moments we shared refreshed my vision of children and fathering. I can only imagine what kind of impact Alli might have had on my life course had I been afforded the chance to develop more of a fatherly presence in her life.

Much to my surprise, my imagination was reawakened in August 2001. After thirteen years of not seeing Alli, I saw her walking toward me as I exercised on a stationary bike at my local gym. Ironically, the timing of this sighting corresponded with the launching of my research project on stepfathering. A bit taller, she had traded in her long hair for a shaved look in keeping with her recent spiritual journey to a Buddhist monastery in Nova Scotia. But even from a distance her bright eyes and smile gave her away. Within seconds I knew I could believe what I saw, as did she. No longer in a position to aspire to the "stepfather-in-the-making" role, I rejoiced in the return of a dear, long lost friend who had grown from a girl into a young woman. Amazingly, without missing a beat, we rekindled our interpersonal chemistry, taking aim at recapping thirteen years worth of our unshared history while reminiscing about the times we spent together. That chance meeting and my new and active friendship with Alli have given me one more personal anecdote to illustrate the fascinating, emotional, and multilayered worlds of fathering and stepfamilies.

Appendix A

STUDY REFLECTIONS, LESSONS, AND RECOMMENDATIONS

For many, wading through a detailed account of how a study is conducted is like listening to someone rant and rave about the endless, mundane details associated with planning a large wedding. When coordinating a wedding, a person first has to determine what type of budget and resources are at his or her disposal while deciding on the location of the wedding ceremony and reception. Then, among many, questions must be answered about the timing and duration of the event, choosing the wedding party, creating the guest list, what caterer to use, the wording of the vows, what to wear, the day's agenda, what music to play, and how the events will be filmed and photographed. Most people aren't particularly thrilled with doing this sort of planning, especially if it isn't their wedding, and few have the patience to listen to a blow-by-blow account of how these decisions were made. Folks are far less interested in how the wedding was organized than they are in showing up on that sunny Saturday afternoon, ready to revel with friends, family, and strangers in the festive atmosphere of a well-planned wedding. But of course, without someone attending to all of these details, the guests probably would not have such a splendid time.

Much like this scenario, I assumed that many of my readers would want to forgo the details of how I planned and conducted my study and move immediately to a description and analysis of men's stories. Because I sought to fashion a book that reached beyond an academic audience, I deferred most of my discussion about my study's details to this appendix. The decisions I made throughout the course of my study, however, are every bit as important to its quality as the wedding planner's decisions are to a wedding's success. Metaphorically speaking, I now direct my comments largely to the researchers, students, and others who have some interest in the planning of the wedding.

I take liberties in how I describe my reflections about the research process in order to make it more accessible to a wide audience. Specifically, I discuss my decision making from start to finish, from designing the study initially to drafting the book. I describe what I did, how I did it, and why I did it, while also commenting on the strengths and weaknesses of my research project as a process. Among my key challenges and choices: how to frame my research questions and develop an interview guide that would enable me to address them most effectively using a qualitative approach, what kind of sample to use, which recruitment and interviewing strategies to select, and how to analyze and write about the participants' stories. Reflecting on these decisions and the fruits of my labors, as I do here, I am able to shed light on some of the key interviewing issues I encountered and judge my success in exploring the social psychology of men's lives as stepfathers. Finally, with an eye toward the future, I spell out how my research led me to sharpen the conceptual tools relevant to the study of men's lives as stepfathers while generating new research avenues relevant to stepfathering, and more generally, to the men who act in a fatherly way toward children who are not their offspring. By reflecting on these matters, I provide others with a behind-the-scenes view of my study, enabling them to develop a keener sense of my work and evaluate it from an informed perspective. The lessons I share should give qualitative researchers the chance to clarify their own research on stepfathers, their partners, and stepchildren.

FRAMING THE RESEARCH QUESTIONS

As I mentioned in chapter 1, my scholarly and personal interests in fatherhood, as well as my commitment to look at men's experiences through a social psychological lens, informed my study of men in stepfamilies. I therefore framed my research questions around the subjective aspects of how men relate to their romantic partner's child. In particular, my goal was to unravel how men thought, felt, and reacted to the prospects of being involved with their partner's child in a fatherly way. This meant that I explored the social processes affecting how men perceive themselves and their situations as they become involved and stay involved in either a formal or informal kind of stepfamily. My focus is consistent with the notion that multiple paths are available for men to experience themselves as fathers or stepfathers[1] and that scholars and policymakers need to pay more attention to the unconventional forms of fathering.[2]

Because I wanted to look at men's lives through a social constructionist and symbolic interactionist lens,[3] I sought to understand how men's subjective worlds are influenced by others, most importantly their partner and stepchild. In addition to asking men about their experiences, I tried to address questions about stepfatherhood by incorporating additional insights from as many of the men's romantic partners as my limited resources and recruitment time frame permitted.

SAMPLING AND RECRUITMENT CONCERNS

In chapter 1, I describe the main demographics of those who participated in this study so I will not repeat them here. Suffice it to say that the sample is rather diverse with the major exception being that stepfathers who are doing poorly in their stepfamilies may be underrepresented. Recall that I did not attempt to recruit a representative sample that would enable me to document patterns among stepfathers, as one might do in a survey research study. Rather, I used a purposive sampling strategy to ensure that my sample included men with the kinds of diverse experiences that are likely to affect their relationships with children who are not their offspring. Although I did not impose rigid sampling guidelines, I made a concerted effort to recruit a sample that took into account the stepfather's age, race, social class, marriage and residence status, duration and level of relationship commitment with partner, and previous/current experience with his own biological children and the target child's gender and age.

I used a variety of recruitment strategies to secure participants: announcements made in a university hospital newsletter, a listserv directed at various university departments, and a local parenting magazine. Flyers were posted at a variety of sites throughout the community and participants responded to those at a community health center, fire station, homeless shelter, and a few churches. Using my assistants' and my own contacts, I recruited a number of participants through word of mouth. An initial telephone screening was completed to determine participants' eligibility. All eligible men I contacted or who contacted me agreed to participate, although scheduling problems prevented a few from being interviewed.

At the outset, I intended to interview twenty stepfathers and ten partners, along with five "stepfamily units" that included a stepfather, birth mother, and child (who was 13–19 years of age and living with the mother). In the end, however, I secured and completed interviews with fifty-one participants (36 men, 13 partners, and 2 children) between late August and December 2001. Although I interviewed thirteen couples (stepfather-birth mother), I was only able to complete two sets of "stepfamily unit" interviews. One of the reasons I made the adjustment with the "stepfamily unit" interviews was that the recruitment period was compressed from six to three months because of administrative regulations associated with my grant's funding schedule that were beyond my control. The reduced time frame and budget constraints limited my ability to recruit people in a more deliberate, selective fashion because my first priority was to recruit a sufficient number of stepfathers from diverse backgrounds. Some stepfathers didn't have children in the appropriate thirteen to nineteen age range for the three-person stepfamily interviews and some who could not coordinate a time when their partner and child could join them for simultaneous interviews. I decided to interview the men when they volunteered in order to maximize my resources and complete as many interviews with stepfathers as possible. Also, the recruitment process went fairly slowly during the first month, then accelerated during the middle period of the grant. Despite this setback, I believe the quality and scope of the data I gathered on stepfathers and their partners is quite good.

Ideally, those who use the analytic method I describe below stop collecting data when they have reached a point called "saturation"—where the most recent participants are no longer providing significant new insights for the study. In my case, the first twenty-five to thirty participants generated the basic parameters of the key ideas that emerged from this study, though interviews with subsequent participants refined and deepened some of these ideas. In addition, because I was open to interviewing a diverse set of stepfathers with stepchildren at various developmental stages, I suspect that additional, more nuanced insights might have been discovered had I had the resources to interview more than thirty-six men. These observations would most likely be specific to stepfathers' experiences with children in specific developmental stages (infancy, preschool, early or late adolescence).

My experience with trying to recruit children, and actually interviewing two fourteen-year-olds, strengthened my conviction that future qualitative research designs should take special care to incorporate children and conduct in-depth interviews with them about stepfathering issues.[4] I offer several suggestions for how future researchers might incorporate children into their designs. First, it may be necessary to relax the procedural rule that I followed in this project that called for simultaneous interviews. Because many parents and children have busy schedules, interviewing the children at a time separate from the parents may enable researchers to secure stepchildren's participation more easily. This approach obviously would raise questions for some scholars about the possibility of a participant talking to one of the other participants who completed the interview first. Unfortunately, the implications of such contact are unknown. They may also not be particularly relevant to a qualitative study such as mine. If the focus of a future study is stepfathering, then stepfathers should be interviewed first to avoid cases where an interview is completed with a child but an interview with the corresponding stepfather does not occur. Second, it may be worthwhile to complete interviews with children even if the mother is not interviewed. Having data for stepfather–child pairs would be useful with or without interviewing the mother, though including interviews with mothers would be ideal. Third, it is helpful to identify multiple interview sites that can accommodate simultaneous, separate interviews thereby making it more convenient for families to participate. Practical matters such as transportation and lack of nearby parking made it impractical for a few families to participate in my study.

INTERVIEWING

I personally interviewed thirty-two stepfathers, one mother, and two children (boy and girl). After being trained specifically for this project, a male research assistant interviewed the remaining four stepfathers while two female assistants interviewed the twelve birth mothers (one assistant did 10 of these interviews). Most interviews lasted about ninety minutes with a range of 45 to 150 minutes. The interviews were audio-taped and all participants were paid $25.

My assistants and I secured our participants' trust by using strategies common to qualitative researchers. For instance, we arranged to interview participants in one of several private, comfortable settings. Most interviews were conducted in my office and other nearby small conference rooms in the Department of Sociology at the University of Florida. Several were conducted in participants' offices or homes and seven were completed in church offices. We also provided upfront time to discuss the project and the informed consent; emphasized participants' anonymity and the confidentiality of their answers; provided participants the chance to ask questions before and after the interview; told them they could choose to not answer questions; and, at the end of the interview, we asked them how they felt about sharing their thoughts with us.

Interviews were roughly organized according to one of three semi-structured interview guides, one each for stepfathers, birth mothers, and children. Although I include sample guides for each type of participant in appendix B, I focus my comments below on the guide for stepfathers. All interviews with couples, including those with the children, were conducted simultaneously in separate rooms. Following the multiparticipant interviews, my assistants and I had debriefing sessions to discuss substantive and methodological issues.

In addition, after completing seven interviews, I provided my assistants with a copy of an analytic summary of concepts and themes I developed after analyzing the first set of interviews and memos. This summary expanded and refined the original set of issues I discussed with the interviewers prior to their initial interview.

As my assistants and I talked to participants, we sought to uncover how men construct, negotiate, and assign meaning to their evolving identities and life circumstances as stepfathers embedded within social settings shaped by familial definitions and norms. Theoretical perspectives well known to sociologists, social constructionism and symbolic interactionism, guided my line of questioning. The interviews covered a range of broad topics and were flexible enough to focus on related issues participants raised during the course of the interview. For stepfathers, my male assistant and I began the interviews by asking them to describe how they first met and got involved with their partner/wife. In general, the direction of the interviews provided men with an opportunity to describe their experience with their partner and stepchild chronologically, but participants were free to move back and forth while they focused on particular issues and told their stories. Thus, aside from the first question, the direction of the interviews varied somewhat depending on the participants' initial answers and the flow of the exchanges. After the first several interviews, my assistant and I made a more concerted effort to ask stepfathers questions, appropriate to their circumstances, dealing with key issues that had emerged from my ongoing analysis of the previous participants' interviews. These included men's experiences of private and public fathering, reactions (reflected appraisals) men were receiving from others about their stepfathering, feelings about stepfathering being a partial substitute for not being with their own children more, role as parent educators for their partners, possession of a mental map for their stepchildren, attempts to be an ally for the biological father, desires for and experiences with being part of a parenting team, future visions of their stepchildren, and experiences with mindful dating that involved their being aware of how their dating a single mother might influence her child.

At various other points throughout the data collection process, I considered emerging insights and adapted my questions and interviewing style to enhance subsequent interviews. For example, Emmit, the twenty-third stepfather out of thirty-six I interviewed, spontaneously used a grading analogy when I asked him, "How would you evaluate what you've done so far? As a father to him [stepson]?" His reply, "I'd say I'd rate myself as a C. Just average. I need to do a lot more I could improve on." Emmit went on to describe specifically how he could be involved with his stepson more effectively. This exchange led me to ask the subsequent men I interviewed a more direct question along the lines of: "What kind of letter grade, using pluses and minuses, would you give yourself in terms of your involvement with [stepchild's name]?" I often prefaced my question by mentioning that an earlier participant had, on his own, assigned a letter grade to evaluate himself as a stepfather. By using this kind of lead-in, I oriented most of the men to think in terms of their stepfathering roles. Depending on their answer, this format allowed me to ask follow-up questions about what they thought they could do to earn a higher grade. The men appeared to feel at ease with this concrete line of questioning. Because everyone is familiar with grades, it gave them a commonsense way to wrestle in their own way with why they assessed themselves as they did. Although I did not at this point systematically ask the men to comment on whether they were comparing themselves to someone, future researchers might use this opportunity to ask more pointed questions encouraging men to identify the extent to which they arrived at their assessment by comparing themselves to specific persons (the mother, man's own father, child's biological father), cultural images ("deadbeat" dad, nurturing father), or some other reference point.

Another change in the interviewing process began to evolve toward the middle of the data collection phase with the birth mothers. The female interviewer started to ask the birth mother whether the biological father had established any rituals or routines with his child prior to the stepfather getting involved. Although I do not refer to these data in the text, it may be worthwhile in future research to consider how the rituals and routines biological fathers establish and continue with their child influence the way stepfathers relate to the child. Furthermore, do stepfathers try to establish their own set of experiences with the child by going fishing, watching the same TV show together, playing a particular game, going for ice cream on a Sunday night, going to church, and so on? These experiences are akin to the affinity-seeking and -maintaining strategies mentioned in endnote 5 to chapter 1.

To help the interviewer keep the participant focused, interviews tended to deal a bit more with issues related to the oldest stepchild, nineteen years of age or younger, living with the mother. Nonetheless, my assistants and I asked the parental participants numerous questions about all of their children (biological and step). The participants often commented on children other than the oldest stepchild without being asked.

Because I was interested in various aspects of stepfathering as a process, the questions encouraged stepfathers to discuss issues related to the way they navigated the terrain of stepfathering and managed their identities as men who present themselves in a fatherly way or as an adult authority figure. Some of the more prominent areas that were directly covered with stepfathers included:

1. the initial context for getting involved with a woman who had a child
2. language issues, how stepchildren referred to the man (dad, first name, nickname)
3. significant changes in the stepfather's relationship to a child since they first met
4. current relationship with a stepchild, including activities, responsibilities, rights
5. social capital (knowledge of friends, teachers, coaches)
6. visions of oneself as a father, images of the ideal father, self-evaluation of stepfathering experiences, sense of whether and how he made a difference in the stepchild's life, perceptions of how the stepchild affected him
7. experiences with own father (and mother) growing up and now
8. perceptions of partner/wife's involvement in shaping his stepfathering experiences (gatekeeping)
9. difficulties with stepfathering
10. discussions about biological father's level and type of involvement
11. emotional connections with a stepchild, sense of claiming the child as his own

My female assistants and I experimented with different opening questions with the mothers. In the initial interviews, mothers were asked to provide an account of how their relationship with their child evolved over time. The next few interviews with mothers focused their attention initially on their relationship with the biological father and their experiences with him as a father to their child. Finally, the last half of the interviews had mothers focus on how they met their current partner (the stepfather being interviewed for the study) and how he got involved in her child's life. The latter strategy proved to be the most effective in moving mothers into the interview in a comfortable way. After the interview was clearly under way, mothers were probed briefly about the biological fathers. The questions my research team and I asked mothers and their children explored their perspectives on many of the kinds of issues listed above for stepfathers.

INTERVIEWING ISSUES AND OPPORTUNITIES

Throughout the data collection phase, and in a few cases prior to it, I wrestled with a number of issues associated with the interviewing process. To assist others who may wish to interview stepfathers, or other stepfamily members, I reflect on some of the significant challenges I faced when asking questions and managing the interview. These include men "doing gender" during the interview, race-related questions, using labels to identify men's and others' positions, ascertaining distinctions men make between biological children and stepchildren, questions about sexuality and stepdaughters, eliciting comments about negative experiences and challenges, and focusing men's attention on a particular stepchild.

My thinking about the interviews with the stepfathers was in some ways influenced by a recent analysis of how men "do gender" in an interview setting and suggestions for interviewing strategies to address these gender enactments. "Situations that make it difficult to signify control, autonomy, rationality, and sexual desirability may be especially anxiety provoking for men wedded to displaying hegemonic masculinity. In such situations we might expect to see behaviors aimed at countering, or symbolically compensating for, the real or implied threat to the masculine self."[5] Thus interviewing technique is not enough, especially if the research speaks to gender-related issues, focuses on decision making, and explores sensitive topics that are emotionally laden. Interviewers need to be aware of men's need to "signify, in culturally prescribed ways, a creditable masculine self."[6]

The interviews with stepfathers, by having them think about their feelings for and relations with their partner's child, the mother herself, and the biological father, afforded men opportunities to think explicitly and implicitly about issues from a gender perspective. Some of the questions also dealt with the men's involvement in decision making regarding how they got into and managed their relationships with the birth mother, stepchild, and biological father. Others offered men the chance to talk about their feelings. In my view, the interviews with stepfathers did not touch on these masculine issues of self as much as previous interviews I've done with men exploring sex and procreative issues.[7] However, minor concerns about control, autonomy, and rationality were apparent occasionally. Issues of control can come into play during an interview both in terms of how a man attempts to wrestle control of the interview setting as well as how he may exaggerate the degree of control he has or has had over a situation that he is describing. Herman, for example, managed his interview by sharing long, authoritative responses to my questions, consistent with the "take-charge" mentality he associated with himself. He also conveyed an image that he was the head of his stepfamily household, an impression that may very well depict his circumstances accurately. From observing his behavior with his wife and stepdaughter after the interview, and during the photo shoot for the book's jacket cover, I am confident that this is indeed the case. Although Herman's behavior during the interview may reflect how he acts in everyday life, it may still influence the nature of what he shares. Ironically, in some respects, Herman was quite willing to share intimate details about his life and display his vulnerabilities even though he presented himself as an expert.

Being aware of the kinds of conscious and unconscious gender enactments men may display in an interview setting is an important first step. This enabled my assistant and me to make a conscious effort to recognize signs of such displays and respond in a manner that allowed men to feel comfortable and safe while avoiding the need to exaggerate control, autonomy, and rationality. Also, in those instances where the stepfathers talked about struggling with their stepchildren and/or partners, we made a conscious effort to be aware of their anxieties, to present a nonjudgmental attitude, and to convey an impression that we valued their efforts to be candid.

One issue related to the interviewing that I may not have dealt with as well as gender involves race. Although I had not initially conceptualized race as a critical variable for structuring my interview guide, I tried to explore in a preliminary way the importance of race to stepfathering for African American men. I anticipated that the imbalanced gender ratio among African Americans (much higher proportion of single women relative to employed single men living outside of prison) might influence participants' perceptions and feelings about stepfamilies, and stepfatherhood in particular. In addition, I thought that the negative stereotypes often associated with nonresident black fathers might influence how stepfathers saw their family roles.[8] I expected that middle-class black stepfathers might feel more pressure to perform well to combat stereotypes. Alternatively, I reasoned that these men might feel as though they didn't have to do as much as, say, white stepfathers or fathers because the image of the "absent" black father was a ready-made point of comparison that they could easily out-shine. Although I question whether my approach was adequate to the task, I did not find much evidence to support my suspicion that African American men would have a clearer sense of how race mattered to them as step-fathers. Consequently, I did not incorporate race into my written analysis of stepfathers. I suspect that future research with a more refined treatment of race issues may uncover new insights. It may show how racial differences in the social demography of families and relationships influence the subjective aspects of men's lives as stepfathers. To tap into these issues, African American stepfathers might be asked questions like: Can you describe any ways that being aware of what it's like to be a black male in America affects the way you approach being a father/stepfather? To what extent do you feel that people look at you in certain ways when they see you—as a black man—with your (step)family? For those with an African American partner: In what ways, if any, did her being black influence the way she looked at you as a potential male presence or father role model for her child?

At various points in the main text I talked about the social significance of the labels people use to refer to family or stepfamily members. These issues are directly relevant to the interview process because the interviewer needs to discover quickly the participant's comfort level with different labels. This is especially important for rapport building because an interviewer doesn't want to frustrate or alienate the participant. As I alluded to in chapter 7, I sensed a bit of resistance during my interview with Doug when I used the "stepfather" label. My experience talking with Doug and others also underscores the notion that the choice and use of a label should take into account the possibility that various people within a man's circle may have different perceptions about the man's role in a child's life. The man may see himself as "the" father or "a" father, but the child and school-teacher may think of him as the stepfather. Or the child may see the man as "the" father or "a" father, but those outside the family may see him as a stepfather. Thus, in the course of an interviewer's exchange with the participant, the interviewer may need to use different labels to get at the nuances of meanings that people construct and act on. In a practical sense, as the interview exchange unfolds, an interviewer may need to question whether it is appropriate to say, "To what extent does the teacher see you as Sammy's (step)father?" "What kind of (step)father do you think you've been?" "How do Sammy's friends treat you as his (step)father?"

Questions of this sort also surface when an interviewer is trying to get a man who has both biological and stepchildren to comment on only one child, or one set of children (biological or step), or perhaps all of them together. Depending on how clearly the interviewer makes this designation, the man may frame his response in a way that does or does not address the question at hand. On several occasions I needed to ask men explicitly to refocus their comments on their stepchildren because they were thinking of their biological and stepchildren collectively, or they had begun to only think about their biological children.

Similarly, throughout my interview with Danny, the fourteen-year-old boy, I had to make a conscious effort to differentiate between his father and stepdad in a way that did not offend him. Remember that Danny was struggling with feeling abandoned by his biological father, who had moved out of state without telling him a number of years ago. To help me distinguish the two "fathers," for the purpose of doing the interview, I asked Danny fairly early on "what do you, call Thomas," the stepfather who was in another room being interviewed by my assistant. Danny's reply, "He's Dad. That's what I call him." Although he had come to refer to his stepdad as his dad, and he sometimes referred to his biological father by his first name, Danny resorted at times to using "father" or "dad" in the middle of his storytelling when referring to his biological father. As the interview evolved I resorted to the technique of saying "your dad Thomas" prior to asking a question. Danny's situation illustrates the need for interviewers to become familiar with the naming conventions individual kids with complex life histories use to identify the adult men in their lives.

Although the terms of my research protocol in effect prevented me from asking stepfathers if they had ever been physically abusive toward a stepchild, I was free to inquire about how they managed any situations that might have the hint of sexual overtones associated with it, specifically with regard to adolescent stepdaughters. I did not pursue this line of questioning with all the men, but I heard enough to recognize that it is an important area to explore. Getting men to talk candidly about this issue is sometimes challenging, but it was possible to broach the subject tactfully and in a nonthreatening manner. Men appeared to be most receptive to my questions about this topic when I prefaced it by commenting first that other men had spoken about their concerns. This took the form of saying that other men with young stepdaughters have sometimes said that they worried that others might view them suspiciously if they hugged their stepdaughter or gave her a kiss in public.

The final significant challenge I faced involved those stepfathers who had multiple stepchildren or both biological and stepchildren. When men had two or more stepkids, decisions needed to be made constantly about how best to focus stepfathers' attention. As noted above, my assistant and I tended to encourage the stepfathers to focus more of their attention on the eldest stepchild living at home. This provided us with the chance to explore in some detail the father–child trajectory. However, because I recognized that an important element of the stepfathering (or fathering) experience is the diverse relationships the man can have interacting with different kids, men were either encouraged or permitted to discuss their various relationships with different stepchildren. Similarly, men's experiences with stepchildren were often affected by their relationships with their biological children, so the interviews were flexible enough to explore the ways men's fathering and stepfathering experiences overlapped, enhanced, and conflicted with one another.

JUDGING THE INTERVIEWS

With qualitative interviews, there is no precise way to evaluate how well they have been conducted, but it is possible to appraise certain features of the interviewing process. In a previous book, a colleague of mine and I developed a series of qualitative indices to assess our success during and after the interviews we conducted with young men aged sixteen to thirty about issues involving sex, relationships, contraception, and the various procreative events (pregnancy scare, pregnancy, abortion, miscarriage, and birth). I focus on five of these indices: (1) emotional accessibility, (2) view of interviewer as counselor, (3) collaborative behaviors, (4) declarations of comfort, and (5) detailed, dense, personal information. I use these indices to organize my comments about the quality of the interviews I conducted with the stepfathers.

Emotional Accessibility

Generally speaking, most participants seemed at ease during their interviews and developed rapport with my research team and me. Evidence for this rapport came in various forms, including the kinds of conversations participants had with the interviewers prior to and following the interviews, the personal feelings participants shared during the interview—both good and bad—and the joking exchanges and laughter that occurred. In the interviews I conducted, for example, I found men like Monty, Ron, and Allen were willing to talk openly and emotionally about their deep-seated frustrations regarding their stepfamily life. Monty and Ron in particular expressed in no uncertain terms their anger, bitterness, and friction as it related to their stepchildren. They also freely spoke about their disappointment with how poorly their respective partners have handled stepfamily dynamics. Stepfathers did not have an exclusive license on sharing painful memories. Three or four women cried at some point during their interviews (with the female interviewers) as they recalled difficult experiences they had with their children and previous partners. Some spoke of previous abuse at the hands of fathers or previous partners. The interviews were also filled with both stepfathers and birth mothers expressing positive emotions. As I noted in chapter 5, a number of stepfathers were quite proud of their stepchildren and talked openly about their feelings. Similarly, some were eager to convey the depth of their loyalty to their stepchildren and what they anticipated they would feel if harm were to ever come to these children. During the course of the interviews I conducted, I was often struck by how much love the men expressed for their stepchildren. Sometimes the men simply said something along the lines of, "I really love those kids," and at other times they talked about how excited they were to have done something special for their stepchild.

View of Interviewer as Counselor

When the men toward the end of the interview described feeling as though it was good for them to talk about their experiences as a stepfather in an interview setting, they were in some ways acknowledging that the interview had served as an informal therapy session. Birth mothers did not give any clear indication that they viewed the interview as therapeutic, though a few indicated that it was fun to talk about the various issues. Even though my male assistant and I did not intentionally try to provide therapy for the men, our willingness to listen and guide their storytelling in some ways offered them a unique opportunity to express and hear themselves talk about important matters with a neutral party. On several occasions during the interview, Ron asked me what I thought about his partner's behavior. Afterward he even asked me if I could provide him with the name of an inexpensive or free counselor who would be willing to see him and his partner. His question prompted me to locate the names and contact information of several area counselors who were willing to provide their services to the poor. I carried this information with me to all subsequent interviews, though no one asked me for it. Another man, Mark, caught me off guard during one of our exchanges midway through the interview when he stopped talking for a moment and asked me if I minded if he took notes. After the interview we discussed his notes, particularly those involving my question about whether his wife felt that he had influenced her children in any way. He had taken notes on this question because he hadn't thought about this before and he wanted to remember to discuss it with his wife. Mark apparently saw the interview as an opportunity for him to identify relevant stepfamily issues and develop a deeper understanding of his situation.

Collaborative Behavior

A number of the participants, especially the stepfathers, took on the role of being a contributor to the project. They appeared eager to help me understand the nuances of their lives while providing insights that might help others. For example, Eddie spent time working with me in the interview to clarify his relationship with his stepchild's biological father. In response to my question about his possibly being an ally to the father, he discussed his perspective on his understanding of that term and its relevance to his particular relationship with the father. During our exchange, we found ourselves developing a keener sense of the various dimensions associated with stepfathers relationships with biological fathers. For his part, he recognized that he in fact does enable his stepdaughter to have a better relationship with her father. Meanwhile, his commentary helped me refine my thinking about the father ally role; it can be played in either a secretive or an overt manner. Another important collaborative behavior was evidenced when some of the men offered suggestions about how other stepfathers might best navigate the challenging circumstances that often go hand in hand with being involved in a stepfamily. More generally, on a number of occasions, sometimes before the interview but more likely afterward, the men mentioned that they hoped they could be of some help to the project. As mentioned in chapter 10, almost all were willing to participate in a future focus group study if I conducted one.

Declarations of Comfort

This index typically refers to the participant verbally acknowledging that he or she is relaxed and comfortable with the interview. Although the men seldom offered this kind of comment spontaneously, they did provide various nonverbal cues that they were at ease and some admitted afterwards that they felt good. Men's general demeanor in the interview was consistent with Herman's reassurance to me that we need not rush the interview after two and a half hours, even though his wife and stepdaughter were waiting for him. A few men also displayed their comfort during and after the interview by asking me personal questions about my own experiences with fathering. Only two of the men gave any indication of being anxious about being in the interview. One became aware after about forty minutes that his three-year-old daughter was getting impatient as she waited in the church facilities for his interview to end. The other participant had taken medication for a serious neck injury that would require surgery in a few days.

Detailed, Dense, Personal Information

Evidence for this index is best witnessed by examining the depth and quality of the excerpts I've included in the book. Throughout, I have offered numerous examples of how stepfathers, birth mothers, and even two children elaborated on the nuances of their experiences and feelings. For some individuals, it was commonplace for them to provide an elaborate description of different facets of their personal life that occurred prior to, as well as during, their current stepfamily relationships. In lots of other instances, the stepfathers and birth mothers simply needed a nudge to get them going; once they understood the level of detail that was desired, they typically accommodated the interviewer by elaborating on their thoughts and feelings.

ANALYZING WHAT PARTICIPANTS HAD TO SAY

One important assumption underlying my research approach is that men are capable of representing the experiences, thoughts, and feelings they have had about stepfathering. In other words, I assume there is "something" about stepfathering that exists independent of the interview setting that I can direct the stepfathers to tap into and describe. I treat language as reflecting stepfathers' social reality. As I discuss below, this assumption influenced not only how I analyzed the transcripts but also how I wrote about the men's experiences.

Consistent with a grounded theory approach to qualitative research, I used the constant comparative method that emphasizes an iterative process of data analysis by comparing incident with incident, category with incident, and category with category.[9] This technique also calls for simultaneous data collection and analysis. My aims for the conceptual analysis presented in this book were more modest than what is typically associated with classic grounded theory—the generation of a theory with explicit phases, dimensions, and properties that is then compared and contrasted to existing theories. In my case, the principal objective was to refine and generate

meaningful substantive and theoretical codes (concepts attached to participants' textual excerpts) relevant to the social psychology of stepfathering.
Consequently, I used the grounded theory method for two main reasons:
(1) to deepen, expand, integrate, and ground in empirical data previously
proposed theoretical notions concerning men as either stepfathers or fathers
and (2) to generate new concepts and their properties relevant to stepfathering. My aim, then, unlike most grounded theorists who wish to produce a full-fledged grounded theory, was to sharpen a conceptual lens for
exploring how men develop and express their identities as stepfathers over
time and in different situations.

Sensitizing concepts have influenced the way I conceptualized and
carried out this project.[10] In general, these concepts provide a starting point
for researchers to collect and consider some class of data without drawing
any definitive conclusions about the material. Some of the more significant
sensitizing concepts that influenced the direction and scope of my interview
questions and analysis of men's replies include: social capital, generativity,
anticipatory socialization, coparenting, looking-glass self, reflected appraisals, compensatory/emulating fathering, and comparative appraisals. In
some cases, I integrated these precise terms into the book, other times not.
I anticipate that my efforts to refine these and related concepts, as well as
my work to generate new ones (father ally, family dance, private/public fathering), will help guide future studies based on a more narrowly defined
sample (stepfathers with 13–15-year-olds, stepfathers of teenagers with involved biological fathers).

Immediately after conducting the interviews, my research team and I
prepared extensive theoretical, methodological, and personal memos. When
interviews were conducted with couples or family units, the interviewers
discussed their experiences immediately afterwards. In addition, interviews
were transcribed within a few days after they were completed and I coded
them upon receipt. In those cases where an assistant completed an interview,
I distributed a copy of the transcript to him or her. By transcribing and coding interviews shortly after they were conducted, my preliminary analysis of
the interviews informed subsequent interviews in a timely fashion.

One of the shortcomings of my coding procedure is that I was the
only person who coded the interviews. Being the sole interpreter of these
data may reduce the dependability of the results.[11] I did, however, have five
participants (Emmit, Herman, Jackson, Randy, and Terry) review all
sections of the draft manuscript that dealt with their individual interviews
and my interpretation of them. I chose these men because I used their material extensively throughout the book. In each case I asked them to de-

scribe how well I had depicted and interpreted their experiences, and to suggest any changes they felt were needed to have my presentation reflect more clearly their view of what they experienced. Aside from a few minor changes, none of the participants asked me to change the text. The minor changes were of the following variety. Herman clarified that he had never been married to the mother of his biological child (I had referred to this woman originally as his wife), and Terry informed me that there is always *fighting* and cursing going on in Zack's biological father's house, not just "cursing" as he had mentioned in his original interview. All of the participants' enthusiastic feedback reassured me that my description and analysis captured their lives in a meaningful way. Herman, in fact, commented that he was going to think about doing things a little differently after reading about himself through my eyes. In addition, prior to contacting the five participants, I had two student assistants read transcripts for nine interviews (7 stepfathers—including Monty and Ron, 2 birth mothers) for those participants who represented exemplars in my study. They reviewed my analysis for those interviews and agreed with my interpretations. One cautionary note about the dependability of my interpretations is that, after reflecting at length on whether to contact Monty and/or Ron, the two men whose comments about their lives were the most negative, I chose not to seek their feedback. My assistant had interviewed the frustrated partners of these two men, the birth mothers of the men's stepchildren, so I was reluctant to add more friction to their lives by creating a situation in which members of these couples might read or ask to read each other's comments. Consequently, participants' feedback on the interviews comes only from those who were largely content with their stepfathering experience.

Although my coding system was informed in some ways by sensitizing concepts I have worked with in my previous research,[12] new codes were incorporated into this analysis as well. Throughout the project I focused on identifying substantive and conceptual themes. During the later stages of data collection, I had an assistant enter the coded data into a qualitative software package (N-vivo) designed for data retrieval and analysis, though I only used the data management features of this program.

An issue relevant to my coding technique and the semistructured interview questions is that questions related to the sensitizing concepts often appeared to lead directly to specific codes, affecting how I interpreted the data. For example, I asked, "Can you describe any experiences you've had caring for other children prior to getting involved with your partner's child?" and then coded many answers as "anticipatory socialization." Although using semistructured questions helped direct the interviews in ways

I found useful, and they deepened and grounded in empirical data some of the sensitizing concepts, this approach may preclude certain kinds of insights from being discovered.

A key facet of my analytic approach was to look at stepfathers' lives with an eye toward the chronology of how men met their current partner, got involved, met the stepchild, and then became increasingly involved (or eventually disengaged) in both their partner's and her child's life. My analytic focus was on the dynamic ways men's perceptions and actions changed as a result of their ongoing exchanges with the birth mother, stepchild, and others.

Another feature of my interviewing and analysis technique was to focus on the factors that either enabled or curtailed their evolving stepfather/father identity and integration into the stepfamily. Somewhat surprisingly, only a few men had serious adjustment problems (Monty, Ron) so I paid particular attention to these men's experiences and treated them as "negative cases" that deviated from the typical pattern found in my data.

Based on the previous literature cited throughout this book, I was aware that several life course, family structure, and personal variables (age, marital/cohabiting status, gender ideology) might influence the conditions and context affecting men's thoughts, feelings, and actions in relation to their partner's child. My analyses took these factors into account.

WRITING ABOUT PARTICIPANTS' LIVES

I vividly recall my interview with Terry, one of the participants whom I treated as an exemplar in the previous chapters. I had the good fortune of having Terry be the second person I interviewed. Shortly into the interview I knew that his story, rich with detail and revealing insights, would play prominently in how I developed my subsequent interviews and wrote about stepfathers' lives. Terry's story of how he first befriended his wife and then Zack was idyllic. Everything fell into place for these three. Most importantly, Terry's commitment to Zack was palpable; he seemed as proud of Zack as any father I've ever met.

Fortunately, Terry was not an isolated case; other men quickly followed suit and showed me that they too were willing to open up about the experiences and feelings they had as stepfathers. Before long, I realized that in addition to having plenty to write about, I would be able to use the literary device of showcasing several men as exemplars to illustrate the processes and challenges men experienced. Men like Terry, Herman, Jackson, John, Kevin, Randy, Monty, and Ron, as well as the others, stood out by what they had experienced and how they were able to share it. They also exemplified stepfathers' diversity in terms of social and personal characteristics as well as family circumstances.

I still needed to make decisions about how I would represent the participants and their stories. These decisions were affected by the analytic strategies I used to make sense of each participant's comments individually, as well as collectively. My decisions were also influenced by how I defined my audience and my perception about what would resonate most with them.

Thinking about how I wanted to describe the participants in the text, I recognized the power of providing the reader with a mental image of the person. Bringing the participant to life is clearly a useful literary tool. Part of this process, though, relies on the reader's conscious and unconscious efforts to categorize and process information. When presented with only limited descriptive information about a person's background, people tend to fill in the gaps by using cognitive strategies that may draw from stereotypical or ideal images. Thus a researcher's use of descriptive information to make the person seem like a real person and not just a faceless, unknown research participant has the potential consequence of prompting the reader to construct what may prove to be a distorted image because it is based on stereotypical thinking. My decision about what descriptors I should use was also complicated by my intent to keep the participants' identities anonymous, at least to those outside their immediate family.

I needed to make basic decisions about whether to report a person's race, occupation, age, family background, and details about stepchildren's gender and age. From an analytic standpoint, and to my surprise, I found that race issues were generally not critical to the way the men framed their experience as stepfathers. As mentioned previously, my attempts to provide African American participants the opportunity to talk about how race affected the way they experienced stepfathering were not productive. Consequently, I typically chose not to use race descriptors to portray my participants in the text. Likewise, I rarely mentioned the participants' previous or current occupations. On those few occasions where I did, my purpose was to show how work-related experiences with kids provided men with unique opportunities that influenced how they related to children. I did, however, consistently mention participants' ages and stepchildren's ages and gender. This made sense because parent–child relations are often influenced by developmental, life course, and gender issues, both from the parent's and child's perspective.

Like all qualitative researchers, I was faced with typical decisions about how best to present the participant's stories and self-reflections. I chose to make extensive use of relatively long quotes throughout. This decision was partly influenced by the broad audience I wanted to reach, including single mothers, remarried mothers, and stepfathers. I reasoned that these individuals would be interested acutely in knowing what their counterparts specifically had to say about their transitions into stepfamilies and what their life experiences were like once they got involved. Also, I found no study in the scholarly literature, especially outside of clinical and journalistic samples, that provides scholars and students with expansive, penetrating accounts of the subjective aspects of stepfatherhood. Stepfathers' stories, told in their own words, are rare. Rosin's journalistic book from the 1980s appears to be the most extensive source of in-depth, qualitative accounts of stepfathers' inner worlds.[13] Moreover, I quickly learned that my student assistants who read early drafts of this manuscript were thrilled to read the participants' firsthand, detailed narratives about their thoughts, feelings, and experiences. Thus I made a concerted effort to give men sufficient opportunity to speak for themselves on a wide range of issues.

As alluded to earlier, I assume that stepfathers are capable of experiencing aspects of their lives as stepfathers in their minds and hearts, experiences that exist prior to their participation in an interview. In addition, I assume they are capable of sharing their perspectives on what has been going on in their lives as stepfathers. Given these assumptions, I did not systematically attempt to interpret what men said by considering explicitly how these statements were connected to features of the interview setting, including personal characteristics of those who interviewed them. My use and interpretation of the participants' quotes therefore represents both an analytic and a literary style. I suggest later how future researchers might broaden their approach by using some form of narrative model to collect and analyze data about stepfathers' lives.

FUTURE RESEARCH AND KEY CONCEPTS

By design, I cast a wide net when identifying male participants for this study because I wanted to ensure that I was able to consider various aspects of the process of stepfathering that arise for men in different kinds of settings. Future research will benefit by streamlining sample designs so that researchers can hone in on more homogeneous subsamples of stepfathers. This strategy will allow researchers to scrutinize particular substantive issues more intensely and generate a deeper understanding of specific concepts, while controlling for potentially confounding factors. Such an approach will enable researchers to say more about the properties, conditions, and contexts associated with how certain types of men develop, negotiate, and express their identities as stepfathers. Although there are plenty of worthy categories of men that deserve closer scrutiny, three categories stand out.

First, those who may not be fully recognized by persons, especially those outside the family, as formal stepfathers, but who act in a fatherly way toward their romantic partner's child. In particular, men who live apart from their partners but have become a prominent figure in a stepchild's life as well as those cohabiting with their partner and her child.

Second, men who have established meaningful ties with the biological father to the point of engaging in what might be defined loosely as some form of cooperative cofathering. Based on my interviews, this subset of men is rather small, but important discoveries most likely await those who study these men. These situations will include stepfathers like those I identified as acting like father allies, although being an ally does not necessarily mean that a stepfather will establish an engaged, reciprocal cofathering alliance.

Third, some stepfathers will find themselves, as Terry did, in situations where a biological father resists and perhaps attempts to undermine a stepfather's efforts to act in a fatherly way toward a child.[14] Currently, this competitive scenario representing the antithesis of cofathering is probably as common or more so than cofathering. More rigorous analyses of fathers' competitive interpersonal tactics should go hand in hand with the study of cooperative strategies used by men involved in cofathering. These analyses need to be sensitive to the possibility that stepfathers may engage in competitive tactics of their own. They may wish to discredit the biological father and push him out of the picture. Monty, for example, had the urge to do this but apparently did not say anything directly to his stepdaughter. Unearthing the details of stepfathers' tactics to undermine the biological father will require skillful interviewing. Although I did not probe specifically for this kind of information, my impression is that stepfathers in my study either avoided such activity or would have been initially hesitant to admit it.

In discussing the private and public faces of stepfathering I underscore the importance of learning more about how individuals identify, navigate, sustain, challenge, modify, and accept the various boundaries, spoken and unspoken, that define the stepfathers' interactions and relationships with stepchildren. My work provides preliminary insights about specific properties associated with the private and public scenarios where men's concrete fathering (stepfathering) or more abstract roles are displayed. Thinking of both the physical and social dimensions of these scenarios reminds us that much of fathering can be seen as occurring within particular sites—physical locations imbued with symbolic meanings (home, school, extended family homes, neighborhoods). As I discussed in chapter 8, fathering occurs in various settings. Some are one-on-one experiences between the man and child without an audience. Others include a select familial audience, perhaps the mother and/or a sibling(s). And some include different types of mixed audiences where some combination of family, friends, professionals, strangers, neighbors, and so on are present.[15] Much can be learned by studying how men move from one type of setting to another, managing their identities and relationships relative to the stepchildren in the process. Questions that focus on men's experiences in and between these different settings are critical in light of the ambiguity of the norms associated with stepfathering.

When viewed broadly, an important piece of the stepfathering puzzle involves men who were once stepfathers but are no longer. My sampling strategy directed my attention to those currently engaged in some form of stepfathering. But what about those countless men whose romantic involvements with single mothers have ended? Notwithstanding a few notable exceptions, the insights gleaned from my study are largely based on stepfathers who perceive themselves as doing rather well in their stepfamilies. Also, I only have limited data on several men's previous experiences with stepfathering in earlier relationships that have ended. Thus one way to extend my work is to recruit men who recently experienced stepfathering in a romantic partnership that subsequently dissolved, perhaps in the past couple of years. Research with these men could produce rich insights about the more difficult aspects of stepfathering, ones that are less likely to be discovered using only a sample of stepfathers currently involved in a stepfamily. Ideally, a future design would include a subset of men who have sustained relationships with a "former" stepchild despite severing their romantic ties with the child's mother. Examining this unique form of stepfather–stepchild relationship should shed light on how personality characteristics and interpersonal dynamics foster some of the strongest stepfather–stepchild bonds.

My approach to studying stepfathers assumes that much can be learned about their subjective lives through interviewing, without focusing specifically on how elements of the interview setting and language may play a fundamental role in constructing knowledge. But some qualitatively oriented scholars would look at stepfathering through a decidedly different methodological lens. For example, those who emphasize some form of narrative analysis[16] would focus on the ways in which stepfathers (and birth mothers and their children) construct stories or share less storied forms of talk in the confines of an in-depth interview. This approach can take various forms, but the underlying notion is that stepfathers, and others who talk, and especially tell stories about stepfathering in an interview setting, actively construct the meaning of the events and experiences as they participate in the interview.[17] Researchers guided by this broad tradition would want to examine more closely how men use different narrative strategies and cultural resources to convey who they are and what they do as stepfathers. When and how are "rescue," "intrusion," "individual achievement," and "teamwork" storylines used? In what ways do participants frame their stories and comments by drawing on social discourses?[18] These discourses provide people with "coherence structures" that offer ways of knowing an aspect of the world, framing a message, and supplying a specific vocabulary to tell a story.[19] The resources relevant to stepfathers may come from such places as media-driven pop culture, therapeutic models of personal and family development, or special interest groups and organizations (stepfamily associations). The images conveyed are likely to be associated with matters like nuclear family and gender ideologies, divorce culture, single mom and deadbeat dad stereotypes, and notions of stepfamily adjustment. Part of the analysis of the way men represent their experiences as stepfathers to an interviewer might also focus on how what the men articulate is co-constructed with the interviewer's help. The narrative approach would broaden the qualitative perspectives used to examine the complex lives of stepfathers and their family members, especially the way they produce meanings about their subjective selves. It may be particularly useful in focusing attention on the different strategies and resources individuals from specific subcultures, neighborhoods, and family backgrounds use to construct stories about their experiences with stepfathering.

Though time and resources limited me to interviewing only two fourteen-year-olds, their stories were rich and revealing. Children can provide a critical perspective on stepfathers' experiences and serve to round out the picture of the interpersonal, stepfamily dynamics associated with men's efforts to assume and develop some type of fatherly presence with children who are not their biological offspring. Whenever possible, their voices, along with those of the birth mothers, should be incorporated into future research.

Last, I outline a series of concepts and thematic issues that proved to be important for my analysis of stepfathers' experiences from a social psychological perspective. I have explicitly or implicitly discussed these concepts in the book at various points, but I reproduce them here to provide those interested in doing research in this area with a more accessible listing of these conceptual tools.

Initial context for involvement. This has different aspects including (1) interaction with partner (platonic, then romantic), (2) interaction with child, (3) first interaction with child when the child is aware that the man is affectionate toward or romantically involved with the mother, and (4) experiences where the stepfather begins to act in a fatherly way toward the stepchild (from the perspective of the stepfather, mother, and child).

Family dance. Birth mothers will have a preexisting set of experiences, rituals, shared knowledge, interpersonal dynamics, emotional memories, and so on, that define their relationship with their children as part of a family unit. Stepfathers who come into contact with a preexisting family must grapple with their own perceptions of how they fit in and how others see them. Understanding how the family dance is perceived and then negotiated into a stepfamily dance is critical.

Mother's identity. A birth mother's sense of self as a mother, as well as a romantic partner, influences the way stepfathers are encouraged or discouraged to participate in stepfathering. Understanding the circumstances that leads her to separate or merge those identities may be important for understanding her gatekeeping activities.

Mother's representations of the biological father. A birth mother can shape a stepfather's image of a biological father by portraying him in particular ways, both initially and over the course of time. The timing, emotional energy, and descriptive aspects associated with these representations can influence men's stepfather identities and how they relate to the birth mother's family dance and individual stepchildren.

Logistical concerns. There are a number of practical considerations that come into play in how stepfathers get involved, stay involved, negotiate their place in children's lives, and sometimes sever their ties with stepfamily members. One of the more important ones involves living accommodations and decisions surrounding how partners manage physical space issues related to spending time together and in many instances living together.

Anticipatory socialization. Some men have had their own children or experiences of being involved with other children. These experiences can sometimes empower men, prompting them to feel confident they know what's going on regarding child care. The adult–child attachments they have established in the past may help shape their perceptions of themselves as a family-oriented person—with a certain set of skills and mindfulness. Thus men who enter a stepfather situation with previous experience being around children may feel more empowered or at least they may feel they have a legitimate reason to believe they deserve respect as a parental figure. Knowing more about the types of anticipatory experiences men have had and their evaluation of them is useful.

Comparative processes. These are related in some ways to anticipatory socialization because they provide stepfathers opportunities to evaluate their experiences. Men with their own children can more easily judge their feelings for and treatment of stepchildren. Stepfathers can also use comparative processes to evaluate their performance as stepfathers by comparing themselves to the birth mothers, biological fathers, their own father, or other fathers.

Naming process ("the name game"). Because language both defines and is shaped by social experience, it is important to consider how the names/labels family members use related to stepfamily ties emerge, are negotiated, and take on meaning. Stepfathers' perceptions, as well as those of the mothers and children, and their use of the "daddy/dad" label are highly relevant in some stepfamilies. Understanding the processes associated with the naming decisions can provide insight into how different people define family and navigate the rituals associated with family life.

Process of paternal claiming. This concept is closely tied to the naming process in many instances. It involves transitions that some men make in their level of commitment to being a father figure to a stepchild. When, how, and why do men begin to see stepchildren as their own? How do men weave financial, emotional, and practical issues into their perceptions? What types of struggles do men have with the idea that they will never be the "real" father? How do they resolve them?

Stepfather–stepchild bonding. Related to the process of claiming are experiences that enable stepfathers to bond with stepchildren. These expressions convey an emotional connection the men have with these children and in some cases are tied to their sense of making a difference in their children's lives. Stepfathers' expressions of pride in their stepchildren and their perceptions of similarities they share with their stepchildren are relevant. The literature exploring "affinity-seeking" and "affinity-maintaining" actions is closely associated with issues of bonding.[20] In addition, stepfathers may attempt to establish special interpersonal rituals and personalized cultural capital as part of the bonding process.[21] This type of capital includes a memory component that exists between people based on their jointly shared discussions and experiences. Finally, this stepfather–child bonding process is likely to be intertwined with men's commitments to a stepchild's mother.

Moral standing and entitlement concerns. Some stepfathers describe being frustrated with stepchildren not giving them the respect they feel they deserve as father figures. They in many ways emphasize their belief that they are entitled to have the children treat them as fathers. This notion is related to the process of claiming and the emphasis on the nuclear family model.

Mental imaging of stepchildren. This concept focuses on the different aspects of how stepfathers think about their stepchildren, both when they are in each other's company and when apart. Some of the key dimensions include the frequency, type, impetus and associated circumstances, depth, and accuracy of men's reflections. Exploring this concept is one way of getting a handle on how invested men may be in particular stepchildren. On average, biological and stepfathers probably engage in mental imaging to a different degree and in a different way than birth mothers. Understanding these differences is important, as is exploring the potential differences between stepfathers and biological fathers.

Mindfulness regarding stepfamily dynamics (romantic relationship, stepchild, biological father, self). The key aspect of this concept involves stepfathers' level of awareness about various stepfamily dynamics (potential or real) as they relate to particular people: birth mother, stepchild, biological father, and their own sense of self. For example, do stepfathers consider the mother's feelings regarding their potential involvement in her life and her child's life? To what extent and in what ways are men conscious of the potential consequences their romantic partner and her child might experience if they were to become attached to them and the relationship ends? To what extent are stepfathers aware of how their involvement with a woman and her child is interrelated with the biological father's connections with these people? To what extent and in what ways are stepfathers aware of how they feel about being involved with a single mother and her child?

Reflected appraisals. Stepfathers' perceptions of the way they believe others are perceiving and treating them in reference to their role in their stepchildren's lives are important to consider when examining stepfathers' identities.

Family support. Related to reflected appraisals is the degree and type of family support offered to stepfathers (the birth mother's and father's side) that help solidify or restrict men's sense of being stepfathers or the kind of relations they have with their stepchildren.

Fathering philosophy. Men's views on various aspects of fathering, including discipline. Some elements of this philosophy are generic to fathering in general whereas some are more specific to stepfathering.

Compensatory/emulative fathering. As with biological fathers, stepfathers often use their relationships with their own fathers as a reference point to guide how they are involved with stepchildren.

Future paternity options. An important issue to consider is men's fertility intentions and their sense of whether their partner can have or wants to have more biological children.

Private and public stepfathering contexts. Thinking about the private and public faces of stepfathering provides a way to think about the sites within which stepfathers "do fathering." There are both physical and social dimensions or properties to this concept. The different kinds of sites stepfathers experience will introduce them to different types of challenges. In these different contexts, stepfathers are likely to experience different kinds of reflected appraisals. Birth mothers and stepchildren are likely to play an important role, as are friends, extended family members, schoolteachers, coaches, camp counselors, shopkeepers, and people on the street.

Parent educator. In stepfamilies, the new male has to navigate the terrain of who is knowledgeable about children's needs. Men who come in with hands-on experience working with kids (their own or perhaps others within a professional context) have resources (cultural capital) available to them that give them legitimacy. Understanding mothers' type and degree of flexibility in recognizing a stepfather's potential contribution is important, as are concerns about mothers "pulling rank."

Coparental teamwork. Desires for and management of parental teamwork are particularly relevant to stepfathers' experiences. Key questions address the conditions and processes associated with stepfathers feeling as though they are part of a parental team with the birth mother, and perhaps the biological father in some instances.

Generativity. Like biological fathers, stepfathers can have adult developmental needs to play a nurturing role in children's lives.

Stepfather impact and child impact. Stepfathers can have impressions of how they have affected their stepchildren as well as perceptions about how their involvement in stepfathering has affected their own lives.

Social capital. Where appropriate, it is useful to consider stepfathers' motivation and ability to develop the knowledge and personal connections necessary to provide stepchildren resources that are linked to the larger social network within which the stepchildren operate.

Stepfathering as substitute/alternative arrangement. Some stepfathers talk about their involvement with stepchildren as providing them some comfort in being around children when they cannot be around their own children.

Father ally. This notion has to do with how stepfathers directly or indirectly provide support for biological fathers to remain active in a positive way in their children's lives. Stepfathers can make overtures because of their concerns about the biological father, birth mother, or the stepchild. Depending on the circumstances, these gestures can be directed at one or more of these persons. Stepfathers' own experiences with being a nonresident father often affect how they deal with their stepfather situation.

Appendix B

SAMPLE OF "KEY ISSUES" FOR SEMISTRUCTURED INTERVIEW GUIDES: STEPFATHER, BIRTH MOTHER, CHILD

STEPFATHER INTERVIEW

Explore aspects of the PROCESS whereby stepfather has gotten involved in the child(ren)'s and partner's lives and CONDITONS, CONTEXT, CIRCUMSTANCES, PERCEPTIONS, NEGOTIATIONS, and FEELINGS related to that involvement.

1. Early history of father–child relationship (and RELATIONSHIP with mom)
   See yourself as a father? LANGUAGE ("DAD" Focus on PROCESS)
   Circumstances that reinforced self-perceptions (nuclear episodes)
   Circumstances that brought about change (turning points)
2. Current relationship
   Specific things they do
   Responsibilities
   Rights
3. Family rules (social capital)
   Friends (social capital)
   Teachers/coaches (social capital)
4. Earlier father visions: Perceptions about biological fatherhood
   Ideal father images/relationship with own father
   Self-evaluations/ratings (fathers, child, partner)
   Make a difference?

5. Conversations about parenting with partner
Relationship with partner
Partner facilitating or hindering (gatekeeping)
6. Other possible difficulties with stepfathering (issues with bio dad)
Other possible things that help stepfathering
Things to make person feel connected to child
Future relationship with child
7. Methods questions
   a. recruitment comfort
   b. substantive issues comfort
   c. how mother's presence would have affected
   d. new questions of stepfatherhood

BIRTH MOTHER INTERVIEW

Explore aspects of the PROCESS whereby stepfather has gotten involved in the child(ren)'s and partner's lives and CONDITONS, CONTEXT, CIRCUMSTANCES, PERCEPTIONS, NEGOTIATIONS, and FEELINGS related to that involvement.

1. History of mother–child relationship INCLUDING INTRODUCTION OF PARTNER
Biological father's involvement
Name issue (first name, dad, daddy, father—FOCUS ON PROCESS and actual names, feelings)
Circumstances that reinforced perceptions/involvement (nuclear episodes)
Circumstances that brought about change in perceptions/involvement (turning points)
How does this relationship compare to other mother–child relationships she has
2. Turning points in life as mother; also with partner as stepfather
3. Relationship with own father or stepfather (clarify if both)
4. Her current relationship with child
Specific things they do
Responsibilities
Rights
Connection to child

Things that help/hurt ability to be mother (issues related to BIO DAD)
5. Friends (social capital)
   Teachers/coaches (social capital)
   Neighbors (social capital)
6. Perception of child's relationship with stepfather
   Perception of stepfather's responsibilities/rights
   Perception of how stepfather has made a difference in child's life
   Perception of stepfather-child disagreements
   Encouragement for stepfather to be affectionate, talk more
   Desires for stepfather to be more involved
7. What should stepfathers ideally do
   Rate stepfather's performance, standards for comparisons
   Conversations with stepfather about parenting
   Similarities/differences in mother/stepfather parenting styles
8. Description of mother's relationship with stepfather
   What does future hold for relationship with partner and coparenting
9. Methods questions
   a. recruitment comfort
   b. substantive issues comfort
   c. how mother's presence would have affected
   d. new questions about stepfathering

CHILD INTERVIEW

Explore aspects of the PROCESS whereby stepfather has gotten involved in the child's and mother's lives and CONDITONS, CONTEXT, CIR-CUMSTANCES, PERCEPTIONS, NEGOTIATIONS, and FEELINGS related to that involvement. Issues of the CHILD'S acceptance.

1. History of child–stepfather relationship INCLUDING EARLY PERIOD, NAMING issue (first name, dad, daddy, father—FOCUS ON PROCESS and actual names, feelings)
   Circumstances that have reinforced/changed perceptions
2. Relationship with own father
   Specific things they do
   Things that help/hurt relationship
   Major changes in relationship

3. Current relationship with stepfather
   Specific things they do
   Perception of stepfather's responsibilities
   Perception of stepfather's rights
   Things that help/hurt relationship (issues related to BIO DAD)
4. How and to what extent has stepfather made a difference in child's life
5. Disagreements
   Things that annoy
   Level of comfort talking, seek advice/permission
   Affection
   Family rules, stepfather's involvement in discipline and monitoring
6. Does stepfather know child's friends, nature of relationships (social capital)
7. Perception of stepfather's efforts as parent
   How is stepfather judged (point of comparison—mom, bio dad, other dads)
   Stepfather's personality or other traits (like and dislike)
   Nature of conversations with mother about stepfather
   Compare stepfather's to mom's parenting style
   What should stepfathers ideally do for children their age
8. Description of mother's relationship with stepfather
   What does future hold for relationship with stepfather
9. Methods questions
   a. recruitment comfort
   b. substantive issue comfort
   c. other's presence would have affected
   d. new questions about stepfathering

NOTES

CHAPTER 1   TALKING TO STEPDADS

1. Dowd 2000; Marsiglio 1998; Marsiglio, Day, and Lamb 2000. I have talked about social fatherhood in broad terms to refer to men who play an active role in raising children who are not biologically related to them. Rothman (1989) and other scholars have discussed similar kinds of issues involving the multiple ways of conceptualizing the different categories of motherhood (ovum, gestational or birth, legal, and social).

2. Dowd 2000, 176. See also Garbarino (2000) for an accessible essay on the need to reinvent fatherhood at the social level by encouraging men and fathers to become more nurturing. To accomplish this goal, he emphasizes the need to consider three discourses about fatherhood: social science, human studies, and soul searching.

3. Dowd 2000, 214.

4. For exceptions, see Coley 1998; Eggebeen, Crockett, and Hawkins 1990; Hawkins and Eggebeen 1991; Jayakody and Kalil 2002.

5. Some qualitative researchers have identified different stepparenting styles, strategies, or roles with some of this work focusing specifically on stepfathers. Drawing on data from 32 remarried couples from Israel, Erera-Weatherley (1996) discusses five styles (biological parent, detached, uncertain, friendship, and "super good" stepmother). Examples of the first four are found in my study of stepfathers. A stepparent who approaches stepparenting using the biological style believes that there are essentially no emotional or behavioral differences between being a biological or stepparent. Being detached captures a stepparent's decision to remain emotionally and behaviorally distant from the stepchild. This may be the only style the stepparent has used or it may emerge after the stepparent has become frustrated with trying to use a different style. Someone who expresses the uncertain style is basically confused. This stepparent doesn't have a clear sense of what others expect or want from him or her and is likely to experience distress. This person will have

a difficult time establishing a clear identity as it relates to the stepfamily and stepchild. Not having previous experience as a parent may accentuate the probability of this style being adopted. The friendship style enables the stepparent to develop a strong bond with the child, but the connection is characterized as friendship rather than part of a parental role.

Levin (1997a, 179–80) uses data collected in Oslo, Norway, from sixty-three persons (men and women) who had been living in a stepfamily arrangement (married or cohabiting) for two to eight years to generate three patterns of stepparenting experience: "reconstructors," "wait-and-see," and "innovators." Reconstructors "have a notion of reconstructing a family similar to the one they had before." These persons try to become a "father or mother substitute." Those who wait and see tend to "go slowly and learn from experience." They tend to be more pragmatic and try to develop a realistic perspective on their family circumstances. As a result they perceive their role as being "a friend and an adult person." Finally, the innovators approach their experience by expressing a clear sense of what they do not want. They are not interested in having the nuclear family as a positive model for their behavior; if anything it's an "antimodel." Their approach resembles that of an "uncle or an aunt."

Other scholars have explored the various strategies stepfathers (Stern 1982) and stepparents (Ganong, Coleman, Fine, and Martin 1999) use to develop friendships and affinity with stepchildren. Ganong and his colleagues, for example, discuss five broad types of strategies: "group activities," "having fun together one-to-one," "communicating one-on-one," "advocating for the stepchild," and "making them feel like family." Although I did not attempt to study these strategies systematically, they were represented in the stepfathers' stories about their involvement with their stepchildren.

6. Because my questions emphasize the subjectivities of men's lives, their thoughts, feelings, and the meanings they assign to aspects of their lives, I selectively use a number of theoretical perspectives well known in the social sciences to frame my analysis: social constructionism, symbolic interactionism, scripting, life course, and identity theory (Blumer 1969; Stryker 1980). In other writings I have used and discussed these perspectives in connection with men's procreative experiences and fathering (Marsiglio 1995a, 1998; Marsiglio and Hutchinson 2002). I do not explicitly introduce these perspectives here because I wish to enhance the readability of this book to a wide audience and avoid redundancy.

7. Griswold 1993.

8. Beckerman, Lizarralde, Ballew, Schroeder, Fingelton, Garrison, and Smith 1998; Crocker and Crocker 1994; Hill and Hurtado 1996; see also McDonald 1999. For an extensive discussion of these and other cultures, see the collection of ethnographic studies presented in Beckerman and Valentine (2002).

9. Researchers have concluded that some cultures in South America recognize partible paternity without evidence that benefits accrue to the children who have multiple fathers (Beckerman and Valentine 2002).

10. Some scholars suggest that a sizable number of Western women actually engage in behavior that is not dissimilar from the South American women anthropologists have studied. R. Robin Baker, a former zoology professor at the University of Manchester, is quoted as saying, "One in 10 children don't belong to their mother's long-term partners, they don't belong to their putative fathers. The take-home message is that if you compare a British woman with a Barí woman, the difference is one of degree rather than kind. We're dealing with a genetic legacy that is the result of 60 million years of primate evolution" (McDonald 1999, A20). Whether women are looking for better genetic material or hoping to secure some residual obligations to their children, women in various cultures may engage in reproductive strategies that incorporate multiple men into their lives and those of their children.

11. Marsiglio 1998.

12. As I describe in appendix A, I had intended to interview several more children in my study on the social psychology of stepfathers but funding and logistics made that unrealistic. I include comments in this book from the two children I interviewed because they are compelling.

13. Jayakody and Kalil 2002; Marsiglio, Day, and Lamb 2000.

14. In the course of writing about the "subjective core" associated with a social scientific approach to fatherhood, Garbarino (2000, 15–16) makes a keen observation relevant to my decision to focus on a particular subset of social fathers—the men who are romantically involved with the child's mother. "The subjective experience of fatherhood is tied to the power that lies in the emotional intensity and psychological ramifications of making love with a child's mother. Being 'sexually active' with a child's mother is at the core of it because it affects a step-father's feelings (for whom the child represents that inescapable fact that the child's mother used to have sex with another man); a divorced father's feelings (for whom the central fact is that his child's mother may be having sex with someone else); and a child's feelings (for the child must cope with the fact that his [or her] mother may be sleeping with someone who is not his [her] father and that his [her] father may be sleeping with someone who is not his [her] mother)."

15. Blankenhorn 1995; Booth, Carver, and Granger 2000; Claxton-Oldfield, Goodyear, Parsons, and Claxton-Oldfield 2002; Daly and Wilson 1988.

16. Blankenhorn 1995, 40.

17. Giles-Sims 1997.

18. Malkin and Lamb 1994; Sedlak and Broadhurst 1996; see also Silverstein and Auerbach 1999. Researchers do not know for sure whether stepfathers' hypothesized lower incentive to invest in their nonbiological children, according to an evolutionary perspective, explains any of the possible differences between biological and nonbiological fathers' abuse patterns. This is one area where less rhetoric and more careful analysis and sober discussion is clearly needed. Exuberant ideological support of heterosexual marriage, when based on muddled findings regarding nonbiological fathers' mistreatment of children, is misleading. At the very least, such an

argument overlooks the reality that domestic violence and sexual abuse would be higher if women and their children were encouraged to stay in "bad" and/or abusive marriages.

19. Using data from the 1997 *Child Development Supplement* (CDS) to the *Panel Study of Income Dynamics* (PSID), Hofferth and Anderson (2003) profiled fathers and stepfathers who were involved with children 0–12 years of age. For this sample of male parental figures, the average age of fathers and father figures was thirty-seven; stepfathers were slightly younger than biological fathers (less than a year). Married stepfathers and cohabiting stepfathers have significantly lower levels of education than biological fathers, and cohabitating stepfathers work about five fewer hours per week on average than biological fathers. Compared to married biological fathers' yearly earnings, married stepfathers and cohabitating father figures make about 70 and 75 percent less, respectively.

CHAPTER 2   A LENS FOR STEPFATHERING

1. For reviews relevant to the social demography of stepfamilies and the key issues facing stepfamilies see Booth and Dunn 1994; Bumpass and Raley 1995; Bumpass, Raley, and Sweet 1995; Cherlin and Furstenberg 1994; Manning and Smock 2000; Seltzer 2000; Smock 2000; Stewart 2001. For a related and more general review of family demography, see Teachman, Tedrow, and Crowder (2000). Phillips (1997) provides a historical portrait of stepfamilies.

2. Eggebeen 2002; Hogan and Goldscheider 2001; see also Eggebeen and Knoester 2001.

3. Fragile Families Research Brief 2002.

4. Smock 2000.

5. Hogan and Goldscheider 2001.

6. Bumpass, Sweet, and Cherlin 1991.

7. Lancaster and Kaplan 2000.

8. Stepparenting and foster parenting are common features of many current preindustrialized societies around the world. For a review of demographic and childcare patterns in fifty-seven societies, see Hewitt 1991.

9. Bumpass, Raley, and Sweet 1995.

10. Manning and Lichter 1996.

11. Anderson 2000.

12. Hofferth and Anderson 2003.

13. Hofferth and Anderson 2003.

14. Marsiglio and Hutchinson 2002.

15. See Woodhouse (1993) for a detailed legal analysis of what she refers to as "gestational fathering." Her clever discussion draws on narratives from children's stories, literature, popular culture, and case law. By focusing on issues associated with men's experiences during a partner's (or perhaps friend's) pregnancy, she crit-

ically reviews what she perceives to be significant deficiencies in family law that stem from viewing parents' as having parental rights based on genetic factors. Similar to Dowd's (2000) emphasis on the significance of nurture to definitions of social fatherhood, Woodhouse articulates a child-centered approach she labels "generism" that goes beyond the "best interest of the child" legal standard. This perspective "would evaluate parents' authority over children and their obligations to children, and to each other, through the lens of children's needs and experiences. It would situate nurturing, especially of the next generation, at the center of family law" (1749).

16. Marsiglio, 2003; Marsiglio and Hutchinson 2002.

17. Glaser 1978; Glaser and Strauss 1967.

18. McAdams 1990; Strauss 1969.

19. Marsiglio and Hutchinson 2002.

20. Hawkins and Dollahite 1997; McAdams 1990; Snarey 1993.

21. Peterson and Jenni 2001.

22. Markus and Nurius 1986; Oyserman and Markus 1990; Strauss and Goldberg 1999.

23. Fox and Bruce 2001.

24. The second and third trajectories are closely tied to men's parenting identity and their perceptions of "self-as-solo-parent" and "self-as-co-parent" (Stueve and Pleck 2001).

25. For an extensive discussion of different aspects of coparenting, shared parenting, and "tag team" parenting, see Dienhart (1998).

26. Allen and Hawkins 1999.

CHAPTER 3   GETTING STARTED

1. Montgomery, Anderson, Hetherington, and Clingempeel (1992) discuss children's role in the "courtship" process that leads to remarriage. See also Ganong and Coleman (1994a, 41–68) for a more general discussion of aspects of dating among those who get remarried.

2. Discussing the increasing diversity of adults' life courses experiences in the United States, the social demographer Andrew Cherlin (1990, 148) succinctly summarized this pattern over ten years ago: "many adults will move into and out of several different unions during their life course. It will not be unusual for someone reaching adulthood in the 1990s to form a cohabiting union, end it, form another one, marry the cohabiting partner, subsequently divorce that partner, enter another cohabiting relationship, and then remarry."

Unions or serious relationships formed in recent years are also more likely to involve what Rindfuss (1991) calls "blurred transitions." In previous eras, the transition from being single to married was much clearer. People were in either one or the other stage. But now people are more likely to drift into relationships, become more serious, perhaps move in with their partner and stay in this arrangement for some time, and then either get married or move apart for a while and then get back together and eventually marry. Sometimes children will accompany the individuals through the entire experience, or they will be born into the evolving relationship and experience only some of the transitions.

3. Furstenberg 1995a; Furstenberg and Cherlin 1991; Manning and Smock 2000; Weinberg and McCarthy 1998. Not only are children exposed to their parent's new romantic relationships, they can often influence the outcome. As Hertherington and Kelly (2002, 190) point out, "Parenting is a two-way street, and the behavior of stepchildren has an important influence on the responses of stepparents and the quality and duration of a new marriage. Disobedient, contentious, hostile stepchildren can make a misery of family relations."

4. Cited in Winslow 2000, 15A.

5. When a woman who is pregnant with her first child gets involved with a man not responsible for the pregnancy, the man could have a stepfathering type of experience.

6. My use of the "family dance" metaphor was inspired by Dienhart's (1998) discussion of the "dance of father involvement" metaphor in her work focusing on men's and women's efforts to coconstruct their meanings of father involvement and parenting more generally. My perception of the family dance incorporates children's contribution to the construction of family meanings as well as the performance of rituals and routines associated with family life.

7. Berger and Kellner 1964.

8. Therapists have noted the importance for new stepparent couples to recognize the preexisting alliances, coalitions, and family history that a resident single parent (most often the mother) has established with her child. Most who write about stepfamily development and counsel couples involved in stepfamilies theorize and work with stepfamilies where the couple already has a fairly well-established relationship (Bray and Kelly 1998; Papernow 1993; Visher and Visher 1996). My analysis emphasizes the importance of also looking at how individuals make the transition to developing a friendship and dating relationship where one or both of the adults is a parent, and how the stepfather begins to associate with the mother's child.

9. Pasley 1987, 206; see also Boss and Greenberg 1984.

10. Goldner (1982) suggests that for stepfamilies to do well, they often need to integrate the nonresident parents and other key relatives into a "new family culture." See Ganong and Coleman (1994a, 120–47) for a useful discussion of issues related to how boundaries are managed between a stepfamily and the other biological parent and his/her family.

11. Ahrons and Rodgers (1987), using data from a sample of postdivorce parents, describe a typology depicting the type of relationship the former partners currently exhibit: dissolved duos, perfect pals, cooperative colleagues, angry associates, and fiery foes.

12. In chapters 5 and 10 I explore more fully how some stepfathers relate to the biological father and the prospects for developing initiatives that would enhance their ability to work cooperatively as parental figures.

13. Consistent with Levin's (1997b, 125) thoughts about how some individuals view the prospects of establishing a stepfamily as a "project," some women in my study were interested in reconstructing their experience. As such, they were motivated to "succeed" while avoiding a new "failure." When the subsequent experience proves successful, it "has retrospective power and helps to permanently frame the first experience."

14. An important avenue for future research is to consider what types of traits single mothers look for in a dating partner and if their preferences differ from those of childless single women. I suspect that single mothers will have a strong tendency to emphasize nurturing qualities as they incorporate a potential dating partner's treatment of her children into their preferences. Some researchers examining heterosexual dating preferences among college students suggest that unlike men, who are more likely to emphasize sex-related qualities, women are more likely to prefer nurturing qualities in selecting dating partners (Fischer and Heesacker 1995). Although single mothers may emphasize nurturance more than single women, the gender difference found among single individuals may be less prominent for single resident parents. In other words, single men with children may emphasize nurturance as much or perhaps even more in a dating partner than do single mothers.

15. Therapists are aware of the unique dilemmas stepfamilies sometimes encounter when a stepfamily is formed after the death of a parent. Papernow (1993, 362) suggests that these types of families are vulnerable to being dominated by either the biological parent–child subsystem or the adult couple subsystem. In the latter situation, issues associated with being a stepfamily are not acknowledged. In many of these cases, "the stepparent adopts his or her stepchildren, further sealing the fantasy, for the adults at least, that this family can operate as if it were a first-time family."

16. This type of confidence is related to the fathering skills in Pleck, Lamb, and Levine's (1986) model of the conditions that affect fathering.

CHAPTER 4   OPENING DOORS, BEING INVOLVED

1. See Coleman, Ganong, and Fine (2000) for a general review relevant to stepparent–stepchild interactions and Amato (1994) for a detailed review focusing on outcomes for children in stepfamilies.

2. Hetherington and Henderson 1997; Kurdek 1990; Kurdek and Fine 1991; Skopin, Newman, McKenry 1993.

3. Cherlin and Furstenberg 1994; Marsiglio 1995b.

4. A related area that I do not explore systematically in this study involves the relationship between how stepfathers' previous and current marital life is related to

their adjustment to being stepfathers (Bray, Berger, and Boethel 1994; Orleans, Palisi, and Caddell 1989; Palisi, Orleans, Caddell, and Korn 1991). One of the key questions related to this body of research involves how stepfathers' decision-making styles with respect to stepchildren are related to the marital (or relationship) bond. This relationship is likely to be reciprocal in some respects. The type of bond romantic partners have may lead the stepfather to assert himself with a stepchild in particular ways and how the stepfather is involved in this type of decision making is likely to either strengthen or weaken his ties with the mother. It would be useful to understand the dynamic aspects of how stepfathers and their partners develop early on their decision-making patterns regarding children, ideally prior to the partners' identifying themselves as a stepfamily.

5. Data from the National Survey of Families and Households reveals that about half of all married stepfamilies started out as cohabiting unions (Bumpass, Raley, and Sweet 1995). These researchers find essentially no difference in the stability of stepfamilies begun by marriage versus cohabitation. Looked at from the child's perspective, other researchers (Graefe and Lichter 1999) have found that children living in cohabiting stepfamilies are more likely to experience multiple family transitions during their lives. See also Stewart 2001; Wineberg and McCarthy 1998.

6. However, moving out, or having a partner and stepchild move out, does not mean that the situation will remain that way forever. As Mott (1990) has shown with national longitudinal survey data, a number of men are living in the home with a child at one interview date, then not living there for one or more years, but present in the home at a later survey. In some cases these transitions involve men leaving the child's home; in other instances the child leaves, usually with the mother. Whether stepfathers are more or less prone than biological fathers to engage in these types of back-and-forth transitions is unclear. A few of the stepfathers in my study mentioned that they had initially cohabited with their current partner, then the living arrangement changed back and forth. See also Wineberg and Mc-Carthy 1993.

7. Men who meet their future romantic partner while she's still experiencing the process of uncoupling from a marriage or serious relationship may be most likely to perceive the single mother as being inconsistent with the way she disciplines her child. Researchers have commented that because single parents are often exhausted from dealing with their own emotional, psychological, and financial needs during and immediately after an uncoupling, they may experience a "diminished capacity to parent" (Wallerstein and Kelly 1980). The marital or relationship conflict the mother experienced while she was with the biological father of her child may persist after the relationship ends, affecting both the child's adjustment and the quality of the mother's parenting (Kline, Johnston, and Tschann 1991).

8. Erera-Weatherly 1996; Fine, Coleman, and Ganong 1998; Fine and Kurdek 1994; Fine, Kurdek, and Hennigen 1992; Marsiglio 1995b; Schwebel, Fine, and Renner 1991. Fine and his colleagues have developed and worked with a model that focuses on stepfamily members' cognitions of their roles and their adjustment

to stepfamily life. This model focuses on the "content" of being a stepparent—what sorts of things the stepparent should do, as well as the "clarity" of those beliefs—how confident a person is that the content in question is appropriate for a stepparent to express. Fine et al. (1998, 823), using separate questionnaire data from parents, stepparents, and stepchildren in forty midwestern stepfamilies, concluded that there was "no consensus among step-parents, parents and stepchildren about how the step-parent *should* and *does* function." They also found that the children's perceptions of the stepparent role were significantly different from those of the parents and stepparents. Other research indicates though that there may be some agreement between stepparents and parents about childrearing. In one study, mothers and stepfathers tended to agree about their relative responsibility for childrearing (Bray, Berger, and Boethel 1994), and in another stepparents and parents raising adolescents had similar views about the stepparent's level of responsibility in raising the stepchild (Ganong and Coleman 1994b).

In an earlier study of mine using data from the 1987–1988 National Survey of Families and Households, I found that 18 percent of stepfathers indicated that it was at least somewhat true that "stepparents don't have the full responsibility of being a parent," with an additional 14 percent indicating that this statement was "neither true nor false." Thirty-one percent believed it was at least somewhat false that "it is just as easy to discipline stepchildren as it is your own children" (Marsiglio 1995b).

9. Cherlin 1978.

10. Hetherington 1993; Hetherington and Clingempeel 1992; Hetherington and Kelly 2002.

11. Hetherington and Jodl 1994.

12. Bernard 1998.

13. Hetherington and Kelly (2002) provide a related discussion of how stepfathers' involvement in stepfamilies can be affected adversely by "maternal resistance."

14. Allen and Hawkins 1999.

15. See Dollahite (1998) and Palkovitz (2002) for discussions of fathers' faith-based efforts to be involved with their children. Although research to my knowledge has not explored stepfathers as spiritual leaders within the home per se, I suspect that the same types of issues would apply to both fathers and stepfathers.

16. An important area of research dealing with financial matters focuses on the economic consequences of divorce, as well as the financial implications of remarriage and cohabitation, on family income. Researchers have estimated that mothers and their custodial children experience a 21–30 percent decline in family income during the first year postdivorce depending on the particular study and measures used (Bianchi, Subaiya, and Kahn 1999; Bianchi and McArthur 1991; Hoffman and Duncan 1988; Peterson 1996). In general, divorced mothers who remarry improve the financial resources available to them (Morrison and Rituallo 2000). Given high rates of cohabitation in recent decades, researchers have begun

to ask whether single mothers who live with a romantic partner improve their financial resources in a manner similar to those who marry (Manning and Lichter 1996). Morrison and Rituallo (2000) review the literature relevant to this question and conduct a comparative analysis of married and cohabiting persons using national data. Their study focuses only on mothers who have been divorced. They concluded, "while in absolute terms, remarriage is economically more advantageous than cohabitation, cohabitation and remarriage are equivalent in their ability to restore family income to prior levels (560)." Women who cohabit, on average, start out in a weaker financial position prior to divorce. See also Anderson, Kaplan, and Lancaster 1999, 2001.

17. Some research indicates that married stepfamily couples expect or assume that the stepparent will help support the stepchildren financially while the stepfamily is intact (Ganong, Coleman, and Mistina 1995; Mason, Harrison-Jay, Svare, and Wolfinger 2002). In their study of forty Midwestern stepfamilies, Fine, Coleman, and Ganong found that stepfathers were actually more likely than either mothers or children to report that they have the same obligations as fathers. This is partly consistent with the previous research.

18. Christiansen and Palkovitz 2000; Marsiglio and Pleck,forthcoming.

19. Because cultural expectations of fathers' direct involvement with their children tend to be lower than those for mothers, stepfathers are more likely to feel comfortable than stepmothers comparing themselves to a relatively low standard for parental involvement (Keshet 1988).

CHAPTER 5   OVERLOOKED ASPECTS
OF STEPFATHERING

1. For national survey studies of what stepfathers do with children, see Hofferth and Anderson 2003; Hofferth, Pleck, Stueve, Bianchi, and Sayer 2002.

2. Amato 1998; Coleman 1988, 1990; Furstenberg 1998; Furstenberg and Hughes 1995; Marsiglio and Cohan 2000; Seltzer 1998a; Teachman, Paasch, and Carver 1996.

3. Recent conceptual discussions about fathering using a systems or ecological approach (Doherty, Kouneski, and Erickson 1998) or a scripting perspective (Marsiglio 1995a, 1998) are also relevant to stepfathers.

4. Although there is some disagreement between the way parents and stepparents perceive the stepparent's role in a stepfamily, the greatest discrepancy is found when comparing stepchildren's perceptions and parents/stepparents (Fine, Coleman, and Ganong 1998, 1999).

5. Cherlin 1978; Ganong and Coleman 1997.

6. Stepfathers' opportunities for providing social capital, as well as their involvement with their stepchildren in other ways, are likely to be affected by the same

four factors outlined by Pleck, Lamb, and Levine (1986) dealing with fathers: motivation, skills, social supports, and institutional barriers.

7. Brown-Smith 1998.

8. Clinton 1996.

9. Ahrons and Wallisch (1987) provide one of the few empirically based discussions of the relations between biological fathers and stepfathers, biological mothers and stepmothers, and stepfathers and stepmothers. They use longitudinal data from a sample of 98 pairs of former spouses and their current partners, identified initially in 1977 from divorce court records in Wisconsin. About 75 percent of the biological parents described the same gender stepparents as being "acquaintances rather than friends or relatives" (241). But the authors add, "few reported arguments, anger, or hostility in their contact." About half of the biological parents described the stepparent to be "supportive of the biological parent's special needs as a parent" (241–42). Among biological fathers specifically, 65 percent reported that the stepparent was "usually" or "always" a "caring person" toward the children and 40 percent thought the stepfather was a good influence on the kids. Finally, 78 percent of the fathers were "mostly satisfied" with the stepfather with only 6 percent saying they were "mostly dissatisfied."

10. A considerable amount of research in recent years has focused on different aspects of nonresident fathers' involvement with their children, especially visitation and child support (Arendell 1995; Braver and O'Connell 1998; Cooksey and Craig 1998; Manning and Smock 1999; Seltzer 1991, 1998b; Seltzer and Brandeth 1995; Leite and McKenry 2002). A number of studies have also focused on how nonresident fathers' actions are related to child outcomes (for a review, see Amato and Gilbreth 1999). The main conclusion from these latter studies is that it is not how much time nonresident fathers spend with their kids that matters, but how they interact with them. In an important related study, White and Gilbreath (2001) look at how children's outcomes are influenced by the kinds of relationships they have with their resident stepfather and nonresident father. Using national data, they conclude that "many children have good relationships with both fathers and that, even controlling for quality of relationship with the mother, good relationships with both fathers are associated with better child outcomes" (155). The outcomes they address include internalizing (unhappy, sad, depressed, feels worthless or inferior) and externalizing (impulsive or acts without thinking, restless or overly active, cannot sit still) problems.

11. Fragile Families Research Brief 2002.

12. MacDonald and DeMaris 2002.

13. Although researchers have done little to explore systematically how becoming a stepfather influences men's personal lives—beyond marital adjustment, several researchers have explored the implications of biological fathers getting involved actively with their children, especially in a marital context. Hawkins and Belsky (1989) argue that by being involved in their young children's lives, fathers develop more nurturing traits. However, some research indicates that positive father

involvement may lead men to experience conflict, stress, and a lower self-esteem (especially with sons), although these patterns do not appear to be related to fathers' level of satisfaction with fathering (Pleck 1997). Finally, Snarey (1993, 98) suggests that fathers are more likely to express their capacity for "establishing, guiding, or caring for the next generation" (in the community at large separate from their own children). In the latter study, being a father is interpreted as encouraging men to play a more significant role in their communities. I suspect that these types of patterns may influence stepfathers as well, though to a lesser degree.

CHAPTER 6   THE NAME GAME

1. Ganong and Coleman 1983, 1997; Ganong, Coleman, and Kennedy 1990.
2. For a related study, see Furstenberg and Talvitie 1979.
3. Furstenberg 1995a.

CHAPTER 7   CLAIMING AND BONDING

1. For a broader discussion of individuals' perceptions about family ties and responsibilities in different family structures, see Ganong and Coleman 1999.

2. For a related discussion of stepfathers' loyalty conflicts involving biological and stepchildren see Clingempeel, Colyar, and Hetherington 1994.

3. Ganong and Coleman (1994a, 83) suggest that stepfathers who also have children of their own "feel more companionship with their stepchildren, experience more intimate stepfather–stepchild interactions, are more involved with their stepchildren's friends, feel fewer negative feelings about stepchildren, and have fewer desires to escape." In a similar vein, I once found using national data that stepfathers who lived with both stepchildren and biological children, compared to their counterparts who only lived with stepchildren, were more likely to report perceptions consistent with having a fatherlike identity (Marsiglio 1995b).

Although some stepfathers genuinely care for and love their stepchildren as much as they do their own offspring, there is reason not to expect this to happen. As Glenn (1994, 49) observes, "Stepparents and stepchildren do not ordinarily choose one another; they enter into a relationship that is incidental to the attraction of two adults to one another. The probability that there will be strong mutual liking is rather low because the screening and testing for compatibility that usually precede the bonding of adults—as occurs in friendship or marriage—often has not occurred. And whatever it is that tends to bond a parent and an infant to one another has not been present either."

4. Cherlin and Furstenberg 1994; Lee, Burkan, Zimiles, and Ladeswki 1994; MacDonald and DeMaris 1996; Quick, McKenry, and Newman 1995.

5. Hetherington and Kelly 2002.

6. I address social policy and legal issues related to stepfathers (stepfamilies more generally) in chapter 9. For commentaries on issues directly or indirectly related to stepparent adoption, see Chambers 1990; Chase-Lansdale 1994; Dowd 2000; Fine 1989 1994; Fine and Fine 1992; Katz 1999; Mahoney 1995; Mason, Fine, and Carnochan 2001; Mason, Harrison-Jay, Svare, and Wolfinger 2002; Mason and Mauldon 1996; Mason and Simon 1995; Woodhouse 1993.

7. Ganong, Coleman, Fine, and Martin (1999) provide a valuable analysis of "affinity-seeking" and "affinity-maintaining" strategies that some stepparents use to encourage their stepchild to accept and like them (see chapter 1, note 5). They categorize stepparents into three types, those that never sought affinity, those who sought it early but then discontinued—shortly after they began to live together in many cases—and those who sought affinity early and continued their efforts throughout the stepparent–stepchild relationship. Although I did not use this model to orient my interviews in any systematic way, the men's comments about their involvement with their stepchildren provide me with a fairly good sense of how they have treated their stepchildren. A few of the men did not seem particularly assertive in their efforts to develop affinity, but the vast majority seem to have made some effort, and only a couple had stopped completely. I revisit this issue in chapter 10 when I discuss ways to enhance stepfathers' relationships with their stepchildren.

8. Strauss 1969. I anticipated that more of the stepfathers would recall turning point experiences that led them to see themselves in a fundamentally different way with respect to their fathering roles. Elsewhere, a colleague and I identified various properties associated with men's procreative turning points, but there were too few cases in the present study of stepfathers to develop a deeper understanding of how the properties of the turning point process more generally may be relevant to stepfathers' experiences (Marsiglio and Hutchinson 2002).

9. If we think of stepfather involvement broadly, there is reason to consider certain types of mental images as a form of involvement. Some cognitive images of stepchildren can simply be flashes of a face, a specific event, or a comment. Or images may be along the lines of a stepfather spending a considerable amount of time imagining certain aspects of a child. The style of thinking that can most easily be thought of as a form of involvement includes a stepfather anticipating and figuring out how he can best serve a child's needs. This may mean the stepfather spends time thinking about ways of solving a problem the child is having at school, with friends, family members, or a personal problem. In one study of couples that had recently became parents, Walzer (1998) found that fathers were much less likely to think about their newborns than were mothers.

10. Collins 1988.

11. Hetherington and Kelly 2002.

12. This is consistent with the finding that, compared to stepparents and biological parents, stepchildren are more likely to perceive the stepparent as a friend rather than a father (Fine, Coleman, and Ganong 1998).

CHAPTER 8   FATHERING VISIONS, PHILOSOPHY, AND CONTEXT

1. An analysis based on two waves of data from the National Survey of Families and Households (1987–1988; 1992–1994) found that spouses think about each other's children when they develop their own fertility intentions. However, unlike stepmothers, stepfathers' fertility intentions are influenced as much by their partner's children as their own previous biological children (Stewart 2002). This finding contradicts Anderson's (2000) findings that men with lower socioeconomic status who become stepparents gain a "fertility benefit" because their partner is more likely to have a child with them. Instead, Stewart's results suggest that men may forgo the chance to have their own children in exchange for securing a partner.

2. During the past ten years, increasing attention has been given to understanding various aspects of men's procreative consciousness and role in family formation (Forste 2002; Goldscheider and Kaufman 1996; Marsiglio 1998; Marsiglio and Hutchinson 2002). In my previous writings, I focused on different aspects of how men develop and then manage their awareness of their actual or presumed ability to create human life. Typically, the desire or aversion to becoming a father, especially early in life, is connected to men's perceptions about having their own children. This consciousness may in some instances influence how men approach the kind of stepfathering that is the focus of this book, or it may pertain to a different type of social fathering in which the children are not biologically related to them or their romantic partner.

3. Alan Guttmacher Institute 2002. This publication provides a social demographic profile of men's life course experiences related to sexual, reproductive, and family life. See also Bachu 1996.

4. See Marsiglio and Hutchinson (2002) for a discussion about fatherhood readiness that deals primarily with biological fatherhood. In some ways, this material can be adapted and applied to men's experiences about being a stepfather.

5. See Thomson (1997) for social demographic analysis of issues related to couple's fertility desires and intentions.

6. Stewart 2002.

7. Kaufman 1997; Mackey, White, and Day 1992; see also Schoen, Kim, Nathanson, Fields, and Astone 1997; Seccombe 1991.

8. Although the common assumption is that women are more likely than men to become pregnant in an effort to solidify a relationship, research with teenagers reveals that some young men also feel the urge to have a child with someone whom they care about in order to secure their involvement with the person (Sugland, Wilder, and Chandra 1997). See also Ganong and Coleman 1988.

9. Daly 1993.

10. Palkovitz 2002.

11. Erikson 1982; Hawkins, Christiansen, Sargent, and Hill 1993; Hawkins and Dollahite 1997; Snarey 1993.

12. Some cross-cultural research has shown that men act differently toward children when the children's mothers are not present (Mackey 1985).

13. From a sociological perspective, I have discussed elsewhere some of the key aspects associated with the contextual nature of father involvement and paternal influence (Marsiglio and Cohan 2000). This work is relevant to stepfathers' experiences as well.

14. Ganong and Coleman 1983, 1997; Ganong, Coleman, and Kennedy 1990.

15. In chapter 9, I elaborate on how school administrators and teachers treat stepfamilies and the need to develop a more receptive policy for including stepparents.

CHAPTER 9   LAYERS OF STEPFATHERING

1. The one exception to this criterion was Ray. He had been married to the mother of his two stepchildren and one biological child, but was now divorced and not sexually involved with her.

2. Marsiglio and Cohan 2000.

3. I suspect that an ethnographic study of stepfathering in a local community or cultural enclave might unearth additional social processes and layers of meaning that shape how the men define, negotiate, and experience stepfathering. In addition, if I had worked with a clinical sample of stepfamilies, persons involved in therapy, I would have generated more and deeper insights about the problems stepfamilies encounter. Because several of my participants were in difficult situations, I was able to tap into a number of important issues. But the breadth and depth of my analysis in this regard is somewhat limited by the small number of cases.

4. Cherlin 1996.

5. Fine, Ganong, and Coleman 1997; Lansford, Ceballo, Abbey, and Stewart 2001.

6. For an analysis of the relationship between the strength of a man's stepfather identity and stepfamily interactions, see Degarmo and Forgatch 2002.

7. Ganong and Coleman 1994a.

8. This discussion is informed by Goffman's (1963) work with people possessing some form of stigma—an undesirable state of difference in the eyes of others. Individuals who have stigmas at some point become acquainted with the larger cultural perceptions of people who have stigmas in a general way. They also learn on a personal level what it's like to possess and manage a stigma, a process that involves their reaction to the way others respond to them.

9. Another recent movie, *The Stepfather,* aired on Bravo June 5, 2002, depicting a stepfather as menacing, violent, and mentally deranged.

10. Booth and Dunn 1994; Bumpass and Raley 1995; Bumpass, Raley, and Sweet 1995; Cherlin and Furstenberg 1994; Manning and Smock 2000; Seltzer 2000; Smock 2000; Stewart 2001.

11. MacDonald and DeMaris 2002.

12. This process is not unlike the experience of an adopted child who is told of his or her birth status after many years of relating to a particular man as father and thinking about himself or herself as the father's biological child.

13. In light of family demographic patterns highlighted previously, an increasing proportion of adult stepfathers are likely to bring some firsthand childhood experience with them into their stepfamilies. For now, the exact implications of having this earlier experience is not clear, but researchers should focus attention on unraveling its relevance.

14. Ahrons and Wallish 1987.

15. Marsiglio 1991.

16. Emery 1994; Visher and Visher 1996.

17. Amato and Rezac 1994; Kline, Johnson, and Tschann 1991; see also Amato 2000.

18. Hetherington 1999; Pasley and Ihinger-Tallman 1994.

19. Friend 2001.

20. Another letter written by a biological father, Tom Wohlmut, and posted on the Stepfamily Network web page in 2001 expresses a similar sentiment about a father's appreciation for the stepfather who is raising his daughter.

> On this Father's Day I believe not only biological fathers should take a bow but also stepfathers. As the biological dad in a stepfamily, I am acutely aware of the fact that my daughter spends part of her time with her stepdad and mom, too. She is shared by two families who love her.
>
> When Father's Day rolls around, I get all the gifts and recognition as her dad. That's great and I eat it up and enjoy my breakfast in bed to the fullest. And while I am like the bright sunshine for my daughter, she also enjoys delightful moonlight. So on this Father's Day, I want to recognize the efforts of my daughter's stepdad.
>
> His name is Richard and I hardly know him. Although we share fatherly duties, we share very little else. I know his birthday and his last name. We hardly ever talk beyond the handful of sentences a year at school functions or when calling my daughter over the phone. What do you think about my daughter? Does she make you happy with her vivacious ways? Can she make you laugh with her jokes? Do you hurt inside when she cries? Do you read her stories when she goes to bed? You are a mystery to me, but of the few things I do know about you I am grateful.
>
> When my daughter comes home, she sometimes relates a story about how Richard did a nice thing for her. How you took her miniature golfing, let her steer the car in the parking lot, took her out for ice cream.
>
> She thinks your parents are great, and she loves the horseback riding lessons your job helps buy her. It's not hard to see that she has come to love you in a special way as a very important member of her extended family.

I know the difficulty you must have experienced with her in the beginning because, you see, my daughter has a stepmother, too. It was hard for all of us to get used to the changes whirling around us, especially her at such a young age. Only time and patience has helped heal old wounds. I just want to encourage you not to take it hard whenever my daughter gets upset about you. She does that to me and her stepmom, too! It's all part of growing up—no matter what one's age.

So while I'm going to enjoy this Father's Day to the fullest, please accept my gratitude. You are an important male influence for my daughter, and I appreciate your kindness and love towards her. I hope one day society will have the courage to face up to the reality of stepfamily situations. My dream is for stepfathers—and stepmothers—to each have their own special day of honor.

21. Similar kinds of insights might apply to a biological father if his relationship with the stepfather is taken into account. In some cases, a father's coparental identity may include not only his experiences with the mother of the child but her current partner as well. Although my discussion focuses on heterosexual couples and stepfathers, the mother's current partner could be a woman. From the father's perspective, these scenarios are likely to be different because any competition he might experience with the stepparent would not be based on male-male competition.

22. MacDonald and DeMaris 2002.

23. Cherlin 1978.

24. Birth mothers often play a significant role in shaping nonresident fathers' relationships with their children, but fathers who have some type of formal legal agreement will be in a stronger position to demand that they be given an opportunity to see and maintain a relationship with their child (see Braver and O'Connell 1998).

25. Dallos 1991; Ganong 1993; Ganong and Coleman 1997.

26. Pasley 1987.

27. Ganong and Coleman 1997.

28. Kravets 2002.

29. Chambers 1990; Chase-Lansdale 1994; Crosbie-Burnett, Skyles, and Becker-Haven 1988; Dowd 2000; Fine 1989, 1994; Fine and Fine 1992; Hans 2002; Katz 1999; Mahoney 1995; Mason, Fine, and Carnochan 2001; Mason, Harrison-Jay, Svare, and Wolfinger 2002; Mason and Mauldon 1996; Mason and Simon 1995; Woodhouse 1993. For a more general discussion of family policy indirectly relevant to stepfamilies, see Bogenshneider 2000; for a legal analysis of family/household, see Woodhouse 1996.

30. Fine 1994. See also Coleman, Ganong, and Fine 2000.

31. Stepfamilies can organize themselves in various ways, including "reconstituted nuclear families, as integrated but distinct cultures, as binuclear systems, and as separate units" (Coleman, Ganong, and Fine 2000, 1299). Berger (1995, 39–42) discusses a typology including three types of stepfamilies: "integrated" ("combine old and new

perspectives"), "invented" ("new present-oriented family-focused unit, into which the past is absorbed, as if nothing existed before"), and "imported" ("function as if they are continuing the original family rather than creating a new family. Adults come together for the marital relationship and they are involved in raising each other's children as if they were born in the current marriage"). See also Erera-Weatherely 1996.

32. Cretney and Masson 1990; Fine 1994.

33. Fine 1994.

34. Mason, Harrison-Jay, Svare, and Wolfinger 2002, 519.

35. The authors suggest that alternative processes might be put into place for long-term cohabitors. Hans (2002) also describes a third and problematic category, "estoppel," that falls between the de facto and legal parent.

36. Emery, Klitzmann, and Waldron 1999.

37. Crosbie-Burnett, Skyles, and Becker-Haven 1988.

38. Furstenberg 1987.

39. Crosbie-Burnett 1992, 1994.

40. See Manning and Wootten (1987) for a summary of stepparents' suggestions for how school personnel could relate better to stepfamily members.

41. LexisNexis (July 18, 2001), FERPA Stepparent has FERPA rights when natural parent is absent. *School Law Bulletin,* Administrative Rulings 5 (3).

CHAPTER 10   TAKING ACTION

1. Coleman and Ganong 1987; see also Claxton-Oldfield 1992 for a more mixed conclusion.

2. Coleman, Ganong, and Fine 2000.

3. Dowd 2000, 189.

4. See also Garbarino 2000.

5. Kimmel 1994.

6. Brody 1985; Goodey 1997.

7. LaRossa 1988; Pleck 1997.

8. Pickhardt 1997, x. This easy-to-read guidebook to stepfathering within a marital context focuses on a variety of issues stepfathers often face involving their self-perceptions, interactions with a stepchild, and involvement with the child's mother. A former editor of *Parents* magazine, Mark Rosin, wrote a useful journalistic guidebook in 1987 based on interviews with fifty stepfathers. He discusses ten considerations stepfathers should keep in mind when developing relationships with stepchildren. These considerations deal with stepfamily adjustment issues and his belief that the biological father's involvement in a stepchild's life is ever present despite each unique stepfamily situation.

9. Pickhardt 1997, 113.

10. Ganong, Coleman, Fine, and Martin 1999.

11. Bertoia and Drakich 1995.

12. Tad Benson, the founder of this site, reports in a personal communication (July 8, 2002) that he had over 12,000 recorded visits to his site in the past twelve months. He also comments, "The main aspect of the site that gets used is the bulletin board. And that's usually people looking for help. Originally, I had an e-mail mentor program on the site, but I only received requests to get mentors and only one person willing to be a mentor. So I scrapped the program. The site is definitely mainly used by new stepdads and their wives (a large female audience) and some veteran ones who are going through difficult times."

13. The mission statement of the CoMamas Association, as presented on its website (June 20, 2003) is to "teach stepwives and their families how to develop cooperative and respectful relationships so they can end their war and get along for the sake of the children." The founders of this organization, with the assistance of a licensed psychologist, share their ideas for enhancing the relationship between a child's biological mother and the current romantic partner of the child's father. (Oxhorn-Ringwood, Oxhorn, and Krausz 2002). Although no comparable book to my knowledge has been written from a man's perspective, many of the ideas relevant to women can be applied to assist men in a similar situation.

14. Another recent addition to the Internet world of stepfamily organizations is *Step Together,* which was originally developed as a website for stepmoms in 2000 and grew out of *Stepmothers International.* According to Katherine McMillan, the retreat coordinator, *Step Together* has about 800 members, with fewer than twenty stepfathers. But she adds, "We had more stepfathers come to our board after a May 7, 2002, *USA Today* article on stepmothers. What we have found is that men don't reach out to other men (as stepfathers) the same way women reach out to each other as stepmothers. I'm thrilled that more stepfathers are finding our site though."

15. See the website for the Stepfamily Association of America for an extensive list of nonacademic links for information pertaining to stepfamilies, stepmother/second wives, stepfather/biofather, and divorce support.

16. I flag this label "father absence." Although it is the term often used by the National Fatherhood Initiative and other organizations and commentators, it is a fuzzy concept that does not capture the complexity of many families' and fathers' lives. For example, some nonresident fathers may be quite active in their children's lives, even more so than some resident fathers, yet be lumped into this "father absence" category. See Marsiglio and Pleck (forthcoming).

17. See Hughes and Schroeder 1997 for a review of programs targeting stepfamilies. Some of these programs focus on children and others are adult focused.

18. Cowan 1988; Cowan and Cowan 1992.

19. Hanson, McLanahan, and Thomson 1996.

20. Marsiglio 1998; Marsiglio and Hutchinson 2002. For other discussions of interventions designed to increase males' awareness of their roles in pregnancy prevention and fathering, see Levine, Murphy, and Wilson 1993; Levine and Pitt 1995; Sonenstein, Stewart, Lindberg, Pernas, and Williams 1997.

21. King 1998. See also syndicated columnist Ellen Goodman's op-ed piece

(June 15, 2003) discussing men's potential for providing services similar to those depicted in the movie, *Daddy Daycare*, with Eddie Murphy.

22. Because prevailing cultural expectations often differ about how mothers and fathers should be involved with children, the pressures stepmothers face may be more demanding than those placed on stepfathers.

23. Woodhouse 1993.

APPENDIX A

1. Marsiglio 1998.

2. Dowd 2000.

3. Marsiglio 1995a, 1998; Marsiglio and Hutchinson 2002; see also note 5 in chapter 1.

4. See Ganong, Coleman, Fine, and Martin (1999) for another example in which multiple-person stepfamily units (including a stepparent, biological parent, and at least one child between ten and nineteen living in the household) were recruited for a study where participants apparently were interviewed separately and simultaneously.

5. Schwalbe and Wolkomir 2002, 205.

6. Schwalbe and Wolkomir 2002, 203.

7. Marsiglio and Hutchinson 2002.

8. For a discussion of related issues, see Furstenberg 1995b; Tucker and Mitchell-Kernan 1995.

9. Glaser 1978, 1992; Glaser and Strauss 1967; Strauss and Corbin, 1998.

10. Van den Hoonaard 1997.

11. Lincoln and Guba 1985.

12. Marsiglio 2003.

13. Rosin 1987.

14. I want to thank MacGregor Meyer for pointing out the need to focus on this third category of stepfathers.

15. Marsiglio and Cohan 2000.

16. Holstein and Gubrium 1995, 2000; Richardson 1990; Riessman 1993.

17. For a review of the alternative forms of narrative analysis, see Cohan 2002.

18. Plummer 1995.

19. Holstein and Gubrium 2000.

20. Ganong, Coleman, Fine, and Martin 1999.

21. Collins 1988. I have taken the liberty to alter Collins's original label of "particularized" cultural capital to make it more user-friendly.

REFERENCES

Ahrons, C. R. and Rodgers, R. H. 1987. *Divorced families: A multidisciplinary developmental view.* New York: Norton.

Ahrons, C. A. and Wallish, L. 1987. Parenting in the binuclear family: Relationships between biological and stepparents. In K. Pasley and M. Ihinger-Tallman, *Remarriage and stepparenting: Current research and theory,* 225–56. New York: Guilford.

Alan Guttmacher Institute. 2002. *In their own right: Addressing the sexual and reproductive health needs of American men.* New York: Alan Guttmacher Institute.

Allen, S. M. and Hawkins, A. J. 1999. Maternal gatekeeping: Mothers' beliefs and behaviors that inhibit greater father involvement in family work. *Journal of Marriage and the Family* 61: 199–212.

Amato, P. R. 1998. More than money? Men's contributions to their children's lives. In A. Booth and N. Crouter, eds., *Men in families: When do they get involved? What difference does it make?* 241–78. Mahwah, N.J.: Erlbaum.

———. 2000. The consequences of divorce for adults and children. *Journal of Marriage and the Family* 62: 1269–87.

Amato, P. R. and Gilbreth, J. G. 1999. Nonresident fathers and children's well-being: A meta-analysis. *Journal of Marriage and the Family* 61: 557–73.

Amato, P. R. and Rezac, S. J. 1994. Contact with nonresident parents, interpersonal conflict, and children's behavior. *Journal of Family Issues* 15: 191–207.

Anderson, K. G. 2000. The life histories of American stepfathers in evolutionary perspective. *Human Nature* 11: 307–33.

Anderson, K. G., Kaplan, H., and J. B. Lancaster. 1999. Paternal care by genetic fathers and stepfathers I: Reports from Albuquerque men. *Evolution and Human Behavior* 20: 405–31.

———. 2001. *Men's financial expenditures on genetic children and stepchildren from current and former relationships.* PSC Research Report no. 01-484. Population Studies Center at the Institute for Social Research, University of Michigan.

Arendell, T. 1995. *Fathers and divorce.* Thousand Oaks, Calif.: Sage.

Bachu, A. 1996. *Fertility of American men.* Population Division Working Paper no. 14. Washington, D.C.: U.S. Census Bureau.

Beckerman, S. Lizarralde, R., Ballew, C., Schroeder, S., Fingelton, C., Garrison, A., and Smith, H. 1998. "The Barí partible paternity project: Preliminary results." *Current Anthropology* 39: 164–67.

Beckerman, S. and Valentine, P. 2002. *Cultures of multiple fathers: The theory and practice of partible paternity in lowland South America.* Gainesville: University of Florida Press.

Berger, P. and Kellner, H. 1964. Marriage and the construction of reality. *Diogenes* 46: 1–23.

Berger, R. 1995. Three types of stepfamilies. *Journal of Divorce and Remarriage* 24: 35–50.

Bernard, J. 1998. The two marriages. In K. Hanson and A. Garey, eds., *Families in the U.S.: Kinship and domestic politics,* 449–57. Philadelphia: Temple University Press.

Bertoia, C. E. and Drakich, J. 1995. The fathers' rights movement: Contradictions in rhetoric and practice. In W. Marsiglio, ed., *Fatherhood: Contemporary theory, research, and social policy.* Thousand Oaks, Calif.: Sage.

Bianchi, S. M. and McArthur, E. 1991. Family disruption and economic hardship: The short run picture for children. U.S. Bureau of the Census, Current Population Reports, Series P-70, no. 23. Washington, D.C.: U.S. Government Printing Office.

Bianchi, S. M., Subaiya, L., and Kahn, J. R. 1999. The gender gap in the economic well-being of nonresident fathers and custodial mothers. *Demography* 36: 195–203.

Blankenhorn, D. 1995. *Fatherless America: Confronting our most urgent social problem.* New York: Basic.

Blumer, H. 1969. *Symbolic interactionism.* Englewood, Cliffs, N.J.: Prentice-Hall.

Bogenschneider, K. 2000. Has family policy come of age? A decade review of the state of U.S. family policy in the 1990s. *Journal of Marriage and the Family* 62: 1136–59.

Booth, A., Carver, K., and Granger, D. A. 2000. Biosocial perspectives on the family. *Journal of Marriage and the Family* 62: 1018–34.

Booth, A. and Dunn, J. 1994. *Stepfamilies: Who benefits? Who does not?* Hillsdale, N.Y.: Erlbaum.

Boss, P. and Greenberg, J. 1984. Family boundary ambiguity: A new variable in family stress theory. *Family Process* 23: 535–46.

Braver, S. L. and O'Connell, D. 1998. *Divorced dads: Shattering the myths.* New York: Tarcher/Putnam.

Bray, J. H., Berger, S. H., and Boethel, C. L. 1994. Role integration and marital adjustment in stepfather families. In K. Pasley and M. Ihinger-Tallman, eds., *Stepparenting: Issues in theory, research, and practice.* Westport, Conn.: Greenwood.

Bray, J. H. and Kelly, J. 1998. *Stepfamilies: Love, marriage, and parenting in the first decade.* New York: Broadway.

Brody, L. R. 1985. Gender differences in emotional development: A review of theories and research. *Journal of Personality* 53: 102–49.

Brown-Smith, N. 1998. Family secrets. *Journal of Family Issues* 19: 20–42.

Bumpass, L. L. and Raley, R. K. 1995. Redefining single-parent families: Cohabitation and changing family reality. *Demography* 32: 97–109.

Bumpass, L. L., Raley, R. K., and Sweet, J. A. 1995. The changing character of stepfamilies: Implications of cohabitation and nonmarital childbearing. *Demography* 32: 425–36.

Bumpass, L. L., Sweet, J. A., and Cherlin, A. J. 1991. The role of cohabitation in declining rates of marriage. *Journal of Marriage and the Family* 53: 913–27.

Chambers, D. L. 1990. Stepparents, biologic parents, and the law's perceptions of "family" after divorce. In S. D. Sugarman and H. H. Kay, eds., *Divorce reform at the crossroads*, 102–29. New Haven: Yale University Press.

Chase-Lansdale, P. L. 1994. Policies for stepfamilies: Crosswalking private and public domains. In A. Booth and J. Dunn, eds., *Stepfamilies: Who benefits? Who does not?* Hillsdale, N.J.: Erlbaum.

Cherlin, A. J. 1978. Remarriage as an incomplete institution. *American Journal of Sociology* 84: 634–50.

———. 1990. Recent changes in American fertility, marriage, and divorce. In S. H. Preston, ed., *World population: Approaching the year 2000*, 145–54. The Annuals of the American Academy of Social Science, Sage.

———. 1996. *Public and private families: An introduction.* New York: McGraw-Hill.

Cherlin, A. J. and Furstenberg, F. F. 1994. Stepfamilies in the United States: A reconsideration. *Annual Review of Sociology* 20: 359–81.

Christiansen, S. L. and Palkovitz, R. 2000. Why the "good provider" role still matters: Providing as a form of paternal involvement. *Journal of Family Issues* 22: 84–106.

Claxton-Oldfield, S. 1992. Perceptions of stepfathers: Disciplinary and affectionate behavior. *Journal of Family Issues* 13: 378–89.

Clingempeel, W. G., Colyar, J. J., and Hetherington, E. M. 1994. Toward a cognitive dissonance conceptualization of stepchildren and biological children loyalty conflicts: A construct validity study. In K. Pasley and M. Ihinger-Tallman, eds., *Stepparenting: Issues in Theory, Research, and Practice*, 151–73. Westport, Conn.: Greenwood.

Clinton, H. R. 1996. *It takes a village.* New York: Simon & Schuster.

Cohan, M. 2002. Discourse, narrative, and the construction of male adolescent heterosexuality. Ph.D. diss., University of Florida, Gainesville.

Coleman, J. 1988. Social capital in the creation of human capital. *American Journal of Sociology* 94: S95–S120.

———. 1990. *Foundations of social theory.* Cambridge: Harvard University Press.

Coleman, M. and Ganong, L. 1987. The cultural stereotyping of stepfamilies. In K. Pasley and M. Ihinger-Tallman, eds., *Remarriage & Stepparenting: Current research and theory*, 19–41. New York: Guilford.

Coleman, M., Ganong, L., and Fine, M. 2000. Reinvestigating remarriage: Another decade of progress. *Journal of Marriage and the Family* 62: 1288–1307.

Coley, R. L. 1998. Children's socialization experiences and functioning in single-mother households: The importance of fathers and other men. *Child Development* 69: 291–30.

Collins, R. 1988. *Theoretical sociology*. New York: Harcourt, Brace & Jovanovich.

Cooksey, E. C. and Craig, P. H. 1998. Parenting from a distance: The effects of paternal characteristics on contact between nonresidential fathers and their children. *Demography* 35: 187–200.

Cowan, C. P. 1988. Working with men becoming fathers: The impact of a couples group intervention. In P. Bronstein and C. P. Cowan, eds., *Fatherhood today: Men's changing role in the family*, 276–98. New York: Wiley.

Cowan, C. P. and Cowan, P. A. 1992. *When partners become parents: The big life change for couples*. New York: Basic.

Cretney, S. and Masson, J. M. 1990. *Principles of family law*. 5th ed. London: Sweet & Maxwell.

Crocker, W. H. and Crocker, J. 1994. *The Canela: Bonding through kinship, ritual, and sex*. Fort Worth, Tex.: Harcourt Brace.

Crosbie-Burnet, M. 1992. The interface between non-traditional families and education: Empowering parents and families. *Family Science Review* 5: 52–63.

———. 1994. The interface between stepparent families and schools: Research, theory, policy, and practice. In K. Pasley and M. Ihinger-Tallman, eds., *Stepparenting: Issues in theory, research, and practice*, 199–216. Westport, Conn.: Greenwood.

Crosbie-Burnett, M., Skyles, A., and Becker-Haven, J. 1988. Exploring stepfamilies from a feminist perspective. In S. M. Dornbusch and M. H. Strober, eds., *Feminism, children, and the new families*, 297–326. New York: Guilford.

Dallos, R. 1991. *Family beliefs systems, therapy, and change*. Philadelphia: Open University Press.

Daly, K. J. 1993. Reshaping fatherhood: Finding the models. *Journal of Family Issues* 14: 510–30.

Daly, M. and Wilson, M. 1988. *Homicide*. New York: Aldine de Gruyter.

Dienhart, A. 1998. *Reshaping fatherhood: The social construction of shared parenting*. Thousand Oaks, Calif.: Sage.

Doherty, W. J., Kouneski, E. F., and Erickson, M. F. 1998. Responsible fathering: An overview and conceptual framework. *Journal of Marriage and the Family* 60: 277–92.

Dollahite, D. C. 1998. Fathering, faith, and spirituality. *Journal of Men's Studies* 7: 3–15.

Dowd, N. 2000. *Redefining fatherhood*. New York: New York University Press.

Eggebeen, D. J. 2002. The changing course of fatherhood: Men's experiences with children in demographic perspective. *Journal of Family Issues* 23: 486–506.

Eggebeen, D. J., Crockett, L. J., and Hawkins, A. J. 1990. Patterns of adult male coresidence among young children of adolescent mothers. *Family Planning Perspectives* 22: 219–23.

Eggebeen, D. J. and Knoester, C. W. 2001. Does fatherhood matter for men? *Journal of Marriage and the Family* 63: 381–93.

Emery, R. E. 1994. *Renegotiating family relationships: Divorce, child custody, and mediation.* New York: Guilford.

Emery, R. E., Kitzmann, K. M., and Waldron, M. 1999. Psychological interventions for separated and divorced families. In E. M. Hetherington, ed., *Coping with divorce, single parenting, and remarriage: A risk and resiliency perspective,* 323–44. Mahwah, N.J.: Erlbaum.

Erera-Weatherly, P. I. 1996. On becoming a stepparent: Factors associated with the adoption of alternative stepparenting styles. *Journal of Divorce & Remarriage* 25: 155–74.

Erikson, E. 1982. *Identity and the life cycle.* New York: Norton.

Fine, M. A. 1989. A social science perspective on family law: Suggestions for legal reform. *Family Relations* 38: 53–58.

———. 1994. Social policy pertaining to stepfamilies: Should stepparents and stepchildren have the option of establishing a legal relationship? In A. Booth and J. Dunn, eds., *Stepfamilies: Who benefits, who does not?* Hillsdale, N.J.: Erlbaum.

Fine, M. A., Coleman, M., and Ganong, L. H. 1998. Consistency in perceptions of the step-parent role among step-parents, parents, and stepchildren. *Journal of Social and Personal Relationships* 15: 810–28.

———. 1999. A social constructionist multi-method approach to understanding the stepparent role. In. E. M. Hetherington, ed., *Coping with divorce, single parenting, and remarriage: A risk and resiliency perspective.* Mahwah, N.J.: Erlbaum.

Fine, M. A. and Fine, D. R. 1992. Recent changes in laws affecting stepfamilies: Suggestions for legal reform. *Family Relations* 41: 334–40.

Fine, M. A., Ganong, L. H., and Coleman, M. 1997. The relation between role constructions and adjustment among stepfathers. *Journal of Family Issues* 5: 503–25.

Fine, M. A. and Kurdek, L. A. 1994. Parenting cognitions in stepfamilies: Differences between parents and stepparents and relations to parenting satisfaction. *Journal of Social and Personal Relationships* 11: 95–112.

Fine, M. A., Kurdek, L. A., and Hennigen, L. 1992. Perceived self-competence and its relations to stepfamily myths and (step)parent role ambiguity in adolescents from stepfather and stepmother families. *Journal of Family Psychology* 6: 69–76.

Fischer, J. M. and Heesacher, M. 1995. Men's and women's preferences regarding sex-related and nurturing traits in dating partners. *Journal of College Student Development* 36: 260–69.

Forste, R. 2002. Where are all the men? A conceptual analysis of the role of men in family formation. *Journal of Family Issues* 23: 579–600.

Fox, G. L., and Bruce, C. 2001. Conditional fatherhood: Identity theory and parental investment theory as alternative sources of explanation of fathering. *Journal of Marriage and Family* 63: 394–403.

Friend, T. 2001. Make room: Father and stepfather work to keep the kids grounded. *USA Today,* July 14, 10D.

Furstenberg, F. F., Jr. 1987. The new extended family: The experience of parents and children after remarriage. In K. Pasley and M. Ihinger-Tallman, eds., *Remarriage and stepparenting: Current research and theory.* New York: Guilford.

———. 1995a. Changing roles of fathers. In P. L. Chase-Lansdale and J. Brooks-Gunn, eds., *Escape from poverty: What makes a difference for children?* 189–210. Cambridge: Cambridge University Press.

———. 1995b. Fathering in the inner city: Paternal participation and public policy. In W. Marsiglio, ed., *Fatherhood: Contemporary theory, research, and social policy.* Thousand Oaks, Calif.: Sage.

———. 1998. Social capital and the role of fathers in the family. In A. Booth and N. Crouter, eds., *Men in families: When do they get involved? What difference does it make?* 295–301. Mahwah, N.J.: Erlbaum.

Furstenberg, F. F., Jr. and Cherlin, A. 1991. *Divided families: What happens to children when parents part.* Cambridge: Harvard University Press.

Furstenberg, F. F., Jr. and Hughes, M. E. 1995. Social capital and successful development among at-risk youth. *Journal of Marriage and the Family* 57: 580–93.

Furstenberg, F. F., Jr. and Talvitie, K. 1979. Children's names and paternal claims: Bonds between unmarried fathers and their children. *Journal of Family Issues* 1: 31–57.

Ganong, L. H. 1993. Family diversity in a youth organization: Involvement of single-parent families and stepfamilies in 4-H. *Family Relations* 42: 286–92.

Ganong, L. H. and Coleman, M. M. 1983. Stepparent: A pejorative term? *Psychological Reports* 52: 919–22.

———. 1988. Do mutual children cement bonds in stepfamilies? *Journal of Marriage and the Family* 50: 687–98.

———. 1994a. *Remarried family relationships.* Thousand Oaks, Calif.: Sage.

———. 1994b. Adolescent stepchild–stepparent relationships: Changes over time. In K. Pasley and M. Ihinger-Tallman, eds., *Stepparenting: Issues in theory, research, and practice,* 87–104. Westport, Conn.: Greenwood.

———. 1997. How society views stepfamilies. *Marriage & Family Review* 26: 85–106.

———. 1999. *New families, new responsibilities: Family obligations following divorce and remarriage.* Mahwah, N.J.: Erlbaum.

Ganong, L. H., Coleman, M., Fine, M., and Martin, P. 1999. Stepparents' affinity-seeking and affinity-maintaining strategies with stepchildren. *Journal of Family Issues* 20: 299–327.

Ganong, L. H., Coleman, M., and Kennedy, G. 1990. The effects of using alternate labels in denoting stepparent or stepfamily status. *Journal of Social Behavior and Personality* 5: 453–63.

Ganong, L. H., Coleman, M., and Mistina, D. 1995. Normative beliefs about parents' and stepparents' financial obligations to children following divorce and re-marriage. *Family Relations* 44: 306–15.

Garbarino, J. 2000. The soul of fatherhood. *Marriage and Family Review* 29: 11–21.

Giles-Sims, J. 1997. Current knowledge about child abuse in stepfamilies. *Marriage & Family Review* 26: 215–30.

Glaser, B. 1978. *Theoretical sensitivity.* Mill Valley, Calif.: Sociology Press.

———. 1992. *Basics of grounded theory analysis.* Mill Valley, Calif.: Sociology Press.

Glaser, B. and Strauss, A. 1967. *The discovery of grounded theory: Strategies for qualitative research.* Hawthorne, N.Y.: Aldine de Gruyter.

Glenn, N. D. 1994. Biology, evolutionary theory, and family science. In A. Booth and J. Dunn, eds., *Stepfamilies: Who benefits? Who does not?* 45–51. Hillsdale, N.J.: Erlbaum.

Goffman, E. 1963. *Stigma: Notes on the management of spoiled identity.* Englewood Cliffs, N.J.: Prentice Hall.

Goldner, V. 1982. Remarriage family: Structure, system, future. In J. C. Hansen and L. Messinger, eds., *Therapy with remarried families,* 187–206. Rockville, Md.: Aspen.

Goldscheider, F. K. and Kaufman, G. 1996. Fertility and commitment: Bring men back in. In J. Casterline, R. Lee, and K. Foote, eds., *Fertility in the United States: New patterns, new theories,* 87–99. New York: Population Council.

Goodey, J. 1997. Boys don't cry: Masculinities, fear of crime, and fearlessness. *British Journal of Criminology* 37: 401–18.

Goodman, E. 2003. Mr. mom to daddy day care. Boston Globe, H11, July 15.

Gottman, J. M. and DeClaire, J. 2001. *The relationship cure: A five step guide for building better connections with family, friends, and lovers.* New York: Crown.

Graefe, D. R. and Lichter, D. T. 1999. Life course transitions of American children: Parental cohabitation, marriage, and single motherhood. *Demography* 36: 205–17.

Griswold, R. L. 1993. *Fatherhood in America: A history.* New York: Basic.

Hanson, T. L., McLanahan, S. S., and Thomson, E. 1996. Double jeopardy: Parental conflict and stepfamily outcomes for children. *Journal of Marriage and the Family* 58: 141–54.

Hawkins, A. J. and Belsky, J. 1989. The role of father involvement in personality change in men across the transition to parenthood. *Family Relations* 38: 378–84.

Hawkins, A. J., Chistiansen, S. L., Sarget, K. P., and Hill, E. J. 1993. Rethinking fathers' involvement in child care: A developmental perspective. *Journal of Family Issues* 14: 531–49.

Hawkins, A. J. and Dollahite, D. C. 1997. *Generative fathering: Beyond deficit perspectives.* Thousand Oaks, Calif.: Sage.

Hawkins, A. J. and Eggebeen, D. 1991. Are fathers fungible? Patterns of coresident adult men in martially disrupted families and young children's well-being. *Journal of Marriage and the Family* 53: 958–72.

Hetherington, E. M. 1993. An overview of the Virginia Longitudinal Study of

Divorce and Remarriage: A focus on early adolescence. *Journal of Family Psychology* 7: 39–56.

———. 1999. *Coping with divorce, single parenting, and remarriage: A risk and resiliency perspective*. Mahwah, N.J.: Erlbaum.

Hetherington, E. M. and Clingempeel, W. 1992. Coping with marital transition: A family systems perspective. *Monographs of the Society for Research in Child Development* 57, 2–3, serial no. 227.

Hetherington, E. M. and Jodl, K. M. 1994. Stepfamilies as setting for child development. In A. Booth and J. Dunn, eds., *Stepfamilies: Who benefits? Who does not?* Hillsdale, N.J.: Erlbaum.

Hetherington, E. M. and Henderson, S. H. 1997. Fathers in stepfamilies. In M. E. Lamb, ed., *The role of the father in child development*, 212–26, 369–73. New York: Wiley.

Hetherington, E. M. and Kelly, J. 2002. *Divorce reconsidered: For better or worse*. New York: Norton.

Hewitt, B. S. 1991. Demography and childcare in preindustrial societies. *Journal of Anthropological Research* 47: 1–37.

Hill, K. and Hurtado, M. A. 1996. *Ache life history: The ecology and demography of a foraging people*. New York: Aldine de Gruyter.

Hofferth, S. L. and Anderson, K. G. 2003. Are all dads equal? Biology versus marriage as a basis for parental investment. *Journal of Marriage and Family* 65: 213–32.

Hofferth, S. L., Pleck, J., Stueve, J. L., Bianchi, S., and Sayer, L. 2002. The demography of fathers: What fathers do. In C. S. Tamis-LeMonda and N. Cabrera, eds., *Handbook of father involvement: Multidisciplinary perspectives*, 63–90. Mahwah, N.J.: Lawrence Erlbaum Associates.

Hoffman, S. D. and Duncan, G. J. 1988. What are the economic consequences of divorce? *Demography* 25: 641–65.

Hogan, D. P. and Goldscheider, F. 2001. Men's flight from children in the U.S.: A historical perspective. In S. L. Hofferth and T. J. Owens, eds., *Children at the millennium: Where have we come from, where are we going?* 173–91. Amsterdam: JAI.

Holstein, J. A. and Gubrium, J. F. 1995. *The active interview*. Thousand Oaks, Calif.: Sage.

———. 2000. *The self we live by: Narrative identity in a postmodern world*. New York: Oxford University Press.

Hughes, R., Jr. and Schroeder, J. D. 1997. Family life education programs for stepfamilies. *Marriage & Family Review* 26: 281–300.

Jayakody, R. and Kalil, A. 2002. Social fathering in low-income, African American families with preschool children. *Journal of Marriage and Family* 64: 504–16.

Kaufman, G. 1997. Men's attitudes toward parenthood. *Population Research and Policy Review* 16: 435–46.

Katz, S. N. 1999. Establishing the family and family-like relationships: Emerging models for alternatives to marriage. *Family Law Quarterly* 33: 663–75.

Keshet, J. K. 1988. The remarried couple: Stresses and successes. In W. R. Beer, ed., *Relative strangers: Studies of stepfamily processes*, 29–53. Totowa, N.J.: Rowman & Littlefield.

Kimmel, M. 1994. Masculinity as homophobia: Fear, shame, and silence in the construction of gender identity. In Harry Brod and Michael Kaufman, eds., *Theorizing masculinities*, 119–41. Thousand Oaks, Calif.: Sage.

King, J. R. 1998. *Uncommon caring: Learning from men who teach young children*. New York: Teacher's College Press, Columbia University.

Kline, M., Johnson, J. R., and Tschann, J. M. 1991. The long shadow of marital conflict: A model of children's postdivorce adjustment. *Journal of Marriage and the Family* 53: 297–309.

Kurdek, L. A. 1990. Effects of child age on the marital quality and psychological distress of newly married mothers and stepfathers. *Journal of Marriage and the Family* 52: 81–85.

Kurdek, L. A. and Fine, M. A. 1991. Cognitive correlates of satisfaction for mothers and stepfathers in stepfather families. *Journal of Marriage and the Family* 53: 565–72.

Kravets, D. 2002. Non-biological father wins parental rights. LexisNexis, June 7.

Lancaster, J. B. and Kaplan, H. S. 2000. Parenting other men's children: Costs, benefits, and consequences. In L. Cronk, N. Chagnon, and W. Irons, eds., *Adaptation and human behavior: An anthropological perspective*, 179–201. Hawthorne, N.Y.: Aldine de Gruyter.

LaRossa, R. 1988. Fatherhood and social change. *Family Relations* 37: 451–58.

Lee, V. E., Burkan, D. T., Zimiles, H., and Ladeswki, B. 1994. Family structure and its effects on behavioral and emotional problems in young adolescents. *Journal of Research on Adolescence* 4: 405–37.

Leite, R. W. and McKenry, P. C. 2002. Aspects of father status and postdivorce father involvement with children. *Journal of Family Issues* 23: 601–23.

Levin, I. 1997a. The stepparent role from a gender perspective. *Marriage and Family Review* 26: 177–90.

———. 1997b. Stepfamily as project. *Marriage & Family Review* 26: 123–33.

Levine, J. A., Murphy, D. T., and Wilson, S. 1993. *Getting men involved: Strategies for early childhood programs*. New York: Scholastic.

Levine, J. A. and Pitt, E. W. 1995. *New expectations: Community strategies for responsible fatherhood*. New York: Families and Work Institute.

Lincoln, Y. and Guba, E. 1985. *Naturalistic inquiry*. Beverly Hills, Calif.: Sage.

MacDonald, W. L. and DeMaris, A. 1996. Parenting stepchildren and biological children: The effects of stepparent's gender and new biological children. *Journal of Family Issues* 17: 5–25.

———. 2002. Stepfather–stepchild relationship quality: The stepfather's demand for conformity and the biological father's involvement. *Journal of Family Issues* 23: 121–37.

Mackey, W. C. 1985. *Fathering behaviors: The dynamics of the man–child bond*. New York: Plenum.

Mackey, W. C., White, U., and Day, R. 1992. Reasons American men become fathers: Men's divulgences, women's perceptions. *Journal of Genetic Psychology* 153: 435–45.

Mahoney, M. 1995. *Stepfamilies and the law.* Ann Arbor: University of Michigan.

Malkin, C. M. and Lamb, M. E. 1994. Child maltreatment: A test of sociobiological theory. *Journal of Comparative Family Studies* 25: 121–34.

Manning, D. T. and Wootten, M. D. 1987. What stepfamilies perceive schools should know about blended families. *Clearing-House* 60: 230–35.

Manning, W. D. and Lichter, D. T. 1996. Parental cohabitation and children's economic well-being. *Journal of Marriage and the Family* 58: 998–1010.

Manning, W. D. and Smock, P. J. 1999. New families and nonresident father–child visitation. *Social Forces* 78: 87–116.

———. 2000. Swapping families: Serial parenting and economic support for children. *Journal of Marriage and the Family* 62: 111–22.

Markus, H. and Nurius, P. 1986. Possible selves. *American Psychologist* 41: 954–69.

Marsiglio, W. 1991. Paternal engagement activities with minor children. *Journal of Marriage and the Family* 53: 973–86.

———. 1995a. Fathers' diverse life course patterns and roles: Theory and social interventions. In W. Marsiglio, ed., *Fatherhood: Contemporary Theories, Research, and Social Policy,* 78-101. Thousand Oaks, Calif.: Sage.

———. 1995b. Stepfathers with minor children living at home: Parenting perceptions and relationship quality. In W. Marsiglio, ed., *Fatherhood: Contemporary theory, research, and social policy,* 211-29. Thousand Oaks, Calif.: Sage.

———. 1998. *Procreative man.* New York: New York University Press.

———. 2004. Studying fathering trajectories: In-depth interviewing and sensitizing concepts. In R. D. Day and M. E. Lamb, eds., *Measuring and conceptualizing father involvement,* 61-82. Mahwah, N.J.: Erlbaum.

Marsiglio, W. and Cohan, M. 2000. Contextualizing father involvement and paternal influence: Sociological and qualitative themes. *Marriage & Family Review* 29: 75–95.

Marsiglio, W., Day R. D., and Lamb, M. E. 2000. Exploring fatherhood diversity: Implications for conceptualizing father involvement. *Marriage and Family Review* 29: 269–93.

Marsiglio, W. and Hutchinson, S. 2002. *Sex, men, and babies: Stories of awareness and responsibility.* New York: New York University Press.

Marsiglio, W. and Pleck, J. H. Forthcoming. Fatherhood and masculinities. In R. W. Connell, J. Hearn, and M. Kimmel, eds., *The handbook of studies on men and masculinities.* Thousand Oaks, Calif.: Sage.

Mason, M. A., Fine, M. A., and Carnochan, S. 2001. Family law in the new millennium: For whose families? *Journal of Family Issues* 22: 85–88.

Mason, M. A., Harrison-Jay, S., Svare, G. M., and Wolfinger, N. H. 2002. Stepparents: De facto parents or legal strangers? *Journal of Family Issues* 23: 507–22.

Mason, M. A. and Mauldon, J. 1996. The new stepfamily requires a new public policy. *Journal of Social Issues* 52: 11–27.

Mason, M. A. and Simon, D. 1995. The ambiguous stepparent: Federal legislation in search of a model. *Family Law Quarterly* 3: 445–83.

McAdams, D. 1990. Unity and purpose in human lives: The emergence of identity as a life story. In A. I. Rabin, R. A. Zucker, R. A. Emmons, and S. Frank, eds., *Studying persons and lives*, 148–200. New York: Springer-Verlag.

McDonald, M. A. 1999. Shared paternity in South American tribes confounds biologists and anthropologists. *Chronicle of Higher Education,* April 9, A19–A20.

McGraw, P. C. 2000. *Relationship rescue: A seven step strategy for reconnecting with your partner.* New York: Hyperion.

Montgomery, M. J., Anderson, E. R., Hetherington, E. M., and Clingempeel, W. G. 1992. Patterns of courtship for remarriage: Implications for child adjustment and parent–child relationships. *Journal of Marriage and the Family* 54: 686–98.

Morrison, D. R. and Ritualo, A. 2000. Routes to children's economic recovery after divorce: Are cohabitation and remarriage equivalent? *American Sociological Review* 65: 560–80.

Mott, F. L. 1990. When is a father really gone? Paternal–child conduct in father-absent homes. *Demography* 27: 499–517.

Orleans, M., Palisi, B. J., and Caddell, D. 1989. Marriage adjustment and satisfaction of stepfathers: Their feelings and perceptions of decision-making and stepchildren relations. *Family Relations* 38: 371–77.

Oxhorn-Ringwood, L., Oxhorn, L., and Krausz, M. V. 2002. *Stepwives.* New York: Simon & Schuster.

Oyserman, D. and Markus, H. R. 1990. Possible selves and delinquency. *Journal of Personality and Social Psychology* 59: 112–25.

Palisi, B. J., Orleans, M., Caddell, D., and Korn, B. 1991. Adjustment to stepfatherhood: The effects of marital history and relations with children. *Journal of Divorce & Remarriage* 14: 89–106.

Palkovitz, R. 2002. *Involved fathering and men's adult development: Provisional balances.* Mahwah, N.J.: Erlbaum.

Papernow, P. 1993. *Becoming a stepfamily: Patterns of development in remarried families.* San Francisco: Jossey-Bass.

Pasley, K. 1987. Family boundary ambiguity: Perceptions of adult stepfamily members. In K. Pasley and M. Ihinger-Tallman, eds., *Remarriage and stepparenting: Current research and theory,* 206–24. New York: Guilford.

Pasley, K. and Ihinger-Tallman, M. 1994. *Stepparenting: Issues in theory, research, and practice.* Westport: Conn.: Greenwood.

Peterson, A. and Jenni, C. 2001. Men's experiences of making the decision to have their first child: A phenomenological analysis. Department of Educational Leadership and Counseling, University of Montana. Unpublished manuscript.

Peterson, R. R. 1996. A re-examination of the economic consequences of divorce. *American Sociological Review* 66: 528–36.

Phillips, R. 1997. Stepfamilies from a historical perspective. In I. Levin and M. B. Sussman, eds., *Stepfamilies: History, research, and policy*, 5–18. New York: Haworth.

Pickhardt, C. E. 1997. *Keys to successful step-fathering*. Hauppauge, N.Y.: Barron's Educational Services.

Pleck, J. H. 1997. Paternal involvement: Levels, sources, and consequences. In M. E. Lamb, ed., *The role of the father in child development*, 123–67, 325–32. 3d ed. New York: Wiley.

Pleck, J. H., Lamb, M. E., and Levine, J. A. 1986. Epilog: Facilitating future changes in men's family roles. *Marriage & Family Review* 93: 11–16.

Plummer, K. 1995. *Telling sexual stories: Power, change and social worlds*. London: Routledge.

Quick, D. S., McKenry, P. C., and Newman, B. M. 1995. Stepmothers and their adolescent children: Adjustment to new family roles. In K. Pasley and M. Ihinger-Tallman, eds., *Stepparenting: Issues in theory, research, and practice*, 105–25. Westport, Conn.: Praeger.

Richardson, L. 1990. Narrative and sociology. *Journal of Contemporary Ethnography* 19: 116–35.

Riessman, C. K. 1993. *Narrative analysis*. Newbury Park, Calif.: Sage.

Rindfuss, R. R. 1991. The young adult years: Diversity, structural change, and fertility. *Demography* 28: 493–512.

Rosin, M. B. 1987. Stepfathering: Stepfathers' advice on creating a new family. New York: Simon & Schuster.

Rothman, B. K. 1989. *Recreating motherhood: Ideology and technology in a patriarchal society*. New York: Norton.

Schoen, R. J. K., Young, C. A., Nathanson, J. Fields, and Astone, N. M. 1997. Why do Americans want children? *Population and Development Review* 23: 333–58.

Schwalbe, M. L. and Wolkomir, M. 2002. Interviewing Men. In J. G. Gubrium and J. A. Holstein, eds., *Handbook of interview research: Context and method*, 203–19. Thousand Oaks, Calif.: Sage.

Schwebel, A. I., Fine, M. A., and Renner, M. A. 1991. A study of perceptions of the stepparent role. *Journal of Family Issues* 12: 43–57.

Seccombe, K. 1991. Assessing the costs and benefits of children: Gender comparisons among childfree husbands and wives. *Journal of Marriage and the Family* 53: 191–202.

Sedlak, A. J. and Broadhurst, D. D. 1996. *Third national incidence study of child abuse and neglect*. Washington, D.C.: National Center on Child Abuse and Neglect, U.S. Department of Health and Human Services.

Seltzer, J. 1991. Relationships between fathers and children living apart: The father's role after separation. *Journal of Marriage and the Family* 53: 79–101.

———. 1998a. Men's contributions to children and social policy. In A. Booth and

N. Crouter, eds., *Men in families: When do they get involved? What difference does it make?* 303–14. Mahwah, N.J.: Erlbaum.

———. 1998b. Father by law: Effects of joint legal custody on nonresident fathers' involvement with children. *Demography* 35: 135–46.

———. 2000. Families formed outside of marriage. *Journal of Marriage and the Family* 62: 1247–68.

Seltzer, J. and Brandeth, Y. 1995. What fathers say about involvement with children after separation. In W. Mariglio, ed., *Fatherhood: Contemporary theory, research, and social policy*, 166–92. Thousand Oaks, Calif.: Sage.

Silverstein, L. B. and Auerbach, C. F. 1999. Deconstructing the essential father. *American Psychologist* 6: 397–407.

Skopin, A. R., Newman, B. M., and McKenry, P. C. 1993. Influences on the quality of stepfather–adolescent relationships: Views of both family members. *Journal of Divorce and Remarriage* 19: 181–96.

Smock, P. J. 2000. Cohabitation in the United States: An appraisal of research themes, findings and implications. *Annual Review of Sociology* 26: 1–20.

Snarey, J. 1993. *How fathers care for the next generation: A four-decade study.* Cambridge: Harvard University Press.

Sonenstein, F. L., Stewart, K., Lindberg, D. L., Pernas, M., and Williams, S. 1997. *Involving males in preventing teen pregnancy: A guide for program planners.* California Wellness Foundation, The Urban Institute.

Stern, P. 1982. Affiliating in stepfather families: Teachable strategies leading to stepfather–child friendship. *Western Journal of Nursing Research* 4: 75–89.

Stewart, S. D. 2001. Contemporary American stepparenthood: Integrating cohabiting and nonresident stepparents. *Population Research and Policy Review* 20: 345–65.

———. 2002. The effect of stepchildren on childbearing intentions and births. *Demography* 39: 181–97.

Strauss, A. 1969. Turning points in identity. In *Mirrors and masks: Transformations of identity*, 92–100. New York: Macmillan.

Strauss, A. and Corbin, J. 1998. *Basics of qualitative research: Grounded theory procedures and techniques.* Thousand Oaks, Calif.: Sage.

Strauss, R. and Goldberg, W. A. 1999. Self and possible selves during the transition to fatherhood. *Journal of Family Psychology* 13: 244–59.

Stryker, S. 1980. *Symbolic interactionism.* Menlo Park, Calif.: Benjamin/Cummings.

Stueve, J. L. and Pleck, J. H. 2001. "Parenting voice": Solo parent identity and co-parent identities in married parents' narratives of meaningful parenting experiences. *Journal of Social and Personal Relationships* 18: 691–708.

Sugland, B. W., Wilder, K. J., and Chandra, A. 1997. Sex, pregnancy, and contraception: A report of focus group discussions with adolescents. Washington, D.C.: Child Trends. Unpublished paper.

Tannen, D. 1990. *You just don't understand: Men and women in conversation.* New York: Quill.

Teachman, J. D., Paasch, K., and Carver, K. 1996. Social capital and dropping out of school early. *Journal of Marriage and the Family* 58: 773–83.

Teachman, J. D., Tedrow, L. M., and Crowder, K. D. 2000. The changing demography of American families. *Journal of Marriage and the Family* 62: 1234–46.

Thomson, E. 1997. Couple childbearing desires, intentions, and births. *Demography* 34: 343–54.

Tucker, M. B. and Mitchell-Kernan, C. 1995. *The decline in marriage among African Americans: Causes, consequences, and policy implications.* New York: Russell Sage.

Van den Hoonard, W. C. 1997. *Working with sensitizing concepts: Analytical field research.* Thousand Oaks, Calif.: Sage.

Visher, E. B. and Visher, J. S. 1996. *Therapy with stepfamilies.* New York: Brunner/Mazel.

Wallerstein, J. S. and Kelly, J. B. 1980. *Surviving the breakup: How children and parents cope with divorce.* New York: Basic.

Walzer, S. 1998. *Thinking about the baby: Gender and transitions into parenthood.* Philadelphia: Temple University Press.

White, L. and J. G. Gilbreth. 2001. When children have two fathers: Effects of relationships with stepfathers and noncustodial fathers on adolescent outcomes. *Journal of Marriage and the Family* 63: 155–67.

Williamson, M. 1992. *A return to love: Reflections on the principles of a course in miracles.* New York: Simon & Schuster.

———. 2000. *Healing the soul of America: Reclaiming our voices as spiritual citizens.* New York: Simon & Schuster.

Wineberg, H. and McCarthy, J. 1993. Separation and reconciliation in American marriages. *Journal of Divorce and Remarriage* 20: 21–42.

———. 1998. Living arrangements after divorce: Cohabitation versus remarriage. *Journal of Divorce & Remarriage* 29: 131–46.

Winslow, J. M. 2000. The perils of dating a child's parent. *USA Today,* January 6, 15A.

Woodhouse, B. B. 1993. Hatching the egg: A child-centered perspective on parents' rights. *Cardozo Law Review* 14: 1747–1865.

———. 1996. Toward a communitarian theory of the nontraditional family. *Utah Law Review* 570: 569–612.

INDEX

abuse, 238, 258; household, 142; physical, of child, 140, 200, 256, 279n18; sexual, 280n18; spousal, 54, 57, 66

Ache tribe of Paraguay, 7, 8

ADHD (attention deficit hyperactivity disorder), 100

adoption, 4, 5, 9, 18, 83, 93, 101, 128, 130, 132, 152, 155–56, 175, 180, 207, 218, 221, 237, 283n15, 292n11

adult–child attachments, 269

affection, 96, 164, 276; physical, 162, 165

affinity-maintaining, 232, 270, 289n7; strategies, 251. *See also* claiming

affinity-seeking, 270, 289n7; gestures, 232. *See also* claiming

African Americans, 15, 27; participants in study, 264; stepfathers, 254–55

androgynous personalities, 233–34

anthropologists, 7

authority: claim to, 194; positive, 230, 233

authority figure, 73, 224; adult, 209, 252

Bari tribe of Venezuela, 7–8

behavioral problems, 100, 103

betrayal, feelings of, 136

binuclear systems, 293n31

biological fathers, 4–7, 64, 88, 165, 270; ally for, 250; character of, 45; involvement of, 104, 106, 139, 220, 252, 274;

representation by mother, 269; relationship with stepfathers, 105

Boy Scouts, 104

Canela tribe of Brazil, 7

Cherlin, Andrew, 281n2

childbirth, 25, 37; out-of-wedlock, 5, 208; preparation classes, 23

child care, 207, 240, 269; agent of, 71, 94; experience with, 62; provider of, 208

children: adjustment of, 73, 284n7, 287n10; caring for, 58, 120, 175, 239–40; claiming of, 21, 128, 137, 146, 157, 159, 197; commitment to, 222, 241; crisis for, 101; decision-making patterns regarding, 284n4; desire to have, 3, 170, 173–75, 183; development of, 83, 248, 264; identification with, 148; outcomes for, 223, 272, 283n1, 287n10; relationship with, 4, 7, 174; school-age, 99, 100; social networks, 98

Children Act 1989, 220

child support, 50, 106, 170, 181, 287n10; obligations of, 9

claiming, 155–56, 176, 204, 217, 252; children, 8, 128, 142, 144, 218; process of, 10, 145, 270. *See also* affinity-maintaining; affinity-seeking

coding systems, 262

ABOUT THE AUTHOR

William Marsiglio, professor of sociology at the University of Florida, has written extensively on the social psychology of men's sexuality, fertility, and fatherhood. His most recent books, *Sex, Men, and Babies: Stories of Awareness and Responsibility* (2002) and *Procreative Man* (1998) explore in novel ways how men anticipate, create, and nurture human life. Professor Marsiglio lectures at national and international conferences on fatherhood and consults for national surveys about male sexuality and fatherhood in the United States and Canada. References to his work have appeared in major newspapers including the *New York Times, Los Angeles Times,* and the *Washington Post.*